Quality Promotion in Europe

Gower

QUALITY PROMOTION IN EUROPE

Edited by Brendan Barker

A REVIEW OF EUROPEAN
COMMUNITY MEMBER STATES'
NATIONAL AND REGIONAL
SCHEMES AND MEASURES IN
THE FIELD OF QUALITY

COMMISSIONED BY

the Strategic Programme
for Innovation and Technology
Transfer of the European Communities

Published by
Gower Publishing
Gower House
Croft Road
Aldershot
Hampshire GU11 3HR
England

Gower
Old Post Road
Brookfield
Vermont 05036
USA

British Library Cataloguing in Publication Data

Quality Promotion in Europe: Review of
European Community Member States'
National and Regional Schemes and
Measures in the Field of Quality
  I. Barker, Brendan
  658.5

ISBN 0-566-07512-1

Typeset in Times by PREST and printed in Great Britain
by the University Press, Cambridge.

Contents

Page

Part One: Quality Improvement and Competitiveness

Part Two: Overview of Study Findings

Part Three: Country Reviews

Part Four: European Quality Activities

List of Tables

List of Figures

Lists of Quality Organisations

List of Contributors

Brendan Barker: Research Fellow within the Programme of Policy Research in Engineering Science and Technology (PREST) at the University of Manchester, UK

Mark Boden: Research Fellow within the Programme of Policy Research in Engineering Science and Technology (PREST) at the University of Manchester, UK

Jean-Jacques Chanaron: Research Fellow within the National Centre for Scientific Research Insitute for Economic Research on Production and Development (CNRS IREP-D), Grenoble, France.

Allan Naes Gjerding: Doctoral Student, The IKE Group, Department of Production, Aalborg University, Denmark.

Paul Kunst: Senior Research Fellow with the Maastricht Economic Research Institute on Innovation and Technology (MERIT), University of Limburg, The Netherlands.

Jos Lemmink: Assistant Professor of Marketing, Faculty of Economics and Business Administration, University of Limburg, The Netherlands.

Nicola de Liso: Research Fellow at the National Research Council Research Insitute for the Dynamics of Economic Systems (CNR-IDSE), Milan, Italy.

Nikolaos Kastrinos: Research Associate within the Programme of Policy Research in Engineering Science and Technology (PREST) at the University of Manchester, UK

Zulema Lopes Pereira: Assistant Professor, Department of Industrial Engineering, Faculty of Science and Technology (FCT), New University of Lisbon (UNL), Portugal.

Ruth Prins: Doctoral Student within the Faculty of Economics and Business Administration, University of Limburg, The Netherlands.

Markus Schroll: Doctoral Student with the Fraunhofer Institute for Technical Systems and Innovation (Fraunhofer ISI), Karlsruhe, Germany

Jurgen Wengal: Research Manager with the Fraunhofer Institute for Technical Systems and Innovation (Fraunhofer ISI), Karlsruhe, Germany.

Foreword

Quality is considered to be a critical factor to the competitiveness of companies and countries as it stimulates and accelerates the pace of structural changes. Hence, quality promotion in industry and the service sector, not only for large enterprises but also small and medium-sized enterprizes (SMEs), has become a challenge for all governments.

In this field, Europe lags behind its major competitors. In the last few years, public bodies in the member states have, however, launched a number of actions to stimulate a better approach to quality in the private sector.

This book has been prepared on behalf of the European Union Programme on Innovation and Technology Transfer (SPRINT) to provide analytical and practical tools to increase policy exchange in the field of quality. The need for such a compilation was based on the diversity of approaches and interventions relevant to quality promotion, the large number of different bodies (public organizations responsible for normalization and certification) and the variations in policy experience at the national level.

There is, nevertheless, a number of common policy instruments which, although given different emphasis, are virtually the same in all member countries:

- In the first instance, a mainly technical *infrastructure* (standardization, certification of products and systems, metrology, testing and inspection) provides the basis for national quality policies in all countries. This infrastructure also encompasses a second range of supporting organizations such as R&D institutes, national and regional bodies for quality promotion, consultants, trade and training organizations, large enterprises as well as local and regional governments, the latter being increasingly active in the quality domain.

- As a second common element, *information and motivation* campaigns are conducted not only on a national level but also now at a local level by the sharing of experience among companies. the creation and increasing importance of quality awards should also be mentioned as an efficient approach to motivation complementary to certification.

- Greater use of *consulting services* appears to be an indispensable way to give companies full access to information and the widespread implementation of quality activities.

- A large number of *specific projects* aiming towards demonstration have been launched to enhance the exchange of experience, especially at a sectoral level.

- A recent SPRINT survey has identified *training* as one of the major constraints for quality implementation in companies to be addressed by the Member Sates

- Last but not least, there is a scarcity of research studies which could gather data in order to convince policy makers and lay the foundation for political decisions (ie. costs of non-compliance, measuring client satisfaction, non-destructive measuring methods). This is also true for evaluations of public policies and their impact at the company level.

This report also emphasizes several themes which should be at the heart of any debate on quality promotion. Some of these have already been developed at the SPRINT conference in Aachen of April 1993. In particular, the following points seem relevant to me:

- Emphasis should pass from quality control to quality assurance and then to total quality management (TQM). This requires the implementation of new promotion tools, some of which are already being established in some member states.
- The current system based on standards should evolve towards a philosophy of continuous quality improvement.
- European academic research and training providers must adapt to quality management.
- TQM criteria need better adaptation to SMEs.
- Environmental preoccupations and the human dimension of quality will be major trends of the future.

Quality is firstly a company's own responsibility, most of the vital elements necessary are under its control. Nevertheless, governments still have an important role to play:

- to create an environment favourable to the development of quality (harmonization and clarification of the standards and certification mechanisms, mutual recognition, etc.).
- to develop research and training bodies, and especially links between these bodies in order to foster the diffusion of good practice.

The influence of the European framework in this area is increasing. It should assert itself in the organization of a true Union quality policy, co-ordinated with regard to its instruments but decentralised with regard to its implementation.

Robin MIEGE
Commission of the European Communities

Preface

This report examines public policies and schemes introduced throughout the European Union in order to improve quality.[1] Ultimately, the performance of any economy depends on the success with which its individual firms produce products and services that are more competitive than those of their international competitors. High quality has long been recognized as an important element in achieving this competitive success. In an increasingly competitive world the existing quality management approach of many European firms is no longer sufficient to guarantee quality that is superior (or even equal) to that of their competitors.

Surveys conducted in many of the countries examined in this report show that typically firms are already well aware (and becoming more so) of the relationship between quality and competitiveness. However, this is not always matched by effective attempts at quality improvement. There are a number of reasons for this. Firms, particularly small and medium-sized enterprises (SMEs), may well be aware of the importance of quality, but may lack awareness of appropriate quality-improving approaches. Even when they are aware, they may lack the resources (both financial and human) necessary to implement and exploit those approaches. Both situations may justify government involvement.

Most European governments have recognized that unassisted market forces cannot be relied upon to ensure that best practice quality-management will effectively diffuse throughout an economy. For this reason, governments have supported public policies directed towards the promotion of quality improvement within the private sector.

The study, on which this report is based, was undertaken during 1992 in order to review European Community member states' national and regional schemes and measures in the field of quality. The study was conducted as part of the European Innovation Monitoring Initiative (EIMS) within the Strategic Programme for Innovation and Technology Transfer (SPRINT) Programme of the EC Directorate-General on Information Technologies and Industries, and Telecommunications (DG XIII). The organizations involved in the study, were:

- **PREST**, the Programme of Policy Research in Engineering Science and Technology at Manchester University,
- **ISI**, the Fraunhofer Institute for Systems and Innovations Research from the Fraunhofer-Gesellschaft for the Promotion of Applied Research,
- **MERIT**, Maastricht Economic Research Institute on Innovation and Technology at the Faculty of Economics and Business Administration, the University of Limburg, and
- **IKE**, the programme on research in economic, technical and institutional change at the Department of Production, Aalborg University.

The first part of this book sets out the background to the study and the methodology employed. The main aim of the survey was to identify the rationale, objectives, orientation, target groups and priority sectors, of the various public schemes and initiatives employed to promote quality. The study covered national and selected regional schemes within the twelve European Union member countries as well as relevant initiatives undertaken by the European Commission. Although the primary focus of the survey was public sector initiatives it was recognised that a significant role is played by private organizations (particularly large firms) in shaping the quality 'environment'. Furthermore, industrial and professional associations are actively involved in quality promotion schemes which complement public sector activities. Examples of these activities are therefore also mentioned in the report where relevant.

Part One discusses the concepts of quality and quality management, their relationship to innovation and competitiveness and the role of public policy in promoting quality. Quality promotion is defined as the set of policies involving government intervention in the economy with the intent of improving the quality of firms' products and services. European countries have shown significant national differences in their approach to quality policy formulation and implementation. To a large extent this reflects different national traditions in government-industry relations. Policies range from the 'direct' promotion of quality, quality management guidelines (including standards) and training schemes, to more general training, financial incentives and innovation promotion schemes that may include a significant quality element.

Public promotion of quality has an important role in industrial policies. There is a relationship between the development of quality management philosophy and the development of new industrial paradigms, and it is possible to identify stages in the development of the various government schemes and initiatives. Thus, in general terms, government policy has tended to move (or is moving) from policies that support quality control and inspection to the adoption of minimum product standards, through to those which support quality assurance management systems and most recently to those which promote total quality management within companies.

Part Two summarizes and analyses the findings of the individual country surveys. Quality promotion both determines and is determined by the institutional environment as part of an interactive process. For this reason an understanding of the quality 'infrastructure' is crucial to understanding quality promotion. The quality infrastructure is defined as the array of public and private institutions and organisations within the economy that fund and promote quality improvement. (We argue that the quality infrastructure is part of the wider innovation supporting infrastructure.) A wide diversity of organizations form the quality infrastructure. The quality promotion system results from the interplay between these different organizations at different levels within the national industrial framework.

Quality-promoting activities typically occur through multilayer networks, including interfirm, intersectoral, interindustry, government and university and other networks. Exchange of information and experience takes place through the networking of individuals and organisations at the regional, national and European level. At these levels the quality infrastructure is emerging both through the creation of new institutions and the coordination of existing ones.

These are categorized as follows:

- industrial policy-making bodies

- public organisations involved in specifying and monitoring standards (i.e. third party certification)
- education organisations
- training organisations
- industrial associations
- professional associations
- consultancies
- large companies.

A range of different quality-related functions are undertaken. These are characterized as follows:

- quality policy
- quality standards
- quality monitoring
- consultancy
- promotion of quality awareness
- education and training
- evaluation of quality policies, schemes and initiatives

Public sector initiatives in quality promotion support one or more of these functions and usually involve a number of different types of organization.

Part Three reviews quality promoting activities at national and regional levels in each of the countries surveyed. In addition to the above categories, quality promotion activities are characterized in terms of those which support research; those which promote awareness; those designed to increase the rate of adoption (through the use of subsidized consultancy, standards etc.); and those supporting education and training. Historically, many governments of the countries surveyed have directly attempted to improve quality by means of procurement, technical regulations referring to safety, environment, consumer protection etc., support to the research and development infrastructure, support to small businesses and general macro-economic policies.

In addition, schemes and initiatives to improve awareness of quality issues are found in most countries. Such schemes are a necessary precursor to the effective diffusion of quality improvement techniques. Similarly, policies to encourage the adoption of good quality management practices are found in most countries. The schemes differ in terms of their quality target level (testing, quality control, quality assurance, or total quality management), coverage (all sectors or some, all companies, or only SMEs), and whether they operate directly or indirectly (i.e. directly through the use of consultants or publicity, or indirectly through large firms encouraging quality improvement in their suppliers).

The specification of quality management process standards (specifically derived from defence requirements) has been particularly important. The success of this approach is indicated by the subsequent adoption of similar standards at an international level. In many cases governments and other actors within national production systems have launched campaigns to increase the awareness of companies of these standards, and even to enforce them on to industries.

It is apparent that in many of the more 'advanced' countries in Europe there is a growing emphasis on quality as a process of continuous improvement (although usually building on the base of an established standards infrastructure). Thus in many countries quality promotion activities are not conducted in isolation, but as part of a much wider attempt at improving all activities of the firm (technical, social and economic).

The need for a competent workforce skilled in quality related activities has been widely recognized. Thus, quality management training programmes have been initiated by various organizations, often as part of government programmes. Indeed professional training is a rapidly expanding area of activity in all of the countries investigated. Accordingly, higher education programmes are increasingly incorporating quality management studies. Furthermore, education and training activities are seen as one of the ways to promote awareness, and thus to complement quality awareness campaigns.

In spite of the importance of product and service quality to corporate and national well-being there is, with a few notable exceptions (Denmark and France standing out), a paucity of good-quality academic research on quality management in many European countries. Quality management is a new field of enquiry in which more research needs to be carried out.

Part Four reviews quality promoting activities at the European level. From the country surveys it is apparent that large imbalances in quality culture exist across Europe. Nevertheless moves towards harmonization in recent years are beginning to see a convergence of national, European and international approaches. Current changes in technology-related legislation, standardization and quality assurance throughout Europe are far-reaching. The recent past and immediate future will be dominated by the major task of harmonization between European Union member countries. Prior to this effort, most technical legislation was at the national level, and was different in every country and often formed a significant non-tariff barrier to trade. Voluntary standards were produced by the national standards bodies and few European standards existed; although, in a few areas such as IT, standardization was international. Conformity testing and certification were even more fragmented, with most action taking place at the sector level within countries. Other aspects of quality assurance were mainly internal to enterprises, and concentrated on manufacturing defects. With the development of the European Single Market (and with it the harmonization of European standards), it is likely that European bodies (including the European Commission) will come to play an increasingly important role in the promotion of quality throughout Europe.

1. Note:

Following ratification of the Maastricht Treaty in 1993 the official name of what had been the 'European Community' was changed to 'European Union'. The earlier term remains in widespread use and the two terms are typically used interchangeably. In this book we typically use 'European Community' when discussing past activities and 'European Union' when discussing current and future ones.

Acknowledgements

I would like to thank the many people throughout Europe who contributed to the study described in this book. Jose Ramon Tiscar, Gerhard Braunling and Robin Miege of SPRINT commissioned the original study on which this book is based and continued to provide useful advice and feedback throughout the preparation of the report. I would also like to thank my colleagues within PREST for their help while I prepared the book. Finally, I would like to thank Solveig Servian of Gower for her patient support and Jeanne Brady for her heroic proof-reading.

Brendan Barker
PREST
December 1993

Part One:

Quality Improvement and Competitiveness

Quality Improvement and Competitiveness

Brendan Barker and Nikolaos Kastrinos

1. Introduction

Ultimately, the performance of any economy depends on the success with which its individual firms produce products and services that are more competitive than those of their international competitors. Achieving high quality has long been recognized as an important element in achieving this competitive success. It is also increasingly evident that quality has given impetus to the creation of employee commitment and flexible management systems which also underpin success. In an increasingly competitive world the existing quality management approach of many firms is no longer sufficient to guarantee quality that is superior to that of their competitors. To remain competitive these firms need to adopt a system of quality management that better ensures that the performance of their products or services satisfies and continues to satisfy customer requirements. These requirements do not remain static, as new products come onto the market and as fashions change, they develop over time. In order to survive and prosper, firms need to position their products or services so that they consistently fall within the boundaries of these developing requirements. Recognition that quality is not a static concept, but rather a dynamic one, involving a process of continuous improvement and founded upon organizational innovation represents a paradigm shift, first understood by a number of Japanese companies and clearly articulated in the concept of Total Quality Management (TQM). In attempting to match the success of these companies, an increasing number of organizations in the West have adopted approaches based on the TQM concept.

The clear competitive significance of quality, together with the fact that best practice quality management does not always effectively diffuse throughout the economy, has led to public sector involvement in a range of quality promotion initiatives.

This report describes the results of a study undertaken to review in European Community (now European Union) member states national and regional schemes and measures in the field of quality. The study was conducted as part of the European Innovation Monitoring Initiative (EIMS) during 1992 within the Strategic Programme for Innovation and Technology Transfer (SPRINT) Programme of the EC Directorate-General on Information Technologies and Industries and Telecommunications (DG XIII). The organisations involved in the study, were:

3

- **PREST**, the Programme of Policy Research in Engineering Science and Technology at Manchester University;
- **ISI**, the Fraunhofer Institute for Systems and Innovations Research from the Fraunhofer-Gesellschaft for the Promotion of Applied Research;
- **MERIT**, Maastricht Economic Research Institute on Innovation and Technology at the Faculty of Economics and Business Administration, the University of Limburg; and,
- **IKE**, the programme on research in economic, technical and institutional change at the Department of Production, Aalborg University.

2. The Study Methodology

Information was collected through a detailed literature review, supported and informed by interviews with key actors. The main aim of the survey was to identify the rationale, objectives, orientation, target groups and priority sectors, of the various public schemes and initiatives employed within the twelve Community countries (together with the activities of the European Commission) to promote quality. Specifically, the study was intended to generate an 'inventory and review of national and selected regional support schemes to promote quality standards'. The survey covered:

- The mainly public organisations involved in the whole range of activities from standards definition and certification to promotion of total quality management. The inventory includes an analysis of their roles/ objectives and the processes through which they formulate and implement their policies; their policy guidelines i.e. perceptions of quality and what quality promotion means to them; and how, if this is so, their policies fit into a more general policy framework.
- A classification of these organizations: in the public-private dimension encompassing a range of actors from the state to industrial firms, and in the central-regional dimension. Although the enquiry concentrates on the public end of the spectrum, major actors include industrial associations and even single firms. These are not ignored if they play an important role but are not a major focus of the study. The second dimension expresses the administrative traditions (in industrial policy in the various countries).
- In addition, quality related schemes and initiatives are classified in a specific-systemic orientated dimension concerning the stage of development of the quality management philosophy which they reflect, as well as global-sectoral and national-regional dimensions concerning the scope of their coverage.
- Additional general information on industrial structures and the administrative mechanisms of the state (how the various organizations are related and how policy is formulated and implemented) is included where this is relevant to our understanding of the operation and impact of quality measures.

The emphasis of the survey was on the dynamic nature of the development of quality related activities within particular national and regional contexts. Important trends at the regional, national and international level have been noted. While particular emphasis has been placed upon analysing initiatives in total quality management this is presented in the context of a description of the 'quality infrastructure' in the different countries and regions investigated. Thus, in addition to describing major quality schemes and initiatives, the survey provides an indication of the major actors involved in the specification, certification and improvement of quality and how they interact.

From the outset, it was recognized that problems would be encountered in defining and characterizing those quality schemes which may not be explicitly recognised as such within different national and regional contexts. In practice, ISO (International Standards Organization) 8402 provided a generally accepted definition of quality as the 'totality of features and characteristics of a product or service that bear on its ability to satisfy stated or implied needs'.[1] This was used as a working definition. Similarly, quality promotion was taken to include, as far as possible, all those incentives to firms to improve quality. These range from the 'direct' promotion of specific quality guidelines (including standards) and training schemes to more general training, financial incentives and innovation promotion schemes that may include a significant quality element. From the literature collected and the interviews undertaken these concepts were found to be fully operational. We are confident that the most significant national quality related activities currently found in the European Union have been included.

Beyond the collection and translation of relevant literature, it was not possible to cover all regional schemes in great detail. We therefore cover a selection of regional initiatives where, for instance, they demonstrate the balance of central to regional schemes in the countries looked at, the economic importance of the region, or the typicality or otherwise of the approaches adopted of other regional activities.

Although the primary focus of our survey has been the public sector it is recognised that a significant role is played by private organizations (particularly large firms) in shaping the quality 'environment'. Furthermore, industrial and professional associations are actively involved in quality promotion schemes complementing public sector activities in all of the countries investigated. Examples of these activities are therefore also included in the report where relevant.

3. Quality and the Innovation Process

To understand the policy dimensions of the quality issue it is useful to place it in the broader context of the innovation process and to identify its relationship with international competitiveness. Recent developments in the study of innovation provide a suitable conceptual reference point.

The importance of innovation for economic growth has long been recognized, with writers such as Solow and Mansfield providing extensive evidence of its impact.[2] Since the early part of this century economists have been interested in the factors which differentiate firms and industries, causing some to move on and others to stay behind.[3] Studies of retardation recognized that a major growth impulse is provided by an innovation, generating in turn scope for a sequence of secondary improvement innovations, extending the market, lowering production costs and overcoming specific bottlenecks. Kuznets argued that the pattern of secondary improvement will develop according to Wolff's Law.[4] Wolff's thesis was that the cost of generating incremental improvements would increase over time and would ultimately approach a limit. Nonetheless he argued that many of these secondary improvements would be unforeseen at the time of innovation but that their cumulative impact would often exceed the impact of the initial innovation. Other writers have argued that use promotes improvement. The idea of improvement and feedback provides a close connection between the promotion of quality and the innovation process.

The evolutionary approach to technical change was synthesised by Nelson and Winter, who introduced the concept of a 'natural trajectory', representing the direction of technical change as perceived by those responsible for promoting it.[5] Within this framework, market needs develop within the 'selection environment', a term encompassing market forces and factors such as the regulatory environment. Following the evolutionary analogy, the prevalence of a technological trajectory is determined by its comparative performance within the selection environment. Georghiou et al refined the concept of the selection environment, arguing that trajectories competed within a 'technical corridor' bounded by the range of characteristics sought by the user, the lower boundary being the minimum viable level of performance and the upper boundary the point where improvement would be redundant.[6] According to Lancaster it is these characteristics that define a product.[7] To put it otherwise, a product is nothing more than a set of performance characteristics. The process of competition, which drives innovation, may then be characterized as the efforts of rival firms within and across trajectories to supply characteristics within the range defined by the corridor.

How then does this relate to quality? To clarify the connection we must first turn to definitions. As a number of writers have pointed out, while 'quality' is a term of which most have an intuitive understanding it is usually difficult to define.[8] The problem is that 'quality' has traditionally been used as an adjective (e.g. as in a 'quality product') to imply a high degree of excellence or some other distinguishing attribute - a usage which is misleading. Many writers have provided their own definitions of the term. Crosby defines quality as 'conformance to requirements' - the conformance of all a product's features and characteristics to the product requirement specification.[9] Juran uses the term 'fitness for purpose' because he maintains that the ultimate user's evaluation of quality is based on whether the product is fit for use and not on whether it conforms to specificational requirements (of which the user may not even yet be aware).[10]

ISO 8402 explains that the term 'quality' is not used to express a degree of excellence in a comparative sense, nor is it used in a quantitative sense (as a quality level or measure) for technical evaluations. Quality is defined in ISO 8402 as 'the totality of features and characteristics of a product or service that bear on its ability to satisfy stated or implied needs'.[11] In this definition we come precisely to the situation we encountered in the wider context of innovation, the need to improve characteristics, defined by the market, in order to secure competitive success. The relation between quality and competitive performance is clear.

This exposition may now be extended to quality management. As Teece has argued, innovation generates benefits but innovating alone is insufficient to reap these benefits.[12] To do so a firm requires access to a range of complementary assets such as marketing and manufacturing capability. Competence in quality management is one element of these complementary assets.

Recent contributions by Porter and Chesnais have focused on the idea of structural or systemic competitiveness, whereby the performance of a firm is constrained by the stimuli to innovation and the complementary capabilities available in the environment in which it operates.[13] Within the European context this environment has both Union and national dimensions reflecting the whole range of cultural and institutional practices within the member states. The infrastructure to support and promote quality, together with the cultural values which shape attitudes and practices within firms all form a part of the environment and provide the focus for this study.

There is thus a need to comprehend the wider institutional structures within which innovation occurs. Technical change both determines and is determined by the institutional environment in an interactive process. The analysis of different systems of innovation is fundamental to an understanding of why technological dynamism apparently occurs more rapidly and efficiently in some countries than in others. In recognition of this the concept of 'national systems of innovation' has been recently developed.[14]

There are different approaches to the concept of national systems of innovation. The narrow approach is focused on the institutions in the public and private sectors that are directly concerned with research, development and the diffusion of innovations, involving not only R&D laboratories, but also scientific libraries, standards institutes, patents offices etc. The broader approach embraces, besides these institutions directly concerned with R&D, all the others which affect learning, the assimilation and diffusion of new technologies. Clearly, it can be seen that the array of public and private institutions and organizations within the economy that fund and promote quality improvement form an integral part of the wider national system of innovation.

4. Managing Quality in the Firm

As Lascelles and Dale point out, there is still some confusion over the definition of quality itself and the terms of quality control, quality assurance, quality management, total quality management and company-wide quality control.[15] Common usage in the literature of the terms 'quality control', 'quality assurance' and 'quality management' does not aid such a straightforward interpretation. For example, the terms 'quality control' and 'quality management' are often interchanged. Ishikawa discusses the problems associated with interpreting the meaning of the words 'control' and 'management', and in the end uses 'quality control' for 'quality management'.[16] His statement that quality assurance is the very essence of quality control (implying that quality assurance is a subset of quality control) confuses the matter still further.

Three generic terms are widely used in connection with quality: these are 'quality control', 'quality assurance' and 'quality management'. ISO 8402 defines each of these terms as follows:

- Quality Control: the operational techniques and activities that are used to fulfil requirements for quality.
- Quality Assurance: all those planned and systematic actions necessary to provide adequate confidence that a product or service will satisfy given requirements for quality.
- Quality Management: that aspect of the overall management function that determines and implements the quality policy (overall intentions and direction of the organization as regards quality, as formally expressed by top management).[17]

Quality control can be considered a subset of quality assurance because it is an integral part of those actions required to attain customer satisfaction.[18] Lascelles and Dale, using the same logic, argue that quality assurance may be considered to be a subset of quality management because it is an outcome of the determination and implementation of the quality policy.[19] Further consideration of the definition of quality management leads them to suggest that the process of quality management is no different from the process of management *per se*. Thus, ISO 8402 states that:

> *Quality management includes strategic planning, allocation of resources and other systematic activities for quality such as quality planning, operations and evaluations.*[20]

Conventionally, quality has been dealt with in a static context, in which it is synonymous to the ability of a product to perform the functions it was designed to perform. This is based on an implicit recognition that every production process involves faults that lead to the production of defective products. In this sense the quality of a product is defined by the extent to which the product meets certain specifications or standards. As these specifications are an integral part of a technological corridor, and at lower levels of aggregation they can be seen as corridors themselves, they represent a definite snapshot of a technological corridor at a point of time. The imposition of such specifications imposes a 'freezing' of the technological corridor into a single line as its lower and upper limit coincide.[21]

If technological corridors are firm-specific, freezing them obviously hinders the ability of a firm to innovate. However, as defective products represent a real 'day-to-day' problem for businesses of all kinds and especially for the manufacturing industry, this static approach to quality has, since the early 20th century, predominated in the manufacturing world. While this approach may have hindered innovation, it was compliant with the stability required for the development of mass production. According to Womack et al, mass production (i.e. high-volume manufacturing of standardized, low-cost products using moving assembly lines, hierarchical systems of control, and a radical division of labour) was the 'new manufacturing paradigm' of the late 19th and early 20th centuries, which enabled an explosive growth of labour productivity and of total economic output.[22] As this type of manufacturing organization produces by nature standardized products, strict input specifications are essential for the highly specialized and standardized processes characterizing it. As defective inputs lead to defective outputs, strict product specifications were imposed all the way up the manufacturing chain and methods were devised to ensure that both inputs and outputs were not defective. It is these methods that constitute quality control. As inputs were bought and outputs were sold in bulk, statistical sampling techniques were devised to perform this task under the title of statistical quality control.

According to Hill recent years have witnessed a fundamental change in the organization, conduct, and dynamics of industrial production.[23] Hill terms this new environment, new-era industrialization. Its major characteristics are:

- The overriding search for opportunities to make revolutionary technological substitutions seems to have been supplanted by a striving for continuous incremental improvements in product, process and every other aspect of the firm. Seeking to do a little bit better every day what one was already doing is now seen as the secret to product and process improvement and profitability. It is not that breakthroughs are no longer looked for, but that their role has been put in a different perspective.

- Flexible production, short production runs, high product variety, and frequent product change (i.e. economies of scope) are all characteristics of new-era industrialization. These require considerably greater access to information and greater coordination within the production system at all levels.

- Integration of functions, decentralization of responsibilities, and worker empowerment demand extensive networking of groups and individuals. Since more decisions are pressed downward in the organization, the frequency and the extent of communication among disparate elements is much greater than in old-era functionally separated hierarchical organizations. Top-down control is being replaced by horizontal coordination.

- Competition between manufacturers in the new era is based less on price and more on product quality, on the range of product function, and on the timeliness with which new and improved products are brought to market. Costs matter, but perceptions of value tend to matter even more. New-era producers seek to meet or exceed customer expectations.

- Major manufacturers in the new era are typically engaged in webs of strategic alliances and joint ventures, both domestic and international. These networks extend not only to suppliers and downstream customers, but also to competitors, universities, and government research laboratories. They may focus on production, R&D, information sharing, or developing common agendas for public policy. Effective use of external networks requires a complementary internal network structure to manage and act on the information that crosses the firm's boundary from the external networks.

- In addition to the points made above, new-era firms engage in the kinds of supplier and customer relations described as key elements of lean production. Suppliers are encouraged to invest in their plant, equipment and people, and they are given greater responsibility to be technically competent. Suppliers are made part of new product design and development teams. Long-term contracts lead to a lessening of direct competition among suppliers and to a reduction in the number of suppliers with which an assembler does business.

9

- Finally, as compared with old-era behaviour, new-era firms are increasingly 'internalizing' what have previously been treated as externalizable costs in the old era. Increasingly sophisticated customers have begun to equate their purchasing decisions with wider social and environmental issues. The discipline of managing all costs internally while simultaneously pursuing quality can lead to better and lower-cost products, more satisfied and productive workers, and better relationships with neighbours and the community, as well as with customers and suppliers.

Similarly, Vos in a recent book, also describes the emergence of a new manufacturing paradigm.[24] He lists the characteristics of manufacturing systems by stage of evolution, as below in Figure 1:

Figure 1: Evolution of manufacturing systems

	Craft	Industrial	Post-industrial
Social system			
Value orientation	Skill	Product	Customer
Norms	Workmanship	Efficiency/productivity	Product development and throughput time
Work system			
Equipment resources	Flexible hand tools	Capital intensive, special purpose	Capital intensive, flexible
Nature of work	Skilled manual work	Unskilled manual work/ functionally specialized intellectual work	Information intensive intellectual work
Work group organization	Task-oriented groupings	Functionally specialized work groups	Self-organizing and self-directed work groups
Control system			
Performance measures	Customary standard	Single and task specific	Multiple and global
Information systems	Informal and based on learning from experience	Formal information systems to control task execution and coordinate sequential activities	Formal and informal systems for control, mutual adjustment and learning
Control mechanism	Craftsman	Hierarchical authority structure	Modified market mechanisms (i.e. long-term cooperation)

Source: Vos[25]

This fundamental change in industrial philosophy and practice is closely related to the ever increasing pace of technical change and the subsequent destabilization of markets. These place increasing demands on the flexibility of industrial production systems that have to respond rapidly to change. This, in turn, has led firms to increasingly integrate their production structures. (This integration also generated cost-savings as it eliminated the need for inventories in intermediate production stages.)

However, increasing integration of production increased the cost of defective inputs and intermediaries, as well as the costs of defective outputs. Thus, new-era manufacturing systems are designed to provide perfection first time, thus avoiding waste in time and materials. These systems are populated by well-trained employees who are encouraged to measure their own performance and to suggest ways to regularly and continuously improve both product and process. New improved quality management systems that are oriented to 'zero-defect' and 'continuous improvement' are therefore necessary underpinning characteristics of new-era manufacturing.

This is not to say that the new manufacturing paradigm is simply the result of the rapid pace of technical change. Indeed, it can be argued that it is one of the factors that has enabled the pace of technical change to increase. Japanese industry adopted novel manufacturing systems on a large scale in the pursuit of industrialization, and achieved the high rates of technical change that brought about the fall of mass production. Not surprisingly Japanese competitive strategies usually involve large quality management systems that are very different to statistical quality control. The thoughts of the so-called 'Quality Gurus', a relatively small number of highly influential experts, were first widely transferred into practice in post-war Japan.[26]

The distinctive contributions of these experts (Crosby, Deming, Feigenbaum, Juran, Ishikawa etc.) are essentially variations on a theme. (The essential elements of these different approaches are briefly described in Appendix One). Each approach has its strengths and weaknesses and they are all demonstrably effective. However, it is ultimately the senior management team's commitment to making quality improvement work, understanding what they are doing, changing behaviour, attitudes and fostering the 'quality spirit' that is the key to long-term success. Several commentators have compared and contrasted the approaches of the four experts.[27] In general, these different approaches are compatible. The common theme running through their philosophies is the concept of quality as a fundamental business strategy permeating the culture of the entire organization. In particular, Fine argues that the teachings of Crosby, Deming and Juran have four points in common:

- the importance of top management support and participation;
- the need for workforce training and education;
- quality management requires careful planning and a philosophy of company-wide involvement; and,
- quality improvement programmes must represent permanent, ongoing activities.[28]

These ideas were adapted to the Japanese corporate culture and led to the development of Company-Wide Quality Control, or as it is often referred to, Total Quality Management (TQM). While the origins of TQM are American it was the Japanese who first adopted it on a large scale; and it is considered a central ingredient of their competitive success. TQM refers to a new quality management philosophy which is based on a pursuit of excellence in production, organizational and inter-organizational relationships. It incorporates this vision of excellence, together with an increase in the responsibility of shop-floor employees for decisions concerning the day-by-day operation of the shop floor as well as with possible improvements in both the product and the production process. However, what characterizes Japanese TQM and distinguishes it from its Western versions is a commitment to excellence as a moving goalpost. For the Japanese the pursuit of excellence in quality concerns 'anything that can be improved'.[29]

5. Public Policy in the New Era of Industrialization

It has been widely observed that unassisted market forces cannot be relied upon to ensure that best-practice quality management will effectively diffuse throughout an economy.[30] This observation has led to the formulation of government policies directed towards quality improvement. However, European countries have shown significant national differences in their approach to quality policy formulation and implementation. To a large extent this reflects different national traditions in government-industry relations. In countries such as France, state involvement in industry is seen as a major part of a process of national strategic planning. In other countries, industrial policy is seen as part of a general economic policy, aiming to create a favourable climate for industrial development. Within Europe, the UK most clearly articulates such a policy. Throughout the 1980s and thus far into the 1990s, UK public policy has been essentially of a hands-off nature, being directed towards creating an environment conducive to industrial development.[31]

Public policy needs to take into account broad developments in industry such as the 'paradigm shift' discussed in previous sections; otherwise, it will be neither appropriately supportive nor effectively regulating. In the process of paradigm shift one cannot forecast the appropriateness of proposed policies by examining how well they did in the past, owing to the qualitative nature of change in the very character of the system being addressed, and the likely responses to particular public policy initiatives. Instead, one must be open to new thinking and to experimentation. Hill identifies some of the implications of new-era industrialization for government policy:

- Government programmes intended to stimulate or to control industry need to become more time conscious. Procedures that require months or even years to approve and implement are becoming increasing inadequate to industry needs.
- Another dimension of public policy needing major change in response to the new paradigm is the nature and organization of public education at all levels. If workers are to make effective use of opportunities to improve the systems in which they work, they need not only to be able to read but to carry out complex calculations and, even more important, to conceptualize abstractly the response of complex systems to their interventions. At advanced levels, support for graduate education and research in engineering and management is needed not only for specific technical topics but also for research and studies that elucidate the characteristics of the new manufacturing paradigm and train technical people and managers to work in it effectively. Thus the new era of industrialization suggests the need for economic development policies to focus on people as much, if not

more, as on firms. Continuous investment in the capabilities of workers throughout their entire careers is required not only of workers themselves but also of their employers and of the government on behalf of society.

- Support for the timely transfer of technology and management best-practice also becomes much more important under the new paradigm of production.
- Another task of public policy in the new era of industrialization is legitimization of, and support for, networking among individuals, companies, government agencies, and other bodies.[32]

5.1 Quality in the Context of European Industrial Policy

The concept of industrial policy has been the subject of repeated controversies for many years in the Union. The issue of global competitiveness is often put forward as the objective for industrial policy. Underlying this concern with competitiveness is a perception that it is of primary importance in determining standards of living both absolutely, and relatively across nations. Competitiveness is recognized as the key to gaining a greater share of world wealth generation and with it a higher standard of living. Moreover, there are good reasons to expect competitive success to be cumulative for considerable periods of time. However, it is also true that competitive success can be reversed - nations and firms which have been highly competitive at one stage of history can lose their advantage over time (of course, the opposite is also true).

The competitiveness of nations is nothing more than an appropriate aggregate of the competitiveness of the firms which they contain (measured either in terms of production or in terms of ownership, for in a world of direct investment and capital mobility, the two can differ substantially). To understand competitiveness, its link to quality and the role of industrial policy, we have to recognise the different levels at which competitiveness is generated and of the important feedbacks which link the various levels. A useful starting point is the recent work by Michael Porter who draws attention to competing explanations of competitiveness.[33] His own preferred definition is in terms of national productivity, where productivity is broadly defined:

A nation's firms must relentlessly improve productivity in existing industries by raising product quality, adding desirable features, improving product technology, or boosting production efficiency.[34]

The basis for enhanced competitiveness can be found in increasing investments in physical, human and knowledge capital, developing closer links between firms, their suppliers and customers, encouraging the diffusion of technology to smaller firms and through public support for the development of risky long-term technologies. In a similar vein, Rothwell and Zegveld in their review of technology policies, identify three elements of a balanced and integrated technology policy to restore industrial competitiveness.[35] These are:

13

- Technical opportunity; this defines the capacity to change the ways in which things are currently done and includes, for example, the technical and scientific infrastructure.
- The structure and dynamics of the industrial sector in terms of propensities to innovation and propensities to grow; crudely, this links 'demand pull' to 'technology push'.
- The size and structure of market demand; i.e. the incentives to innovate.

Together these factors constitute the most significant structural dimensions of competitiveness. Governments can intervene to influence each of these elements as well as their interdependence.

Within the European Union itself there has been a growing consensus on the type of policy needed to lay down the conditions for a strong and competitive industry. The main issue is which conditions need to be present in order to strengthen the optimal allocation of resources by market forces, towards accelerating structural adjustment and towards improving industrial competitiveness and the industrial and particularly technological long-term framework. While it is recognized that the main responsibility for industrial competitiveness must lie with firms themselves, there is a role for public authorities in providing the framework within which this can most effectively happen.

Thus the European Community document, 'Industrial Policy in an Open and Competitive Environment (COM(90)556)', argues that Community industrial policy should be built around an adequate balance between the following elements:

- the laying down of stable and long term conditions for an efficiently functioning market economy;
- the provision of the main catalysts for structural adjustment; and
- the development of the instruments to accelerate structural adjustment and to enhance competitiveness.[36]

The document recognizes that industry adapts on a permanent basis to the signals provided by the market through a process of structural adjustment. Structural adjustment and international competitiveness are closely linked since the ability to produce effectively for markets comes precisely from the speedy adjustment of resources to demand which is at the basis of structural adjustment. Three main areas cover the principal stages of structural adjustment:

- the prerequisites required for structural adjustment to get under way;
- the catalysts, which act on the willingness of business to undertake adjustment in reply to pressures and opportunities; and,
- the accelerators, which further develop structural adjustment.

European Community industrial policy is addressing these three stages. Within this policy the importance of quality (and specifically quality management systems) has been explicitly recognized. Quality systems underpin the dynamic adjustment of resources to demand and are seen as a significant source of competitive advantage by firms and governments alike. Standards and third party certification add credibility to quality systems and are a major reason for national government and European Commission involvement. In addition, a range of other quality promotion approaches have been adopted - these are discussed in the next section.

5.2 Public Promotion of Quality

Governments typically promote quality through a range of schemes and initiatives. Quality promotion can be defined as the set of policies involving government intervention in the economy with the intent of improving the quality of firms' products and services. These range from the 'direct' promotion of quality, quality management guidelines (including standards and certification) and training schemes to more general training, financial incentives and innovation promotion schemes that may include a significant quality element. Public promotion of quality has an important role in industrial policies, as there is a relationship between the development of quality management philosophy and the development of new industrial paradigms, and it is possible to identify stages in the development of the various government schemes and initiatives. Thus, in general terms government policy has tended to move (or is moving) from policies that support quality control and inspection of adoption of minimum standards, through to those that support quality assurance and finally those which are promoting total quality management within companies.

5.2.1 Quality Standards

Rothwell and Zegveld listed in broad terms the means by which governments influence technological innovation as: procurement; technical regulations referring to safety, environment, consumer protection etc; support to the R&D infrastructure; support to small businesses; and general macro-economic policies.[37] Little reflection is needed to realize that the first three categories are inherently related to standards. Procurement typically involves compliance to standards, regulations refer to standards, and finally, standards are actually specified by engineering communities through bodies that are part of the R&D infrastructure.

For most of the 20th century standards have been an integral part of industrial policies of the developed countries affecting innovation and accordingly their competitive performance. National product specifications provided for a rapid diffusion of innovation through the engineering communities, provided the basis for national standards specification bodies, and, through their links with the relevant communities, provided for a rapid generation and diffusion of the necessary skills.[38] Furthermore, this diffusion effectively and sometimes mandatorily excluded foreign products from domestic markets. Needless to say, national standards irrespective of whether they concern safety, or other characteristics of product use, were essentially quality standards. Accordingly, the quality management techniques of companies were adapted to ensure that their products satisfied these standards.

National production systems with innovation policies organized around national product specifications faced immense problems in the environment of the 'new era'.[39] First, standards can only effectively perform their role as a means of industrial policy in technologically leading countries. In countries that are technological followers the imposition of standards would either exclude local production from new industries or simply destroy local production. Second, national standardization mechanisms had to cope with shortening product life-cycles. This meant that standards would have to be constantly devised, updated and diffused at an increasing pace. In such a situation, conventional product quality standards became increasingly inadequate.

As a response to this situation quality management process standards have been increasingly adopted. This approach has been adopted in the ISO 9000 and EN 29000 series. These standards specify quality assurance mechanisms for firms rather than the quality specifications of their products. Thus, their definition can be seen as part of a strategy to diffuse, through engineering communities, quality management practices that will increase the flexibility of firms to adopt product improvements. In many cases governments and other actors within national production systems have launched campaigns to increase the awareness of companies of these standards, and even to enforce them on to industries.

It is questionable whether the quality management techniques promoted by these standards are appropriate for all companies and sectors. The first issue is, indeed, whether quality management itself is an activity suitable to all. Here, a number of analysts and consultants have argued that consumers accustomed to Japanese products now demand quality in everything.[40] A few years ago the label 'Made in Germany' was enough to guarantee 'high-quality' for consumers. This is no longer the case. Thus, the quality demanding culture that seems to be emerging in modern societies has been identified by Lascelles and Dale as a shift in the market paradigm.[41] As Feigenbaum argues: 'quality has become a central area of basic economic and social emphasis'.[42]

The second issue concerning the adoption of quality management standards is whether they are accompanied by an improvement orientated culture. Lascelles and Dale argued that TQM is a set of management prescriptions that ought to be observed by companies wishing to survive in a competitive environment in which quality control becomes a prime competitive strength.[43] However, if TQM is approached as the introduction of intermediate quality control layers in the production process, then it becomes a very difficult cost-saving exercise in which the cost installing a TQM system and detecting defective intermediaries has to be greater than the cost of the defective products. As Watanabe argued, it is the commitment to quality improvement that makes the difference between Japanese and Western versions of TQM.[44] Only when employees become responsible and committed to improvement, can competitive gains be realized through innovation and the flexibility and innovativeness of firms increase through TQM practices.

5.2.2 Incentives and Awards

In this context it is useful to look briefly at awards given by a number of private organisations with the intention of promoting good quality management practice. Typically, these cover a much wider scope than the standards discussed above. The most prestigious awards and those with the highest profiles are the Deming Prize, Malcolm Baldrige Award, and most recently, the European Foundation for Quality Management (EFQM) Award.

- *The Deming Prize* is awarded by the Japanese Union of Scientist and Engineers. There is no limit to the number of awards which can be given in any particular year, since it is not a prize as such but rather marks an advanced stage in an organization's development towards total quality improvement.

- *The Malcolm Baldridge National Quality Award* was established by the United States Congress in 1987 as a presidential award and recognizes the quality achievements of American companies. Its examiners look at seven criteria as part of the award procedure. Up to two awards can be given each year in each of three categories:

    – manufacturing companies or their subsidiaries;

    – service organisations of their subsidiaries; and,

    – small businesses.

- *The EFQM Award* was founded in 1988 by the presidents of 14 leading European companies. At its first meeting in London in 1990, members of the Foundation decided to instigate a European Quality Award in association with the European Commission and the European Organisation for Quality (EOQ). Candidates for the award are evaluated against eight criteria.

The essential difference between the ISO 9000 series and the EFQM, Baldridge and Deming auditing procedures is their scope; the area which they are trying to audit. The ISO 9000 series is intended to judge quality assurance systems. It has little to do with the quality of a total organization or its strategy. Only ISO 9004 looks at the management of quality in depth, rather than only the quality systems. However, ISO 9004 only has the status of guidelines, which are not assessable and will not be used as a base for certification. The ISO judges against the standards and specification, as laid down by the organisation itself. Thus, it will certify the implementation of the quality plan as documented in the organization's own quality handbook. It will not certify the adequacy of the quality handbook.

In contrast, the basis for the Deming, Baldridge and EFQM procedures goes far deeper. Not only do they cover the same aspects that are present in ISO 9001, 9002 and 9003, but they also attempt to assess the factors raised in ISO 9004. The essence of these audits is that quality improvement has to be seen in its relationship to the total strategy of the business. The ISO places far less emphasis on examining the actual quality improvement process itself, as opposed to its results. Deming, Baldridge and EFQM lay much greater stress on the management of the actual process.

The second major difference between ISO and the Deming, Baldridge and EFQM audits involves the reference system used - that is, the norms and standards forming the basis for assessment. The ISO norms and standards have been externally defined by ISO technical committees and formulated for their relevance to all business situations, and as such the usefulness of ISO standards for many organizations, such as the service or software industries, is open to question (see, for instance, the UK TickIT initiative which is specifically related to the software industry).[45] The issue is currently under discussion in a number of national and international fora.

Deming, Baldridge and EFQM are far more encompassing. Their guidelines for assessment are clear. The basis of both these awards is that every organization is different. Organizations operate in different market situations, with different people, and different business histories and cultures. Therefore, there is no best way to improve a quality process. As long as the organization can justify why a particular approach is being taken, then it may well be judged quite acceptable. The essence of these awards is that the organization will be judged upon its ability to understand its own market position and the role which quality can play within its total business strategy.

The third difference between the ISO procedures and the Deming, Baldridge and EFQM lies in the auditing process itself. In some respects, all of the procedures are similar. For example, all auditors are externally appointed and the organization has no choice, either in who is appointed or in the procedures which they subsequently follow. There are some important differences in the types of individuals used as auditors by the four bodies.

ISO auditors have been selected and certified as approved bodies for auditing. Unfortunately, these auditing organizations are, in most cases, also consulting or advisory organizations in quality improvement. There is therefore, in theory at least, the possibility of a conflict of interest.

A fourth area of difference between ISO and the Deming, Baldridge and EFQM Awards lies in the actual role which the auditor fulfils. The ISO procedure involves passive auditing. The external auditor carries out his assessment on non-compliances. A non-compliance is any incident which, in practice, does not conform to that specified in the quality plan or quality handbook. In contrast, Deming, Baldridge and EFQM have within their procedures a clear element of active auditing. Discussion and learning can occur with the result that the auditing process can become an extremely effective form of cheap consultancy.

5.2.3 Other Quality Promoting Activities

Governments as well as other actors engage in a number of other measures and schemes with the intent of improving the quality of firms' products and services. These complement the 'direct' promotion of quality management guidelines (including standards) and range from training schemes to more general training, financial incentives and innovation promotion schemes that may include a significant quality element. In general terms quality promotion activities can be characterized in terms of those which support research, those promoting awareness, those designed to increase the rate of adoption through the use of subsidies, those supporting education and training, and, those which attempt to improve quality through public procurement practices.

Research

Although a considerable body of literature exists on subjects such as the techniques of quality management and certification-based quality assurance systems, there are notable gaps, including how to assess the effectiveness of quality assurance, modelling the progress an organization is making towards developing a total approach to quality, supplier development, and quality improvement change agents.[46] Despite the importance of product and service quality to corporate and national well-being, there is, with a few notable exceptions, a lack of academic research on quality management in many European countries. Quality management is a new field of enquiry and, until more research is carried out, will remain a problematic academic subject.

Awareness

Aschner and Pataki analyzed more than a thousand journal articles, conference papers, studies and other documents.[47] In summarizing their results they produced an international picture of quality consciousness and knowledge of managers. An adapted version of their findings is presented below in Figure 2. The figure indicates that quality aspects do not play a central role in managerial activities in many regions of the world, and in some countries quality is only of peripheral importance

Figure 2: Quality consciousness of managers in different countries

Country or region	Role of Quality in Management	Level of Quality Consciousness
Japan	Quality is the focus of management.	Excellent
US	The role of quality is gaining importance; in several companies it will soon be the focus.	Good
Western Europe	Quality is considered a special professional problem of the management. In several countries government measures are taken to emphasise the role of quality.	Satisfactory
Eastern European countries and some developing countries	Quality is treated as a special problem focused mainly on workmanship.	Limited
Other countries	Quality is a secondary issue or not part of managerial activities.	Incidental

Source: adapted from Aschner and Pataki

Adoption

Policies to encourage the adoption of good quality management practices are found in most countries. Questions arise as to whether these schemes should cover all sectors or some, all companies, or only SMEs or whether such schemes should operate directly or indirectly (i.e. directly through the use of consultants or publicity, or indirectly through large firms encouraging quality improvement in their suppliers).

Education and Training

One of the consequences of rapid technological progress has been the need for constantly upgrading the skills in the labour market. In the field of quality, this need has resulted in quality management training programmes initiated by various organizations, often as part of government programmes. Indeed professional training is a rapidly expanding area of activity in all of the countries investigated. Accordingly, higher education programmes are increasingly incorporating quality management studies to provide up-to-date and useful skills to their students. Furthermore, education and training activities are seen as some of the ways to promote awareness, and thus to complement quality awareness campaigns.

References

1. International Standardization Organization (1987), *ISO 8402 - Quality Vocabulary*, Geneva.

2. Solow, R. (1957), 'Technical Change and the Aggregate Production Function', *Review of Economics and Statistics:*, Vol X, 313-320.

    Mansfield, E. (1968), *The Economics of Technical Change*, New York, Norton;

    Mansfield, E. (1977), *The Production and Application of New Industrial Technology*, New York, Norton.

3. Schumpeter, J. A. (1912), *The Theory of Economic Tradition*, Cambridge Mass., Harvard University Press, (translated in 1934).

4. Kuznets, S. (1930), *Secular Movements in Production and Prices*, New York, Houghton Mifflin.

    Kuznets, S. (1971) *Economic Growth of Nations*. New York, Belnap Press.

5. Nelson, R. R. and S. G. Winter (1977), 'In search for a useful theory of innovation'. *Research Policy*, Vol. 6, 36-76.

6. Georghiou, L. G. et al., (1986), *Post-innovation Performance*. London, Macmillan.

7. Lancaster, K. J. (1966), 'A new approach to consumer theory', *Journal of Political Economy*, Vol. 74, 132-157.

8. Lascelles, D.M. and Dale, B. (1988), 'A Review of the Issues Involved in Quality Improvement', *International Journal of Quality and Reliability Management*, Vol. 15, 76-94.

9. Crosby, P.C. (1979), *Quality is Free*, Sevenoaks, Hodder and Stoughton.

10. Juran, J.M. (1979), *Quality Control Handbook*, McGraw-Hill, New York.

11. ISO 8402, op. cit.

12. Teece, D. J. (1986), 'Profiting from Technological Innovation: Implications for Integration, Collaboration, Licensing and Public Policy', *Research Policy* , Vol. 15, 285-305.

13. Porter, M. E. (1985), *Competitive Advantage*, New York, Free Press.

    Porter, M. E. (1990), *The Competitive Advantage of Nations*. New York, Free Press.

    Chesnais, F. (ed); (1992), *Technology and the Economy: the Key Relationships*, Paris, OECD.

14. Lundvall, B-A. (1993), National Systems of Innovation, London, Pinter.

15. Lascelles and Dale, op. cit.

16. Ishikawa, K. (1985), *What is Total Quality Control? The Japanese Way*, New York Prentice-Hall.

17. ISO 8402, op. cit.

18. Lascelles and Dale, op. cit.

19. Lascelles and Dale, op. cit.

20. ISO 8402, op. cit.

21.   Georghiou, L. et al, op. cit.

22.   Womack, J.P., Jones, D. and Roos, D. (1990), *The Machine that Changed the World*, London, Macmillan.

23.   Hill, C.T. (1992), 'New Manufacturing Paradigms, New Manufacturing Policies?', *Technological Forecasting and Social Change*, Vol. 41, 351-363.

24.   Vos, C. A. (1992), *Manufacturing Strategy: Process and Content*, London,Chapman and Hall.

25.   Ibid.

26.   The prestige which these 'Quality Gurus' enjoy is such that no reference to quality can ignore them. Thus a short profile of their approaches is attached as an annex.

27.   For example see:

      Fine, C.H. (1985), *Managing Quality: A Comparative Assessment, Manufacturing issues*, New York, Boon Allen and Hamilton.

      Geeruliet, V. (1984), *Three of a Kind: A Reflection on the Approach to Quality*, Corporate Quality Bureau, Philips Group NV.

      Main, J. (1986), 'Under the Spell of the Quality Gurus', *Fortune*, 18 August.

28.   Fine, op. cit.

29.   Watanabe, S. (1990) 'Work-organization, Technical Progress and Culture with Special Reference to Small Group Activities in Japanese Industries', Paper presented in the Technology and Competitiveness Conference, The French Ministry for Industry and Regional Planning, The French Ministry for Research and Technology, OECD, Paris, 24-27 June.

30.   Stoneman, P. and Vickers, J. (1988), 'The Assessment: The Economics of Technology Policy', *Oxford Review of Economic Policy*, Vol. 4, i-xvi, 1988.

31.   Ibid.

32.   Hill, op. cit.

33.   Porter, M. E. (1990), op. cit.

34.   Ibid.

35.   Rothwell, R. and Zegveld, W. (1981), *Industrial Innovation and Public Policy*, London, Pinter

36.   CEC (1990), *Industrial Policy in an Open and Competitive Environment*, COM(90)556, Luxembourg.

37.   Rothwell and Zegveld, op. cit.

38.   Kastrinos, N. (1993) National Strategies for Quality Improvement: the Case of Greece, Paper for the 4th International Conference on Productivity and Quality Research, Miami 9-12 February 1993.

39.   Hill, op. cit.

40.   Friesecke, R. F. (1983), 'The Quality Revolution: a Challenge to Management', *Managerial Planning*, Vol 32, 7-9, 26.

41.   Lascalles and Dale, op. cit.

42.   Feigenbaum, A.V. (1983), *Total Quality Control*, New York, McGraw-Hill.

43.   Lascelles and Dale, op. cit.

44.   Watanabe, op. cit.

45.   TickIT, (1991), Department of Trade and Industry, London.

46.   Lascelles and Dale, op. cit.

47.   Aschner and Pataki, op. cit.

Part Two:

Overview of Recent Developments

Overview of Recent Developments

Brendan Barker

1. Introduction

This section presents a short overview of recent developments in the twelve European Community (now European Union) member countries. These are reviewed in more detail in Part Three of the report. It is organized in terms of the framework used to collect information in each of the countries on quality promoting activities. First, the emergence of quality as an issue is examined. Second, the 'quality infrastructure' found in the different countries is discussed. Third, examples of significant quality promoting schemes and initiatives are reviewed. Finally, the trajectories of future developments at regional, national and European levels are highlighted.

2. Emergence of Quality as an Issue

It is apparent that concern over quality has emerged at different times and for different reasons within the countries surveyed. To some extent, the emphasis of programmes and initiatives adopted has been heavily influenced by the time at which concern with quality was first expressed reflecting the dominant quality ideology at the time. Essentially it is possible to identify three waves of interest: those countries where concern with quality emerged in the 1960s and 1970s (here the emphasis was on quality assurance systems and the establishment of a standards and certification infrastructure); those where it emerged in the 1980s (when the emphasis was more on the development and introduction of total quality management-based systems); and those in which it is only just emerging now. The *British* (closely followed by the *Irish*) and *French* governments were amongst the first in Europe to become aware of the importance of quality and, in particular, that there was a role for government in promoting improved quality throughout the economy. The British government had long been active in quality issues related to defence procurement. During the 1960s and 1970s its attention was increasingly drawn to the importance of quality in industry in general. Similarly, public involvement with quality in France began with the quality requirements of the purchasing bodies of the Ministry of Defence in the late 1940s and the early 1950s. From the beginning of the 1970s, the French government began to express concern about the key role of product quality in competitiveness and became aware of the necessity of public involvement in the definition of a national policy toward quality.

In *Belgium* the first initiatives in the field of quality originated in the department of Flanders in 1970, following a visit to Japan. This visit led to the creation of a provincial centre for education, training and support in quality management.

Subsequently, similar centres were opened in the other regions. Initiatives at the national level occurred much later - a national accreditation act was passed only in July 1990. In the *Netherlands* the first concerns regarding quality were expressed in a memorandum from the Ministry of Economic Affairs in 1976. The approach adopted by the Dutch government has changed over time. It is possible to distinguish roughly three phases in government policy. In the first, activities emphasized quality control and assurance. In the second, quality management was emphasized. Finally, in the third and current phase, companies are actively encouraged to take on responsibility for quality improvement themselves, rather than relying on a package of activities provided by the government - reflecting what seems to be an indirect approach by government to promote total quality management in companies.

Danish initiatives reflect the gradual evolution of industrial policy to take account of the development of 'new era' manufacturing. The core of this approach is an emphasis on: cooperation within and between companies and other organizations; an integrative approach to technical and organizational innovation; and the importance of human resource management in developing the technical and organizational competencies of both management and employees. This three-point approach has begun to underpin the entire Danish national system of innovation. It is strongly conducive to the evolution of the national quality infrastructure and the diffusion of total quality control principles.

The general situation in *Germany* was characterized by a lack of concern with quality as a competitive problem. Compared to other industrial countries, the German recognition of quality as an issue occurred rather late. Industry (to a certain extent justifiably) relied on the reputation of products made in Germany. From late 1987, quality began to emerge as an issue with increasing recognition of the threat posed by superior quality goods from Japan.

In both *Spain* and *Portugal* the emergence of the European Single Market has been perceived as a serious challenge by both government and industry. Both countries have responded with large-scale national programmes, which in the case of Spain is directed primarily towards establishing the necessary infrastructure for quality monitoring but also encompasses more general quality promotion activities. Portugal has been able to build on an (already) existing infrastructure.

In the *Greek*, *Italian* and *Luxembourg* cases only now is there effective recognition (and action) that quality is an issue to be tackled at the national level, again pushed by developments at the European level.

2.1 The Diffusion of Quality Concepts

Most of the country reviews present evidence of the diffusion of quality concepts throughout the economy. Surveys conducted in the countries show that typically firms are already well aware (and becoming more so) of the relationship between quality and competitiveness. However, this is not always matched by effective attempts at quality improvement. There are a number of reasons for this. Firms (particularly SMEs) may well be aware of the importance of quality, but may lack awareness of appropriate quality improving approaches. Even when aware, they may lack the resources (both financial and skills) necessary to implement and exploit those approaches. Both situations may justify government involvement.

A useful proxy measure of quality awareness is provided by the uptake of quality standards. This uptake has been much greater in the UK than in other European countries, largely reflecting the greater past emphasis on standards in the UK and the fact that the framework supporting their use has been in existence for very much longer. However, it is apparent that certification by firms to internationally accepted quality standards is rapidly increasing throughout Europe (see Figure 3, page 28). While the use of such standards has undoubtedly been effective in raising the average level of quality awareness (and indeed the average level of quality) throughout Europe, it is important to recognize the limitations of quality standards (as discussed in the previous chapter).

Evidence for the diffusion of TQM and related approaches is, by its very nature (representing fundamental cultural shifts specific to individual firms), much more difficult to determine. Nevertheless, a number of surveys have presented some evidence that these approaches are increasingly diffusing through large firms. Unfortunately, the evidence for the diffusion of TQM techniques in SMEs is not so positive and indeed is one reason why SMEs are a particular focus of most promotion activities.

3. The Quality Infrastructure

Although in this study we are primarily interested in public sector schemes and initiatives, it is usually the case in the countries investigated that private bodies have a significant involvement in defining and/or implementing those schemes and initiatives. Furthermore, industrial and professional associations in some countries often initiate quality promotion schemes, performing a role more usually undertaken by the public sector in other countries.

By defining, as Mowery does, innovation as 'any change in the sociotechnical systems of design, manufacture, distribution, and/or use which improves the performance of the entire system with regard to cost and quality of product, or of service to users and/or employees' it follows that improvements in quality necessarily depend on innovations in the sociotechnical system.[1] Thus quality promotion is one of the many activities undertaken within a national innovation system. Adapting Mowery's definition of national innovation systems, the quality infrastructure can be defined as the array of public and private institutions and organizations within the economy that fund and promote quality improvement.

Figure 3: Diffusion of quality standards (ISO 9000 or equivalent) in selected EU member countries

- Adoption of BS 5750 (equivalent to ISO 9 000, EN 29,000, etc.) by UK companies (scale is in thousands).

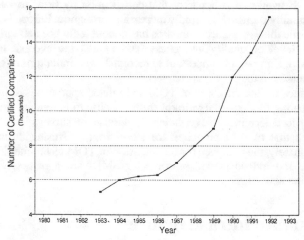

Source: BSI

- Adoption of ISO 9000 (or equivalent) by organizations in a number of European Countries.

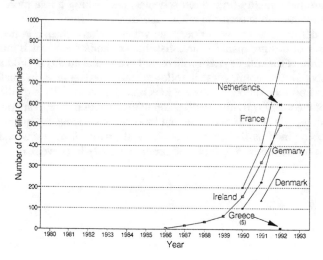

Various national sources

28

A wide diversity of organizations form the quality infrastructure. The quality promotion system (as we have argued, a subset of the innovation system) results from the interplay between these different organizations at different levels within the national industrial framework. Quality-promoting activities typically occur through multilayer networks, involving firms within and between sectors, government and universities, and other networks. Exchange of information and experience takes place through the networking of individuals and organizations at the regional, national and European level. At these levels the quality infrastructure is emerging both through creation of new institutions and the coordination of existing ones. These were categorized as follows:

- industrial policy-making bodies;
- public organizations involved in specifying and monitoring standards (i.e. third party certification);
- education organizations;
- training organizations;
- industrial associations;
- professional associations;
- consultancies; and,
- large companies.

In looking at the quality promoting infrastructure, perhaps the most important dimension is that of the public-private sector. Some countries have a significant degree of state involvement in virtually all aspects of quality promotion. By contrast, within Germany for example, there are no broad-based actions to increase public awareness. In this regard, the semi-public and non-profit private sectors have taken the initiative. Thus, unlike other countries, the public sector in Germany does not award promotion prizes, rather the initiative lies in private hands (the DGQ 'Walter-Masing-Preis').

3.1 Quality Policy-Making Bodies

Quality is an issue involving most areas of national life. For this reason, a large number of public bodies can have a policy interest in the area. However, quality issues in the civil sector first arose in relation to manufacturing. For this reason, the main quality policy-making responsibility usually resides within those organizations having responsibility for industrial policy. To a large extent, the level at which this occurs depends on the wider political structure of the countries investigated. Thus, in Belgium, recently agreed constitutional arrangements have led to departmental governments (Flanders, Walloonia and Brussels) being able to define and implement industrial policies with respect to their regions. By comparison, over the last few years France has adopted a comprehensive quality promotion strategy at the national level, with the French Ministry of Trade and Industry (MICE) - through its quality directorate, SQUALPI - being the main public body supporting French public policy on quality management and standards. However, even in France there are significant regional quality-promoting activities operating within the national framework. For this reason, the Rhône-Alpes region is of particular interest because of its official position as a 'pilot region' for most of the bodies and associations dealing with quality promotion.

To a greater or lesser extent in all of the countries investigated, responsibilities for quality promotion are shared between national and regional bodies. The degree of freedom given to regional activities depends on the historical relationship between central government and the regions. Figure 4, below, summarizes the situation in each of the countries investigated.

Figure 4: Main actors in quality policy formulation

Country	Main Actors in Policy Formulation
Belgium	Departmental governments
Denmark	Ministry of Industry through National Agency of Industry and Trade
France	Ministry of Industry and International Trade through Quality Directorate (SQUALPI)
Germany	Federal Ministry of Science and Technology (BMFT)
Greece	Ministry of Industry, Energy and Technology
Ireland	Irish Science and Technology Agency (EOLAS) and the Training and Employment Authority (FAS)
Italy	Little from central government, some active regional governments
Luxembourg	None
Netherlands	National Ministry of Economic Affairs, increasing regional involvement
Portugal	National Ministry of Industry and Energy
Spain	MICYT very active, much regional activity within context of National Quality Plan
UK	Department of Trade and Industry (DTI), some regional activity

3.2 Organizations Involved in Specifying and Monitoring Standards

At the heart of the national infrastructure for industrial quality are those institutions with responsibilities for standardization, certification, calibration, testing and inspection.

Many major purchasers in the public and private sectors (see below) require their suppliers to meet and document their compliance with certain criteria with regard to process quality, inspection and administration, and to permit regular checks and process audits. During the 1960s and 1970s throughout Europe a number of these organizations introduced quality schemes.

However, the emphasis in these schemes was still on inspection, and the direct costs of the scheme were borne by the purchaser (second party certification). While such arrangements can operate effectively in a simple, single customer-supplier relationship, they become increasingly complicated the more complex such relationships become. It was often necessary for larger manufacturers to submit to multiple assessments of their manufacturing and management capabilities by several major customers each year.

Recognition of this problem has led to the development of a widely accepted standard for quality management which can not only be applied by a customer to assess the capabilities of its supplier, but can be operated by independent third-party certification bodies (i.e. third party certification).

The route to achieving approval to ISO 9000 is through independent third party assessment and certification by an accredited certification body. The certification body is an independent organization which will assess a company's quality system against published criteria - ISO 9000. Where these criteria are met, a certificate is issued indicating this achievement. Accreditation is granted to a certification body following successful assessment of its technical competence and the effectiveness of its own quality system by an accreditation body.

Suitably endorsed ISO 9000 certificates will be recognized throughout the European Union and the European Free Trade Association (EFTA). However, since being adopted by the European Union and its member states, it is becoming clear that there are some limitations with the quality standard's broad-base application throughout Europe. The major limitation currently concerns the level of implementation of the 'Global Approach' to be found across Europe. The United Kingdom and the Netherlands are two of the most advanced member states with regard to the formation of national councils for the registration and supervision of certification bodies. Within the UK, certification bodies have been active for several years with the result that many thousands of organizations are certified to the standards. At the other end of the spectrum, some countries within the EU have yet to publish their intentions or timing plans for testing and certification as adopted by EFTA and EU members. This is manifested at present by some national councils refusing to accept certification across some of the boundaries, although both practices are not in the spirit of the 'Global Approach'. Without a European umbrella organization to oversee the national authorities and ensure common standards of interpretation, there will inevitably be disputes about standards of assessment and credibility of certification bodies and their assessors. Although the 'Global Approach' has been adopted by the EC, its introduction across Europe is likely to be slower than industry would like.

National quality standards infrastructure arrangements are briefly described below and listed in Figure 5 (page 33).

The National Quality Standards Infrastructures

- The BNI-IBN (Belgisch Institut voor Normalisatie-Institut Belge de Normalisation, Belgium Standards Institution) is the national organization for standards specification, and the National Council for Accreditation and Certification is the national organization for the accreditation of certification organizations.

- The DS (Dansk Standardiseringsråd, Danish Standards Association) is responsible for setting quality standards, while the National Agency of Industry and Trade acts as the national accreditation body.

- Within France, AFNOR (Association Française de Normalisation, French Standards Association) is responsible for standards specification, and AFAQ (Association Française pour l'Assurance Qualité, French Association for Quality Certification), has responsibility for accreditation.

- In Germany, standards are established centrally by DIN (Deutsche Institut für Normung, German Institute for Standards), while the recently established DAR (Deutsche Akkredittierungerat, German Accreditation Organization) and TGA (Trägergeminschaft für Akkredittierung, Society for Accreditation) have responsibility for accreditation. Currently, four certification bodies are accredited, with the DQS (Deutsche Gesellschaft für Qualität, German Society for Accreditation of Quality Assurance Systems) and TÜVCERT (Zertifizierungsgemeinschaft für Qualitätssicherungssysteme des Technische Überwachungsvereine, Association for the Certification of Quality Assurance Systems) undertaking most certifications.

- In Greece, ELOT, the Hellenic Organisation for Standardization, is the organization responsible for standardisation and certification. An accreditation council was set up in 1989.

- In Ireland, certification is performed by the NSAI (National Standards Authority of Ireland). Accreditation is undertaken by the EOLAS (Irish Technology Agency), which also has a consultancy division undertaking certification.

- In Italy, UNI (Ente Nazionale Italiano di Unificazione, Italian Standards Institute) is the standards body, while SINCERT (Sistema Nazionale per l'Accreditamento degli Organismi di Certificazione, National System for the Accreditation of Certifcation Organizations) has responsibility for accreditation. Five certification bodies were accredited by 1992.

- As yet, Luxembourg has no standardization, accreditation and certification bodies. A quality Act was due to be agreed in 1993. The Act will prepare the infrastructure required to implement international quality agreements.

- In the the Netherlands the NNI (Nederlands Normalistic Institut, Netherlands Standards Institute) is the national organisation responsible for standardisation. The accreditation body - RvC (Stichting Raad voor Certificate, Council of Certification) - was created in 1981. There are currently 14 recognized certification bodies.

- In Portugal, the IPQ (Instituto Português da Qualidade, Portuguese Institute for Quality) is responsible for standardization activities. Within the scope of the SNGQ (Sistema Nacional de Gestão da Qualidade, National Quality Management System), the IPQ carries out accreditation and certification.

- In Spain, AENOR (Asociación Española de Normalización y Certificación, Spanish Association for Standards and Certification) was established in 1985 as the body responsible for implementing standards and certifying companies.
- The BSI (British Standards Institution) is responsible for setting standards, while the NACCB (National Accreditation Council for Certification Bodies) is the national statutory body established by the government in 1985 to undertake assessment of British certification bodies.

Figure 5: National Quality Standards Infrastructures

Country	Standards	Accreditation	Monitoring
Belgium	BNI/IBN	NAC-QS	7 third Party
Denmark	DS	National Agency of Industry and Trade	third Party
France	AFNOR	AFAQ	AFNOR + 32
Germany	DIN	DAR/TGA	DQS TUVCERT + 2
Greece	ELOT	Accreditation Council	ELOT
Ireland	NSAI	EOLAS	third party
Italy	UNI	SINCERT	?
Luxembourg	IBN	?	?
Netherlands	NNI	RvC	14 third party
Portugal	UNP	IPQ	IPQ
Spain	UNE	AENOR	AENOR
United Kingdom	BSI	NACCB	BSI 28 other third party

3.3 Other Components of the Infrastructure

As well as the formal quality bodies, a number of other actors are important in the promotion of quality.

3.3.1 Education and Training Organizations

These organizations are primarily universities, technical colleges and commercial schools at various levels of education, as well as centres for vocational training. An increasing trend in a number of countries (e.g. Denmark and the UK) is for these centres to operate as independent bodies selling educational and training services (e.g. professional development seminars, workshops courses) to the business sector.

3.3.2 Consultancies

The importance of consultancies in diffusing best practice amongst firms (particularly SMEs) is widely recognized. In many countries private consultancies have been active in the field of quality for a number of years, and recently there has been a rapid expansion in the number offering support in the area. Some public support may be provided where the market for quality consultancy is not yet properly developed. Thus, in the UK, public support is justified in terms of market failure (i.e. without such support smaller firms would find consultancy services to be costly, relevant consultants difficult to identify, and advice difficult to incorporate into their activities). In other countries, as in Greece, the public sector plays the major role in the consultancy domain. However, even in Greece there has been a growing private quality consultancy business.

3.3.3 Industrial and Professional Associations

Associations of employers play an important role in diffusing quality concepts through industries. In the same way, professional associations (including employee associations, trade unions, technical and managerial associations), play an important role in diffusing quality concepts at the level of individual actors.

In particular, national quality associations - often in conjunction with the EOQ - have taken the initiative in the formulation of education and training concepts and measures, partly due to the stimulus of recommendations from international organizations (for instance, the IAQ).

3.3.4 Large Companies

Many large companies have evolved their own sophisticated methods of supplier quality system evaluation (so-called second party certification). Often these involve rating assessed suppliers. The ratings enable the customer to rank all of its potential and existing suppliers from 'unacceptable' through 'acceptable' to 'preferred' or some other level of 'excellence'. A weakness of the ISO 9000 series is that it provides only a 'pass' or 'fail' certification. In the early stages of certification, and until industry gains confidence in the third party system, second party audits are likely to continue in many industries.

Essentially, the process of second party certification reflects the exercise of power on the part of the certifying organization. Normally, a buyer-supplier relationship exists between the two organizations in question, with the buyer auditing and certifying the supplier. This process is usually asymmetrical in favour of the buying organisation, which is in a position to impose quality control requirements on the supplier. This situation might be expected to cause resistance on the supplier side, but another kind of asymmetry in favour of the buyer might counteract this - the fact that the buyer, who as a normal rule is more competent in the field of quality control than the supplier, offers assistance in the development of quality control practices within the supplying company.

The crucial role of large industrial corporations in the diffusion of the TQM philosophy was widely observed. Large companies diffuse good practice in three main ways:

- through their own quality strategy with their suppliers;
- by focusing their own organization on total quality issues, they are constantly increasing the pressure on their suppliers; and,
- through their involvement in standardization and certification decision-making processes.

In Greece and Italy in particular, where the public promotion of quality is perhaps least developed, TQM initiatives have largely been limited to a relatively small community of subsidiaries of multinationals and large national firms.

4. Emphasis of Quality Activities

The nature of activities emphasized within quality-enhancing schemes differ in terms of coverage and level. Schemes may cover some or all sectors, and/or some or all companies. Typically, schemes have been targeted at the manufacturing sector. Increasingly the emphasis is shifting to include the service sector. In most cases, small and medium-sized enterprises have been a particular focus of programmes.

The level at which quality-enhancing activities operate also differs. In general terms, inspection, quality control, quality assurance and total quality management can be considered as a hierarchy in the evolution of quality management techniques. Thus in France, quality is defined in a comprehensive way ('Qualité Totale').

Figure 6 (page 36), provides a graphical representation of the main emphasis of current quality-promoting activities. Although necessarily simplistic, it is useful in helping to distinguish between those relatively 'advanced' European countries where the emphasis is on TQM, and those less advanced where the emphasis is on inspection and quality control. Typically, in the more advanced countries the quality infrastructure has been in place for a number of years. This, together with relatively widely diffused experience in quality control and quality assurance techniques, is leading to an increasing emphasis on TQM.

Figure 6: Emphasis of quality activities

Country	Activity			
	Inspection and testing	QC	QA	TQM
Belgium	**	**	***	**
Denmark	*	**	***	***
France	***	****	****	**
Germany	*	*	**	*****
Greece	*	*	*	*
Ireland	**	***	***	**
Italy	*	*	*	*
Luxembourg	*	*	*	*
Netherlands	*	*	***	****
Portugal	****	****	***	*
Spain	****	****	***	*
UK	**	**	*****	**

5. Quality Promoting Schemes and Initiatives

The quality-promoting organizations discussed in the previous section undertake and/or support a range of different quality related functions. It is possible to characterize these in the following way:

- Quality policies.
- Quality standards.
- Other quality promoting activities.
    - consultancy;
    - promotion of quality awareness;
    - research;
    - education and training.
- Evaluation of quality schemes.

Public sector initiatives in quality promotion will support one or more of these functions and usually involve a number of the types of organization described above.

5.1 Quality Policies

Quality policies are now usually seen as an integral part of industrial policy. Most governments explicitly recognize the relationship between quality and competitiveness at the firm, and ultimately national, levels. Policies usually relate to the development of an appropriate quality-supporting infrastructure (see above), procurement, improvement of quality awareness, research in support of quality improvements or diffusion, and education and training. In most of the countries investigated these are the responsibilities of many different organizations, and coordination of activities is sometimes problematic. A few countries, notably Spain, have or are developing an explicit overarching quality framework specifically to coordinate national and regional quality activities.

Public sector procurement practice is important in promoting quality. More of the major organizations are seeking contractual obligation to ISO 9000 as a condition of supply. In the UK, the Local Government Act of 1988 requires local authorities to put contracts for essential services out to competitive tender. A number of authorities have included ISO 9000 certification as a condition of tender.

5.2 Quality Standards

Public policy promotion initiatives in all of the countries have emphasized the use of quality standards. While recognizing that there is more to good quality management than simply achievement of certification, it is argued that the development and application of standards represents one of the most effective ways to approach the problem of improving quality across the economy as a whole.

The origins of these standards can be traced to attempts to combine quality assurance with the pursuit of technological superiority characterizing the US defence industry. Thus, the first management standard was devised in 1959 within the framework of the US military programme MIL-Q-9858 'Quality Program Requirements'. MIL-Q-9858 was revised in 1963 and was adopted by NATO in 1968 as Allied Quality Assurance Publication 1 (AQAP-1). In 1970, the British Ministry of Defence adopted the provisions of AQAP-1 as their Management Program Defence Standard DEF/STAN 05-8.

In 1979, the British Standards Institution used these predecessor standards to develop the world's first successful market-acceptable quality management standard designated, BS 5750. (DEF/STAN 05-8 was further revised to conform to the provisions of the then proposed BS 5750 and took on the designations of DEF/STAN 05-21, 22, 23, 24).

Drawing on the development of such standards in the UK, France and Germany, the International Standards Organization (ISO) introduced the quality management standard ISO 9000. In 1987, the two standards were reconciled making them essentially identical documents. In the same year the EC adopted the same standard as EN 29000. Figure 7 (page 38) lists equivalent national and international quality assurance standards.

In parallel with the introduction of internationally agreed standards, there was a recognition of the need to achieve a greater degree of coordination in the way compliance is assessed. The coupling of national standards to international ones (ie ISO 9000/EN 29000) has the further effect of reducing barriers to trade. Thus in 1989, the EC adopted a resolution that endorsed the key points of the Commission document 'A Global Approach to Certification, and Testing - Quality Measures for Industrial Products COM(89)209'. The objective of the Global Approach is to eliminate multiple checks on manufacturers and products caused by differing national regulations or by the behaviour of buyers, users and consumers. The cornerstone of this policy is the promotion of ISO 9000 and the necessary systems to support it, nationally and at the Union level.

Figure 7: International quality standards

Standards body (country)	Quality management and quality assurance standards: Guidelines for selection and use	Quality systems: Model for quality assurance in design/development, production, installation and servicing.	Quality systems: Model for quaity assurance in production and installation	Quality systems: Model for quality assurance in final inspection and test	Quality management and quality system elements: Guidelines
ISO	ISO 9000: 1987	ISO 9001: 1987	ISO 9002: 1987	ISO 9003: 1987	ISO 9004: 1987
European Community	EN 29000	EN 29001	EN 29002	EN 29003	EN 29004
Belgium	NBN X 50-002-1	NBN X 50-003	NBN X 50-004	NBN X 50-005	NBN X 50-002-2
Denmark	DS/ISO 9000 DS/EN 29000	DS/ISO 9001 DS/EN 29002	DS/ISO 9002 DS/EN 29002	DS/ISO 9003 DS/EN 29003	DS/ISO 9004 DS/EB 29004
France	NF X 50-121	NF X 50-131	NF X 50-132	NF X 50-133	NF X 50-122
Germany	DIN ISO 9000	DIN ISO 9001	DIN ISO 9002	DIN ISO 9003	DIN ISO 9004
Greece	ELOT EN 29000	ELOT EN 29001	ELOT EN 29002	ELOT EN 29003	ELOT EN 29004
Ireland	IS 300 Part O/ ISO 9000	IS 300 Part 1/ISO 9001	IS 300 Part 2/ISO 9002	IS 300 Part 3/ISO 9003	IS 300 Part 0/ISO 9004
Italy	UNI/EN 29000 - 1987	UNI/EN 29001 - 1987	UNI/EN 29002 - 1987	UNI/EN 29003 - 1987	UNI/EN 29004 1988
Luxembourg	NBN X 50-002-1	NBN X 50-003	NBN X 50-004	NBN X 50-005	NBN X 50-006
Netherlands	NBN-ISO 9000	NEN- ISO 9001	NEN-ISO 9002	NEN-ISO 9003	NEN-ISO 9004
Portugal	NP-EN 29000	NP-EN 29001	NP-EN 29002	NP-EN 29003	NP-EN 29004
Spain	UNE 66 900	UNE 66 901	UNE 66 902	UNE 66 903	UNE 66 904
United Kingdom	BS 5750: 1987 Part 0: Section 0.1 ISO 9000/ EN 29000	BS 5750: 1987 Part 1: ISO 9001/ EN 29001	BS 5750: 1987 Part 2: ISO 9002/ EN 29002	BS 5750: 1987 Part 3 ISO 9003/ EN 29003	BS 5750: 1987 Part 0: Section 0.2 ISO 9004/ EN 29003

5.3 Other Quality Promoting Activities

5.3.1 Consultancy

Consultancy support may take the form of advice to companies on specific quality assurance systems (ie how best to achieve certification to ISO 9000, or equivalent), or more general help in the implementation of a fully-fledged TQM system. A survey conducted in the UK in 1991 found that 78% of companies employ consultants to help implement a quality programme. The main reasons given were that they lacked in-house expertise and wished to speed up the process of gaining certification. Public authorities have been active in promoting consultancy as a means of transferring best-practice.

5.3.2 Quality Awareness and Promotion

A wide range of public and semi-public, professional and industrial associations are involved in quality promotion activities. Many countries have begun to introduce national quality awards. Some examples are given below.

The British Quality Awards scheme was launched in 1984 to give impetus to the government's initiatives arising from the 1982 White Paper. The intention was to create a national award which would encourage the adoption of TQM. Since its inception, 22 companies have won the award. At the beginning of 1991, the DTI announced that it had set up a committee to examine the scope for a new national award for quality. The committee has now reported and has recommended the introduction of a quality award based on similar criteria to those of the European Quality Award (see below).

Similarly, the MICYT (Spanish Ministry of Industry, Trade and Tourism) has recently launched the National Quality Award (1992). Following other European initiatives, it aims to develop further the adoption of quality practices and to promote excellence in quality in Spanish firms. The award, which carries no monetary value, is organised by MICYT in conjunction with the AECC (Spanish Association for Quality). Under the scheme, two awards are made: one to firms of more than 250 employees, and another to firms of less than 250 employees.

The European Quality Award is sponsored by the European Commission, The European Foundation for Quality Management (EFQM) and the European Organization for Quality (EOQ). To receive the prize, applicants must demonstrate that their approach to TQM has contributed significantly to satisfying the expectations of customers, employees and others with an interest in the company for the past few years.

The first step in an application for the European Quality Award is the collation of a body of quality management data from within the organization. There is significant value in this process even if the company is not successful in winning the award, as it will enable the company to assess its level of commitment to quality. It will also show the extent to which this commitment is being deployed - vertically through every level of the organization and horizontally in all areas of activity.

When the application is received it is marked by a team of up to six assessors, all of whom have undergone the same training course thus maximizing consistency. The application is scored on the basis of self-appraisal data supplied by the company with its application. The assessment is used to decide which applicants should be visited for further assessment. Visits involve the verification of the application and the inspection of the quality practices of the leading applicants. After the jury's final review and decision the European Quality Award is presented to the companies that demonstrate the highest standards of Total Quality Management. In the year following presentation of the award winners share their experience of Total Quality Management at EFQM seminars. These seminars offer a platform for the promotion of good practice TQM throughout Europe.

5.3.3 Research

Many public initiatives support research into the development and/or implementation of quality systems. The German BMFT's 'Programm Qualitätssicherung' is noteworthy. This measure is intended to promote basic research, practically-oriented research and cross-field cooperative projects, technology transfer for the broad diffusion in practice of scientific knowledge on quality; it also supports the work of standardization and the establishing of norms.

5.3.4 Education and Training

The value of training and education in promoting quality is widely recognized. In France, according to a survey conducted by the Ministry of Education in 1992, around 400 training and education schemes deal with quality-related issues. This major effort is shared among the universities, public and private bodies. By contrast, the education of managers in the UK is generally poor. Most education and training takes place within Higher and Further Education colleges and very little in business schools and university departments of management education. Many of these courses are technician- rather than management-oriented.

Elsewhere throughout Europe, two approaches are discernible at the higher education level:

- specialist technological universities, which teach quality management in the context of their expertise in particular sectors of industry;
- business schools, which teach elements of quality management as a subset of general management programmes.

5.4 Evaluation of Quality Schemes

Many of the quality-promoting schemes and initiatives identified in the survey are the subject of formal evaluations - an increasing trend for all publicly funded programmes. However, because most public measures have only recently been introduced, few formal outputs from these evaluations yet exist. In addition, the relative youth of many of the programmes means that, in many cases, the lessons learnt from earlier evaluations have yet to be fully applied in new programmes. The following section describes a selection of the evaluations and reviews which have been and are being undertaken. The most detailed evaluations have been undertaken in the Netherlands.

In 1988, an evaluation report, 'The Netherlands: Time for Quality!' ('Nederland:

hoogste tijd voor kwaliteit!'), was published with results and recommendations for the period 1988-1990.[2] The main conclusion of the advisory group was that, although much had been achieved in the previous three years, much remained to be done. The advisory group argued that the promotion of quality needed to be continued in order to introduce quality on a permanent basis in Dutch business. In particular, it argued that the Ministry of Economic Affairs should continue its quality policy by means of a total programme aimed at awareness, infrastructure, education and demonstration projects. As a result of the report's conclusions the Ministry launched the 'Quality and Logistics' programme ('Kwaliteit en Logistiek'). An intermediate evaluation of the programme has been undertaken and progress reports published in 1989, 1990 and in 1991 contain an overview of the activities carried out and the programme results.[3]

The evaluation found that the objectives of the information activities have been attained, but that most of the projects were directed to a single business group or industry. It was noted that the final target group, the business community, was not reached at all levels and in all sectors. It argued, however, that the creation of the KDI information and documentation centre, together with the establishment of the 'Dutch Quality' steering group, was likely to lead to an improvement in these activities.

Some projects in the field of knowledge infrastructure were realized with difficulty and results were obtained with considerable effort. The distribution of knowledge to companies often appeared to be a problem. However, there were also a number of very successful projects, - for instance the realization of 16 workshops in the mechanical and electrotechnical industry, instead of the planned eight workshops.

According to the objectives, a lot of attention has been paid to quality and logistics within the teaching programme of schools of Higher and Intermediate Vocational Education (HBO and MBO). In this respect, the ten projects in HBO schools appeared to be very successful, with the link between education and businesses with regard to quality being significantly improved, especially in higher and intermediary vocational education. However, most universities do not currently regard quality as a particular discipline. As a result, projects in universities appeared difficult to realize. This was also the case for schools of Lower Vocational Education.

Most demonstration projects have not yet been completed and there are no products available at this moment. The financial and time requirements demanded from companies, have caused some hesitance from potential companies. Most demonstration projects would not have been realized without the financial support of the programme. The distribution to all industries of knowledge obtained in the demonstration projects needs to continue. Most often, adaptations are needed in order to apply the project results more widely or more specifically to other industries. The programme has been prolonged and an additional budget has been made available for these adaptations.

The results of the programme were determined by means of a questionnaire circulated throughout the Dutch business community. At the start of the programme, it was found that 78% of Dutch companies paid attention to quality. More recent measurements in April 1991 showed that, during the period of the programme, 84% of the companies regarded quality as a central policy issue. In addition, the number of certified quality systems has increased significantly. In 1989, approximately 80 new certificates were granted and 370 were granted in 1991. TQM, however, is applied or fully developed in only 1% of all businesses.

In the UK, the Quality Consultancy scheme undertaken as part of the DTI Enterprise Initiative was the subject of a formal survey by the scheme contractors (Pera International and Salford University Business Services Limited) in 1991 (the results were published in 1992).[4] The survey was conducted against a background of increasing popularity of the scheme - around 200 companies each week were being referred for consultancy advice - with most companies seeking assistance with the introduction of a quality management system prior to certification to ISO 9000/BS 5750. The aims of the survey were to assess the progress of quality consultancy client companies to ISO 9000/BS 5750 and to undertake a post-consultancy analysis of the perceived benefits to clients of introducing a quality management system.

A total of 2317 firms (representing 34% of clients from the launch of the scheme in January 1988) who had completed a quality consultancy project prior to 31 December 1990 were interviewed by telephone.

The report concluded that certification to ISO 9000/BS 5750 will be achieved by up to 95% of clients who take advantage of a funded quality consultancy project. On average, certification followed 15 to 18 months after the commencement of a project. The report estimated that if demand for the scheme continued to increase at the current rate, about 45,000 UK firms will have achieved certification by 1995 following a DTI funded consultancy.

Firms saw a number of additional benefits arising directly from their introduction of a quality management system: 89% saw an improvement in operational efficiency; 76% in marketing; 48% in profitability; and 26% in export sales.

Concern that major competitor countries were engaged in nation-wide quality campaigns led to a 1989 study comparing quality related measures in a number of industrial countries with Germany.[5] Although not a formal evaluation, this study provides a decision base for policy measures in the field of quality in Germany. In addition, a number of broad empirical studies have been carried out to examine quality related activities in companies.

It is general practice in Germany to evaluate federal programmes. In the case of the CIM programme, which preceeded the current 'Qualitätssicherung' programme, the evaluation was completed during 1992 and provided an input into the later programme. The 'Industrielle Gemeinschaftsforschung' (industrial cooperative research programme) - the framework in which the AIF initiative 'Querschnittsforschung Qualitätssicherung' and the following projects have taken place has only recently been evaluated but this evaluation has not as yet covered quality related projects.

In Portugal, the PEDIP programme (launched with support from the EC) is intended to aid the development of Portuguese industry. It has a special sub-programme for quality (Programme 6). In addition, the other sub-programmes have also contributed to the development of quality infrastructures in Portugal in the past three years. At the moment, the PEDIP head office is undertaking an evaluation of the results of the programme. The analysis will encompass three components: direct audits of promoting entities, inter-sectoral analysis to evaluate the impact of PEDIP in Portuguese industry, and the influence of PEDIP on the attitudes of managers.

6. Overview and Outlook

From the individual country reports it is apparent that large imbalances in quality culture exist across Europe. In the previous chapter the concept of a 'national system of innovation' was introduced, namely the need to comprehend the wider institutional structures within which innovation occurs. Thus, developments in quality promotion (an activity we include within the broad definition of innovation) both determine and are determined by the institutional environment in an interactive process. For this reason the description of different national systems of innovation is fundamental to an understanding of why quality improvement has apparently occurred more rapidly and efficiently in some countries than others.

6.1 Emerging Trends at the National Level

Although *Belgium* is currently in a period of political transition, the network of organizations in the field of quality is clearly structured. The network consists of different levels which are closely interrelated. At the provincial/regional level several centres for quality are responsible for promotion and support of quality activities in companies. These organizations operate almost identically and are all autonomous. At the national level the Belgian Centre for Quality (BCK-CBQ) is the umbrella organization of all provincial and departmental quality centres.

Largely as a result of the efforts of the various independent quality organizations, the departmental governments have begun to recognize the importance of quality for their relative economic position. The quality organizations in Flanders are discussing with the Flemish government the creation of new programmes to stimulate TQM. The proposed programmes are based on a model of 'sharing quality management' for small and medium-sized companies in which several companies share a quality manager (subsidized by the Flemish government) for a given period. In the department of Walloonia, new developments in the field of quality are being realised within the scope of the national Act on Economic Expansion. Although, within the Act, loans were given for market research activities, these did not cover quality improvement activities. Following its increase of political power the Walloon government has reexamined the fields of application of the Act. The Walloon government will subsidize consultancy to small and medium-sized companies. The consultancy service will include quality audits with the purpose of certification of the company following the international standards.

The approach taken by the *Danish* government at the national level is unlikely to change significantly. At the regional level, it is presently difficult to identify future trends in the field of quality, although a second initiative in North Jutland may be taken in the short term (this remains speculation). At the national level, initiatives focusing solely on the field of quality are not being prepared. The Ministry of

Education is likely to be an increasingly important actor in the Danish quality infrastructure as the issue of quality becomes a major focus of courses within the legislation on vocational retraining.

It seems reasonable to suggest that the future development of the Danish quality infrastructure will see significant changes. The activities at the levels of industrial policy and the training and education system will continue to stimulate the diffusion of total quality control principles, thus contributing to the dynamism of the quality infrastructure. Furthermore, the establishment of a Danish national accreditation system, and the effects of learning-by-doing-and-interacting in the consultancy sub-system, are contributive features which encourage manufacturing and other companies to engage in total quality projects.

In *France*, the quality community is characterized by a clear division of responsibility. Public bodies are only concerned with promotion of quality awareness at a 'global' level (and at a sectoral level where there is a specific government responsibility). Public associations deal with the 'hard core' of the implementation process of total quality management systems: standardization, certification, accreditation, tests and control, training, consultancy and research. MFQ (Mouvement Française pour la Qualité) is the most active organization in quality promotion, training and development. The private sector is strongly involved both in implementing TQM and in consultancy.

Over the next five years, MICE (the French Ministry of Industry and Commerce)'s strategy is likely to remain unchanged. This will involve the promotion of a greater awareness of quality by all economic sectors, the fostering of an efficient technical and cultural institutional environment and support for firms in their efficient use of quality management systems. MICE will emphasize several priorities: the development of education and adult training; support for research in quality management concepts and methods; the creation of a national award for quality achievement; support for the MFQ; expansion of the operation 'Partnership 92'; and support for the AFAQ in increasing the number of certified firms.

Institutions for the promotion of quality assurance in *Germany* are extremely heterogeneous in their aims and structure. At present, the only general public promotion measures in the area of quality assurance are at a national level. The promotion activities of the BMFT and the BMWi are run nationwide via centrally acting project administration bodies. Other important activities at a national level are the promotion measures of the AIF, the DFG, the FQS and the Volkswagen Foundation, which make funds available for research projects in the area of quality assurance. New institutions have been founded such as the 'Deutsche Gesellschaft zur Zertifizierung von Qualitätssicherungssysteme mbH' (DQS), the 'TUV Zertifierungsgemeinschaft für Qualitätssicherungssysteme' (TUVCERT), the 'Forschungsgemeinschaft Qualitätssicherung e.V' and, at the regional level, the several Steinbeis-Transfer Centres for Quality in Baden-Württemberg. With respect to eastern Germany, the quality issue is definitely more difficult since the standard of product quality has to be considered as relatively low.

Even though few of the specific promotion programmes planned have yet reached the state of concrete projects the general awareness of and commitment to quality related activities seems ubiquitous. There is a growing concern for quality management and an orientation towards total quality management concepts. This can particularly be observed in the changes and growth of the DGQ and its activities, as well as in the growing supply of private commercial organizations in the quality management field.

As in most European countries, the automobile industry and to some extent the electrical industry are the forerunners in quality related activities. Their requirements urge even small suppliers to think about advanced quality systems. The 'innovation support infrastructure' which in Germany consists of a very broad mixture of differently organized, financed, and specialized organizations has obviously already largely adapted to the growing demand in the quality field.

Quality improvement is currently an emerging issue in *Greece*. The discussions are focusing on the development and adaptation of the Greek infrastructure to the demands of the European Community standardization system and on the promotion of TQM amongst Greek firms. These discussions involve the promotion of an infrastructure able to satisfy the needs of industry in quality control through testing and standard certification developments in the public sector. While a number of developments have taken place, the quality community in Greece is still small, and Greek firms are characterized by a lack of awareness about the importance of quality in competitive performance. It is hoped that an increasing number of institutions and organizations will take part in these discussions resulting in a widening of the quality community and a diffusion of quality management practices that will increase the competitiveness of Greek firms.

The *Irish* Quality Association 'Quality Strategy for the 1990s' identified the means by which quality was to be improved in Irish manufacturing and service industries in the 1990s. It focused on a number of new initiatives in education and training and support for quality awards and other promotional activities.

In *Italy*, a national 'unifying law' does not yet exist, but Parliament is working on the creation of the Italian certification system. The Italian scene is already characterized by a series of bodies which set and recognize standards and certification schemes. Similarly, research into quality-related issues is carried out in both private and public organizations which are in some cases already connected, often by participating in joint projects or because they are member of UNI. Not enough time has passed for the creation of established networks, and government involvement seems to be more reactive than proactive. The situation remains fluid. Despite acknowledging the relevance of quality to the production system and the economy, however, a unifying law has not yet been passed by the Parliament, although specific areas have been covered by *ad hoc* legislative measures. National and regional bodies, as well as regional associations for quality, are organizing a rapidly growing number of initiatives.

Similarly in *Luxembourg*, there is no national quality scheme or initiative, although there are several bodies dealing with sectoral product and process quality control. A government working group undertook preliminary work prior to the publication of an official 'Quality Act' in 1993.

In contrast, the *Netherlands* has been extremely active in the promotion of quality. The scope of activities has changed over time. Recently, the quality concept has been extended to include environmental and labour aspects. The environment in particular is the subject of an increasing number of quality programmes, partly as a result of the increasing pressure for environmental awareness.

The increasing competitiveness of world markets has been perceived by the Portuguese government, industry and services as a serious threat. The past few years in *Portugal* have seen the creation of several infrastructures for quality improvement, the development of new technological sectoral centres and regional industrial associations, and an increasing awareness of the importance of quality for the forthcoming competitive market and the activities already carried out by industrial and services companies for quality improvement. In 1983, the SNGQ (National Quality Management System) was created to supervise all activities and methods related to quality. The SNGQ is coordinated by the IPQ (Portuguese Institute for Quality).

The continuing efforts developed byIPQ and other national organizations, as well as the cooperation between sectoral-regional entities, universities-industry, and supplier-client, will have short and medium-term results on quality and productivity improvement. For the past five years many activities such as the national quality campaign, the establishment of quality awards, seminars, conferences and other awareness initiatives have taken place throughout the country and have contributed to a change in the managerial attitude.

In response to industrial change in *Spain* over the past decade and the perceived need for Spain to increase its international competitiveness, particularly with the development of the Single European Market, the role of improving industrial quality in support of increased competitiveness has been given particular attention in recent Spanish technology policy. A number of Spanish institutions have been established during the past decade to develop the core of the quality infrastructure. At present, the Ministry of Industry, Trade and Tourism is enacting a Framework Programme for the promotion of technology and competitiveness, which aims to review the normative situation with regard to standardization.

The MINER (Spanish Ministry of Industry and Energy), now reorganized as the MICYT (Ministry of Industry, Commerce and Tourism), formulated a comprehensive national plan to promote and fund the awareness and adoption of all aspects of quality practices by Spanish industry and to develop and strengthen the infrastructure for industrial quality in Spain. The PNCI (National Plan for Industrial Quality) is being implemented over the course of the three-year period 1991-1993 with a total budget in excess of Pta 12,000 million. The objectives of the Plan are to:

- create demand for quality products and services;
- contribute to the diffusion and international recognition of the quality of Spanish products and services;
- introduce systems of quality management; and,
- introduce demonstrations of quality.

A key aim of *United Kingdom* government policy has been to support the development of a comprehensive quality supporting infrastructure. This has meant closer involvement in standards-setting, and encouraging the adoption of quality management systems, together with assessment, certification and accreditation schemes. The UK DTI (Department of Trade and Industry) Enterprise Initiative is primarily concerned with spreading best-practice management methods in small and medium-sized enterprises (SMEs) in England and Wales (similar schemes have been introduced in Scotland and Northern Ireland). It has two main elements: awareness and consultancy help. A third main strand of DTI activity in the field of quality has been promotion of BS 5750 and support for the quality infrastructure. The main focus of the Enterprise Initiative, however, is the provision of subsidized consultancy services. The aim is to help companies identify and resolve barriers to their competitive performance.

The current DTI Enterprise Consultancy Initiative is due to end in March 1994. The original aim of encouraging a self-sustaining market amongst SMEs for consultants is felt to have been very successful. As yet there is little indication as to what, if anything, will follow it, although any follow-up scheme is likely to place more emphasis on TQM.

6.2 Strengths and Weaknesses of National Policies

In the previous chapter it was noted that governments typically promote quality through a range of schemes and initiatives. Furthermore, quality promotion was defined as the set of policies involving government intervention in the economy with the intent of improving the quality of firms' products and services. These range from the 'direct' promotion of quality, quality management guidelines (including standards) and training schemes, to more general training, financial incentives and innovation promotion schemes that may include a significant quality element. Public promotion of quality has an important role in industrial policies, as there is a relationship between the development of quality management philosophy and the development of new industrial paradigms, and it is possible to identify stages in the development of the various government schemes and initiatives. Thus, in general terms, government policy has tended to move (or is moving) from policies that support quality control and inspection of adoption of minimum standards, through to those that support quality assurance and finally those which are promoting total quality management within companies.

Historically, many governments of the countries surveyed have directly attempted to improve quality by means of procurement; technical regulations referring to safety, environment; consumer protection etc.; support to the R&D infrastructure; support to small businesses; and general macro-economic policies. The first three areas have been particularly important.

The specification of quality management process standards, again specifically derived from defence requirements in the UK and France, has been particularly important. The success of this approach is indicated by the subsequent adoption of similar standards at an international level. In many cases governments and other actors within national production systems have launched campaigns to increase the awareness of companies of these standards, and even to enforce them on industries.

However, a major issue concerning the adoption and promotion of these standards is whether they are accompanied by a quality improvement-oriented culture. As Watanabe argued, it is the commitment to quality improvement that makes the difference between the Western emphasis on quality assurance and the Japanese emphasis on total quality management. In this context it is useful to mention again the increasing number of awards given by governments and quasi-private organisations with the intention of promoting good quality management practice. Typically, these cover a much wider scope than the criteria required in quality standards.

More generally, however, it is apparent that in many of the more 'advanced' countries in Europe there is a growing emphasis on quality as a process of continuous improvement, although usually building on the base of an established standards infrastructure. Thus in many countries, Denmark being a good example, quality promotion activities are not simply conducted in isolation, but as part of a much wider attempt at improving all activities of the firm (technical, social and economic).

Following the discussion in the previous chapter, quality promotion activities are characterized in terms of those which support research; those which promote awareness; those designed to increase the rate of adoption through the use of subsidies; and those supporting education and training.

Schemes and initiatives to improve awareness of quality issues are found in most countries. In addition to being cheap, they are a necessary precursor to the effective diffusion of quality improvement techniques. Similarly, policies to encourage the adoption of good quality management practices are found in most countries. The schemes differ in terms of their quality target level (testing, quality assurance, or total quality management), coverage (all sectors or some, all companies, or only SMEs), and whether they operate directly or indirectly; directly through the use of consultants or publicity, or indirectly through large firms encouraging quality improvement in their suppliers.

The need for a workforce skilled in quality related activities has been widely recognized. Thus, quality management training programmes have been initiated by various organizations, often as part of government programmes. Indeed professional training is a rapidly expanding area of activity in all of the countries investigated. Accordingly, higher education programmes are ever more incorporating quality management studies to provide students with up-to-date and useful skills. Furthermore, education and training activities are seen as one of the ways to promote awareness, and thus to complement quality awareness campaigns.

In spite of the importance of quality to corporate and national well-being, academics in many European countries have been relatively slow to study the area (with some notable exceptions such as Denmark and France). Quality management is a new field of enquiry and, until more research is carried out, will remain a problematic academic subject.

6.3 European Actions

Large imbalances in quality culture exist across Europe. Nevertheless moves towards harmonization in recent years are beginning to see a convergence of national, European and international approaches. Current changes in technology related legislation, standardization and quality assurance throughout Europe are far-reaching. The recent past and immediate future are dominated by the major task of harmonization among European Union member countries. Prior to this effort, most technical legislation was at the national level, was different in every country, and often formed a significant non-tariff barrier to trade. Voluntary standards were produced by the national standards bodies and few European standards existed; although in a few areas such as IT, standardization was international. Conformity testing and certification were even more fragmented, with most action taking place at the sector level within countries. Other aspects of quality assurance were mainly internal to enterprises, and concentrated on manufacturing defects. With moves towards the European Single Market (and with it the harmonization of European standards), it is likely that European bodies (including the European Commission) will come to play an increasingly important role in the promotion of quality throughout Europe.

Already the Commission has established the Certification Unit of DG III as an umbrella organization dealing with quality issues in a 'horizontal' way across the areas of Commission interest. Other DGs support activities which directly impinge upon quality-related activities. Thus, DG XII has launched programmes to support collaboration between the testing laboratories of the Member States (BCR), to examine the interface between developments in science and technology and standards setting and observance (SAST project 2); and a pilot project intended to assist SMEs to identify and assess the impact of new European standardization, certification, and quality requirements SMEs will have to master in order to attain the benefits of the internal market. Two DG XIII lines of action within the SPRINT programme also have relevance for the promotion of quality. Two of the main objectives of the SPRINT programme are to strengthen the European infrastructure for innovation support services and to ensure a rapid diffusion of new technologies to firms throughout Europe. One strand within SPRINT is supporting the formation of transnational networks of Research and Technology Organisations (R&TOs). Another strand is geared towards helping SMEs Manage the Integration of New Technologies (MINT). Finally, the PRISMA programme of DG XVI is aimed at establishing a quality infrastructure in less favoured regions of the EU. These are discussed in some detail in Part Four of the report.

References

1.   Mowery, D.C. (1989), Collaborative Ventures Between US and Foreign Manufacturing Firms, *Research Policy*, 18, 1, pp 19-33.

2.   Ministerie van Economiche Zaken, projectgroep Kwaliteitsbeleid (1987), *Nederland: Hoogste tijd voor Kwaliteit*, Den Hag, 11 November.

3.   Ministerie van Economiche Zaken, projectgroep Kwaliteit en Logistiek (1992), *Voortganrapportage 1991, Kwaliteit en Logistiek*, Den Hag.

4.   PERA International and Salford University Business Services Limited (1992), *A Survey of Quality Consulatncy Scheme Clients, 1988-1990*, Report to the DTI, London.

5.   Pfeiffer, T. et al (1990), *Untersuchung zur Qualitässicherung*, Kernforschungszentrum Karlsruhe, KfK-PFT 155.

Part Three:

Country Reviews

Belgium

Paul Kunst, Jos Lemmink and Ruth Prins

1. Introduction

In Belgium, the political situation has an important bearing on policy in the field of quality. In recent years there has been a significant change in the relationship between the national government and the three regions of Flanders, Walloonia and Brussels. As a result, the responsibilities of the three regional governments with respect to business policy has increased significantly. Consequently, quality promotion is almost entirely the responsibility of the regional governments, while the national government in Brussels has no significant role. In this report, quality activities and support schemes are clearly distinguished for the different regions. In respect to quality, the three regions may almost be considered as three individual countries.

The role of the national government in Brussels with respect to quality is, however, very important in (but also limited to) the field of accreditation and certification. In 1990, the national government passed a law, on the initiative of the National Ministry of Economic Affairs, concerning the accreditation of certification and inspection bodies as well as testing laboratories. The law supports the creation, through Royal Decrees, of an official accreditation structure, which guarantees a credible, neutral and objective system for accreditation and certification at the national and European level. Under this law, the first seven certification bodies were accredited in 1992.

2. The Emergence of Quality as an Issue

The first initiatives in the field of quality originated in the region of Flanders in 1970. Several West-Flemish entrepreneurs visited Japan and witnessed the impressive expansion of Japanese businesses, the result of a sustained application of quality products and services. The visit led directly, in 1971, to the creation of a provincial centre for education, training and support with respect to total quality management in companies: CKZ (Centrum voor Kwaliteitszorg, West Flanders Centre for Quality). The second provincial centre for quality, CKZ Antwerp was established the same year, the initiative for this centre being taken by industry representatives, especially from the mechanical and electrotechnical industries. Two years later CKZ Brabant was established. During the 1980s three more centres for quality were established in Flanders: CKZ East-Flanders (1981), CKZ Limburg (1982) and CKZ Flemish Brabant (1986). Similar centres were established in the Walloon region: CQ Liège-Luxembourg (Centre pour le Gestion de la Qualité Liège-Luxembourg, Liège-Luxembourg Quality Centre) and the CQ Hainaut-

Namur. In this respect the influence of Fabrimetal (Federation of the Mechanical and Electrotechnical Industry) has been very important. Within the country, Fabrimetal has played a pioneering role with regard to quality. Most centres were established on the initiative of Fabrimetal companies. Fabrimetal also provided secretarial support for several of the centres in their first few years of operation.

In 1973, the BCK-CBQ (Belgisch Centrum voor Kwaliteitszorg-Centre Belgique pour la gestion de la Qualité, Belgium Centre for Quality) was established as a national umbrella organization in order to provide national representation in the EOQC (European Organization for Quality Control). At that time Belgium was the only country in Europe which was not a member of EOQC.

Public initiatives in the field of quality are rare. The first public initiative was taken by the Flemish government in 1982. The Minister of Education provided financial support in order to implement TQM in the field of secondary education. A policy committee 'Total Quality Management in Education' was established to carry out the programme. More information about the programme is given in Section 5.1. The initiative gave the impulse to the establishment of several Acts (Decreten) by the Flemish government concerning quality in education. An Act (Decreet) is, in this respect, not national law but has force in the region in which it was passed. One Act determined that quality had to be a part of the curriculum of schools and universities and another obliged the training of teachers in the field of quality. Also, the DOO (Dienst Onderwijs Ontwikkeling, Flemish Ministry of Education) in Flanders established standards with respect to quality in school organizations.

In 1984, the Flemish government explicitly recognized the importance of quality to the economy. The Flemish government agreed with the need for a quality policy which: promoted total quality management in businesses; and developed an image of Flemish quality in other countries.

A consequence of this decision was the establishment in 1985 of the VCK (Vlaams Centrum voor Kwaliteitszorg, Flemish Centre for Quality) as an umbrella organization for the provincial quality centres in Flanders. This establishment was supported by the Flemish government with a financial contribution of ECU 1.4 million in total for a period of five years up to 1990. A condition of this support was that VCK and the centres for quality should eventually become self-supporting and maintain their level of activity in the years following.

The most recent development in the field of quality has been the agreement of a national law concerning the accreditation of certification and inspection bodies, as well as testing laboratories.[1] This Act was established on the initiative of the National Ministry of Economic Affairs in July 1990. The Belgian business community and certification organizations had wanted the law for several years. Its passing at last allowed official certification and accreditation to be undertaken.

In March 1992, the first seven certification bodies were officially accredited by the National Committee for the Accreditation of Certification Bodies which certify Quality Assurance Systems (NAC-QS). The NAC-QS had been created in 1989 on the initiative of the BIN/IBN (Belgisch Institut voor Normalisatie-Institut Belge de Normalisation, Belgian Standardization Institute) together with the VCK, the AWQ (Association Wallone pour la gestion de la Qualitè, Walloon Quality Association), the KCGB-CQRB (Kwaliteitscentrum Gewest Brussel-Centre pour la Gestion de la Qualitè de la Règion Bruxelloise, Brussels Quality Centre) and a number of other organizations in order to provide the necessary framework for the official recognition of Belgian certification bodies according to NBN (Belgisch NormBelge, Belgain standards).

NAC-QS plays an important role in implementing the law concerning accreditation and certification. The rationale for the statutory regulation of accreditation is that the credibility, neutrality and objectivity of systems for certification and accreditation are best guaranteed by law. The law of July 1990 covers only the basic principles of accreditation and certification. Because of its simple structure the law allows different accreditation and certification structures to be defined and implemented. In this way, it is easy to adapt to changes in the international certification and accreditation structure. Also, the accreditation structure provides, from the start, the possibility of cooperation between the different national governments, regions and provinces while allowing each to retain their own competencies. The law is based on the following principles:

- The law is voluntary in nature, eg it is not supposed to impose rules on all companies or institutions, but only on those companies who wish to provide credible references indicating that they are operating in accordance with internationally recognized standards.
- The law is based on a simple and pragmatic approach: maximum transparency and coherence is guaranteed, and takes into account, as far as possible, existing systems (on condition that these provide a coherent whole which can be coordinated at the national level).

The establishment of a National Council for Accreditation and Certification in January 1991 was a logical first step leading from the Accreditation Act of July 1990. The overall objective of the Council is to guarantee the realization and coordination of the accreditation system.[2] The task of the Council is:

- to coordinate the principles and procedures concerning accreditation and certification;
- to accumulate, distribute and publish information with respect to activities in the field;
- to ensure that all interested parties are involved in activities of accreditation and certification;
- to promote and coordinate all efforts which lead to agreements of mutual recognition at international level; and,
- to give advice with respect to coordination and certification. The Council was officially installed in July 1991 and is composed of representatives from the National Ministry of Economic Affairs and other national ministries, the Flemish, Walloon and Brussels regional governments, the BNI, the BKO (Belgian Calibration Organization), together with

representatives from many other industrial and consumer organizations, trade unions, and accredited certification bodies.

2.1 Diffusion of Quality

In 1989 a study was carried out by PRACK (Vereniging voor Praktijkgericht en Participatief Management en Integrale Kwaliteitszorg, Association for Practice-Oriented and Participative Management and Total Quality Management), in conjunction with the Belgian National Bank and some large companies, to investigate the situation in Belgium with regard to Total Quality Management.[3] About 1400 companies of all industries were questioned. 600 (42%) of the companies replied. 28% of the companies said that total quality management was applied. Two-thirds of these companies had applied TQM for over two years. 73% of the respondents defined TQM as 'to better control the quality of our products', 60% as 'to motivate and involve employees in the company' and 52% regarded TQM as 'a global strategy'. The companies were also questioned about their motives for the implementation of TQM. Approximately 70% answered that the implementation of TQM was a strategic choice for a new management approach; 40% considered it as a good selling argument and 35% implemented TQM under the pressure of clients. Other findings of the study were that small companies had enough capacity for a systematic TQM policy, that TQM activities have least progressed in medium-sized companies, and that time appeared to be the most important reason (51%) for difficulties with the implementation of TQM, ie TQM was not given the highest priority.

According to W. de Pril (vice-president of the CKZ East-Flanders) 'The life cycle of TQM, as it was introduced fifteen years ago, is nearly at its end'.[4] Four phases can be distinguished: an awareness phase, an implementation phase, an audit phase and finally a certification phase. The awareness and implementation phase is considered to be completed and the audit and certification phase has now been entered. Companies are less dependent on the support of quality centres. The organizations that promote quality have to adapt to the new situation and should concentrate less on promotion and awareness. Training and the exchange of experiences are important nowadays. An exception is the service sector with the observation that 'Total Quality Management stops at the factory gate', ie TQM is mainly applied in the product industries and barely developed in the service sector.[5] The introduction of quality in the service industry is an increasingly important issue for the regional and provincial quality centres. The Flemish centres are already developing initiatives for the introduction of TQM in the service industry, but little progress has so far been made.

The question has arisen as to whether the government should play a more important role in the field of quality.[6] For instance should the government support companies financially, as in other countries? The opinion often expressed is that if companies regard quality as important, they will undertake quality improvement activities by themselves. It is argued that the best service government can provide for companies is to implement TQM itself in order to function more efficiently; thus saving companies time in their dealings with government.

56

The most significant developments in quality promotion are listed below in Figure 8, below.

Figure 8: Review of developments in the field of quality1970-1992

1971:	Establishment of first (provincial) quality centre: West-Flanders
1973:	Establishment of the Belgian Centre for Quality as umbrella organization of all regional and provincial centres, membership of Belgium in EOCQ
1982:	First public initiative: 'implementation of TQM in Education' subsidized by the Flemish government
1985:	Establishment of VCK, subsidized by the Flemish government
1989:	Establishment of National Committee for the Accreditation of Certification Bodies (NAC-QS)
1990:	Establishment of the Accreditation and Certification Law
1991:	Establishment of the National Council for Certification and Accreditation
1992:	First official accreditation of seven certification organizations by NAC-QS

3. The Quality Infrastructure

The network of organizations in the field of quality is clearly structured. The network consists of different levels which are closely interrelated. At provincial level eight centres for quality - 'CKZs-CQs' - are responsible for the promotion and support of quality activities in companies. These organizations operate almost identically and are all autonomous. At regional level the Flemish, Walloon and Brussels Centres for Quality, respectively VCK (Vlaams Centrum voor Kwaliteitszorg), AWQ (Association Wallone pour la Gestion de la Qualité) and KCGB-CQRB (Kwaliteitscentrum Gewest Brussel-Centre pour la Gestion de la Qualité de la Région Bruxelloise) are active. These are the umbrella organizations for the provincial centres found in Flanders, Walloon and Brussels. At the national level the BCK-CBQ (Begisch Centrum voor Kwaliteitszorg-Centre Belge pour la Gestion de la Qualité, Belgian Centre for Quality) is the umbrella organization for all of the provincial and regional quality centres. It is responsible for the international representation of Belgium. Additionally, the BIN-IBN and the NAC-QS are the two national organizations responsible for the preparation of standards and for the accreditation of certification organizations.

3.1 Certification

Quality systems are certified by several national and foreign certification bodies. In 1989, NAC-QS was established to accreditate certification bodies of quality assurance systems. NAC-QS is composed of representatives from BIN-IBN, VCK, AWQ and KCGB-CQRB. NAC-QS contributes to the execution of the accreditation and certification law, and continues to play an important role in defining and creating the accreditation structure.

NAC-QS and the Dutch Council for Certification agreed in 1991 to assist each other in the accreditation of certification organizations of quality systems. This cooperation will lower the costs of accreditation.[7] Another advantage is the reinforcement of the position of Belgium in the field of accreditation and mutual recognition of certification bodies. The first seven certification bodies were accredited by NAC-QS in March 1992. These included BQA (Belgian Quality Association), Bureau Secco, AIB-Vinçotte, Bureau Veritas Quality International, SGS European Quality Certification Institute, Det Norske Veritas and Eurosym. In the near future, the acknowledgement and withdrawal of accreditation will be determined by Royal Decree within the terms of the law on accreditation and certification of July 1990. From this point accredited certification bodies will be notified to international or foreign institutions in view of the conclusion of agreements for mutual recognition.

3.2 Standardization

Belgian standards (NBN) are established by the Belgian Standards Institute (BNI-IBN). The institute collaborates with other standardization institutions such as BEC (the Belgian Electrotechnical Committee). BIN-IBN allocates the BENOR-mark of conformity (for the electrotechnical norms this is the CEBEC-mark). In addition, BIN-IBN is the Belgian centre for information on technical regulations and standards.

BIN-IBN is nationally and internationally active at different levels. At the national level BIN-IBN has close contact with private sector and governmental organizations. At the international level the institute is a member of the ISO and CEN. There is also close contact with the Dutch standards institute NNI as part of the Benelux cooperation. BIN-IBN is a non-profit organization and is one-third financed by the Government, one-third by industry and one-third by revenue raised by the sales of standards etc.

In the European context for accreditation and certification (EOTC and the EQS - the European Committee for Quality Systems), an advisory committee on the certification of quality systems - BQS (Belgian Committee for Quality Systems) was installed within BIN-BNI. It was on the initiative of this committee that the Council for Accreditation and Certification was installed in 1991 in conjunction with AWQ, KCGB-CQRB and VCK.

The relationship between the different parts of the accreditation and certification system in Belgium is shown below in Figure 9.

Figure 9: The accreditation and certification system in Belgium

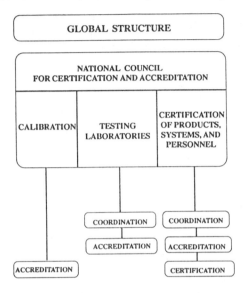

Source: Lathuy, I.B., Ministry of Economic Affairs, 'L'Accreditation et la Certification en Belgique', July 1991.

3.3 Promotion, Awareness and Consultancy

As mentioned above, organizations undertaking these activities are primarily located at the regional level. These will be described in the relevant sections, below.

3.3.1 Provincial Organizations for Quality

The nine Belgian provinces are covered by eight provincial centres for quality. The Flanders region contains five provincial centres (CKZ West-Flanders, CKZ Antwerp, CKZ East-Flanders, CKZ Limburg and CKZ Vlaams-Brabant); the Brussels region has one (CQ Brabant) and Walloonia two (CQ Liège-Luxembourg and CQ Hainaut-Namur). The first centre was established in 1971 (CKZ West-Flanders) and the other centres were established in the following years. The centres are responsible for most activities developed in the field of quality for regional companies. The objective of the centres is to promote and support TQM in all industries. Target groups are all companies located in the area. In looking at the activities undertaken by the centres, it is possible to distinguish between services and products. The services package includes the following activities:

- Awareness: organization of information sessions, courses, seminars, study days etc.
- Consultancy: advice and support with respect to implementation and improvement of TQM.
- Working groups: working groups are installed within the centres to deal actively with specific problems (eg new developments), and to exchange information with companies by means of publications or other activities.

The products that are made available by the centres are publications, magazines, books, audio-visual material (eg video tapes) etc. The Walloon centres appear to be less developed than the Flemish centres. They fulfil awareness, information and training activities, but provide little advice and support to companies. About 1700 companies are members of one of the Flemish or Walloon provincial quality centres.

The centres have non-profit status and are mainly funded by membership fees from companies while receiving no financial contributions from the public sector. Evidence suggests that the centres are happy with the financial autonomy this arrangement guarantees.

3.3.2 Regional Centres for Quality

Because of the linguistic and new administrative structure of Belgium, the Walloon and Flemish regions each have their own umbrella organization. In Flanders this is the Flemish Centre for Quality (VCK) and in Walloon the Walloon Association for Quality Management (AWQ). In addition, there is a 'regional' centre for the capital Brussels, KCGB-CQRB (Kwaliteitscentrum Gewest Brussel - Centre pour la Gestion de la Qualité de la Région Bruxelloise). This centre is closely related to CQ Brabant.

VCK promotes and extends TQM in Flanders in cooperation with the provincial centres for quality. In its function as an umbrella organization VCK is not directly involved with businesses, but is more oriented to sector associations and top management. VCK carries out a number of activities:

- Project certification: to encourage certification of businesses.
- Project education: introduction of TQM in the field of education to increase quality awareness.
- Promotion: promotion activities in the Flemish region; contact with sister organizations in Belgium and abroad.

Additionally, VCK has a particular task as an interlocutor with the national government and the Flemish government. In the other direction VCK is the transfer-point to the Flemish provincial centres for information about European and international developments in the field of quality (EOQ, ISO). VCK is totally private and autonomous. It was established with financial support from the Flemish government (see Section 2), but, at present, neither the national nor Flemish governments provide financial support. VCK's income consists of contributions from the Flemish provincial centres for quality and from its own activities.

AWQ is the Walloon counterpart of VCK. Its mission and objectives are identical to those of VCK. AWQ was established on the private initiative of several industrialists and was not subsidized (in contrast with VCK) by the Walloon government. The activities of AWQ are mainly awareness, information and training, but its activities are less developed than the activities of VCK.

AWQ does not offer consultancy to companies in the field of quality management. Within AWQ three working groups operate. The working groups concentrate on certification, training and measurement. From early in its creation AWQ has tried to draw the Walloon government's attention towards the importance of quality. The two provincial centres for quality 'Liège-Luxembourg' and 'Hainaut-Namur' in Walloonia are members of AWQ.

An important activity of both VCK and AWQ is the presentation of TQM awards in the regions of Flanders and Walloonia. These awards are granted every two years. Companies which have obtained remarkable results in the field of TQM are considered for the quality award. There are two awards available, one for a SME and one for a multinational company. In addition, VCK presents an award for the best quality managers of the year. The main purpose of these awards is to improve company awareness of TQM activities.

3.3.3 The National Centre for Quality

The Belgian Centre for Quality (BCK-CBQ) was established in 1973 in order to represent Belgium in the EOQC. The centre is now the umbrella organization of the three regional centres AWQ, VCK and KGCB-CQRB. The objective of BCK is 'to stimulate with all appropriate means the use and implementation of techniques and way of thoughts of quality control, in order to increase in this way the quality and security of goods and services'.[8] In its regulations the most important task of BCK-CBQ is described as follows: 'To be the coordinator between the provincial centres and to be the official interlocutor between national and international institutions'.[9] Through membership of the provincial and regional centres about 1700 companies are members of BCK. In 1992, BCK organized, in cooperation with VCK, the EOQ'92 conference in Brussels.

The organization (see Figure 10, page 62) of the quality infrastructure has been criticised. It is said that there are too many circles and too many activities, such as seminars, working groups, congresses etc. However, the main reason for this situation is that a decentralized structure is thought to be necessary to effectively promote TQM in Belgium. A disadvantage of the decentralized structure is that the centres cannot act as one unity to the public.[10] Activities of the different provincial associations overlap sometimes.

3.3.4 Sectoral Organizations

In addition to the regional and provincial centres for quality a number of private sector organizations exists. In the building industry WTCB (Wetenschappelijk en Technisch Centrum voor het Bouwbedrijf, Scientific and Technical Centre for Building Industry) coordinates the activities of the Belgium Building Department of the EOQ. eg the promotion of ISO 9001 norms in the building industry. In 1990 nineteen companies in the chemical industry established their own quality organization, called Qualichem. The objective of Qualichem is to spread information and to organize courses and meetings in order to transfer experiences in the field of quality. The target group of the organization is not only the chemical industry, but also suppliers and clients of the industry. In addition, some provincial centres for quality have sectoral working groups, eg for the software, graphic and textile industry. Working groups within VCK operate towards the implementation of TQM in the health sector and education.

Figure 10: Structure of Quality Centres in Belgium

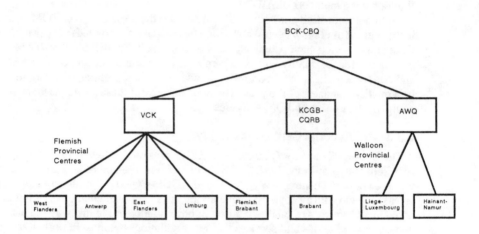

PRACK (Association for Practice-Orientated and Participative Management and Total Quality) was originally established in 1983 for the regions of Walloon and Brussels. Today it operates nationally. PRACK organizes people and companies who want to 'to promote the alertness of companies and other organizations in Belgium by means of practice-oriented development of quality circles, participative management and Total Quality Management'.[11] About 200 companies are members of PRACK. PRACK is a member and co-founder of the EFQCA (European Federation of Quality Circles and Quality Management Associations). EFQCA organizes a European congress every two years and develops research projects at the European level.

In 1989, the national broadcasting organization BRT-RTBF (Belgian Broadcasting Organization) ran eight television programmes on TQM. The broadcasts were the result of an initiative by VCK in conjunction with BRT-RTBF and the government. The programmes were directed to the general public, employees, managers, in industry and services, in the commercial and public sectors.

3.4 Research

Limited information on quality research is available through a research project carried out in 1988-89 by UMIST (University of Manchester Institute of Science and Technology, UK) and SQMI (Strategic Quality Management Institute, Erasmus University, the Netherlands).[12] The purpose of this project was to establish the 'state-of-the art' in teaching and research in European higher education as a basis for future developments of TQM. The project was initiated by the EFQM (European Foundation for Quality Management). EFQM stressed that more attention needed to be given to quality and quality management in Europe, and especially to the role of European universities, business schools and polytechnics in education and the teaching of TQM. In Belgium only three universities responded to the research questionnaire: the University of Gent, the Catholic University of Leuven and the University of Antwerp. Research was carried out in the three universities on the subjects of customer satisfaction, 'Just-in-Time', performance measurement, etc. At the moment, there is no overview of recent research activities in the field of quality.

3.5 Training and Education

The provincial centres for quality and several commercial consulting firms specializing in the area offer internal training to companies implementing Total Quality Management. In addition there are a number of external training possibilities. The centres for quality offer a large number of courses, seminars etc. For example, CKZ Antwerp organizes about 24 courses on subjects such as Quality, Philosophy, Methodology and Organization, Statistical Process Control, Quality Assurance Systems etc. As a result of the project 'Total Quality Management in Education' and consequent to the establishment of the Act on quality in education (see Section 2), quality management has been incorporated into the curriculum of schools and universities. Education on TQM is also provided at post-graduate level. In October 1986, CKZ Limburg and the Limburg University Centre established together with the Post-graduate Centre the first MSc in 'Total Quality Management' programme in the Benelux countries.[13,14] The programme was originally directed towards the production sector, but was extended to the service sector in 1988-89. The target group of the programme are managers and responsible staff personnel, eg quality managers and top managers, in production companies, service industries, and the public sector. The programme intends to introduce participants to the TQM philosophy and in the large number of applications of TQM in different situations. The lectures are given by professors and teachers of the Limburg University Centre, the Higher Economic School Limburg (from 1990 part of the Limburg University Centre), and other universities in Belgium and from abroad. The teaching languages are Dutch and English. In 1989 the University of Mons in Walloonia established its own post-graduate programme - an MSc in 'Total Quality Management' - identical to the programme provided by the Post-graduate Centre in Flanders.

4. National Quality Schemes and Initiatives

At present there are no national quality schemes or other schemes in which stimulation of quality improvement plays a major role. The establishment of schemes for quality purposes by the national government remains unlikely. Ongoing developments in the political structure are resulting in business policy being increasingly defined and implemented at the regional government level.

5. Regional Quality Schemes and Initiatives

Three quality schemes have been distinguished in the region of Flanders. Two schemes are global and concern education and promotion. The third scheme is sectoral and is aimed at consultancy in the field of quality in the industrial sector.

5.1 Global Schemes

5.1.1 Flanders

The programme 'Total Quality Management in Education' was started about ten years ago to implement TQM in secondary education in the Flanders region. The programme is carried out by the policy committee 'TQM in Education' in conjunction with six industrial companies. These companies already have experience in TQM. They motivate and support TQM activities in schools of secondary education and assist in the training and education of management, teachers and students. The short term objective of the programme was to work step by step on quality improvement. The objectives in the long run were:

- to optimize the school organization through the introduction of TQM;
- to teach and train TQM as a specialism;
- to engage education and industry to cooperate intensively; and,
- to realize a substantial mentality change.[15]

The programme started in late 1982 and is still continuing. In 1992 about 173 schools were involved.

The most important quality promotion scheme has been 'Subsidies of the Flemish Government for Quality, Durability and Product Improvement with Respect to the Ecology Criterion'.[16] The scheme's Ecology Criterion was established in 1990 by the Flemish government for large companies and SMEs. The scheme was established as a consequence of the Act of the national government concerning economic expansion. The application of this Act is determined by the departmental governments. The Flemish government desired to take into account in its economic policy the main goal of the Brundtland report; i.e. sustainable development. Thus the objective of the Ecology Criterion Scheme is to stimulate investments in more environmentally responsible products and production processes. Five components form the basic elements of the scheme:

- raw materials economization;
- energy economization;
- production improvement;
- fire security and security of labour conditions; and,
- reduction of environmentally aggravating effects.

Work towards the five components can attract financial support of up to 15% of investment costs. Target groups are small, medium and large companies. Quality is an essential element of the 'production improvement' component. Importance is attached to the increase of quality and durability of products and production processes. The technical requirements of products are gauged against Belgian norms or European and international standards. An improvement in the production component has to be confirmed by a quality assurance system according to the ISO 9000 standards.

5.1.2 Walloonia

In the region of Walloonia no specific quality programme of the Walloon government exists. The only development in the field of quality on the part of the Executive has been the establishment of an Act (Decreet) of September 1989 concerning the attribution of a Walloon quality label; appellation of local origin or appellation of Walloon origin.[17] This quality label is a collective mark determined by the Walloon government which indicates that a product produced or transformed in Walloon possesses a certain quality level. This Act concerns principally product quality and does not refer to TQM.

5.2 Sectoral Schemes

One sectoral scheme in the field of quality was identified in Flanders. This scheme was called Horizon '92 and is based in the province of Limburg. Horizon '92 was developed by GOM-Limburg (Provincial Development Society) and began in 1989. The purpose of the programme was to reinforce strategically, in view of European unification, SMEs in Limburg by means of external advice. This advice corresponded to both external and internal aspects of the firm. Examples of external aspects included: market research and strategic market planning, export organization (transnational) collaboration with other companies and the implemention of quality systems according to ISO 9000 standards. The internal aspects concerned: TQM, production control, planning and innovation (products, technology). 70% of the consulting costs were provided by the EFRO (Europees Fonds voor Regionale Ontwikkeling, European Fund for Regional Development) and the province of Limburg. The remaining 30% of the costs had to be financed by the participating companies themselves. By 1992, 59 projects had been carried out under Horizon '92, with 35 in the area of quality management. Fifty companies were involved in one or more of these projects. Table 1 (page 66) provides a breakdown of study participation. The majority of the studies were devoted to quality management.

Table 1: Overview of studies in Horizon '92

Year	QM	Export marketing	Total
1989	1	11	12
1990	3	11	14
1991	31	2	33
Total	35	24	59

Source: Gewestelijke Ontwikkelings Maatschuppij (GOM), Limburg Horizon '92.

The content of the quality studies was:

- information and awareness of employees in companies;
- company diagnosis directed to quality activities in each department;
- definition of quality action plans;
- support of employees in the company who are responsible for the development of quality organization, working procedures and instructions; and,
- support and evaluation of the implementation of quality systems within the company.

The task of GOM consisted of registering consulting firms and assisting companies in problem definition and the choice of appropriate consultants. The programme was accessible for companies in the industrial sector, with less than 200 employees, situated in the province of Limburg and with a market abroad. In 1991, 31 of the 33 study projects concerned support for the implementation of quality systems according to ISO 9000 (EN 29,000) standards in SMEs. Of the 59 studies, 24 finished in 1991. Most of these studies were carried out in the building materials, mechanical-electrotechnical, transport and chemical industries. The primary budget of Horizon '92 was already exhausted in August 1991. However, an enlargement of the project was possible, thanks to increased financial contributions from the Flemish government and EFRO.

6. Overview and Outlook

Belgium is at the moment in a politically transitional period. Regional governments have gained more political power and influence and have recently started to determine business policy.

In the field of quality, the national government takes important measures with respect to the establishment and development of a national accreditation structure.

The law of July 1990, concerning the accreditation of certification and inspection bodies, as well as testing laboratories, has offered the possibility to create a structure which can participate as a full partner at the European level.

With respect to the regional governments there have been, until now, only incidental initiatives in the field of quality and no consistent quality policy has really existed. However it seems likely that important new developments in the field of quality will emerge in the near future. The efforts of the quality organizations have persuaded regional governments to realize the importance of quality for their economic position relative to each other and to others (companies, countries).

At the moment the quality organizations in Flanders, especially VCK, are deliberating with the Flemish government on starting a couple of new programmes in order to stimulate TQM. In 1992 the Flemish government will decide upon these programmes. For example, one of the proposed projects is the implementation of TQM in public services. The proposed programmes are not aimed at large company quality improvement/TQM actions and campaigns, but are based more on 'sharing quality management' between SMEs. The idea is to employ a quality manager for several companies for a certain period. The quality manager supports these companies in quality improvement activities with the final objective of achieving ISO 9000 certification. The Flemish government will subsidize a percentage of the costs of employing the quality manager.

With respect to the Walloon region, new developments in the field of quality are being realized in the context of the national Act on Economic Expansion. This Act provides loans for economic expansion. At the business level, loans were given for market research activities. However the application of the Act did not concern quality improvement activities. As a result of the increase of the political power of the regional governments, the Walloon government recently started redefining the scope of application of the Act. One application (in preparation at the time of writing), will partly apply to quality. The Walloon government will subsidize consultancy services to small and medium-sized companies. One of the subjects of the consultancy service will be quality audits undertaken with the purpose of certifying the company to international standards.

In conclusion, it is likely that there will be new developments in the field of quality as the regional governments develop plans to stimulate quality improvement activities. The scope of these plans is not clear enough at this moment to draw definite conclusions about future developments.

7. List of Organizations

Name	Address	Telephone/Fax
Quality Policy Bodies		
National Government Ministry of Economic Affairs	23 Square de Meeus B-1040 Brussels	(32) 25 50 52 09
Flemish Government Ministry of Economic Affairs	Jozef II-straat 30 B-1040 Brussels	(32) 22 18 12 10
Walloon Government, Ministry of Economic Affairs	Rue Mazy 25-27 B-5100 Jambes	(32) 81 33 12 11
Brussels-Capital Government Ministry of Economic Affairs	Stefanietoren 1 Louizalaan 54 B-1050 Brussels	(32) 25 17 12 59
Belgian Institute for Normalization (BIN)	Avenue de la Brabanconne 29 B-1040 Bruxelles	(32) 27 34 92 05
Council for Certification and Accreditation	23 Square de Meeus B-1040 Brussels	(32) 25 50 52 09
Policy committee 'TQM Education'	UIA-Universiteitsplein 1 B-2610 Wilrijk	(32) 38 20 29 66
Programme 'Masters in TQM'	Post University Centre Limburg, Universitaire Campus B-3590 Diepenbeek	(32) 11 22 99 61
National Quality Centre		
BCK-CBQ	Lakenweverstraat 21 B-1050 Brussels	(32) 25 10 24 33
Regional Quality Centres		
VCK	Research Park de Haak B-1731 Zellik	(32) 24 76 56 00
AWQ	Rue Puissient 15 B-6000 Charleroi	(32) 71 32 57 11
KCGB-CQRB	Lakenweverstraat 21 B-1050 Brussels	(32) 25 10 24 35
Provincial Quality Centres		
CKZ Antwerp	Commandant Weynstraat 85 B-2710 Hoboken	(32) 32 22 12 80
CKZ West-Vlaanderen	Doorniksesteenweg 220 B-8500 Kortrijk	(32) 56 20 36 23
CKZ Oost-Vlaanderen	Martelaarslaan 49 B-9000 Gent	(32) 91 35 88 53
CKZ Limburg	Kunstlaan 18 B-3500 Hasselt	(32) 11 22 79 09
CQ Brabant	Lakenweverstraat 21 B-1050 Brussels	(32) 25 10 24 35

CQ Liège-Luxembourg	Boulevard E. de Laveleye 191 B-4020 Luik	(32) 41 41 04 54
CQ Hainaut/Namur	Chaussée de Jolimont 263 B-7100 Haine-St-Pierre	(32) 64 27 54 11

Sectoral Quality Centres

EOQ, Belgian Department Building	c/o WTCB Aarlenstraat 53 B-1040 Brussels	(32) 22 30 62 82
Qualichem	Leuvensesteenweg 613 B-1930 Zaventem-Zuid 7	(32) 27 59 46 13
PRACK	Washingtonstraat 44 B-1050 Brussels	(32) 26 48 04 89

Accredited Certification Bodies

AIB-Vincotte vzw	Koningslaan 157 B-1060 Brussels	(32) 25 36 82 11
BQA	Monoyerstraat 24 B-1040 Brussels	(32) 22 30 93 30
Bureau Secco	Aarlenstraat 53 bus 2 B-1040 Brussels	(32) 22 38 22 11
Bureau Veritas Quality International	Mechelsesteenweg 128-136 B-2018 Antwerpen	(32) 32 47 95 50
Det Norske Veritas	p/a Buro & Design Center Heizel Esplanada PB 78 B-1020 Brussels	(32) 24 75 23 40
Eurosym vzw	President Kennedypark 23 D B-8500 Kortrijk	(32) 56 76 67 07
SGS EQCI	Noorderlaan 87 2030 Antwerpen	(32) 35 42 46 00

References:

1. Royal Decree of 20 July 1990, on the *accreditation of certification and inspection bodies as well as laboratories*, Official Journal 16124, 22 August 1990.

2. Royal Decree of 24 january 1991, on the *establishment of the National Council for Accreditation and Certification*, Official Journal 2140, 2 February 1991.

3. PRACK, (1989), *De Standaard, Ruim kwart Belgische bedrijven streeft a ktief integrale kwaliteit na*.

   PRACK, (1989), *De Financieel-Ekonomische Tijd, Kwaliteitsstreven strandt op gebrek aan vorming en tijd,*.

4. *De Kwaliteitskrant*, (April 1992).

5. Ibid.

6. Ibid.

7. *De Kwaliteitskrant,* (April 1991).

8. *De Kwaliteitskrant,* (April 1992).

9. Ibid.

10. Ibid.

11. University of Manchester, Quality Management Centre, (1990) TQM in Europe.

13. Post-graduate Centre (Postuniversitair Centrum Limburg) situated in Diepenbeek (Province Limburg).

14. Masters in Total Quality management: Masters in Integrale Kwaliteitszorg (MIKZ).

15. Vlaamse Gemeenschap, (1991), Vlaanderen informatie brochure *Kwaliteitszorg in Vlaanderen'*, Brussel

16. M. Mulder, first advisor Economic Expansion Large Companies, Ministry of the Flemish Community, Het subsidiëren van kwaliteitsprojecten door de Vlaamse gemeenschap, CKZ Oost-Vlaanderen, 1992.

17. Décret (1989) concernant l'*attribution du label de qualité wallon, l'appellation d'origine locale et l'appelation d'origine wallone*, Official journal 9448, 28 November 1989.

Other References:

Vlaams Centrum voor Kwaliteitszorg (1991), 'België-Nederland: samen akkrediteren is goedkoper, *De Kwaliteitskrant*, nr. 3, April 1991, Zellik.

Vlaams Centrum voor Kwaliteitszorg,(1991), Belgische akkreditatie in wettelijk kader, *De Kwaliteitskrant*, nr. 7, Oktober 1991, Zellik.

Vlaams Centrum voor Kwaliteit, information brochure *Met de zorg voor kwaliteit groeit ook de zekerheid''*, Wilrijk.

Lathuy, L.B., *Certificatie in België*, Brussel, August 1991.

Denmark

Allan Naes Gjerding

1. Introduction

This report on Danish national and regional schemes in the field of quality deals mainly with the manufacturing sector. This reflects the main emphasis of national and regional policy initiatives. In addition, some comments on the construction sector are presented as these also fall within the scope of many of the policy initiatives. Furthermore, policy initiatives in relation to consultancy, and training and education, are dealt with at some length, because these initiatives are an important part of industrial policy in the field of quality directed towards the manufacturing sector.

Section 2 analyses the emergence of quality as an issue in Danish industrial policy. It argues that Danish industrial and technology policy in the last part of the 1980s has evolved around a 'new era' systems approach. Three initiatives at the level of national industrial policy have been particularly conducive to the promotion of this integrative approach in the Danish manufacturing sector. The core of this approach is an emphasis on:

- cooperation between parties within the individual company and between the company and organizations in the neighbouring environment;
- an integrative approach to technical and organizational innovation; and,
- the importance of human resource management in the sense of developing the technical and organizational competencies of both management and employees.

Section 3 gives some introductory facts on industrial organization and argues that a strong bias towards small companies in an international context and a relatively high proportion of exports have made Danish industrial managers and industrial policy authorities well aware of the present and future competitive pressures on the Danish economy. This awareness has stimulated the promotion and acceptance of total quality control principles as reflected, in part, by a relatively large number of ISO 9000 certificates in the manufacturing sector. Furthermore, Section 3 argues that the evolution of Danish industrial policy described in Section 2 has stimulated both the number of organizations in, and the dynamism of, the Danish quality infrastructure. The quality infrastructure is analysed, and a detailed inventory is given in Section 7 and illustrated in Figure 11 on page 84. The quality infrastructure comprises seven categories:

- private companies in which the management of total quality control plays an important part in the pursuit of economic survival;
- institutes concerned with research and technology service directed towards the needs of private companies;
- organizations engaged in higher education and vocational training and retraining;
- consultancies;
- industrial and professional associations;
- industrial policy-making bodies; and
- public and private bodies engaged in certification.

Furthermore, an overview of the evolution of the Danish industrial policy-making system is given. Section 3 concludes with a sub-section on second party certification in Denmark. This part of Section 3 reports on some of the results of a survey of nine large companies known to be active in the field of quality promotion.

Section 4 provides an analysis and an overview of the national policy initiatives described in Section 2. Common to these initiatives is an emphasis on:

- an integrative approach to technical and organizational innovation;
- the need to stimulate intra-organizational innovation by inter-organizational cooperation; and
- the importance of disseminating to other organizations the results of the projects subvented by the initiatives.

The fields of interest of the individual initiatives are described, and an overview of the activities undertaken within the initiatives is provided regarding research, training and education, consultancy, and promotion and awareness. It is especially emphasized that the national initiatives focus on the ability of the participating organizations to disseminate their results when granting a public subsidy for the projects in question, and because the principle of public access to the results of the subvented projects is so important, promotion is defined as the dissemination of results and the undertaking of company-specific projects.

Section 5 describes two regional initiatives: a small one in the South of Jutland comprising only seven companies and five consultancies, of which two are technology institutes, and a large one in the North of Jutland comprising 100 companies and 26 consultancies, of which four are technology institutes.

Finally, Section 6 provides an overview of existing initiatives and an outlook for future trends at the levels of national and regional industrial policy in the field of quality. This section focuses on the future dynamism of the Danish quality infrastructure.

2. The Emergence of Quality as an Issue

Although a national Danish association on quality control, Dansk Forening for Kvalitetsstyring, was established as early as 1960, the issue of quality did not appear on the political agenda until the mid-1980s. When it did appear, it evolved out of industrial policy initiatives, not based on governmental reports on quality like the ones appearing in the UK during the 1970s and early 1980s, but based on industrial experiences in the Danish economy, to some extent expressed through the National Agency of Industry and Trade acting as secretariat of the Danish Technology Council (Teknologirådet). The following section argues that a succession of industrial policy initiatives has gradually led to total quality control being firmly placed on the political agenda.

In December 1983, the Technology Council proposed an extraordinary national four-year programme on technological development to be known as TUP (Teknologisk UdviklingsProgrammet, Programme for Technological Development). TUP was initiated in order to disseminate frontier technological development, especially in the field of information technology.[1] The argument in favour of this initiative may be summarized as follows:

> *The recent technological development, especially within the fields of microelectronics and information technology, presents new opportunities for the improvement of international competitiveness to an industry comprising the same structure as the Danish industry. At the same time, this development imposes on Danish industry the need for an unprecedented structural change, and the accomplishment of this change is of vital importance to the Danish welfare state. The magnitude of the public and private efforts related to the dissemination of high technology in our neighbouring competitor countries requires an extraordinary Danish effort if Danish backwardness is to be avoided. The rate of industrial structural change will determine the appropriation of benefits regarding employment and the balance of payments. For this reason, a governmental extraordinary initiative seems reasonable.[2]*

(author's translation)

The working committees behind the proposal argued that new technological opportunities, offsetting the advantages of large scale production, had developed within reach of the internationally small Danish industrial companies, especially in the fields of knowledge acquisition, administration, product development and production activities, and could be grasped in a way that developed the production flexibility and non-adversarial labour relations characterizing these companies. The proposal suggested a public investment of Dkr 1525 million in six different fields:

- dissemination of information technology (Dkr 405 million),

- development and implementation of manufacturing production systems based on information technology (Dkr 450 million),
- product development (Dkr 285 million),
- acquisition of knowledge abroad (Dkr 65 million),
- finance for high technology in research, development, technology service and education (Dkr 300 million), and
- technology assessment (Dkr 20 million).

The programme was initiated by the Danish government in 1985, and during the period of 1985 to 1988, 1836 projects were undertaken, consuming a total government funding of Dkr 1311 million.[3] The projects involved a large number of private companies, technology institutes, various organizations and consultancies, and a number of educational organizations. According to an evaluation of the programme, the participating companies, the Danish technology infrastructure, and the relationship between the companies and the infrastructure appeared to have benefited from the programme.[4,5]

One of the main objectives of the TUP programme was to support the general formation of knowledge and competence in participating companies, and three-quarters of the companies experienced an increase in the competence of the work force.[6] However, the primary focus of attention within the TUP programme was on the technical aspects of industrial development and technical innovation, with little emphasis on organizational change. But as the programme proceeded, an initiative regarding consultancy support for the introduction of the management philosophy of computer integrated manufacturing was undertaken, and although this 'newcomer' did not have any significant effect on the participating companies, it did introduce a focus on the organizational aspects of technical innovation.[7]

The organizational aspects became more visible in an initiative on the management of, and cooperation in, technical innovation, proposed in 1988.[8] Arguing that many companies, inspired by recent technological development, had invested in 'hardware' in the form of information and production technology without realizing the expected benefits (regarding the minimization of inputs to the production process, the improvement of productivity, and the development of new products) the proposal emphasized the ability of the company to engage managers and employees in cooperation on organizational change, applying an integrative approach to the aspects of commercial results and financial resources, production, products, marketing, organizational structure, labour relations, and conditions of work.

Although not extraordinary in regarding the level of government funding proposed for the programme (Dkr 30 million during the three-year period of 1988 to 1990), the initiative was remarkable in the sense that nine manufacturing companies had been visited by the working committee during the preparation of the proposal. These companies had invested heavily in technical innovation during the first half of the 1980s in order to achieve the benefits mentioned above. However, a substantial number of the companies had been unable to realize the intended objectives, due to a technical-organizational mismatch created by a lack of management ability to integrate technical innovation and human resource management, especially regarding organizational change and the upgrading of qualifications and skills of the labour force *vis-à-vis* the demands on work organization, and labour force competence posed by the new technology.[9]

The working committee preparing the proposal on management of and cooperation on technical innovation was formed in 1987 by the Technology Council which, at about the same time, appointed a working committee on the promotion of quality. The latter was assigned not to substitute for, but to complement, the proposals of the committee on management of and cooperation on technical innovation.[10] The proposal of the working committee on the promotion of quality, the KUP programme (KvalitetsUdviklings Programmet, Programme for Quality Development), was issued in early 1988, suggesting a government funding of Dkr 55 million to be spent in the period of 1988 to 1990 on activities regarding global and sectoral promotion of total quality control, TQC-projects in specific companies, and improvement of the Danish quality infrastructure.[11] The focus of attention of this initiative may be described as a combination of the Deming philosophy and an emphasis on organizational interactive learning.

Finally, prior to the termination of the KUP programme, the Technology Council launched an initiative on improved utilization of production systems, the BUP programme (Bedre Udnyttelse af Produktionssystemer, Improved Utilization of Production Systems), with suggested government funding of Dkr 50 millions to be spent in the period of 1990 to 1992. The task of the working committee preparing the proposal was to define fields of interest in relation to the improved utilization of existing resources of manufacturing companies, regarding the development of market possibilities, process technology, capital assets, human resources, procurement, and internal information systems aimed at the measurement and control of the utilization of inputs and resources. The proposal defined the production system of a manufacturing company as the interplay between the technical, administrative, and social systems, and argued, in relation to the lack of productivity growth in the Danish manufacturing system despite a rapid diffusion of new advanced process technology, that the realization of the productivity potentials associated with new advanced process technology depends on the improvement of the interplay between the sub-systems within the production system.[12]

Summing up, in a medium-term historical perspective, two features of the evolution of the industrial policy initiatives can be identified:

- an increasing emphasis on the interplay between technical and organizational innovation, and
- an emphasis on projects involving cooperation between companies, technology institutes, consultancies, industrial associations, and organizations for education and vocational training and retraining, among others.

Thus, it seems reasonable to argue that during the TUP programme and subsequent initiatives, a 'new era' systems approach to technological development gradually became the focus of industrial policy. In fact, the analysis above shows that this approach comprises both the interplay between sub-systems within the individual company and the interplay between the different entities of the national system of innovation. The core of this approach is an emphasis on:

- cooperation between parties within the individual company, and between the individual company and organizations in the neighbouring environment;
- an integrative approach to technical and organizational innovation; and
- the importance of human resource management, in the sense of developing the technical and organizational competencies of both management and employees.

The intra and inter-organizational principles of this three-point approach is not only a set of organizational beliefs at the level of policy formation, but is also, to an increasing degree, a view shared by managers of Danish industrial companies. In fact, the TUP programme and the subsequent policy initiatives are, to a large extent, reflections of the needs and expressed wants of Danish industrial managers. Consequently, important parts of the Danish national system of innovation have been, or are becoming, pervaded by the three-point approach, which is strongly conducive to the evolution of the national quality infrastructure and the diffusion of total quality control principles described in the next section. This trend, and not only the national and regional schemes and measures in the field of quality, may explain the rapid growth in the number of ISO-certified Danish companies. (see below).

2.1 The Diffusion of Quality

Regarding the number of ISO 9000 certificates, Denmark appears as a pioneer amongst EC member states, primarily in the field of manufacturing activities and, as argued above, the diffusion of these certificates might be perceived as an indicator of the diffusion of the organizational principles of total quality control. It is, at present, difficult to trace the relationship between the diffusion of total quality control principles during the last three or four years, and the technology policy initiatives undertaken in the same period, because evaluation at the levels of policy and programme administration is still to come. However, bearing in mind the number of companies, organizations, research and technology institutes, consultancies, and industry and labour market organizations which have participated in national and regional initiatives during the period 1988 to 1992, one might, reasonably, state the proposition that the rate of total quality control principles measured by the rate of diffusion of ISO 9000 certificates is bound to increase in the near future. This point of view seems to be validated by the statistical evidence presented below.

Examining Tables 2 and 3 (page 77) leads to two main observations as to the industrial organization of the Danish manufacturing sector:

- a strong bias towards small and medium-sized companies in a national context, and small companies in an international context.

- a relatively high proportion of exports, measured by the export shares of turnover in the various industries.

Table 2: Distribution of companies according to size

Number of Employees	Number of Companies	Percentage
6-19	3406	48.5
20-49	2020	28.8
50-99	819	11.7
100-199	427	6.1
200-499	264	3.8
500+	81	1.1

Sources: The statistical ten-year review 1991, and calculations from the general statistical review of trade and commerce 1991:6 (June). Both publications by the Danish Central Statistical Office

Table 3: Share of exports in various industries

Sub-sectors	%Export in Turn-over	% of Total Exports
Mining and quarrying	83.7	5.6
Food, beverages and tobacco[a]	18.4	16.8
Textile, clothing and leather	44.1	5.7
Wood products and furniture	33.0	4.7
Paper, printing and publishing	17.2	4.4
Chemicals and petroleum	50.0	16.5
Non-metallic mineral products	19.1	1.9
Basic metal industries	54.5	1.7
Fabricated metal products[b]	49.2	40.1
Other manufacturing industries	60.3	2.6

a. including dairies

b. excluding repairs of machinery

Sources: The statistical ten-year review 1991, and calculations from the general statistical review of trade and commerce 1991:6 (June). Both publications by the Danish Central Statistical Office

The rapidly growing interest in Danish manufacturing companies in adopting principles of total quality control is, to some extent, rooted in an awareness of these structural configurations, which make the Danish manufacturing sector vulnerable to changes affecting the international competitiveness of the companies in question. The realization of the European Single Market is, by the top management of many exporting companies, and by industrial and technology policy authorities, often mentioned as a serious challenge due to the expected increases in competitive pressures at the product markets. The expectations of an increase in competitive pressures are somewhat intermingled with the belief that the rate of diffusion of total quality control principles in European countries comprising the most important Danish export markets and foreign competitors is much higher than the Danish rate of diffusion thus undermining the relative position of Danish international competitiveness *vis-à-vis* an international trend towards customization, flexibility, and high speed of delivery as competitive assets at the international product markets. Consequently, in the public debate on international competitiveness and industrial and technology policy, the acquisition of an ISO 9000 certificate is often mentioned as a necessary means to:

- satisfy customer confidence in the quality of Danish products;
- support marketing; and
- improve on the internal efficiency of the company.

Furthermore, the current development (partly inspired by US legislation) and harmonization at the EC level of legislation regarding producer responsibility for products have, in some instances, been brought to the attention of top management in private companies by the Danish authorities in charge of industrial and technology policy. The anticipation of legislation in the field of producer responsibility for products was one of the arguments stated in favour of the Danish national programme on promotion of quality presented in Section 4.

Regarding the diffusion of ISO 9000 standards, the strategic disposition of the certified companies has, to some extent, been defensive in nature.[13] It seems as if the diffusion of ISO certificates has been spurred by the fear of top management in manufacturing companies of losing competitive strength, and, consequently, the rate of diffusion is high, perhaps even surprisingly so, considering the distribution of company size in the Danish manufacturing sector.

Table 4 (page 78) summarizes the number of ISO certificates issued to Danish manufacturing companies by the end of September 1991. The level of diffusion of ISO 9000 certificates in Denmark seems rather high, by international standards (see Part Two), especially when one considers the relative size, on average, of Danish manufacturing companies (see Table 2, page 77). The second column in the table indicates a presently high rate of diffusion of ISO 9000 certificates. This estimate is based on the number of ISO certificates issued by the DS (Dansk Standardiseringsråd, Danish Standards Association) since the end of September 1991. It is based on the assumption that the distribution of certificates issued by certification bodies active in Denmark,[14] and according to the various ISO standards, remain stable. Both this estimate, and the actual figures in the first column show that the growth of the number of manufacturing companies acquiring an ISO certificate has been very strong.

Table 4. Number of ISO 9000 certificates issued to Danish manufacturing companies

	ISO 9001	ISO 9002	ISO 9003	Total
By September 1991	37	28	2	67
End of 1991	63	48	3	114

Source: KvalitetsGruppen (1991), p.7, and own calculations based on the statistical ten-year review 1991 issued by the Danish Central Statistical Office and Standardnyt no.6, 1991. Standardnyt is a journal of standardization issued by the Danish Standards Association (Dansk Standardiseringsråd) every second month.

From discussions with various experts in the field it appears that this estimate is actually too low, partly due to the fact that Det Norske Veritas, which was the only accredited certification body in Denmark, has greatly increased the number of certificates it has issued in Denmark since September 1991. The correct number of ISO 9000 certificates by the end of 1991 could easily have been a total of approximately 140,[15] and according to figures from Trade Book International,[16] the number of ISO certificates by the beginning of May 1992 was approximately 180.[17] This figure had grown to at least 200 by the end of May, indicating a 30 to 45% growth during the first five month of 1992, presumably at an increasing rate.[18]

3. The Quality Infrastructure

The way in which this impressive growth has been supported by the Danish policy initiatives in the field of quality can hardly be assessed, especially because the evaluation stages of the national and regional initiatives are still to come. However, the fact that the policy initiatives have been highly supportive in generating a quality infrastructure in Denmark might indicate that a significant effect of policy initiatives has been at work.

In a Danish setting, the definition of the quality infrastructure touches upon several branches of economic and technological activities, as will appear from the following seven categories. Compiling an exhaustive inventory of the actors of these groups is a major research project that can hardly be done within the time limits of the present study. However, Section 7 contains an inventory of major actors in the Danish quality infrastructure, compiled primarily on the basis of secretarial information from the National Agency of Industry and Trade, the NordTek secretariat (cf. Section 5) and the DS. Bearing in mind the large numbers of projects and participating organizations within these initiatives, the inventory presented in Section 7 touches upon the major part of the Danish quality infrastructure. The seven categories in the Danish quality infrastructure are:

- private companies,
- research institutes,
- higher education institutes/further education institutes,
- consultancies,
- industrial and professional associations,
- industrial and policy-making bodies, and
- certification bodies.

i) Private companies in which the management of total quality control plays an important part in the pursuit of economic survival

This category can be divided into the sub-categories of companies without a certificate and certified companies, which both contains a number of companies engaged in second-party certification. As mentioned above, the number of companies with an ISO 9000 certificate is at least 200, and none of these have been included in Section 7.

ii) Institutes concerned with research and technological service directed towards the needs of private companies

This is a rather heterogeneous category, spanning from public university departments to semi-public technology institutes and private technology service institutes. The semi-public sub-category comprises, at present, approximately 20 technology institutes receiving an annual state subsidy according to the Danish legislation on technological service, and a number of technology information centres (TICs).[19] The semi-public institutes act as independent profit centres servicing primarily the private business sector from which an important part of their annual turnover accrues as payments for services rendered.[20] In order to strengthen the technological and economic capabilities of the technology institute structure, the Technology Council initiated in 1989 a process of merging activity.[21] Consequently, the number of technology institutes has been falling during the past years, from 31 in 1989 to 25 in 1990 and approximately 20 in 1991. The present number of technology institutes is somewhat uncertain due to an ongoing wave of mergers that gained speed especially during 1991.[22] The inventory in Section 7 contains seven licensed technology institutes, which have participated in the national promotion of quality initiative (KUP), and three technology information centres.

iii) Organizations engaged in higher education and vocational training and retraining

These organizations are primarily universities, technical colleges and commercial schools at various levels of education, and a number of centres and schools for vocational training and retraining. Due to legislation on vocational training and retraining initiated in the mid-1980s, the vocational training and retraining organizations have increasingly become independent profit-centres selling educational services to primarily the private business sector. The same tendency can, although not to the same degree, be observed in the cases of universities, technical colleges for higher education and commercial schools. The inventory in Section 7 contains 23 organizations engaged in higher education and vocational training and retraining which have participated in the national promotion of quality initiative (KUP) and, furthermore, three organizations known to be active in the field of quality.

iv) Consultancies

A number of consultancies have been active in the field of quality for some years, and an extremely large number of consultancies have indicated that they are interested in and capable of consultation on total quality control. As part of the promotion of quality initiative (KUP), five information meetings for consultancies were held by the DS as part of their project on establishing a Danish system for the certification of quality control systems (see Section 4), a project that began in May 1988 and ended in April 1990. The participating consultancies, more than 140, were recorded in a register by the Danish Standards Association. However, according to this register not more than 15-17% of these consultancies had actively participated in the development of quality control systems that were or could be certified. The inventory in section 7 contains 29 consultancies which have participated in the development of quality control systems that have been or can be certified. This list contains 24 consultancies from the DS register and five of the consultancies participating in the regional quality initiative in North Jutland. Furthermore, four of the 29 consultancies are, at the same time, licensed technology institutes.

v) Industrial and professional associations

This is another heterogeneous group, comprising labour unions, associations of employers, employees, trades, professionals and various industries, and institutes not licensed. The inventory in Section 7 contains twelve of these organizations, ten of which have participated in the national promotion of quality initiative (KUP).

vi) Industrial policy-making bodies

Regarding the field of industrial policy, one could, of course, argue that the number of policy-making bodies is quite large. However, regarding the field of quality, in Denmark primarily an issue in the manufacturing sector, the number becomes limited. Mainly two ministries are engaged in this field: notably, the Ministry of Industry, the source of the initiatives described in Section 2, but of course also the Ministry of Education which is in charge of the legislation on vocational training and retraining mentioned in relation to category 3 above. Primarily, three policy-making bodies under the auspices of the Ministry of Industry have been active in the national promotion of quality initiative, as described in Section 4. These are the Council for Metrology (Statens Metrologiråd), the Technical Testing Tribunal (Statens Tekniske Prøvenævn) and the Technology Council (Teknologirådet), all of them using the National Agency of Industry and Trade as secretariat. However, as a consequence of the law on industrial development issued in June 1990, a number of councils and committees were merged into the Council for Industrial Development (Erhvervsudviklingsrådet), the Council for Improved Export Performance (Eksportfremmerådet) and the Committee for Appropriation (Bevillingsudvalget), all of which are using the National Agency of Industry and Trade as a secretariat. The Council for Industrial Development acts as an advisory body to the Minister of Industry, while the Council for Improved Export Performance acts as an advisory body to the Council for Industrial Development. Finally, the Committee for Appropriation is a decision-making body in the field of public co-financing of industrial and technological activities under the auspices of the two councils mentioned above. The policy initiatives on promotion of quality (KUP) and improved utilization of production systems (BUP) continue under the auspices of the Council for Industrial Development.[23] None of these policy-making bodies have been included in the inventory in Section 7.

vii) Public and private bodies engaged in certification

The organizations in this category are semi-public or private, with the exception of the National Agency of Industry and Trade, acting as the Danish accreditation body concerning companies engaged in certification regarding products, quality control systems, and personnel, laboratories and companies in the field of technical testing and inspection. As was mentioned earlier, regarding the certification of quality control systems, five organizations are particularly active in the Danish certificates market, also regarding certificates on products and personnel. They have all been included in the inventory in Section 7. Out of these, the Danish affiliation of Det Norske Veritas has been accredited according to the Danish Accreditation System, while the DS is licensed as a technology institute.

In the field of technical testing, we find 59 accredited laboratories, two of which are foreign. Only the 18 laboratories engaged in calibration have been included in the inventory of Section 7, and four of these are licensed technology institutes.

The Danish Accreditation System is quite new. As part of the activities following the law on industrial development in June 1990, the Danish Accreditation System was established by the beginning of 1991. At present the accreditation system covers the fields of technical testing and the certification of products, quality control systems, and personnel.[24] In the field of inspection, the administrative procedures of the accreditation body, the National Agency of Industry and Trade, awaits the final harmonization of the European standards.[25] In the field of technical testing, a Danish national authorization system was established in 1973, administered by the Technical Testing Tribunal (Statens Tekniske Prøvenævn), and when the tribunal was dissolved as part of the legislation on industrial development, the administration of the authorization system was transferred to the National Agency of Industry and Trade. In 1989, the surveillance of the authorized laboratories was transferred to the Danish Institute of Fundamental Metrology (Dansk Institut for Fundamental Metrologi), which continues this work on behalf of the National Agency of Industry and Trade. The authorizations issued within the authorization system have been extended in the form of accreditations within the Danish Accreditation System.

Finally, two things should be mentioned about the Danish accreditation system. First, by the end of 1990, Denmark became the fifteenth member of the Western European Calibration Cooperation (WECC) as part of the attempts to prepare the

Danish accreditation system for the European Single Market.[26] Second, complaints about the decisions on accreditation made by the National Agency of Industry and Commerce are dealt with by the Complaints Board on Public Tenders (Klagenævnet for Udbud), instituted by law in June 1991 to handle complaints on Danish public tender according to EC legislation. Figure 11 (page 84) is a graphical summary of the description of the Danish quality infrastructure, with respect to the enforcement of the promotion of quality initiative (KUP), the Danish Accreditation System, and the major part of the quality infrastructure reflected in the inventory in Section 7. As mentioned in the text of Figure 11, the nexus of the figure is projects undertaken in order to solve company-specific problems of total quality control. Actually, a number of projects involving cooperation between organizations within all of the seven categories in various mixtures were undertaken, and in some cases only a single organization carried out the project. However, Figure 11 reflects the main working of the quality infrastructure, especially in relation to various policy initiatives, with one important exception. This exception, second party certification, is discussed in some detail in the following section.

3.1 Second Party Certification in Denmark

Second party certification has been reserved for 'special treatment', because it is a sub-system within the quality infrastructure which is especially important to the dynamic nature of the infrastructure in the near future. A small survey of nine large Danish companies known to be active in the field of quality was undertaken. The rest of this section briefly describes the main findings of this survey.

The quality control system of seven of the nine companies had been certified, six according to ISO 9001 (and/or its equivalent BS 5750, part I) and one according to ISO 9002. All of the nine companies had an individual or individuals in charge of quality, by management position and/or by management responsibility. Furthermore, all of the nine companies were engaged in different sorts of inter-organizational cooperation on one or more aspects of total quality control, primarily at a national level, ranging from participation in groups of people meeting frequently in order to share experiences and discuss matters,[27] to frequent contacts with business contacts and more formal arrangements.

Regarding cooperation with other manufacturing companies, companies competing directly with the respondent, non-competitors and customers were all mentioned by four respondents, while companies engaged in indirect competition with the respondent were mentioned in two cases. Regarding other types of inter-organizational contact in the field of quality, eight companies responded positively, primarily pointing to industrial organizations and technology institutes, and to organizations engaged in vocational training and retraining servicing the workforce of the company in question.

Figure 11: The Danish quality infrastructure

(with respect to the enforcement of the national promotion of quality initiative (KUP), the Danish Accreditation System, and the major part of the quality infrastructure).

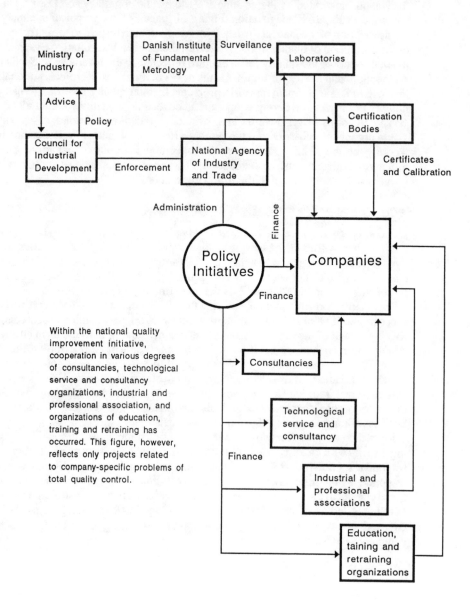

Furthermore, three companies reported to have cooperated with one or more certification bodies. This might indicate that certification bodies participate more actively in the quality infrastructure than one might expect, thus contributing to the diffusion of quality management best practice.

Most frequently, suppliers were mentioned as inter-organizational cooperative parties as reported by six respondents. This was expected, of course, and is not surprising *vis-à-vis* the fact that eight of the nine companies had presented one or more suppliers with quality control requirements. As a general rule, these requirements differed according to the supplier in question, and, furthermore, the companies differed in the degree of formalism and unconditionality related to the requirements. To some extent, the degree of unconditionality and formalism reflected the company's own quality control system, ie the more elaborate the company's quality control system, the more unconditional the requirements to the supplier's quality control system. This correlation was, however, not uni-directional, and was to some extent offset by the fact that the number of suppliers able to satisfy quality control requirements was too small for the procurement needs of the companies in question.

All of the nine companies had, on one or more occasions, assessed the quality control system of one or more suppliers and made an estimate on whether this system showed adequate performance. The eight companies had judged whether the supplier's quality control system was documented according to the requirements of the company, and seven of the respondents had made assessments on the implementation of the system. However, as a rule, suppliers were not required to document their quality control system according to any recognized standard, and the supplier requirements were mainly based on the needs of the company in question. But of course, both the company and the supplier did keep their eyes on the internationally recognized standards, using them as suitable guidelines.

As a main impression gained from the survey, the suppliers submitted themselves to the requirements of the companies. Resistance did occur, but only in a few cases, and in some cases only as a transitory phenomenon. 'Well, they have no choice', as one respondent said, and other respondents argued that most suppliers would welcome the opportunity to improve on their quality control through cooperation with a competent manufacturer. This, and the fact that six of the nine companies plan to present suppliers with quality control requirements in the future, might indicate that the nature of the second party certification sub-system of the Danish quality infrastructure will become more dynamic in the future. However, these future requirements will not, as a rule, correspond closely to one or more internationally recognized standards, except in the medium to long term.

This might be an important feature. Considering the number of ISO 9000 certificates already issued and the number of potential certificates that might be issued within perhaps four to five years,[28] one might argue that the present market for quality control system certificates would approach the level of saturation in the medium term. However, an increased level of activity within the field of second party certification might push the limits of the certificates market by introducing a range of new, potential 'customers' to the 'suppliers' of certificates.

This outlook, further elaborated in Section 6, concludes this section describing the Danish quality infrastructure, presenting a suitable inventory, and analyzing the working of a quality infrastructure sub-system which presumably will become increasingly important in the near future. As argued in Section 2, the evolution of policy initiatives towards some kind of 'new era' system approach has been conducive to the development and improvement of the Danish quality infrastructure, and Section 4 turns to the actual working of these initiatives, while Section 5 examines two regional initiatives of some importance.

According to the common descriptive methodology agreed upon by the organizations undertaking this study, the national and regional quality schemes and initiatives should be classified on a global-sectoral continuum in relation to the scope of their target groups, and the activities within these initiatives in four main areas of activity: research, training and education, consultancy, and promotion and awareness. While Sections 4 and 5 pay due respect to these guidelines, the reader should observe, however, that the global dimension will be almost absent, because the scope of the initiatives described are primarily sectoral.

4. National Quality Schemes and Initiatives

Earlier, Section 2 argued that three policy initiatives have been especially conducive to the promotion of quality at the national level, ie the initiatives on management of, and cooperation in, technical innovation, improved utilization of production systems, and, notably, promotion of quality (KUP). As shown in Table 5 below, a total of Dkr 151.5 million in government funding was provided for these three initiatives during the five-year period of 1988 to 1992, and the initiatives were mainly directed towards the manufacturing sector, thus being of a sectoral rather than a global scope. However, within KUP, there were a number of global schemes aimed at improving the Danish quality infrastructure.

Table 5. Government quality related initiatives

Initiative	Funding (million Dkr)	Period	Target
Promotion of quality	71.5	1988-91	manufacturing construction
Management and cooperation	30.0	1988-90	manufacturing
Improved utilization	50.0	1990-92	manufacturing

Sources: Project Survey, KUP-initiative, June 1990; Project Survey, BUP-initiative, November 1991; Teknologirådet (1988a, 1988b, 1990).

While the management and cooperation and the promotion of quality initiatives supplement each other by introducing, on the political agenda, an integrative approach to technical and organizational innovation, the initiative on improved utilization of production systems has gone a bit further, emphasizing the interplay between the technical, administrative, and social sub-systems. At the same time, all of the initiatives emphasize, in effect, the need to stimulate intra-organizational innovation by inter-organizational cooperation, because mainly projects based mainly on inter-organizational development are subvented within the initiatives.[29] Furthermore, the initiatives stress the importance of disseminating the results of the subvented projects, because the participating organizations are requested to make the results available to the public. These integrative approaches and the emphasis on achieving intra-organizational innovation by inter-organizational cooperation and dissemination of results constitute the core of the three-point approach at the level of policy, described in Section 2. At the level of initiative, the degree of system-orientation varies according to the differences in the fields of interest between the initiatives, and the fact that the rationales of the initiatives differ from one another is the most important feature explaining the evolution of the 'new era' system approach.

The main objective of the management and cooperation initiative is to promote the awareness of managers and employees in the manufacturing sector regarding the need for a non-adversarial approach to the integration of commercial results, financial resources, production, products, marketing, organizational structure, labour relations and work conditions. In order to achieve this aim, priority is given to three fields of interest, especially directed towards small and medium-sized companies:

- activities promoting the formation of knowledge (e.g. research) and experimental work at factories, in projects based on inter-organizational cooperation.
- distribution of knowledge by traditional and non-traditional means,[30] for education, study groups, and the like, and through demonstration projects and experience groups.
- education, training, and re-training of management, employees, and consultants advising the companies on technical and organizational change.

While the management and cooperation initiative focuses on the promotion of awareness of new organizational principles in general, using demonstration projects as an important medium (see the overview below), the activities within the initiative on improved utilization of production systems are devoted to the solution of company-specific problems by the application of best-practice organizational principles, giving priority to four fields of interest:

- activities regarding the definition of productivity targets, methods for the measurement of productivity, and the development of competence and qualifications of management and employees. The focus of this part of the programme is upon the adaptation to company-specific purposes of existing methods and procedures.

- projects regarding the solution of company-specific problems hampering the utilization of company resources, e.g. in the form of human resources, process technology, materials, capital assets, and information.

- the distribution of knowledge through workshops, conferences, demonstration projects, videos and written materials.

- finally, while the initiatives on management and cooperation and improved utilization of production system stimulates the diffusion of best-practice organizational principles at the company and sectoral levels, the promotion of quality initiative (KUP) supplements these activities by stimulating the interplay between, on the one hand, an increased speed of diffusion of total quality control principles at the company level, and on the other hand, the improvement of the quality infrastructure. Four fields of interest constitute the core of the KUP initiative:

  1. an awareness campaign and general information directed towards private companies, the system of education, training and re-training, and authorities in charge of public procurement.

  2. initiatives directed towards companies with the purpose of improving total quality control, in the form of development projects in specific companies, and projects aimed at diffusing knowledge of total quality control principles at the level of industry or sector, e.g. through demonstration projects and experience groups.

  3. improvement of the Danish quality infrastructure by:

     – the development of an internationally approved Danish accreditation system;

     – the development of new procedures for calibration, the improvement of the services offered by Danish calibration laboratories, and the development of courses in measurement and calibration techniques and in auditing as part of a certification process; and

     – an analysis and clarification of the need for standards in the manufacturing and construction sectors.

  4. initiatives regarding education, training, and re-training in the field of quality.

Funding devoted to the various fields of interest within the framework of each initiative appear in Figure 12 (page 89). An additional funding, to be spent in 1991, of Dkr 11.5 million provided within the KUP initiative for consultancy in private companies has been included. This additional funding did, in fact, prolong the KUP initiative by one year.

The cases in question are three projects on the development of productivity measurement undertaken within the initiative on improved utilization of production systems, and involving more than 440 manufacturing companies, two industrial associations, two consultancies and a number of technology information centres. Two of these projects were directed towards the improvement of productivity measurement in twelve companies, and the last project aimed at disseminating some productivity-based accounting principles at a number of seminars (lasting for five days) involving 430 companies.[31]

Figure 12: Funding of the fields of interest within government quality initiatives

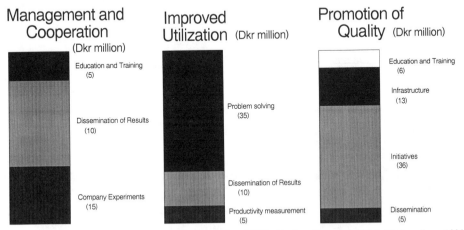

Sources: Elaborated from Teknologirådet (1988); Project Survey, KUP Initiative, June 1990; Newsletter, May 1991; Project Survey, BUR Initiative, Nov. 1991.

In summary, within the three initiatives covered by Figure 12, more than 90 projects has been undertaken with the participation of more than 800 manufacturing and construction companies, and approximately 25 consultancies, 15 technology institutes and technology information centres, 35 industrial and trade associations, 25 organizations engaged in education and vocational training and retraining, and a couple of certification bodies, a total of approximately 900 organizations.[32] Tables 6 and 7 (page 90) indicate that the public funding available for these projects was supplemented by a semi-public and private funding approximately twice as big.

4.1 Research

As the main focus of the initiatives is the promotion of organizational best practice as part of primarily company-specific projects, actual research within the initiatives is absent, despite the large number of projects. One might argue that an element of applied research taking place outside research organizations has been present in some projects, but the nature of these activities is, however, one of consultancies disseminating their skills and methods to the companies involved. Furthermore, no scientific organizations were involved.

Table 6: Funding for the initiative on promotion of quality

Key: (1) public funding available, (2) public funding consumed, (3) total public, semi-public and private investment in the initiative, all in Dkr million and (4) the number of projects undertaken, 1988-90. Compare with Figure 12.

Field of interest	(1)	(2)	(3)	(4)
Dissemination	5	4.559	4.559	1
Initiatives	36	35.745	100.004	28
Infrastructure	13	13.390	17.635	11
Education and training	6	0.637	0.891	2
Total	60	54.331	123.089	42

Source: Project Survey, KUP initiative, June 1990

Table 7: Funding for the initiative on improved utilization of production systems.

Key: (1) public funding available, (2) public funding consumed, (3) total public, semi-public and private investment in the initiative, all in Dkr million and (4) the number of projects undertaken, 1990 to 1992. Compare with Figure 12.

Field of interest	(1)	(2)	(3)	(4)
Measurement	5	4.779	28.274	3
Company problems	35	26.057	124.135	18
Dissemination	10	0	0	0
Total	50	30.836	152.409	21

Source: Project Survey, BUP initiative, November 1991.

4.2 Training and education

In the field of training and education, five projects took place within the promotion of quality initiative.

First, DIEU (Danske Ingenørers Efteruddannelse, the Retraining Association of Danish University Trained Engineers) developed a course in auditing formally qualifying the participants to perform auditing of quality control systems. This course ('audit-2') is a four-day course superimposed on a three-day basic course ('audit-1') required for the participation in audit-2 and comes up to the British IQA criteria for auditing courses.[33]

Second, the technology institute Svejsecentralen (Welding Centre) developed a course aimed at qualifying laboratory staff to institute a quality control system within the licensed laboratories described earlier in Section 3.

Third, the development of an education for 'quality instructors' was undertaken by the national agency for pedagogy in vocational training (Statens Erhvervspæda-gogiske Læreruddannelse). Initially, at a hearing, a number of industrial associations, policy makers and organizations in the field of vocational training and retraining had advocated the need for upgrading the competence of vocational and commercial teachers in the field of quality. The education for quality instructors programme was an attempt to meet this perceived need.

This project took place as three identical pilot project courses in three different parts of the country, each with the participation of 16 persons from four commercial schools, five technical colleges at lower levels, five centres for vocational retraining and eight private companies. Of the 48 persons involved, 47 qualified as quality instructors, and the participants had been selected according to the 'DUR-T principle', i.e. the participants were willing and able to participate (Deltage), they had experience in education (Uddannelse) in fields where the topics of quality control and measurement have some importance, they were respected (Respekt) by their colleagues and managers as professionally competent people, and they enjoyed the confidence (Tilled) of their colleagues and managers.

The objective of the pilot projects was to develop an education programme defining the responsibility of the quality instructor as guiding and supporting colleagues, employees and organization while disseminating concepts, beliefs, control procedures and standards in the field of quality within the functional tasks of the organization to which the quality instructor belongs. Consequently, the quality instructor will serve as a consultant, adviser and mediator, e.g. regarding support for the planning and implementation of the quality control philosophy within instruction sessions and courses, the undertaking of intra-organizational lectures, courses, conferences, seminars and workshops on quality control systems and techniques, and the organization of the accumulation and dissemination of experiences in the field of quality control and measurement techniques among the employees of the company, and teachers within commercial schools, technical colleges and vocational training centres.

The education programme for quality instructors is now being marketed by the national agency for pedagogy in vocational training, and the final education programme (almost similar to the pilot projects) is a two-month modular system comprising an initial four-day course in quality control principles, followed by a project undertaken by the participants in their organization, and a two-day course evaluating and summing up the experiences gained through the projects.

Fourth, a team of nine specialists in the field of quality undertook the production of a basic book in quality control and measurement. The result, *Møltoft et al.*, is intended for education within commercial schools and technical colleges at lower levels, and retraining courses for operators, technicians, middle managers and administrative staff.[34] *Møltoft et al.* is used as a textbook in the education of quality instructors.

Fifth, the Q-Initiative at the island of Fyn (Q-initiativ Fyn) initiated a four-step retraining programme with the objective of disseminating total quality control principles in private companies. Q-Initiative Fyn is a collaboration between six companies, with 34 companies more loosely connected to the initiative. The development of the retraining programme was undertaken in cooperation with the affiliation of the DTI (Dansk Tecknologisk Institut, Danish Technology Institute) at Fyn and a number of educational organizations in Odense (the major city at Fyn), i.e. the vocational retraining centre (AMU-Fyn), the technical college for higher education (Odense Teknikum), the technical college (Odense Tekniske Skole), the university (Odense Universitet) and the commercial school (Tietgenskolen).

The retraining programme has been tested at the six Q-Initiative Fyn member companies and is now being marketed by a consortium (KC, Kvalitetsudvikling-scenter Fyn, Quality Promotion Center Fyn) comprising the DTI affiliate and the educational organizations.

Concluding the overview on training and education, I wish to draw the reader's attention to the effects of the law on retraining initiated in June 1985 (the so-called Law 271). The law enables the Minister of Education to subsidize job-orientated retraining initiated, at the local level, by industry and educational organizations in cooperation. During the five-year period of 1986 to 1990, nearly a thousand experimental and developmental projects (subsidy: Dkr 330 million) and approximately 1600 retraining courses (subsidy: Dkr 60 million) have been undertaken. Naturally, the issue of quality control has slipped into the mass of projects. In 1990, seven of the 21 retraining courses in the field of productivity focused on quality control, subsidized by approximately Dkr 7 million out of the approximately Dkr 27 millions subsidy for new projects in the field of productivity.

Thus, quality retraining has consumed nearly 12% of the total subsidy for retraining courses in the five-year period, although quality did not really become an issue within the Law 271 initiative until 1990. This, and the fact that the issue of quality is increasingly being touched upon in the curriculum of many parts of the educational system, indicates that the Ministry of Industry is becoming a still more important actor in the quality infrastructure.[35]

4.3 Consultancy

In a way, the initiatives described in this section have contributed tremendously to the proliferation of the consultancy component of the Danish quality infrastructure, considering the number of consultancies participating in the company-specific projects. One might argue that the projects undertaken have stimulated the processes of consultancy learning in the field of quality, both by doing, i.e. actually consulting on the company-specific projects, and by interacting, i.e. the mutual exchange of knowledge and needs between the companies and consultancies involved. Thus, the level of competence in the field of quality has benefited enormously from industrial policy initiatives.

This process has been stimulated by a number of activities. The promotion of quality initiative included a Dkr 5 million subsidy arrangement for consultancy assistance directed towards small manufacturing companies (less than 50 employees). In sum, 624 companies benefitted from this arrangement, which is about 10% of all Danish manufacturing companies with less than 50 employees. The consultancy arrangement was administered by the Danish Technology Institute with the participation of the technology information centres.

It should be observed that during the period of administrative restructuring described in Section 3, the subsidies for consultancy assistance under the aegis of the Productivity and Consultancy Committee (Produktivitets- og Konsulentudvalget) have been reduced year-by-year,[36] and the initiative on management of, and cooperation in, technical innovation was, partly, initiated in order to satisfy the gap between the supply and demand for subsidies in the field of consultancy.

4.4 Promotion and awareness

The promotion of quality initiative is, in essence, the most important industrial policy initiative stimulating the diffusion of total quality control principles in Denmark. The objective of the initiative has been to create a number of successful demonstration projects, serving as exemplars in the field of quality and demonstrating that the establishment of a quality control system is both possible and profitable. The initiative has particularly emphasized projects revealing to other companies, especially at the level of industry, the problems of and solutions to total quality control. The aspect of promotion has been present every time an application for subsidies was assessed, especially regarding the dissemination of results by, for instance, visits at companies serving as demonstration projects.

Furthermore, the consultancy arrangement mentioned above has been an important part of the promotion of quality control principles to small manufacturing companies. The subsidy for consultancy has, apparently, been an important means to overcome the resistance of many small company managers to invest money in quality control consultancy, while still being somewhat uncertain about the effect of the investment. In this respect the consultancy subsidy has had an important gearing effect in leading to the initiation of quality control projects which would not have happened otherwise.

The principle of public access to the results obtained in projects at the levels of company, industry and sector, justifies that promotion within the initiatives described in this section is defined as the dissemination of results and the undertaking of company-specific projects. If one applies this definition, it appears from Figure 12 (page 89) and Tables 6 and 7 (page 90) that promotion is the major part of the initiatives. This definition, underpinning this discussion, is validated by the fact that the National Agency of Industry and Trade, as a principle, supports primarily projects based on the cooperation between organizations, and emphasizes the ability of these organizations to transfer to other organizations the knowledge obtained in the course of the project in question.

Thus, the promotion part of the promotion of quality initiative comprised 27 projects. Out of these, 25 were concerned with the manufacturing sector, of which 16 were directed towards specific industries, and two were concerned with the manufacturing sector. Nearly 120 companies participated in the projects, together with seven technology institutes, 15 industry and labour market organizations, a number of consultancies, and, among others, two certification bodies (the Danish Standards Association and Norske Veritas). The Danish Standards Association participated, as one of several consultants, in three projects involving 13 companies, of which one project involving six companies took place within the construction sector. Norske Veritas, cooperating with the employers' organization of the shipbuilding industry, initiated their own Dkr 17 million project within the shipbuilding industry, involving six shipyards.[37]

Regarding the improvement of the Danish quality infrastructure, 11 projects were undertaken. One large project, undertaken by the Danish Standards Association in order to develop and implement an internationally approved Danish accreditation system, involved seven companies aiming for an ISO 9000 certificate.[38]

In the field of developing new procedures for calibration and improving the services offered by Danish calibration institutes, seven projects were undertaken, involving approximately 700 companies for comparative calibration, four technology institutes, and five centres for physical labour conditions, among others. In the field of analysis and clarification of the need for standards in the manufacturing and construction sectors, two projects took place, one aiming at clarifying the use of the ISO 9000 standard in the construction sector, and one aiming at establishing a system of standards in the industry of engineering consultancy.

Within the initiative on improved utilization of production systems, the activities in the field of development of productivity measurement, and the improvement of competence and qualifications of management and employees as part of company-specific projects, involved approximately 15 companies, three labour market organizations, a couple of consultancy companies, and 250 companies as participants in workshops. The activities in the field of company-specific problems, comprising 18 projects of which eight are directed towards the industry level, involved approximately 100 companies, four labour market organizations, ten consultancy companies, a number of institutes, and 25 companies as participants in workshops.

Regarding awareness, understood as public relations, a number of activities have taken place which deserve to be mentioned. Within the promotion of quality initiative, an awareness campaign, undertaken by a campaign committee appointed by the Council for Technology, organized national meetings within the industries of fabricated metal products, textiles, food, beverages, and tobacco, and within the construction sector. Furthermore, a newsletter was issued and a textbook on quality produced.

Within the initiative on improved utilization of production systems, monthly folders on the topic of productivity are issued and mailed to 7000 companies. Within the management and cooperation initiative, a conference was held in October 1991, presenting the results from some of the 150 companies which participated in the initiative. This conference was the starting signal of a major campaign 'Future Days '92' (Fremtidsdage '92), directed towards 1500 manufacturing companies encouraged by mail to organize a 'Future Day'. A 'Future Day' may take one of two forms, either a visit to one of 26 companies selected as demonstration projects, or a visit from one of these companies. In addition, a book on 'Cooperation in Danish' (Samarbejde på dansk) and two videos have been produced. The book summarizes the experiences of the 150 companies which participated in the initiative, and the videos illustrate problems of and solutions to the organizational aspects of technical innovation. The video 'The old man is right' (Hvad fatter gør) shows the possible causes of conflict and communication barriers between persons at different levels within the organisational hierarchy. The video 'The company of the future' (Fremtidens virksomhed) presents the Danish company Oticon (a major world manufacturer of hearing aids), which, as part of the initiative, substituted computer networks for the use of paper in the administrative sub-system and made a number of subsequent organizational changes.

5. Regional Quality Schemes and Initiatives

This section describes the only two known regional policy initiatives in the field of quality: a minor one in the south of Jutland and a major one in the north of Jutland. While the South Jutland initiative involves only seven companies, the North Jutland initiative involves 100 companies striving to establish a total quality control system. The description and analysis of these initiatives follow the methodology of the previous section, i.e. the regional initiatives should be classified on a global sectoral continuum in relation to the scope of their target groups, and the activities within these initiatives in four main areas of activity, i.e. research, training and education, consultancy, and promotion and awareness.

The regional initiatives are similar to the national initiatives in relation to the global sectoral continuum, that is to say the regional initiatives can be located at the sectoral part of the continuum, both being directed towards the manufacturing sector. Furthermore, the regional schemes are similar to the national schemes regarding the absence of research activities. However, the two regional initiatives are quite different. While the South Jutland initiative is part of an arrangement for subsidizing consultancy assistance to private companies, the North Jutland initiative emphasizes the solution to company-specific problems at a more general level. This implies, regarding the field of quality, that the South Jutland initiative, as opposed to the North Jutland initiative, comprises only activities in the field of consultancy, while the North Jutland initiative comprises activities in the fields of training and education, and promotion and awareness, as well. Thus, an overview as the one presented in the previous section will only be provided in the North Jutland case.

5.1 The South Jutland initiative

In 1987, the local county administration in cooperation with the Industrial Council of South Jutland (Sønderjyllands Erhvervsråd) and the local technology information centre initiated an initiative on the diffusion of knowledge, technical innovation and tourism (Vidensspredning, teknologisk udvikling, turisme), also termed SEP (Sønderjyllands EF-programmet, The EC Initiative of South Jutland). The total funding of the SEP initiative is Dkr 95 million for the six-year period of 1987 to 1992 of which Dkr 44 million accrues from EC regional funding, which in a Danish setting is administered by the National Agency of Industry and Trade.

Within the SEP initiative, a subsidy arrangement for consultancy assistance has been provided, funded by Dkr 5 million accrued from the EC regional funding and Dkr 1 million made available by the local county administration. At the beginning of May 1992, Dkr 4.6 million had been spent on 32 projects involving 28 companies, and eight of these projects were in the field of quality, involving eight companies and five consultancies, of which two are technology institutes and one is the local technology information centre. Of the seven surviving companies (one having gone bankrupt) engaged in establishing a quality control system, six were using an ISO 9000 standard as a point of reference, and three indicated in their application for consultancy subsidies that they were aiming at an ISO 9002 certificate. Actually, four of the seven companies received additional funding from the National Agency of Industry and Trade, three within the promotion of quality initiative.[39]

5.2 The North Jutland initiative

In 1986, the county administration of North Jutland initiated the so-called NordTek programme funded by Dkr 137.9 million in the five-year period of 1987 to 1991 and of which Dkr 95 million accrued from EC regional funding and Dkr 42.9 million from EC social funding. The objective of this programme was to stimulate the establishment of industrial networks especially in the field of information technology, to promote technical innovation and the upgrading of skills, to enhance product development in areas of special importance to the public sector (e.g. in the fields of public health and environmental protection), and to market high technology exports from North Jutland companies in the regions of the south of Norway and the west of Sweden. The primary fields of interest within the NordTek programme were the elements of infrastructure, consultancy and education in relation to technical innovation.[40]

During the autumn of 1989, the secretariat of the NordTek programme became aware of the fact that several companies in the region of North Jutland would take an interest in a regional quality promotion initiative, and when three proposals for a quality promotion initiative appeared at the Department of Production at Ålborg University, the local affiliate of the Welding Centre (Svejsecentralen) and the local affiliate of a nation-wide consultancy (T. Bak-Jensen), a working committee supervised by a steering committee.was formed. The working and steering committees, and the subsequently formed steering committee for the quality initiative, engaged quite a number of people from, among others, regional councils for industrial development, the Department of Production at Ålborg University, a number of technology institutes and technology information centres, the science park (NOVI), and a number of manufacturing companies.[41]

The quality initiative was scheduled for a period of one and a half years funded by Dkr 10 million, of which 55% accrued from EC regional funding and 45% from the local county administration. The initiative emphasized activities directed towards the solution of company-specific problems in the field of quality control within the manufacturing sector and was divided into four stages, followed by an evaluation procedure: an awareness campaign stimulating companies to engage in the development of total quality control systems, a preliminary inquiry into the needs of the manufacturing companies in question, the actual undertaking of quality control projects in a number of companies, and activities in the field of education and training. Most of the companies involved in the initiative participated in both the preliminary enquiry and the actual projects.

The awareness campaign was originally scheduled to last for a few months, but in fact, lasted for almost a year. The stage of preliminary inquiries, originally scheduled to terminate in mid-1991, continued until the end of 1992. Similarly, activities in the field of education and training lasted for about one and a half years, about six month more than originally planned. As a result, additional funding was provided. Figure 13, below, presents the final public funding for the quality initiative, in total Dkr 11.3 million.

The North Jutland quality initiative is comparable to the national initiatives in two important respects:

- The industrial policy philosophy is the same, i.e. the industrial policy authorities announce an initiative and expect the companies and consultancies to respond with applications for public subsidy.
- The projects actually undertaken are perceived as part of a large-scale promotion.

However, unlike the national initiatives, the North Jutland initiative did not emphasize the ability of the participating organizations to disseminate their results. Furthermore, unlike the national initiatives, the regional initiative emphasized an integration of the awareness campaign and the projects actually undertaken. The stage of preliminary inquiries served as an integrative device.

Figure 13: Funding of the fields of interest within the North Jutland quality initiative. (1990 to 1992, in Dkr 1000)

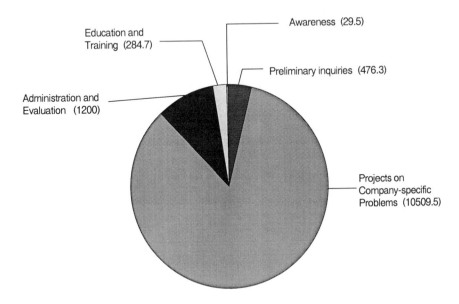

5.2.1 Training and Education

As the objective of this stage, the North Jutland quality initiative was supposed to supplement current activities in the field of training and education. The activities subsidized were supposed to present new forms of education and training regarding form and content, and should, furthermore, have been directed towards white-collar staff (managers, engineers, and economists) only partially included in the national promotion of quality initiative. However, the regional initiative did compromise on this objective. Two projects, both open to blue-collar workers as well, were subsidized: the development of a quality control course at the centre for vocational retraining (AMU) in Ålborg (the capital of North Jutland) and a course combining education and experience groups developed by the North Jutland affiliate of the Danish Technology Institute (Nordjysk Teknologisk). The technology institute course is directed towards companies trying to develop a quality control system (inspired by ISO 9000) and takes the form of monthly meetings over 12 to 18 months, where the companies exchange experiences and receive training in the field of quality. Both courses will continue to be offered by the project organizations.

According to the proposal for the regional quality initiative, a number of training and education activities could be financially supported, e.g. games and role playing stimulating the employees' recognition of quality control-related problems, and courses adapted to specific companies and/or groups of employees, but no one was applied for subsidy regarding these matters.

5.2.2 Consultancy

As part of the NordTek programme, a consultancy, TEKNORD, offering the assistance of managers in the field of technology and marketing, has been established. These managers are leased on a part-time basis to private companies required to pay only 50% of the managers' fees. By the end of 1991, 47 companies had contractual arrangements with TEKNORD, employing nine managers in the field of technology and two managers in the field of marketing. TEKNÓRD has, of course, been involved in the quality initiative, the consultancy sub-system of the Danish quality infrastructure.

Besides TEKNORD, 25 consultancies were involved in the project stage of the regional quality initiative, among these four technology institutes. Of the consultancy expenses defrayed by the participating companies, the quality initiative would reimburse up to 50%, up to a maximum of Dkr 225,000 per company. At the same time, up to 70% of the expenses related to the promotion of quality *vis-à-vis* the company's workforce could be reimbursed. This subsidy, however, was included in the maximum level of Dkr 225,000, and consequently the consultancy subsidy was smaller than appears at first sight.

Finally, the regional quality initiative covered most of the expenses in relation to the preliminary inquiries described below.

5.2.3 Promotion and Awareness

The awareness campaign was initiated by a meeting at the local science park, informing the 'industrial managers' (erhvervschefer) in North Jutland about the activities they were supposed to undertake within the quality initiative.[42] This meeting was followed by three meetings at the science park and the two local technology information centres, respectively, informing a number of company managers about quality control principles, consultancy in relation to quality control projects, and the regional quality initiative. About 800 companies were invited to these meetings, and 150 participated. These meetings were supplemented by arrangements organized by a couple of local industrial offices and associations.

Following the awareness campaign, the stage of preliminary inquiries was set in motion. At each company participating in this stage, three meetings took place. The objective of the first meeting, organized by the local technology information centre or industrial office, was to inform the company about the quality control issue, ISO 9000 and the regional quality initiative, thus stimulating the company to decide whether or not it could benefit from, or should embark on, a quality control project (and what the objectives of the project should be). If the answer was affirmative (which it was not in several cases) a consultancy was selected for the second meeting. At the second meeting, the company was visited by a consultant assessing, together with company representatives, the company's need for quality control and planning the objectives, the schedule and the costs of a quality control project. On account of the second meeting, the third meeting took place in the form of a visit from the local technology information centre or industrial office, with the objective of making a final decision, selecting a consultancy for assistance in the project, and devising an application for subsidy from the regional quality initiative.

Between 110 and 120 companies participated in the preliminary inquiries, of which a many undertook actual quality control projects. In total, 100 companies engaged in the latter, of which several did not participate in the preliminary inquiries because they had already engaged in a project, or decided on a set of quality objectives, a schedule, and a consultancy. In April 1992, about 20% of the project companies had reached the terminal stage.

The awareness campaign was resumed during the autumn of 1992, when a number of meetings took place. At these meetings, directed primarily towards companies not participating in the regional quality initiative, a number of project companies related the problems experienced and the solutions devised during the course of the project in question.

6. Overview and Outlook

The last section of the present study presents a few comments on the development of industrial policy at the national level and the future dynamism of the Danish quality infrastructure.

It is presently impossible to predict future trends in the field of quality promotion at the regional level. It is likely that a second initiative in North Jutland will be taken in a couple of years, but the nature of this possibility is still somewhat speculative.

At the national level, initiatives focusing solely on the field of quality are not being prepared. However, some present trends of the development of industrial policy indicate that the emphasis of industrial policy on the integration of technical and organizational innovation, conducive to the promotion of total quality control principles, will still be present in the near future.

Section 4 described the national promotion of quality initiative as acting in the way as snowflakes forming a snowball that gathered momentum carrying with it a number of companies and organizations. This snowball effect, stimulated by the initiative on improved utilization of production systems, will continue to be at work. At present, a major initiative under the aegis of the Council for Industrial Development (Erhvervsudviklingsrådet) is being prepared in the field of productivity with the objective of following up on the initiatives described in Section 4, directed towards small and medium-sized manufacturing companies, and emphasizing organizational innovation and human resource management. If the proposal for the initiative is approved by the Ministry of Industry, the initiative will be set in motion by the end of 1992.

The advent of the productivity initiative indicates that the Danish industrial policy will continue to emphasize the 'new age' system approach. In fact, the 1991 Danish governmental statement on industrial policy argues that Danish manufacturing companies ought to exploit the productivity potentials of the existing capital stock, rather than investing in new types of high technology, and points to human resource management, improved marketing, effective financial management and the development of producer supplier relationships as means to improve productivity growth.[43] This point of view will, undoubtedly, dominate industrial policy in the fields of technical and organizational innovation.

In addition, Section 4 suggested that the Ministry of Education would become an increasingly important actor in the Danish quality infrastructure due to the diffusion of the issue of quality as a major focus of courses within vocational retraining. In addition, one should observe that the training and education activities within the initiatives described in Section 4 have resulted in courses now being marketed by the participating organizations.

Consequently, it seems reasonable to suggest that the future development of the Danish quality infrastructure will be of a rather volatile nature. The activities at the levels of industrial policy and the training and education system will continue to stimulate the diffusion of total quality control principles, thus contributing to the dynamism of the quality infrastructure. Furthermore, the establishment of a Danish national accreditation system, and the effects of learning-by-doing-and-interacting in the consultancy sub-system mentioned in Section 4, are contributive features, as well, encouraging manufacturing companies and companies in other parts of the private business sector to engage in total quality projects. At present, as argued in Section 3, the rate of diffusion of ISO 9000 certificates in the Danish manufacturing sector might decrease in the medium term, but will probably resume its speed in the long run as a result of the proliferation of producer supplier relationships in the field of quality. This study will conclude by suggesting that this resumption will benefit further from the dynamism of the Danish quality infrastructure, including an increasing awareness of managers and policy-makers of the potential benefits of total quality control.

7. List of Organizations

Name	Address	Telephone/Fax
National accreditation bodies		
Industri-og Handelsstyrelsen	Tagensvej 137, DK-2200 København N	31 85 10 66/31 81 70 68
Dansk Institut for Fundamental Metrologi	Lundtoftevej 100 DK-2800 Lyngby	45 93 11 44
Certification Bodies		
Det Norske Veritas,	Danmark Nyhavn 16, DK01051 København K	33 91 18 00/33 91 18 01
Dansk Standardiseringsråd	Baunegardsvej 73, DK-2900 Hellerup	39 77 01 01/39 77 02 02
Bureau Veritas	Hovedvagtsgade 10 DK-1103 København K	31 42 02 3431/31 26 72 34
Lloyd's London	Meldahlsgade 5, DK-1613 København V	33 14 11 12/33 14 11 15
British Standards Institution	Linford Wood Milton Keynes MK14 6LE	+44 908 221166
Organizations active in the KUP initiative		
Sammenslutningen af Danske Merkonomer	Vestre Voldgade 83 1. th., DK-1552 København V	33 14 69 17
Dansk Stalinstitut	Overgade 21 DK-5000 Odense C	66 13 08 88
Entrepenørforeningen	Nr. Voldgade 106 DK-1358 København K	33 13 88 01
Foreningen for Vaerkstedsteknisk Metrologi	Blomsterager 510 DK 2980 Kokkedal	42 24 94 80
Foreningen af Radgivende Ingenører	Esplanaden 34C DK-1263 København K	33 11 37 37
Foreningen af Danske Kedelfabrikanter	Snaregade 16 DK-1205 København K	33 13 08 44
HK, Odense	Vindegade 72 DK-5000 Odense C	66 12 20 12
Plastindustrien i Danmark	Rådhuspladsen 55, 4. DK-1550 København	33 13 30 22
Traeets Arbejdsgiverforening	Nr. Voldgade 34 DK-1358 København K	33 15 17 00
Foreningen af vindm-IIefabrikanter	Lykkesvej 18 DK-7400 Herning	97 22 47 77

ESF, EDB-Systemleverandørernes Forening	Admiralgade 15, DK-1066 København K	

Technology institutes active in the KUP initiative

Dansk Beklædnings-og Textil Institut	Gregersensvej 5, DK-2630 Tastrup	42 99 88 22
Dansk Teknologisk Institut	Teknologiparken, DK-8000 Århus C	86 14 14 00
BC/BPS	Doktor Neegaards Vej 5 E, DK-2970 Hørsholm	42 86 52 24
Dantest	Amager Boulevard 115 DK-2300 København S	31 54 08 30
Elektronik Centralen	Venlighedsvej 4, DK-2970 Hørsholm	42 86 77 22
Emballage- & Transportinstituttet	Meterbuen 15, DK-2740 Skovlunde	42 84 30 66
Svejsecentralen	Parkalle 345 DK-2605 Brøndby	42 96 88 00

Educational organizations active in the KUP initiative

AMU-centre Fyn	Petermindevej 50 DK-5100 Odense C	66 13 66 70
Danske Ingenørers Efteruddannelse	DtH Bygning 208 DK-2800 Lyngby	45 796 80 45
Odense Universitet	Campusvej 55, DK-5000 Odense C	66 15 86 00
Odense Tekniske Skole	Allegade 79 Dk-5000 Odense C	65 91 50 80
Ingeniørhøjskolen i Odense Teknikum	Niels Bohrs Alle 1 DK-5230 Odense M	66 13 08 27
Tietgenskolen	Nonnebakken 9 DK-5000 Odense C	66 11 57 47
Uddannelsescentret for Aalestrupøegnen	Borgergade 41 DK-9620 Aalestrup	98 64 25 66
Frederikshavn Handelsskole & Handelsgymnasium	Kirkegade 9 DK-9900 Frederikshavn	98 42 33 55
Handelsskolen i Hjørring	Hestkaervej 30 DK-9800 Hjørring	98 92 40 55
Århus Købmandsskole	Vesteralle 8, DK-8000 Århus C	86 12 91 88
Hillerød Handelsskole & Gymnasium	S.Jernbanevej 4, DK34-00 Hillerød	42 26 33 71

102

Holbæk Handelsskole	Slotshaven 1 DK-4300 Holbæk	53 43 41 43
Hjørring Tekniske Skole	Albert Gingesvej 55 DK-9800 Hjørring	98 92 15 44
Aalborg Tekniske Skole	Øster Uttrupvej 1 DK-9000 Aalborg	98 12 94 66
Århus Tekniske Skole	Homstadgade 6 DK-8200 Århus N	86 16 91 00
Hillerød Tekniske Centralskole	Milnersvej 48 DK-3400 Hillerød	42 25 18 15
Holbæk Tekniske Skole	Absalongsgade 20 DK-4300 Holbæk	53 43 46 46
AMU - Centre Aalborg	Postbox 2019 Sofievej 61 DK-9000 Aalborg	98 14 46 77
AMU Centre Vendsyssel	Ringvejen 226 DK-9800 Hjørring	98 92 00 77
AMU Centre Århus	Hasselageralle 2 DK-8260 Viby J	86 28 54 55
AMU Centre Horsens	Strandpromenaden DK-8700 Horsens	75 62 74 88
AMU Centre Hillerød	Milnersvej 43 DK-3400 Hillerød	48 24 15 95
Statens Erhvervspædagogiske Laereruddannelse	Riegensagade 13 DK-1316 København K	33 14 41 14

Other organizations not mentioned elsewhere

Dansk Forening for Kvalitetsstyring, DFK	Henrikshave 59 DK-2950 Vedbæk	42 89 13 05
Textil-og Konfektionscenter Danmark	Uldjydevej 3, Birk DK-7400 Herning	97 12 70 22
Danmarks Tekniske Højskole	Driftsteknisk Institut Lundtofttevej 100 DK-2800 Lyngby	45 93 44 66
Aalborg Universitetscenter	Institut for Produktion Fibigerstraede 13 DK-9220 Aalborg	98 15 85 22
Handelshøjskolen i Århus	Institut for Kvalitetsledelse Fuuglesangs Alle 4 DK-8210 Århus V	86 15 55 88
Sydjysk Teknologisk	Jacob Gades Alle 12 A DK-6600 Vejen	75 36 61 11

Teknologisk Informationscenter	Aabenraa Kilen 6 DK-6200 Aabenraa	74 62 39 15
Teknologisk Informationscenter, Aars	Østtre Boulevard 6 C DK-9600 Aars	98 62 46 00
Teknologisk Informationscenter, Hjørring	Eghomsvej 1 DK-9800 Hjørring	98 92 74 00
PC Laboratoriet A/S	Mågevej 7 DK-9690 Fjerritslev	98 21 32 00
Trade Book International	G. Kongevej 86 A DK-1850 Frederiksberg C	31 24 19 49

References:

1. Teknologistyrelsen (1983), *Et teknologisk udviklingsprogram* (A Programme for Technological Development), København: Teknisk Forlag, December.

2. Ibid. p. 1

3. The TUP programme was, in a Danish setting, an extremely large initiative, and one s not surprised to recognize that the main objectives of the TUP programme were repeated in the discussion paper on growth and structural change issued by the Danish government in 1986 (Arbejdsministeriet et al., 1986).

4. Den Faglige Koordineringsgruppe (1990), *Sammenfatning (Conclusion), Evaluering af Det Teknologiske Udvikling, rapport nr.1*, København: Industriog Handelsstyrelsen.

5. Prodevo Aps. (1990), *TUP's effekt i den teknologiske infrastruktur* (The Effect of TUP on the Technological Infrastructure), Evaluering af Det Teknologiske Udviklingsprogram, rapport nr.3, København: Industriog Handelsstyrelsen.

6. Vilstrup Research (1990), *TUP's effekt i erhvervslivet* (The Effect of TUP on Industry), Evaluering af Det Teknologiske Udviklingsprogram, rapport nr.2, København: Industriog Handelsstyrelsen. (A report on a large questionnaire survey undertaken in order to measure the efficiency of the TUP programme). p. 11.

7. Prodevo Aps. (1990), op. cit. p 13.

8. Teknologirådet (1988b), *Ledelse, samarbejde og ny teknologi* (Management, Cooperation and New Technology), København: Industri- og Handelsstyrelsen, August.

9. In fact, as has been documented by research financially supported by the National Agency of Industry and Trade and the Ministry of Labour, quite a few Danish manufacturing companies during the 1980s were not able to achieve the productivity rates associated with technical innovation based on microelectronics and information technology.

10. The background for these initiatives was, partly, a statement on industrial policy, issued by the Ministry of Industry in 1986, which pointed to quality management as a competitive asset.

11. Teknologirådet (1988a), *Kvalitetsudvikling* (Promotion of Quality), København: Industriog Handelsstyrelsen, February.

12. Teknologirådet (1990), *Bedre udnyttelse af avanceret udstyr* (Improved Utilization of Advanced Equipment), København: Industriog Handelsstyrelsen.

13. This is one of the many interesting results from a series of questionnaires made by KvalitetsGruppen, a private consultancy. The results of this investigation is published in KvalitetsGruppen (1991).

14. ISO certificates in Denmark have primarily been issued by the following five certification bodies, with percentage share of the total number of certificates by the end of September 1991 mentioned in brackets: Dansk Standardiseringsråd (51%), Bureau Veritas (22%), British Standards Institution (10%), Lloyds (9%), and Det Norske (the Norwegian) Veritas (7%), cf. KvalitetsGruppen (1991, p.6). During 1992, the share of Det Norske Veritas has been increasingly growing, according to telephone conversations with various experts.

15. Carstensen, J. (1992), 'Kvalitetsfeber raser videre i Nordjylland' (Continous High Temperature Quality Fever in North Jutland), *Erhvervsbladet*, March 23.

16. Trade Book International is a recently established private company compiling and issuing a register on the number and names of companies with an ISO 9000 certificate in Denmark. The first volume of the register, issued under the name of 'ISO 9000 Denmark', appeared in 1992, and the intention is that the register should contain a list of consultancy companies working in the quality field, as well. The published register will be updated every third month.

17. Industrirådet (1992), '180 firmaer med certifikat i ISO 9000 Denmark' (180 certified companies in 'ISO 9000 Denmark'), *Teknisk Nyt*, no.4.

18. Conversation with Mogens Holm from Trade Book International (estimated that nearly 500 Danish companies were gradually coming close to the final ISO 9000 audit).

19. In fact, according to the law on technological service, the label 'technological institute' may only be used by organizations licensed by the National Agency of Industry and Trade.

20. In 1991, the licensed technology institutes recieved a total subsidy of Dkr 204 millions (Industri-og Handelsstyrelsen, 1992), which is approximately Dkr 35 millions more than in 1990 (Industriog Handelsstyrelsen, 1991). In addition, as part of their activity, the technology institutes recieve quite an amount of money accruing as payments for service rendered within policy initiatives, e.g. approximately Dkr 156 millions in 1990. The TICs recieve approximately Dkr 35 millions each year. Statistics on 1991 are not available at the present moment.

21. Industri-og Handelsstyrelsen (1990), *Årsberetninger 1989* (Annual Reports 1989), København: Industriog Handelsstyrelsen.

22. Industri-og Handelsstyrelsen (1992), *Årsberetning 1991* (Annual Report 1991), København: Industriog Handelsstyrelsen.

23. The dissolved councils and committees were: The Technology Council (Teknologirådet), the Council for Improved Export Performance (Eksportfremmerådet), the Industrial Development Foundation (Udviklingsfondet), the Council for Regional Development (Erhvervsudviklingsrådet), the Committee for State Subsidy to Product Development (Statstilskud til Produktudvikling), the Council for Cooperation between private companies and the public sector (Formidlingsrådet), the Technical Testing Tribunal (Statens Tekniske Prøvenævn), the Council for Metrology, and the Productivity and Consultancy Committee (Produktivitets- og Konsulentudvalget). Prior to this development, in 1988, the secretariat of the Council for Improved Export Performance, the Directorate of Regional Development servicing the Council for Regional Development, the License Office (Licenskontoret) within the Ministry of Industry, and the Technology Administration (Teknologistyrelsen) had been merged into the National Agency of Industry and Trade.

24. Jørgensen, A.P. (1992), *Dansk Akkrediterings Ordning* (The Danish Accreditation System) København: Industriog Handelsstyrelsen, mimeo, May.

25. Until this harmonization is completed, the requirements posed to organizations in want of an accreditation in this field has been stated in a governmental technical regulation.

26. Industri-og Handelsstyrelsen (1991), *Beretninger fra råd og udvalg* (Reports from councils and committees), København: Industri- og Handelsstyrelsen.

27. Primarily the so-called ERFA-groups (experience groups).

28. This number could be quite large, bearing in mind the estimate made by Mogens Holm from Trade Book International, and considering that the time-lag from the initiation of a quality control system project to the certification of the quality control system is, on average, nearly two years (KvalitetsGruppen, 1991).

29. The initiatives have tried to the stimulate the cooperation between private companies, industrial and trade organizations, consultancies, and 'knowledge centres', i.e. technology institutes, universities, technological information centres, science parks and the like.

30. Eg videos, plays, and the like.

31. Those in charge of this project was IA, the national association of industrial employers (Industriens Arbejdsgivere), using Habberstad A/S as consultant. Habberstad A/S is a prime consultancy in the field of productivity control and measurement, relying on the methodology for productivity analysis developed in Sjøborg (1984).

32. Furthermore, within the promotion of quality initiative, approximately 700 companies participated in comparative calibration, giving a total of 1500 companies. However, the number of participating companies is presumably less than 800, because several companies participated in more than one project within the three initiatives.

33. DFK (1991), *Uddannelse inden for kvalitetsstyring* (Education in the Field of Quality Control), DFK publication no.155, Vedbæk: Dansk Forening for Kvalitetsstyring.

34. Møltoft, J. et al. (1991), *Kvalitetsstyring og måleteknik* (Quality Control and Measurement Techniques), København: Industriens Forlag.

35. Unfortunately, the trend towards decentralization and self-regulation, which has pervaded the educational system since the mid-1980s, has made it virtually impossible to find and exploit central sources of information. Thus, mapping quality education activities in the country is a major research project in its own right.

36. The Productivity and Consultancy Committee had at its disposal Dkr 50 millions in 1986, 42 millions in 1987, 40 millions in 1988, and 36 millions in 1989 (Teknologistyrelsen, 1987; Industri- og Handelsstyrelsen, 1988, 1989, 1990).

37. The shipbuilding project has not reached its terminal stage yet, but is due by the end of October 1992.

38. This project lasted from the beginning of May 1988 to the end of April 1990, and by the end of April 1990, 6 of the 7 companies had been certified according to the ISO 9000 standards. The last of the 7 companies was certified in August 1991.

39. The individual company is required to pay at least 20% of the consultancy fee and can recieve a maximum of 40% from the SEP initiative, if an additional amount of public funding is obtained from other public sources. Thus, one might describe the SEP consultancy arrangement as stimulating local companies to exploit public initiatives generated elsewhere.

40. Regarding infrastructure, NordTek has been a prime mover in the establishment of a science park in North Jutland, NOVI (Nordjyllands Videnpark). The NordTek secretariat is located at NOVI.

41. The final initiative was laid in the hands of NOVI's Development and Finance Foundation (Erhvervs- og Finansieringsfond) and administered on a part-time basis by a researcher at the Department of Production, Aalborg University.

42. Denmark is divided into 14 counties, each comprising a number of municipalities (about 270 in total). In general, each municipality and each county has its own 'industrial manager' (erhvervschef) who is supposed to participate in the enforcement of the local industrial policy and take a number of initiatives on his/her own. All counties and most of the municipalities have an 'industrial council' (erhvervsråd) using the industrial manager as secretariat or chief of staff in municipalities which supply the industrial council with an 'industrial office' (erhvervskontor) and acting as policy-making bodies. As a general rule, the industrial councils comprise representatives of the public and private sectors.

43. Industriministeriet (1991), *Erhvervspolitisk redegrelse* 1991 (Statement on Industrial Policy 1991), København: Industriministeriet, April. p. 12

Other References

Arbejdsministeriet, Finansministeriet, Industriministeriet & Undervisningsministeriet (The Ministries of Labour, Finance, Industry, and Education) (1986), Debatoplæg om vækst og omstilling. Krav til strukturpolitikken (Discussion Paper on Growth and Structural Change. Requirements for a Structural Policy), København: Arbejdsministeriet, Finansministeriet, Industriministeriet & Undervisningsministeriet.

Dansk Standardiseringsråd (1988), *DS/ISO 8402. Kvalitet - Ordliste* (Quality-Vocabulary), København: Dansk Standardiseringsråd.

Deming, W.E. (1986), *Out of the Crisis*, Cambridge, Mass.: The MIT Press.

Industri-og Handelsstyrelsen (1988), *Teknologi og effektivitet* (Technology and Efficiency), København: Industriog Handelsstyrelsen.

Industri-og Handelsstyrelsen (1989), *Årsberetninger 1988* (Annual Reports 1988), København: Industriog Handelsstyrelsen.

KvalitetsGruppen (1991), *Fakta om certificering* (Facts on certification), Aarhus: KvalitetsGruppen, December.

Sjøborg, E.R. (1984), *Totalproduktivitet efter POSPAK metoden* (Total Productivity according to the POSPAK Method), Oslo: Bedrifts-konomens Forlag.

Teknologistyrelsen (1987), *Teknologi og effektivitet. Industriministeriets erhvervsfremmeordninger* (Technology and Efficiency. Industrial Development Initiatives by the Ministry of Industry), København: Teknologistyrelsen.

France

Jean-Jacques Chanaron
CNRS

1. Introduction

This chapter describes the activities and measures in the field of quality assurance and management in France. In addition to describing national schemes, initiatives in the Rhône-Alpes, Savoie and Isère regions are covered as examples of regional schemes.

2. The Emergence of Quality as an Issue

The importance of product quality and standards was officially recognised in the establishment of AFNOR (Association Française de NORmalisation, French Standards Association) in 1926. A non-profit organization, AFNOR, has a close relationship with MICE (Ministère de l'industrie et Commerce Estranger, Ministry for Industry and Foreign Trade). The first step in the public promotion of quality came with the quality requirements of the purchasing bodies of the French Ministry of Defence in the late 1940s and the early 1950s. In the 1950s and 1960s, French government policy limited itself to promotion and indirect action through the so-called 'auto-responsabilisation' of quality experts and professionals. 1950 saw the setting up of a National Office for Productivity within the Ministry of Industry. In 1957, the AFCIQ (Association Française pour le Contrôle Industriel de la Qualité, French Association for Industrial Quality Control) was created and in 1961, the ATPCI (Association des Techniciens et Professionnels du Contrôle Industriel, Association of Industrial Quality Control Technicians and Professionals), later renamed AFQ (Association Française des Qualiticien, French Quality Association) was established.

From the beginning of the 1970s, the French government recognised the key role product quality played in competitiveness and became aware of the necessity of a public involvement in the definition of a national policy toward quality. In 1975, SQUALPI (Sous-Direction de la Qualité pour L'Industrie et de la Normalisation, Directorate for Quality of Industrial Products and Normalisation) was set up within the Ministry of Industry (now the Ministry of Industry and International Trade, MICE). In the 1980s, its activities increased in scope and variety and included the provision of information, motivation (education, training, etc.) and finance. MICE has several missions: promoting the concept of quality, structuring the institutional environment, funding and sustaining the implementation of quality management systems in SMEs.

Financial support for quality promotion has come from a variety of sources. In

1984, the FRAC (Fonds Régionaux d'Aide au Conseil, regional Consultancy Funds) was set up. This provided regional funding for SMEs seeking consultancy (covering 50% of the cost).

In 1985 a Club for Teaching and Quality (Enseignement et Qualité) was established with the involvement of the Ministry of Education which also set up a working group on education and training of quality management systems. In 1987, a new body, MEQUI (Mission pour l'enseignement de la qualité industrielle, Mission for Teaching of Industrial Quality) took over the job of the Club and the working group. Other schemes have a significant quality promoting 'element'. These are discussed briefly under the relevant sections.

2.1 Quality Standards

By the early 1970s, there were 22 different quality related standards in the world. Most of these were private and had very specific coverage; examples found in France at this time include those produced by NATO, EDF (the French Electricity Board), and CEA (the French Atomic Energy Agency). Only three countries had specific quality related references: the United Kingdom, Germany and the United States of America. Between 1973 and 1983, major French industrial corporations lobbied AFNOR and MICE to promote a national standardization system.

The first step in quality related standards occurred in 1974 when AFNOR published the X50-110 standard for quality management (based on previous AFCIQ references). AFNOR began to investigate more comprehensive standards in 1980. In March 1983, AFNOR published the French quality standards X50-109, X50-111 and X50-112 which were subsequently absorbed by the ISO 9000 series (EN 29000 series) within the French X50 series in December 1988.

The ISO 9000 standards, published in 1987, after eight years of international negotiation within the ISO Technical Committee TC 176, were largely based on British, French and German national standards. ISO 9000, 9001, 9002 and 9003 were very close to the British standards while ISO 9004 was very much influenced by the equivalent French standard. The quality audit standards ISO 10011 were also influenced by the French standards X 50-112 and X 50-136. (See Figure 14, page 111).

Figure 14: French quality standards

	FRENCH STANDARDS		ISO STANDARDS	
	Code	Date	Code	Date
1. Concepts				
Quality Concepts	X 50-120	Sept. 1987	ISO 8042	Nov. 1988
Metrology Concepts	X 07-001			
Quality & Management Vision 2000	X 50-124	Dec. 1991		
2. Quality Management				
Quality Management & Assurance	X 50-121	Dec. 1988	ISO 9000	Dec. 1988
ISO 9000 Application Guide	X 50-121.2	Dec. 1991	ISO 9000.2	Dec. 1991
Quality in Software	X 50-121.3	Dec. 1991	ISO 9000.3	Dec. 1991
Quality in Management in Services	X 50-122.2	Dec. 1991	ISO 9004.2	Dec. 1991
Evaluation of Cost of Non-Quality	X 50-126	Oct. 1986		
Quality in Design	X 50-127	Jan. 1988		
Quality in Purchasing	X 50-128	Dec. 1990		
Use of Metrology	X 07-010	Oct. 1986		
Test of Instruments	X 07-011	Oct. 1990		
3. Quality Assurance				
Models of Quality Assurance	X 50-131	Dec. 1988	ISO 9001	Dec. 1988
	X 50-132	Dec. 1988	ISO 9002	Dec. 1988
	X 50-133	Dec. 1988	ISO 9003	Dec. 1988
Quality Audits	X 50-136.1	Dec. 1988	ISO 10011.1	Dec. 1991
	X 50-136.2	Dec. 1991	ISO 10011.2	Dec. 1991
	X 50-136.3	Dec. 1991	ISO 10011.3	Dec. 1991

Figure 14 continued.

4. Methods, Instruments and Techniques				
Need to competitivity	X 50-100	Apr. 1987		
Value Analysis	X 50-150	May 1985		
	X 50-151	June 1984		
	X 50-152	May 1985		
	X 50-153	May 1985		
Quality Manual	X 50-160	Oct. 1988		
	X 50-161	Dec. 1988		
	X 50-162	Oct. 1991		
Quality Assurance Plan	X 50-164	June 1990		
Audit Report	X 50-165	Jan. 1990		
Supplier Questionnaire	X 50-168			
Supplier Data Processing	Z 67-131	Oct. 1988		
Supplier Quality Tests	X 50-142	Dec. 1990		

Source: AFNOR (1992), Gérer et assurer la qualité, Paris.

2.2 The Diffusion of Quality Concepts

In the 1980s, several surveys were carried out by national associations and private consultants in order to evaluate the diffusion of quality concepts throughout the French industry. A 1983 report by AFQ (on behalf of MICE) on 'the Cost of Non-Quality in Industrial and Commercial SMEs' reported on a survey of 130 SMEs. The cost of non-quality was estimated to be FFR 150 billion in manufacturing and building and FFR 270 billion in the whole French economy for 1981, i.e. FFR 12,860 per employee every year.[1] This non-quality cost was 4.2% of turnover and 9.7% of total added value. This report was used to justify the setting up of the standard X 50-126 in October 1986 'Quality management: a guide for evaluation of costs resulting from non-quality'. More recently, a AFQ study (1986) revised the estimate of non-quality cost in SMEs to between 5-15% of turnover or 15-40% of added value.[2]

In 1983, the minister for industry, P. Dreyfus, asked C. Germon, MP to carry out a study on standardization as a weapon in competitiveness, i.e. the use of standards to promote product quality and the development of industry, in order to increase exports, and to improve consumer protection and workers safety.[3] The main strategic conclusions were:

- standardization must be integrated with industrial policy;
- standardization must be freely accepted by all actors, i.e. without any constraints;
- partners should be equal in negotiations;
- national standardization must be integrated within international standardization policy.

In 1984, a report by G. Bapt surveyed the conditions for an improvement of quality in French industry.[4] The survey found that the importance of quality was recognized throughout SMEs, large corporations and public institutions. It was also recognized that there was a considerable amount of quality improvement to be achieved. The report concluded that quality improvement had to be dynamic and global, dealing with technology, management methods, human attitudes and behaviour, relationships with suppliers and customers and organizations. The report made several recommendations to the French government in terms of public initiatives: national promotion campaigns, education and training, and fiscal and financial support. These recommendations were later taken into account in the activities of the SQUALPI, AFNOR, AFAQ, MFQ, etc.

More recently, two major surveys were carried out by private consultants on behalf of the French Ministry of Industry and Trade in order to assess the diffusion of quality management systems throughout the French industry:

- The first, 'The Cost of Non-Quality', was carried by private consultants on behalf of the French Ministry of Industry and Trade in order to update estimates of the cost of non-quality in industry (found to be around 10% of turnover).[5]
- The second, 'Quality in SMEs', was published in October 1991. The survey was carried out by NODAL Consultants et Europe Qualité Services and covered 41 SMEs.[6]

At time there were 35,774 SMEs (those firms employing between 10 and 500 workers) in France providing 53.2% of total employment, producing 41.4% of the total added value and investing 36.7% of total industrial investment. From the beginning of the 1980s, a majority (95% in 1986) of French SMEs have recognized the importance of quality in their survival, but most have only implemented formal and structured quality management systems since the mid-1980s. In 1989, a survey by ARACQ (Association Régionale pour l'Amélioration de la Compétitivité par la Qualité) conducted within the Rhône-Apes region found that 45% of SMEs did not use any quality control systems and 71% did not have a quality improvement programme.[7] Another survey, carried out in 1988 by the CNPF (French Confederation of Industry) found that 41% of SMEs which had set up a quality control system did not have a quality improvement programme.[8]

The major conclusions of the 1991 NODAL Consultants 'Quality in SMEs' survey were:

- Most SMEs approached public bodies and quality institutions for help only after an increase in internal awareness on the importance of quality.
- SMEs preferred to go to their relevant technical centres and to public administrations or associations which they felt were independent.
- Amongst the 41 SMEs, there were four reasons for an interest in quality:
    1. management initiative;
    2. prompted through cooperation or partnership;
    3. compelled by customers; and,
    4. attempt at survival following bankruptcy.
- The results of the implementation of quality management system in SMEs were:
    - improvement of internal performances, i.e. employees' motivation; cost reduction; job enrichment; innovation; etc.
    - increase in competitive advantages, i.e. increase in turnover, market shares and profits; access to new markets; up-grading in product portfolio; better corporate image; better supplier-customer relationship (confidence, exclusivity, etc).
- The main obstacles to such results were employees' inertia and organization bottle-necks, and more particularly in training capabilities.

An official document published by SQUALPI in 1992 estimates that 60% of SMEs do not have any formal quality department or policy.[9] It also pointed out that most SMEs often restrict quality management to two issues only: product control and human resources management.

3. The Quality Infrastructure
3.1 Government Bodies

MICE is the main public body supporting French public policy with regard to quality management and standards. Under SQUALPI, information has been disseminated through advertising and more particularly through the so-called 'Train for Quality' operation in which a special train visited 17 cities and attracted 11,000 visitors (SME managers, Quality Circle members etc) with the support of many institutions: local and regional public bodies, local and regional chambers of commerce etc). The 'Train for Quality' promoted a greater awareness of quality, increased the commitment of regional bodies and highlighted the advantages of collective approach to quality management.

In 1986 official recognition was given to several bodies: RNE (Réseau National d'Essais, National Network of Testing Laboratories); AFAQ (Association Française pour l'Assurance Qualité, French Association for Quality Certification); AFAV (Association Française pour l'Analyse de la Valeur, French Association for Value Analysis); MFQ (Mouvement Français pour la Qualité, French Quality Centre).

3.2 Public Associations

Several public associations deal with quality related issues at the national, regional and local level.

The division of responsibility for product quality certification is as follows:

Definition of Standards	AFNOR
Control and Tests	Accredited Laboratories
Certification	AFNOR and Accredited Bodies

Similarly, the division of responsibility for quality assurance certification is as follows:

Definition of Standards	AFNOR
Audit and Control	Consultants
Certification	AFAQ

Finally, the MFQ and AFAV are the most active organizations in quality promotion, training and development.

AFNOR (Association Française de Normalisation, French Standards Association) AFNOR is a publicly-funded body responsible for:

- identification and analysis of the needs for new standards;
- coordination of standardization efforts;
- centralization and analysis of all proposals for new standards;
- dissemination, publishing and advertising of standards;
- training to standards;
- representation of French interests in any non-government international institutions dealing with standards; and
- control of standard application and of agreement to use the NF (norm Française, French standard) label.

AFNOR deals with standards definition and control, product quality certification, training and consultancy in quality-related issues and publishing. A grant from the French Ministry of Industry covers a third of its budget, 10% comes from public contracts, 8% from members' fees and 50% from 'commercial' activities in publishing, training and consultancy.

AFNOR subcontracts standards control to 32 accredited national standardization offices (bureaux de normalisation) and is in contact with provincial enterprises and public bodies through six regional delegations.

For standards definition, AFNOR is organized into 19 GPN (Grands Programmes de Normalisation, Standardization Programmes) each managed by a COS (Comité d'Orientation Stratégique, Strategic Committee) with industry and public body representatives. Each COS has responsibility for defining priorities for sectoral standards and includes several General Commissions (CG) elaborating detailed programmes; Standardization Commissions (CN) defining standards and participating in international standardization bodies (CEN, ISO); and Expert Groups (GE) elaborating appropriate standards.

COS number 12, 'Organisation Techniques and Services for Enterprises' has a General Commission, 'Quality and Management' which has responsibility for quality related issues. There are 3 Standardization Commissions: 'Concepts and Terminology'; 'Management and Quality Insurance'; 'Methods and Techniques', with 20 Expert Groups.

These working groups deal with various issues such as: revision of ISO 9000 (1996); development of ISO 8402 (vocabulary in quality management and certification); coherence of concepts in standards; harmonisation of concepts; process quality (ISO 9004-3); quality improvement (ISO 9004-4); quality in project management; application guide for ISO 9001, 9002 and 9003; revision of ISO 9001, 9002, 9003; revision of ISO 9004; quality planning; configuration management; quality textbook; economics of quality; quality diagnosis; quality data, etc.

AFNOR is strongly involved in the CEN (European Standards Committee) and CENELEC (European Standards Committee in Electrotechnics) in Brussels, ETSI (European Telecommunication Standards Institute) in Sophia-Antipolis, ISO (International Organization for Standardisation) and the CEI (International Electrotechnics Commission) in Geneva.

In the near future, AFNOR will develop standardization according to the ISO TC 176 recommendations. (The Internationational Standards Organization Technical Committee 176 has responsibility for developing international quality management standards.) Thus, future development will be directed toward:

- improving the efficiency of Total Quality Management systems and methods;
- expanding the relevant standards to all functions, from R&D and design to maintenance and services: and,
- exploring new issues, and in particular accounting for the social and ecological environment.

The National Committee for Maintenance is located within AFNOR. The Committee undertakes quality promotion and training. AFNOR also helps the 'Initiatives et Compétitivité' clubs at both the national and local levels. These clubs consist of representatives of both large corporations and SMEs who play an important role in promoting quality related issues.

AFAQ (Association Française pour l'Assurance Qualité, French Association for Quality Certification)

AFAQ is an independent non-profit organisation set up in 1988 with responsibility for quality certification according to international standards ISO 9001/9002/9003. Following a report by a specific committee set up by the Ministry of Industry, AFAQ took over the mission of AFNOR's 3AQ unit which had already certified 30 companies by the end of 1987. AFAQ emphasizes its independent position between suppliers and customers as a third party certification body. AFAQ has three groups of members:

- College A : suppliers (industry federations) with 30 members;
- College B: buyers (major industrial groups) with 32 members;
- College C: quality bodies (technical centres, MFQ, Veritas etc) with eight members.

Its board has nine representatives from Colleges A and B, four representatives from College C and two external experts. As a member to the AFAQ board, MICE has an advisory position. AFAQ is organized according to ISO 45012 standards. AFAQ has 11 sectoral committees (casting and rubber, chemicals, agro-food, transportation, civil engineering, electricity and electronics, engineering and consultancy, mechanical, casting, building industry, electric engineering, and concrete industry).

Although AFAQ has no official monopoly on quality certification it is in effect the only French public body able to certify a company according to the ISO 9000 series (this responsibility having been transferred from AFNOR in 1988). AFAQ has a close relationship with AFNOR and MFQ in France, and with the equivalent certification bodies in Europe. Cooperation agreements have been signed with DQS (Germany), AENOR (Spain), AGA (USA) and DS (Denmark). AFAQ has reciprocity agreements with SQS in Switzerland and QMI in Canada. AFAQ's basic philosophy is not to compete or to replace private quality certification but to provide enterprises with a certificate dealing with the common framework given by the ISO 9000 series, in particular when they have several customers. There were 200 certified companies by January 1991, 350 by November 1991, 438 by January 1992, 500 in March, and 700 by October 1992.

As is apparent in Figure 15 large industrial customers are not all prepared to recognise the AFAQ certificate. Some are still imposing their own audit. But it is expected that the rising cost of certification will lead to a reduction in the number of audits, in particular when a company is supplying several customers, and then a wider recognition of the AFAQ certificate. It is difficult to estimate the cost of the AFAQ certificate. The direct cost could vary from FFR 30,000 to 250,000. There is also the annual cost for improvement and revision (an average of 10 days per year) and training (an average of 40 days per year). Currently, the certification process is very long: 22 months for ISO 9002 and 24 months for ISO 9001.

According to J. Graindorge, chairman of the National Quality Committee, the average total cost of the TQM approach is FFR 2,000,000 and requires 24 working months. FFR 1,000,000 are required every year to improve the quality system.

MFQ (Mouvement Française pour la Qualité, French Quality Centre)
The MFQ is the national body for the promotion of quality related issues in France. It was created in March 1991 with the merger of AFCIQ/AFQ and regional representatives of the AFCERQ (Association Française des Cercles de Qualité, Association of French Quality Circlds) following the national office's bankruptcy in 1989. The MFQ undertakes research (through its four dedicated institutes),

training and promotion of quality. By March 1992, 2,500 individuals and more than 500 firms were registered as members. It is chaired by J.R. Fourtoux, chairman of Rhône-Poulenc and is characterized by the involvement of large French corporations with a strong commitment to promote quality awareness within SMEs. The MFQ has 13 regional agencies, 10 specialized groups (bank/insurance, automotive, building, energy, pharmaceuticals, food-processing, etc), and more than 60 working committees. MFQ is carrying out a feasibility study of a club for ISO 9000 certified firms.

Figure 15: Large industrial customers and AFAQ certification

	FULL OWN CERTIFICATION	SIMPLIFIED CERTIFICATION
PSA-Renault 1st Tier	Yes	No
PSA-Renault 2nd Tier	No if ISO 9001-9002	-
PSA-Renault Machines	No	-
SIAR (Ministry of Defence)		
High Armament Specificity	Yes	No
Medium Specificity	Yes	Yes if AFAQ Audit
Low Specificity	No	-
SNCF	No in most cases	Yes in other cases
EDF Safety Devices	Yes	Yes in some cases
EDF other supplies	No in some cases	Yes in other cases
GDF	No in most cases	Yes in other cases
Cogema Materials	No in some cases	Yes in other cases
Cogema Specific Equipment	Yes	Yes in some cases
France Telecom		
Non-specific products	No	-
Specific products	No	Yes
Thomson-CSF	Yes	Yes in some cases
Merlin Gerin	No	-
Telemecanique	No	-
3M France	No if ISP 9001-9002	-
Usinor Sacilor	No	-
UGAP	No	-
Rhône-Poulenc	No if ISO 9001=9002	-
La Poste	No	-
Elf Aquitaine	Yes	Yes in some cases

Figure 15 cont.

	FULL OWN CERTIFICATION	SIMPLIFIED CERTIFICATION
L'Air Liquide		
Strategic Products	Yes	No
Non-Strategic Products	No in some cases	Yes
Bertrand Faure Auto	No	-
BSN	No	-
CAMIF	No if ISO 9001-9002	-
CEA	Yes	No
Esso Most Suppliers	Yes	No
Esso Other Suppliers	No	
Exxon Chemicals	No if ISO 9001-9002	-
Kodak Pathé	Yes	Yes
Shell	Yes	Yes
Sollac	No in most cases	-
Solvay	Yes	Yes
Total	No in most cases	Yes strategic
Pont-a-Mousson	No	-

*(by 25/3/1992)

3.3 Other Bodies Undertaking Quality Related Activities

AFAV (Association Française pour l'Analyse de la Valuer, French Association for Value Analysis)

AFAV is an independent association set up in 1978 in order to promote the use of value analysis methods in industry. Its 1992 budget is FFR 1.3 million, all from private funds. In 1992, AFAV has 434 members consisting of 90 enterprises, 253 individuals, 41 consultants and 50 professors. Its main mission is the promotion of value analysis through publications, conferences and training, and the improvement of value analysis methods through research. Value analysis is widely applied in industry and could be considered as a valuable method for quality management. According to AFAV's members' evaluation, the cost efficiency could be increased by 10% to 30% for a better quality. AFAV grants certification to value analysis experts. It participates in the Institute for Safety in Operation set up within the MFQ in 1991.

RNE (Réseau National d'Essais, National Network of Testing Laboratories)

The RNE (Réseau National d'Essais) is an independent public association set up in 1979 to certify testing laboratory competence, in particular to the ISO 45000 series, the ISO-CEI 25 and the OECD recommendations for R&D laboratories. By January 1992, there were 282 accredited testing laboratories in France. This number increased rapidly during 1993 with the requirement that laboratories working within the CE scheme be accredited to ISO 45001. For this reason many large industrial corporations are setting up such laboratories despite their high cost.

RNE and AFAQ have signed an agreement of mutual recognition: a testing laboratory with the RNE ISO 45001 certificate will be treated as equivalent to an AFAQ ISO 9002 certificate. RNE has also signed agreements with NAMAS (UK), STERLAB (Netherlands), SWEDAC (Sweden) and DANAK (Denmark). In the United States, RNE is providing American testing laboratories with the French certificate.

CERESTA (Centre d'Enseignement et de Recherchede Statistiques Appliques, Centre for Teaching and Research for Applied Statistics)

Founded in 1952, within the Institute for Statistics in the University of Paris, the Centre for Teaching and Research for Applied Statistics (CERESTA) was transformed into a public association in 1985. CERESTA deals with promotion and diffusion of the applications of statistics in industry, administration and public services. It organizes training seminars with a strong involvement in documentation and advice to ex-students. The CERESTA pays particular attention to SPC (Statisitical Process Control) training. It is a good example of university involvement in quality-related issues.

ACFCI (Assemblée de Chambres Française de Commerce et d'Industrie, National Assembly of Chambers of Trade and Industry)

ACFCI dates from 1898. It is strongly involved in quality related issues for promotion and training at national level but also in coordinating actions at regional and local levels by 161 local chambers (CCI) and 21 regional chambers (CRCI). Since the main mission of ACFCI, CRCI and CCI is to provide support to industry and trade, quality related issues are included in most of their activities. Quality is one area promoted by 680 industry experts, 65,000 students are taught every year in 273 business schools and education centres and 270,000 trainees are taught in 360 training centres.

4. National Quality Schemes and Initiatives

Over the last few years France has adopted a comprehensive quality promotion strategy at the national level. Quality is defined in a comprehensive way ('Qualité Totale'). The service as well as the manufacturing sector is strongly involved. Like the UK, small and medium-sized enterprises have been targeted in state and private initiatives for quality promotion.

4.1. Global

4.1.1 Standards and Certification

AFNOR is responsible for product quality standards, granting the NF certificate when one of the accredited sub-contracting certification bodies has carried out the legal tests and audits. The NF certificate is granted to any voluntary applying product which can satisfy the relevant standards and quality tests. In 1992, a national campaign promoted NF, the AFNOR trademark, emphasizing that it is only granted to high quality products ('NF makes the difference').

AFNOR is strongly involved in the revision process of ISO 9000 series (ISO Vision 2000 Committee) due to be completed by 1996. AFNOR representatives are members of ISO Technical Committee 176 ('Quality Management and Quality Assurance').

Product Quality Certification

There are several bodies accredited in product quality certification including AFNOR, which is the main one. Product quality tests are carried out by more than 280 laboratories which have to be certified by the RNE. The audits are carried out by an audit team (two to six experts during one to two days). They are consultants trained and accredited by the RNE (300 in France). The cost of such an audit varies from FFR 10,000 to FFR 30,000.

Quality Assurance Certification

Although not yet officially accredited AFAQ is the only working certification body for ISO 9000 series standards. Candidates for certification must apply to the AFAQ general secretary and fill in a preliminary identification in order to be analysed by an appropriate sectoral committee. This preliminary application defines which is the relevant ISO 9000 standard and whether the applicant has already a quality assurance system. The company then answers a questionnaire and provides the committee with its quality assurance booklets (ISO 9001/9002) or its quality assurance organisation (ISO 9003). An auditing team then investigates the quality assurance system and provides the committee with an anonymous report that the candidate may object to.

The average cost of such an audit is typically about FFR 50,000 (the cost varies from a minimum of FFR 30,000 to a maximum of FFR 250 000). The audits can last from a day to a week and can involve from one to five experts. Some public and private grants are available to SMEs. The certification process as a whole can last up to six months. The AFAQ certificate is granted for three years with an annual monitoring visit. If problems are found during the visit, the certified company may get a warning, a suspension or even have certification removed.

4.1.2 Promotion and Awareness

There are several schemes and initiatives dedicated to promotion and awareness. At the national level, several tax refund schemes for training, research and development, certification and normalization have been set up. Several such schemes promote quality:

- R&D tax refund scheme: from 1990, this scheme allows companies to deduct 50% of the increase in their standardization expenditures from their operating income. Such expenditures are wages (and related social cost) of employees attending official standardization meetings (AFNOR, accredited standardisation offices, CEN, CENELEC, ISO, CEI) and a contractual amount for other costs (30% of wages).
- ANVAR (Agence Nationale de Valorisation de la Recherche, National Agency for Innovation and R&D), provides grants for quality-related initiatives as far as a new product or a new process is involved. This financial support could start from the market research stage up to certification by a third party. Any company is eligible for this scheme providing a detailed and comprehensive project.

ANVAR is also using the National Fund for Modernization and the Public Technological Venture Capital Initiative to support projects with the aim of improving process quality through investment in automatization, training, quality assurance.

One of the missions of MFQ, AFNOR, and AFAQ, is the general promotion of quality and quality management in order to increase the awareness of quality issues in industry. They organize conferences, seminars and visits, publish books and notes, offering advertising support (posters, videos, etc) and grant awards. The most well-known journals are:

- *Qualité en Mouvement* (formerly *Qualité-Magazine*) published by the MFQ and providing general information; and,
- *Enjeux* published by AFNOR which promotes quality standards.

MFQ is the main quality promoting body within France. In addition, both AFNOR and AFAQ have set up lines on the Minitel system (3616 AFNOR and 3616 AFAQ) to provide their customers with information. AFNOR has responsibility for editing and disseminating standards. On the AFNOR Minitel line, there is access to its NORIANE+ database on French, European and international standards. Having responsibility for the National Committee for Maintenance, AFNOR also publishes a comprehensive list of maintenance enterprises.

There are several national awards granted by the various associations:

- MFQ and MICE have recently instigated the 'Grand Prix Qualité Totale'. The regional award is decided by regional MFQ offices and DRIRE (Direction Regionale pour l'Innovation et la Recherche, Regional Office for Innovation and Research) and the professional award by the Institute of Quality Management (IQM), chaired by M. Hué de la Collombe, director of the Renault Quality Institute.

- AFAV grants the AFAV-INOVA Award to projects using the value analysis method. The projects have to demonstrate innovative products or services.

Many associations are organizing conferences and seminars:

- AFAQ is organising a national conference on quality assurance certification every year in partnership with AFNOR, MFQ and the Club Initiatives et Compétitivité. In 1992, this conference was held in Lyon.
- AFNOR was responsible for the ISO 9000 international symposium in April 1992.

In addition, some quality related databases are worth mentioning:
- NORIANE+ is providing, through Minitel and with an annual subscription, 57,000 different documents on French, European and international standards, unified technical documents, reports, etc.
- NORMATERM is providing, through direct access to Minitel, more than 100,000 French and English concepts and definitions.
- VULCAIN BDM is a database on materials with a quick and cheap access to the Minitel.
- AFNOR is providing all information on French, European and international standardization offices with quick and cheap access to Minitel.
- MARQUE NF is the NF product quality brand database and is also provided through Minitel
- MAINTEL is providing information on maintenance through Minitel.
- PERINFORM is a tri-lingual CD-ROM on all French, British, German, European and ISO standards that can be used on any PC compatible micro-computer. The CD-ROM is up-dated every month and is available through a subscription.

The ACFCI (National Association of Chambers of Trade and Industry) is carrying out two national promotion schemes:

- the RNPQ (Réseau National de Promotion de la Qualité, National Network for the Promotion of Quality) was set up in 1984 by ACFCI, CNPF (Confederation Nationale du Patronat, National Employers Confederation) and CGPME (Confederation Général des PME, National Confederation of SMEs). National, regional and local chambers of trade and industry staff are carrying out pre-diagnosis quality audits. The aim has been to visit more than 4,500 SMEs per year in order to promote both quality management and quality certification.

- A 'sub-contracting' initiative was set up in 1992 to promote quality within the relationship between manufacturers and suppliers: the objective is to first help French SMEs to become suppliers of Japanese 'transplants' in Europe, and then to become suppliers of Japanese manufacturers in Japan.

4.1.3 Education

According to a survey conducted by MICE in 1992, around 400 training and education schemes are dealing with quality related issues. Many universities are involved in quality related education. Figure 16 lists some examples of the main schemes.

In addition, two public bodies deal with quality related adult education. At the Ministry of National Education level, there are 350 GRETA (GRoupements d'ET-Ablissements, Groups of Establishments) of which 65 are permanent dealing with adult training and education. A number teach quality-related issues. Also at the Ministry of Education level, there is the CNED (Centre National pour l'Enseignement à Distance, National Centre for Distance Learning) providing distance training and education. Again some of these are quality related.

Figure 16: Examples of courses in quality

FACULTE DE PHARMACIE D'ANGERS: DESS (Insurance for safety of bio-products).

INSTITUT DE LA Qualité DE L'OUEST: (DEA Quality)

ECOLE CENTRALE DE PARIS: (Masters degree in Quality)

ECOLE SUPERIEURE DE COMMERCE DE PARIS: (Masters degree in Quality)

ECOLE SUPERIEURE DES TRAVAUX PUBLICS: (Masters degreee inQuality)

ECOLE NATIONALE SUPERIEURE DES ARTS ET METIERS: (Masters degree in Quality)

ECOLE DES HAUTES ETUDES COMMERCIALES DE LILLE: (Masters degree in TQM)

UNIVERSITE TECHNOLOGIQUE DE COMPIEGNE: (Quality engineering course)

ECOLE NATIONALE SUPERIEURE DES TECHNIQUES INDUSTRIELLES ET DES MINES DE DOUAI: (Metrology and quality engineer)

INSTITUT UNIVERSITAIRE DE FRANCHE-COMTE: (Quality diploma)

UNIVERSITE PAUL SABATIER DE TOULOUSE: (Quality in SMEs diploma)

UNIVERSITE DE MARSEILLE-3: (DESS Quality in chemical engineering)

FACULTE DE PHARMACIE DE LYON: (DESS quality management)

UNIVERSITE D'ANGERS: (DESS reliability of products and services Electromechanicals and quality management)

INSTITUT UNIVERSITAIRE DE TECHNOLOGIE DE SAINT-ETIENNE: (DUT Quality in business and public bodies management)

INSTITUT EUROPEEN DE LA Qualité TOTALE DE VICHY: (DESTU Animation and management of total quality)

INSTITUT MEDITERRANEEN DE LA Qualité DE TOULOUN: (TQC and TQM diploma)

Other Bodies

The CDAF (Compagnie des Acheteurs Française, Company of French Purchasing Managers), an independent association set up in 1945, is in charge of ESAP 2000, École Supérieure des Acheteurs Professionnels (National School for Professional Purchasing) at which quality is strongly emphasised. ACFCI, CRCI and CCI (Chambre de Commerce et d'Industrie, Chambers of Commerce and Industry) are involved in quality-related education through their 273 business schools and education centres. At university level, the most quality-dedicated centres are: IPIA (Auch), IFCC (Fougères), CFSA (Bourges), École de la Qualité (Charleville-Mézières), EIA (Marseille), CERELOG (Metz), CHAMFOR (Reims), CEFOPE (Troyes) IMT (Toulon) and IEQT (Vichy).

4.1.4 Training

Most of the public associations are heavily involved in training. AFNOR has seven training centres in France: one is in Paris and there is one in each of its regional delegations. In 1991, 4,600 people were trained by more than 210 lecturers. In 1992, there were more than 300 available training seminars in six major topics:

- standardization and strategy;
- quality management and communication;
- quality assurance;
- quality management;
- quality improvement methods; and,
- information technologies.

The cost of such training sessions ranges from FFR 2,500 (for one day) to FFR 8,800 (for three to four days).

MFQ is strongly involved in quality management training. It provides its members with advice in training and organizes more than 50 national training courses in quality control and quality management. Courses are carried out in its Training Centre or in other places when they are organized with partners such as AFNOR, IRDQ (Institut de Recherche et de Developpement de la Qualité, Research and Development Institute for Quality), INA (Institut National Audio-Visuel Mèthodes, National Institute for Audio-Visual Techniques), CERESTA, and INPG (Institut National Polytechnique Grenoble, National Polytechnic Institute of Grenoble). Others are organised in joint venture with specialized consultants.

In 1992, CERESTA organized 18 different training seminars dealing with statistics, quality control, quality management, experiment planning, reliability, data analysis and forecasting. Such training sessions are organised either in the training centre in Paris or for private purposes. They last from 2 to 15 days and cost between FFR 5,200 - 14,200. Lecturers come from industry or public administration.

CDAF is also organising training seminars in its training centre in Neuilly-Plaisance (Paris) or in in-company sessions. Thirty different seminars specialize in purchasing-related issues such as international purchases, sub-contracting purchases, purchases of industrial equipment, buying through telephone, quality in purchasing, international logistics, supplier evaluation, buying negotiation, working in groups, etc.

4.1.5 Consultancy

Several organizations involved in quality related issues are not involved in consultancy but provide enterprises with lists of accredited or selected consultants: that is the case for AFAV, AFAQ,and MFQ. AFNOR is the only nationwide organization dealing with consultancy mainly for product quality management and total quality management, in particular when preparing for certification.

The only national scheme promoting consultancy is the so-called FRAC (Fonds Règionaux d'Aide au Conseil, Regional Consultancy Funds) initiative, which is budget managed at regional level to finance consultancy in quality management, innovation and computer integrated manufacturing.

Since 1984 more than 3,000 FRAC projects have been supported at a total of around FFR 130 million.

4.1.6 Research

There is no national and global research initiative on quality management. Most universities, business schools and schools of engineers are involved in research which has a quality element. The IRDQ (Institut de Recherche et de Développement de la Qualité, Institute for Quality Research and Development) is one of the main research centres which has been quoted by the Ministry of Industry and SQUALPI as of national interest. IRDQ is a public association set up by a group of enterprises (GEC Alsthom, Bull, Solvay, Du Pont, Peugeot) and institutions (AFNOR, local authorities). It is involved in both research and consultancy. Its annual turnover is approximately FFR 4.5 million. There are six research groups: systematic approach to quality, sociology of quality, quality in design, quality and computer science, quality in surface treatment, quality in services. The IRDQ quality-related philosophy is the so-called 'systemic' approach which involves all functions and departments within a company: TQM must be a comprehensive and global approach involving all levels and activities.

Research programmes are emphasizing the development of new methods and techniques: new quality concepts, new TQM approaches and methods, new quality 'products' (i.e. quality implementation techniques) and new training methods and documents for quality management.

Industrial corporations, universities and research institutes are also carrying out research on quality management but at a much smaller level.

4.2. Sectoral Schemes

Sectoral schemes and initiatives mainly deal with promotion and awareness. Some include research, education and training. All sectoral ministries have their own specific quality schemes. The following description of activities found within the Ministry of Defence and the Ministry of Agriculture and Forests, as well as one from the engineering industry are provided as examples.

MOD (Ministère de la Défence, Ministry of Defence)

Within the MOD, the DGA, the Directorate General for Armament, is responsible for quality related issues. Within the DGA, there are seven directorates: land, air, sea, space, electronics, advanced R&D and SIAR (Service de Surveillance Industrielle de l'ARmement, Industry Monitoring Service). Since 1982, at DGA level, the quality-related policy is global and comprehensive. As the final customer for military programmes that it itself has defined, the MOD includes total quality management in its 'management of programme methods'.[11] The DGA has set up a quality infrastructure with both operational and functional responsibilities.

Each directorate is responsible for the quality of its operations while SIAR monitors supplier quality. In 1980, SIAR set up RAQ (Réglement d'Assurance Qualité, Quality Assurance Regulation) in order to control the quality of the MOD's suppliers. Through its 300 locations in France and with 1,500 engineers, SIAR, 'supervises' 7,000 plants (these employ about 160,000 and have a combined turnover of approximately FFR 61 billion). SIAR conducts about 10,000 audits par year.

The number of certified companies is decreasing: 2,500 in 1985, 2,100 in 1991. SIAR is predicting that this will decline further to about 1,500 in the next 5 to 10 years. With the launch of the AFAQ certificate in 1988, SIAR decided to place increasing emphasize quality throughout the design, manufacturing and maintenance phases.

At the functional level, the CGQ (Quality Management Committee) establishes the DGA quality policy. The MAQ (Quality Assurance Mission) is its working arm on a day-to-day basis together with the CMQ (Quality Delegate) of each DGA directorate. The main objective of the MAQ/CMQ structure is to achieve a quality management system which is accepted by all the MOD suppliers. (this has begun with the signing of an agreement between major suppliers, the MOD, the CNES (Centre National d'Etudes Spatiales, French Space Centre) and the Ministry for Transportation through the BNAE (Bureau de Normalisation de l'Aèronautique et de l'Espace, Standardisation Office for Aerospace).

From November 1991, the DGA-AQ 902 document, 'A Textbook of Programme Management Methods' is supposed to have been applied by all MOD suppliers.[12] Thus, the MAQ/CMQ is able to certify that a supplier is using some of the accredited methods in the management of its programs while the SIAR is only able to certify the quality assurance system through its RAQ certificates.

During the next five years, one of the main objectives for DGA is to try to disseminate its program management practices and methods to other European armies, and in particular in the UK and Germany.

MAF (Ministère de l'Agriculture et Forêt, Ministry of Agriculture and Forest)

The Ministry of Agriculture and Forest deals with both product quality and quality assurance.

A quality-related policy for agricultural products is a very old tradition in France and has always been strongly supported, if not initiated at government level. The national certification body is the CPPAQS (Centre pour la Promotion Produit l'Alimentation Qualitè Supèrieur, National Centre for the Promotion of Food

Products with Superior Quality).

A national sectoral scheme for the promotion of quality assurance, AQ 2000, was set up in 1986 within the national R&D promotion scheme 'Aliment 2000' (Food 2000). Between 1986 and 1989, the AQ 2000 programme, undertaken by 20 small and large food suppliers under the leadership of an international consultant, developed a general guide for quality assurance in agro-food business following the ISO 9000 series.

Since 1989, following the conclusions of AQ 2000, MAF, through its own budget for the promotion of quality, and the SQUALPI programme 'Partenaires pour l'Europe' (Partners in Europe) are funding specific applications of the general guide.

In September 1989, a report by P. Creyssel, on behalf of the MAF, had three major conclusions:

- quality assurance in food businesses is absolutely necessary;
- certification is necessary; and,
- certification might be made through a sectoral committee within AFAQ.[13]

Such a committee was set up in January 1991. By March 1992, ten food-related companies had achieved AFAQ certification. The main motivations are the cost-saving provided by total quality management and the requirements of industrial customers when they are supplying their products to other food businesses.

Sectoral audits are made by experts belonging to both AFAQ and DGAL (Direction Générale pour l'Alimentation, General Food Directorate of MAF) and trained to specific sectoral guidelines to the ISO 9000 series.

Since 1990, MAF has supported the 'Aliment 2002' programme in which one of the main issues is the ISO 45011 certification for food-testing laboratories. The project is undertaken by the R&D Mission of the DGAL and the RNE.

At MAF level, quality-related schemes in training and education and research are undertaken by the DGER (Education and Research General Directorate). The main actions are dealing with general quality management training for agro-food employees while some very general courses on product quality are provided within the different schools and universities dealing with agriculture.

The research programme on quality management is the aforementioned ISO 45011 scheme within Aliment 2002.

Engineering Industry

As an example of an industry-led initiative, it is worth mentioning training schemes that were set up in 1986 by UIMM (Union des Industries Métalliques et Minieres), the national body for mines and metal-industry. These training schemes (QUIMM for Quality UIMM) are targeted to SME managers and executives:

- A QUIMM-dirigeant (QUIMM general managers) lasts for two days and mainly emphasizes quality awareness.
- A QUIMM-cadres (QUIMM executives and staff) lasts for four days; the first two days focus on motivation and awareness of quality and the other

two days on quality management methods.

- ADAQUIMM (Self-Diagnosis QUIMM) is the establishment of a steering committee of all quality-related staff in the SME with an independent consultants to carry out a survey of the quality-related problems and needs of the firm and a proposal for training and certification opportunity.
- When the self-diagnosis has been completed, there are two alternatives according to the survey results: investigation of third party certification (e.g. AFAQ) with a full diagnosis and a comprehensive training to quality assurance; or a total quality management approach only (i.e. without any certification objective) with intra-company training.

5. Regional Quality Schemes and Initiatives

Most public and para-public bodies and associations have specific regional offices: MFQ, AFNOR, AFAV. They also use local representatives through chambers of trade and industry and professional and industrial federations. The survey has investigated only a sample of regional quality-related schemes and initiatives. AFNOR has six regional delegations:

- Rhône-Alpes Centre-Est (Lyon)
- Sud-Ouest (Bordeaux-Mérignac)
- Ouest (Nantes)
- Nord (Lille-Marcq-en-Baroeul)
- Est (Nancy)
- Sud (Marseille)

By June 1992, MFQ had nine regional offices:

- Qualité Ouest (Bretagne, Pays-de-Loire)
- Qualité Nord (Nord-Picardie, Haute et Basse-Normandie)
- Qualité Centre-Est (Centre, Champagne-Ardennes, Bourgogne)
- Qualité Est (Lorraine, Alsace, Franche-Comté)
- Qualité Sud-Est (Languedoc-Roussillon, Provence-Alpes-Côte d'Azur)
- Qualité Rhône-Alpes-Auvergne (Rhône-Alpes, Auvergne)
- Qualité Ile-de-France (Ile-de-France, DOM-TOM (Département d'Outre Mer - Territories d'Outre Mer))
- Qualité Sud-Ouest (Aquitaine, Limousin, Poitou-Charentes)
- Qualité Midi-Pyrenées

For practical reasons, the report will present only a sample of regional schemes. In particular, the choice of the Rhône-Alpes region is due to its official position as a 'pilot region' by most of the bodies and associations (MFQ, AFAQ) dealing with quality promotion.

At the regional level, MFQ has several quality promotion initiatives. Once a month, the Ile-de-France delegation organizes a breakfast, a one-day seminar and a visit.

Since 1988, AFNOR, on behalf of SQUALPI, has organized the 'Initiatives et Compétitivité Europe 92' clubs at regional level: such clubs are set up by private companies without legal statute. Their main objective is the promotion and analysis of standards and certification (product and company) through regular meetings in which experienced companies present their strategy.

A national club is headed by the leaders of the biggest French industrial groups (Télémécanique, Saint Gobain, Rossignol, PSA, Pechniney, Thomson, Casino, Elf, Framatome, Aérospatiale, Renault, Bull, Usinor-Sacilor, CFP, Schneider, Casino). Its purpose is to increase awareness of quality in SMEs. This club has proved a great success, with 1,300 members (enterprises) in 20 regions.

At regional and local level, the scheme is supported either by the AFNOR delegation, the chamber of trade and industry, a quality club, DRIRE, the industry confederation or a consultant.

At local and regional levels, chambers of trade and industry are strongly committed to quality promotion. Since they are independent bodies, they are able to develop their own schemes and initiatives: conferences, publications, clubs, awards etc. Some schemes are emphasizing specific sectors such as the food business in Toulouse, or targeting specific goals such as the training of quality technicians in Rennes. All local and regional chambers have at least one quality expert.

Most of the national associations' training courses are organized at regional level. This is the case for MFQ and AFNOR.

As it has been mentioned at national level, there is only one scheme promoting consultancy: the FRAC initiative. FRAC rules and principles have been set up at both national and regional levels to provide SMEs with a specific grant for consultancy in quality, strategy and computer aided manufacturing (CAD-CAM, automation). Applicants are SMEs of less than 500 employees in industry, tourism, construction, transportation, agro-industry, wood and craft industry.

FRAC provides 50% of the consultantancy cost up to a maximum of about FFR 100,000 in most regions. But regional DRIRE have some freedom with maximum levels: in Rhône-Alpes, for instance, and only for quality-related applications, the maximum amount may reach FFR 150,000. For quality diagnosis, the grant could cover 80% of the cost up to FFR 15,000. The decision-making process is as follows:

- Company application with a detailed quality improvement proposal and an economic and financial report;
- Audit by a DRIRE representative; then,
- FRAC Regional Committee with representatives from local chambers of trade and industry, MFQ, SIAR (regional office of Ministry of Defence), AFAV, regional industry confederation, regional council meet every month to make decisions on funding and to consider consultant reports.

The FRAC scheme not only involves DRIRE but also some other regional public bodies involved in such activiities such as Tourism, Building, Agriculture and

Forest, and the Trade and Craft.

MFQ has set up several research groups at regional level in order to improve the common understanding of various quality-related issues and to study new concepts and methods. For instance, in Ile-de-France, there are eight research groups: quality indicators in administrative services, participative management and human resources, management and ethics, quality in commercial function, quality and safety, quality for social workers, quality in transportation, quality in public services.

5.1 Rhône-Alpes

Rhône-Alpes is one of the leading regions in France. Located in the south-east of France, its capital is Lyon. Rhône-Alpes is considered to have the optimal 'European' size and is perfectly located at the junction of North, South and West, East European corridors and part of the so-called 'golden lozenge': Milano, Vienna, Munich, Lyon.

There are 5 million inhabitants, i.e. 9% of the French population. The economic situation of Rhône-Alpes is one of the best in France, with a higher rate of economic growth (0.2% more than the French average between 1975 and 1986) and increasing exports (equipments, steel, chemicals and pharmaceuticals, trucks, consumer goods). 500,000 people are working in industry, i.e. 12% of the total French industrial employment. Rhône-Alpes is also a leading region for research and development: 9 universities, 24 national schools of engineers, 13 technical centres, 20,000 researchers, 130,000 students.

Attention to quality is an old tradition in industry, and in particular in its historic fields of expertise: hydro-electricity (one-third of the French output), nuclear energy (60% of French output), paper, leather, textiles (silk), plastics and tourism.

In its total spending for quality, standardization and certification of the various associations (MFQ, AFNOR, ANVAR etc.), Rhône-Alpes accounts for more than its economic weight, between 15% and 20%. By April 1992 there were 20 companies certified for ISO 9001 out of 68 in France and 34 for ISO 9002 out of 285. That is why Rhône-Alpes was used as a pilot region for quality promotion by the MFQ in 1992.

DRIRE (Direction Regionale pour l'Innovation et la Recherche, Regional Office for Innovation and Research)

The DRIRE Rhône-Alpes, a regional representative of the Ministry of Industry, is one of the leading public bodies dealing with quality through the FRAC (Fonds Régional d'Aide au Conseil, Regional Fund for Consultancy) scheme.

In Rhône-Alpes the FRAC budget for 1991 was FFR 20 million of which 80% are for the quality scheme. This scheme is targeted on quality diagnosis, quality control, certification and quality management.

DRIRE Rhône-Alpes is also in charge of the executive recruitment grant scheme which could help industrial SMEs with less than 80 employees in employing a new manager dealing with marketing finance, manufacturing, R&D and quality. The SME could get a FFR 100,000 grant if the annual cost of the manager is more than FFR 240,000.

Présence Technologique Rhône-Alpes

This is a network of public and para-public bodies: the regional council, DRIRE, ANVAR, ARIST (Agencie Regionale pour l'Information Scientifique et Technique, Regional Agency for Scientific and Technical Information), CRCI, INPI (Institut Nationale pour la Propriété Industrielle, National Institute for Industrial Patent Rights), AFNOR, CRITT (Centre Regionale pour l'Innovation et le Transfer de Technologie, Regional Centres for Innovation and Technology Transfer), and CCIs.

Its main objective is to increase the awareness of SMEs for technology and innovation, including quality. It provides them with a unique source of data and information.

The Quality Charter for Rhône-Alpes

In December 1991, a Quality Charter was signed by all public and para-public actors in Rhône-Alpes: the Préfet, the leaders of the regional council, the regional economic and social council, the MFQ (executive president of Rhône-Poulenc), the regional chamber of trade and industry; and representatives from the regional industry confederation and the SMEs confederation. The charter emphasizes the key role of quality in competitiveness and the necessity of both a general and comprehensive involvement.

In 12 November 1992 there was a 'Week for Quality' during which the first 'Rhône-Alpes Award for Quality Achievement' was presented.

CERTIFI-RA

CERTIFI-RA is a network of companies and public and para-public institutions providing a grant to SMEs of less than 500 employees which apply for quality assurance certification from AFAQ. The grant could reach 40% of the AFAQ invoice up to FFR 20,000 even if the AFAQ certificate is not delivered. In Rhône-Alpes, CERTIFI-RA is acting on behalf of the AFNOR regional delegation.

CDAF

CDAF Rhône-Alpes is organising its ESAP 2000 courses, inter-company training sessions and intra-company seminars at regional level. Regional training sessions are chosen within the national programme.

5.2 Savoie

Savoie is a department within Rhône-Alpes with Chambéry as its capital and Albertville as its most famous city since it hosted the Winter Olympic Games in 1992.

The specific characteristic of Savoie is that there are 1,200 enterprises of which most are SMEs (the biggest one has 1265 employees) and a third are involved in industrial engineering and maintenance. In Savoie, 530 SMEs have less than 5 employees, 450 have 5 to 10 employees, 180 have 11 to 100 employees and only 40 have more than 100 employees. Such a structure fully justifies public and para-public involvement in promoting quality. The department of Industry in the CCI of Chambéry-savoie and the Club Qualité Savoie (Savoie Quality Club), have decided to deal with quality-related issues through two kinds of initiatives:

- direct individual contact for an economic and strategic diagnosis with a target of 100 visits per year. 123 firms were visited in 1991: 100 for a first visit and 23 for a complementary contact. Of these 123 enterprises, more than 50% had a quality-related problem and more than 20% required a certification for ISO 9000 because they are sub-contracting or supplying a bigger company. The others are 'certified' by their own customer according to its specific requirements.
- direct collective awareness through conferences and seminars. 180 managers and executives of more than 100 companies attended the conference on ISO 9000 series and certification in April 1991.

The CCI of Chambéry-Savoie is providing the audited companies with a list of quality consultants and helps them in their contacts with the relevant public bodies, in particular to gain access to public grants such as FRAC Quality.

The CCI is acting in close partnership with the 'Club Qualité Savoie'. This informal organisation, set up in 1986, is managed by the Industrial and Commercial Association of Savoie, a local subsidiary of the National Confederation of Industry (CNPF). With 50 members, the club has three objectives: to increase local SMEs awareness to quality, to promote TQM approach, and to disseminate appropriate information through conferences. It is the local representative of MFQ and it organises two kinds of conferences:

- internal technical meetings (three per year) on quality management systems and methods: TQM, SPC, AMDEC, certification, etc.
- annual public conferences on global issues such as quality circles and certification.

In December 1991 the Club set up the Savoie Quality Award. One award was given to an SME at an early stage in introducing TQM, another was given to an SME with two years experience with TQM.

In Savoie, there is no specific training and education scheme but the club is promoting the involvement of some of its members in lecturing on TQM in technical schools and colleges.

5.3 Isère (Grenoble)

Industry in Isere is very dynamic and heavily involved in high technology. There are both large corporations (Hewlett Packard, Merlin Gerin, Caterpillar, Thomson, Alcatel, etc) and SMEs. By mid-May 1992, twelve local companies had received their AFAQ certificate. Quality is considered a vital issue by most SMEs.

The Grenoble Chamber of Trade and Industry (CCIG) is hosting the local representative of AFNOR, MFQ and Initiatives et Compétitivité. This office, set up in 1991 and headed by a Quality Consultant (Chargé de Mission) is strongly promoting the TQM approach within local industry. Such a promotion scheme is articulated around collective and individual initiatives. It is also involved in training through the CCIG Training Centre. All programmes are analysed and discussed by a steering committee.

Every month, a workshop is organized with a presentation by an expert and a sharing of experiences: in 1992 the meetings emphasized quality in purchasing (January), TQM (February), European standards (March), quality assurance in sub-contracting (April), quality in services (May) and quality environment (June).

Individual promotion is organized through a free preliminary visit. Such a visit is not a quality audit but a promotion and a pre-diagnosis evaluation. A comprehensive list of quality consultants is provided with a set of documents about ISO 9000 series, the AFAQ certification process and MFQ's advice for quality consultancy. Cheap access to the AFNOR database Perinorm is also provided. In 1991, 40 SMEs were visited.

FRAC applications by local SMEs are studied by a DRIRE representative located in Grenoble.

In Isère, AFPI-ASFO 38 and UDIMEC (Union Departmentale de Industrie Mecaniques, Mechanical Industry Union) deal with SMEs in the engineering industry. They are heavily involved in quality-related training applying the QUIMM schemes at local level through the AFPI training centre. They began in September 1991 and have organized four QUIMM-dirigeants and 4 QUIMM-cadre training schemes with seven training consultants accredited by UIMM. By the end of 1992, QUIMM schemes were running every two months and three ADAQUIMM had been completed.

The AFPI 38 basic philosophy is to develop total quality approach in SMEs at the cheapest cost. It is helping SMEs in finding skilled, cheap and reliable consultants through the UIMM network. For the ADAQUIMM scheme, the target is to minimize the cost of consultancy in optimizing the involvement of the company staff. The diagnosis is carried out by them with advice from the consultant (one day a month maximum) and under its guidance.

6. Overview and Outlook

In France, the quality community is characterized by a clear division of responsibility:

- Public bodies are only concerned with promotion of quality awareness at a 'global' level (and at a sectoral level where there is a specific government responsibility). Public bodies are involved in introducing quality in education and promoting research in quality-related issues.
- Associations are dealing with the 'hard core' of the implementation process of total quality management systems: standardization, certification, accreditation, tests and control, training, consultancy and research.
- The private sector is strongly involved both in implementing TQM and in consultancy. Most large corporations have set up total quality management systems to ensure quality from both their suppliers and sub-contractors and their own products. They are heavily involved in the promotion of total

quality management systems through active participation in the various associations dealing with quality-related standardization and certification. This basic pattern of a strictly defined division of responsibility, with a decentralized structure, has been advocated since the 1970s.

Most representatives of French quality-related bodies have emphasized the crucial role of large industrial corporations in the diffusion of the TQM philosophy through two main initiatives:

- Their own quality strategy with their suppliers. Focusing their own organization on total quality issues, they are constantly increasing the pressure on their suppliers. Some of them, such as the car manufacturers (Renault and PSA) and the aerospace industry, have set up their own quality certification process providing SMEs and other industries with a comprehensive and global strategy.
- Their involvement in all standardization and certification decision-making processes: the most active (Merlin-Gerin, BSN, Thomson Renault, PSA, Air Liquide, CIT-Alcatel etc) are attending and even chairing national standardisation committees and strongly lobbying within AFAQ, MFQ or AFNOR steering committees etc.

An increasing number of SMEs are well aware of the importance of TQM for their competitiveness and are accepting such a costly challenge. But most of them are still deeply in need of external pressure. Motivation is provided by three main actors: the Ministry of Industry, the large corporations, and the various national associations involved in the quality-related network: MFQ, AFNOR and AFAQ.

Public institutions are strongly involved in promoting SME's awareness of TQM. According to a meeting held in Lyon in June 1992 attended by 50 SMEs, such schemes are very efficient and must be maintained in the future, if not increased in volume.

AFNOR and AFAQ are essentially 'sovereign' bodies. They act as the operational arms for standardization and third-party certification with an official recognition by public bodies (but without any formal relationship with the government). They have a private statute and a strong involvement of large corporations in their managing statutes.

Other associations, such as AFAV, ACFCI, MFQ, are involved in quality promotion assistance and training schemes for SMEs. Their role is very important since they have constant contact with the 'customers' of TQM.

French administration and industry support such a diversified and widely disseminated involvement because private businessmen and executives prefer a 'parapublic' partner rather than a civil servant to help in TQM implementation. This partly explains why SQUALPI has such a 'light' structure and why the associations are the real operational actors.

6.1 The Future

It is too early to assess the results of most current national and regional schemes and initiatives since most of them have been set up in the last five years. A comprehensive and efficient evaluation is unlikely to be carried out before the mid-1990s.

Over the next five years, MICE's strategy is likely to follow its existing path:

- to promote a greater awareness of quality by all economic sectors;
- to set up an efficient technical and cultural institutional environment;
- to help firms to act efficiently with quality management systems.

MICE will emphasize several priorities:

- developing gradual initial education and adult training;
- developing research in quality management concepts and methods;
- creating a national award for quality achievement;
- supporting the MFQ;
- expanding the operation 'Partners for Europe';
- supporting the effort of AFAQ to increase the number of certified firms.

7. List of Organizations

Name	Address	Telephone/Fax
National Public Bodies		
Sous-Direction de la Qualité pour L'Industrie et de la Normalisation (SQUALPI)	22 rue Monge 75005 Paris	+33 1 43 19 52 17/+33 1 43 19 50 44
Commissariat a la Normalisation	30-32 rue Guersant 75017 Paris	
Agence Nationale de Valorisation de la Recherche (ANVAR)	43 rue caumartin 75436 Paris Cedex 09	+33 1 40 17 83 00,
MAF	175 rue du Chevaleret 75013 Paris	(1) 49 55 58 45
MOD	24 avenur Prieur de la Côte d'Or	(1)49 85 03 69/(1)49 85 14 04
Main National Quality Bodies		
Association Française pour L'Analyse de la Valuer (AFAV)	Tour Europe Cedex 07 92049 Paris La Défense	+33 1 42 91 59 57/+33 1 42 91 56 56
Association Française pour L'Assurance Qualité (AFAQ)	Tour Septentrion Cedex 9 92081 Paris La Défense	+33 1 47 73 49 49/+33 1 47 73 49 99
Association Française pour la Normalisation (AFNOR)	Tour Europe Cedex 7 92049 Paris La Défense	33 1 42 91 55 33
Mouvement Française pour la Qualité (MFQ)	5 Esplanade Charles de Gaulle 92773 Nanterre	+33 1 47 29 09 29/+33 1 47 25 31 21
Institut de Recherche et de Dévelopement de la Qualité (IRDQ)	45 avenue Carnot 25000 Besancon	+33 81 80 97 21/+33 81 53 05 04
Reseau National d'Essais (RNE)	52 rue Madame 75006 Paris	+33 1 45 44 69 66/+33 1 45 44 48 97
Bureau National de Metrologie (BNM)	22 rue Monge, 75005 Paris	+33 1 46 34 48 40
Limited Scope Quality Bodies		
Association Française des Ingenieurs et Responsables de Maintenance (AFIM)	13 rue de Liège 75009 Paris	+33 1 42 80 64 00/+33 1 45 26 81 96
Comité National de la Maintenance (CNM)	Tour Europe Cedex 07 92080 Paris La Défense	+33 1 42 91 56 76
Association de Formation du Transport-Institut de Formation aux Techniques d'Implantation et de Manutention (AFT-IFTIM)	63 Avenue de Villiers 75017 Paris	+33 1 47 66 03 60
Association Française pour la Logistique dans l'Enterprise (ASLOG)	63 Avenue de Villiers, 75017 Paris	+33 1 47 66 03 60

Agence de la Productique (ADEPA)	17 rue Perier. 92120 Montrouge	+ 33 1 46 512 70
Reseau National de Promotion de la Qualité (RNPQ)	31 Avenue Pierre 1er de Serbie 75/84 Paris Cedex 16	+33 1 47 20 26 73
Confederation Française pour les Essais Non Destructifs (CONFREND)	32 Boulevard de la Chapelle 75882 Paris Cedex 18	+33 1 46 07 94 73

Other Important Quality-Related Institutions

Assemblee des Chambres Françaises de Commerce et d'industrie (ACFCI)	45 avenue d'Iena B9 448-16 75116 Paris	+33 1 40 69 37 73
Centre National du Patronat Française (CNPF)	31 avenue Pierre 1er de Serbie, 75784 Paris Cedex 16	33 1 40 69 44 44
Association Française pour la Connaissance et l'application des Normes (ACANOR)	BP 128 24160 excideuil	+ 53 62 04 70,

Accredited Product Certification Bodies

ACERFEU (fireproof materials)	4 avenue du Recteur Poincare 75782 Paris CEDEX 16	(1) 64 68 82 82
ACERMI (isolating products)	4 avenue du Recteur 75782 Paris CEDEX 16	(1) 40 50 28 28
ADAL (aluminium)	30 avenue de Messine 75008 Paris	(1) 42 25 26 44
ADF (dental products)	92 avenue de Wagram 75017 Paris	(1) 42 27 89 00
APSAD (security systems)	26 boulevard Haussmann 75009 Paris	(1) 42 47 90 00
ASQUAL (textiles)	14 rue des Reclettes 75013 Paris	(1) 45 35 24 01
ATG (gas and oil)	62 rue de Courcelles 75008 Paris	(1) 47 54 34 34
Bureau Veritas	17 bis Place des reflets La defense 2	(1) 42 91 52 91/(1) 42 91 52 94
CEMP (plastics)	6 rue Jadin 75017 Paris	(1) 47 64 01 08
CEBTP (building components)	12 rue Brancion 75737 Paris Cedex 17	(1) 45 39 22 33
CTBA (wooden products)	10 avenue de saint Mande 75012 Paris	(1) 43 44 04 20
CTC (leather products)	4 rue Hermann Frenkel 69367 Lyon Cedex 07	78 69 50 12
CEKAL (isolating glassware)	55 avenue Kleber 75116 Parid	(1) 47 55 63 90
CERTIMECA (metal products)	6 rue Anotole France 75017 Paris	(1) 47 66 02 23

CSTB (building materials)	4 avenuedu rectuer Poincare 75782 Paris Cedex 16	(1) 40 50 28 28
FIB (concrete products)	3 rue Alfred Roll 75849 Paris Cedex 17	(1) 47 66 03 64
GTFI (fireproof products)	10 rue du Debarcadere 75017 Paris	(1) 40 55 13 13
ITR (welding)	9 rue la Perouse 75116 Paris	(1) 47 20 10 20
LNE (packaging and general)	1 rue Gaston Boissier 75015 Paris	(1) 40 43 77 00/(1) 40 43 37 37,
OGBTP (building)	55 Avenue Kleber 75784 Paris	(1) 40 69 51 00,
UTAC (automotive)	157 rue Lecourbe 75015 Paris	(1) 48 42 53 90

References

1. AFQ (1983), *Le cout de la non-qualité dans les petites et moyennes entreprises industrielles et commerciales*, Paris, 31 mars.

2. AFQ (1986), *Le cout de la non-qualité dans les petites et moyennes entreprises industrielles et commerciales*, Paris, 31 mars.

3. C. Germon, P. Marano (1983), *La normalisation, clé d'un nouvel essor*, La Documentation française, Paris.

4. G. Bapt (1984), *Les conditions de l'amélioration de la qualité dans l'industrie francaise*, Paris, La Documentation française.

5. C. Doucet (1986), *Rapport d'étude concernant la certification des systémes d'assurance de la qualité des enterprises*, MIPTT, Paris.

6. NODAL-EQS (1991), *La qualité dans les PMI*, Ministére de l'Industrie et du Commerce Extérieur, Paris.

7. GMV (1986), *Perception de la Qualité par les PMI*

8. ARACQ (1989), *Qualité et compétitivé dans les PMI, le cas de la Loire.*

9. GMV (1986) op. cit.

10. SQUALPI (1992), *Textes réglementaries française ayant trait a la normalisation, la certification ou la protection des personnes*, Paris, 10/2.

11. J. Cavaillés (1991), *Manuel des méthodes de management de programme*, Paris, Teknea.

12. Ibid.

13. MAF (1989), *La certification des systémes d'assurance-qualité dans le secteur agroalimentaire*, Paris.

Other References

AFCIQ Quest (1981), *Vous dites : qualité ?*, Groupe de Travail Promotion-Qualité, Nantes.

AFCIQ-Quest (1989), *Terre de qualité QUEST*, Nantes.

AFNOR (1989), *Gérer et assurer la qualité, recueil de normes françaises*, Paris.

AFNOR (1992), *Gérer et assurer la qualité recueil de normes françaises*, tome 1, concepts et terminologie, Paris.

AFNOR (1992), *Gérer et assurer la qualité, recueil de normes françaises*, tome 2, management et assurance de la qualité, Paris.

AFNOR-ISO (1992), ISO 9000: Application symposium, first internation ISO 9000 quality standards application symposium, Paris, 26-27 March.

AFNOR (1992), *Catalogue Formation 92*, Paris, AFNOR.

CCE (1990), *L'analyse de la valeur dans la Communauté Européenne*, SPRINT, DG XII, EUR 13096.

CDAF (1992), *Stages et séminaires 1992*, Paris

CEC (1991), *Value analysis glossary*, SPRINT, DG XII, EUR 13774.

J. Chové (1991), 'Révision des normes ISO 9000, Ne laissons pas passer le train', *Enjeux*, no 115, mai 1991, pp. 40-51.

G. Delafollie (1991), *Analyse de la valeur*, Paris, Hachette.

DGA (1992), *Glossaire des termes utilisés pour le management des programmes d'armement*, MOD, DGA-AQ 914, Paris.

B. Jouslin de Noray (1989), 'Le mouvement international de la qualité : son histoire', *Qualité Magazine*, décembre, pp. 26-35.

R. Lavergne (1992), 'Accréditation et certification', *Enjeux*, mai

Les Echos (1992), 'Assurance qualité : passage obligé mais pas facile a négocier', Dossier spécial, *Les Echos*, 29 avril.

MAF (1989), *De l'assurance qualité a la certification d'enterprise : un impératif pour l'agro-alimentaire*, Colloque, Paris, 21 novembre.

MAF-APAVE (1989), *Programme Assurance Qualité 2000*, Paris, Sadave.

MFQ (1992), *Programme de formation 1992*, Paris.

MRICE (1985), *Les chemins de la qualité, Des expériences, des méthodes, des références pratiques*, Paris.

B. Picoche (1990), 'Un atout pour le marché européen: l'assurance-qualité', *Adria Normandie Information*, No 7.

RNE (1992), *Annuaire 92*, Paris

Strauss-Kahn, Ministre de l'Industrie et du Commerce Exterieur, *Orientation de la Politique de Promotion de la Qualité et de la Securité Industrielles*, Paris 29 April 1992.

Germany

Jürgen Wengel and Markus Schroll

1. Introduction

This chapter describes and analyses the situation and developments in Germany with respect to activities and measures in the field of quality assurance and quality management. Given the current situation as regards the awareness of quality issues (which is reflected in the information available) in Germany, it focuses almost entirely on the industrial sector; the service sector is largely tackled as a peripheral issue.

2. The Emergence of Quality as an Issue

Until recently, the general situation in Germany was characterized by little concern with quality as a competitive problem. Industry relied on the reputation of the 'Made in Germany' mark. Quality assurance was understood as an engineering problem; a task concerned primarily with the performance of the manufacturing process and with quality control techniques (and at best quality control costs). (The limited awareness of the quality issue must not be mistaken for a relative lack of quality-related infrastructure; in particular with respect to testing or education.) According to this 'philosophy', certification of quality systems in firms only played a limited role. Little concern was given either to explicit or to comprehensive quality concepts such as total quality management. Only a few sectors (for instance aerospace, military and nuclear) had a more intensive approach to quality involving comprehensive quality systems with specific quality standards).[1] This situation is now changing.

From late 1987 more coordinated initiatives started to raise the profile of the quality issue in Germany. Even though it is difficult to identify the prime movers behind such initiatives they come primarily from the representatives of academic and intermediate bodies (focusing in particular on the research area) rather than from industry. However, some of these bodies undoubtedly represented industrial interests.

The causes for these initiatives were obviously diverse. There was certainly a disruption of the German position as regards 'quality competition'. At the popular level this might be indicated by the way Japanese cars began to appear at the head of lists of the most reliable automobiles, compiled by the largest German automobile club (ADAC) from statistics gained through its break-down service.

However, the problem was not a general lack of quality of German products but the fact that quality no longer provided a competitive advantage which could outweigh generally higher prices. Major competitor countries were engaged in nation-wide quality campaigns. This caused concern, which was reflected in the approach of a study in 1989 comparing quality related measures in a number of industrial countries with Germany.[2] The results of this study have provided the decision base for policy measures in the field of quality in Germany.

The activities in Germany also relate to EC actions such as the adoption of a new approach to harmonization, a global approach to certification and testing, and consideration of a European directive on product liability (see Part Four).[3,4] The adoption of the ISO 9000 series as DIN (Deutsches Institut für Normung e.V., German Institute for Standardization) standards must be mentioned in this context as well, though it is itself rather a reaction to the growing awareness of quality issues. The previous 'resistance' to certification which was probably based on a misunderstanding of it as a standardization of the firm's quality system is turning into acceptance (if not a conviction) that a certified quality system is a factor in international competition.

Against this background, the above mentioned study was launched, and several memoranda were issued.[5,6] A broader discussion of quality started which finally led to a high-level conference 'Initiative Qualität' (Quality Initiative) in 1990 which was jointly organized by the RKW (Rationalisierungskuratorium der Deutschen Wirtschaft e.V., the rationalization board of German industry), AIF (Arbeitsgemeinschaft Industrieller Forschungsvereinigungen e.V., the working group of industrial research associations), BDI (Bundesverband der Deutschen Industrie e.V., the national association of German industry), and the DGQ (Deutsche Gesellschaft für Qualität e.V., the German Society for Quality).[7] It brought together the ministers responsible for the BMFT (Bundesministerium für Forschung und Technologie, the Federal Ministry of Research and Technology), the BMWi (Bundesministerium für Wirtschaft, the Federal Ministry of Economic Affairs), heads of relevant organizations and representatives of industry, including the unions.

A number of activities started in this context. The major one was the 'Rahmenkonzept Qualitätssicherung' (frame concept for the promotion of quality assurance) issued in 1990 for the promotion of quality assurance of the BMFT managed by the KfK-PFT (Kernforschungszentrum Karlsruhe- Projektträgerschaft Fertigungstechnik und Qualitätssicherung, the nuclear research centre Karlsruhe- project administration body for manufacturing technology and quality assurance). This frame concept included different types of promotion measures such as cooperative research projects, the promotion of groups of researchers from different disciplines mainly at universities, and technology transfer. It took almost two years before the frame concept was transformed into a proper promotion scheme. The budget increased from ECU 100 to 175 million and slight amendments were made in the light of several consultations of interested parties mainly via workshops and experiences with first calls for tender.[8]

This new programme phase signaled a slight change in focus; a change indicated by the addition of 'and quality assurance' in its name. Previously, the task had concentrated on the promotion of advanced manufacturing technology (e.g. computer aided design and manufacture) mainly by the use of so-called 'indirect-specific' programmes which aim to accelerate the broad application (diffusion) of a specific technology (most recently computer integrated manufacture) in a specific target group (in this case, the manufacturing technology industries).[9]

Originally the indirect-specific concept was also considered for the promotion of quality-related measures, it being initially envisaged that subsidies would be provided for certification according to the DIN 9000 standards. For various reasons (in particular, a lack of funds, a growing belief that the indirect-specific concept was incompatible with a free market policy, and expected problems in achieving acceptance by the EC) a programme of this form was not launched. Instead a cooperative research project in the field of certification was launched. This was aimed at improving and supporting the applicability and implementation of ISO 9000 standards in SMEs.[10] Owing to high expectations the call for tender received 168 applications with 790 partners of which around 600 were firms (90% of which were SMEs). A further call for tender provided support for groups of researchers.

Experience with the cooperative project led to amendments in the frame concept (and an increase in budget). Applicants to the first call for tender were allowed to participate in a cross-sectoral or sector-specific cooperative project or to seek a subsidy for the implementation of ISO 9000 in their company. 400 to 500 firms were expected to take advantage of this last offer. With the strengthening of the transfer component, the programme is now much more broadly based and less research orientated.

In general, national public measures largely concentrate on research, mainly in the engineering disciplines. The BMWi is involved in discussions but has not yet launched any specific programme. However, it has financed cross-sectoral quality research with the AIF which was additional to the usual subsidies to this organization under the heading 'Industrielle Gemeinschaftsforschung' (industrial cooperative research). The scheme has been running since 1989 and is now entering a stage where activities will probably be left to the sector-specific organizations and follow the procedure as it is generally applied to publicly funded projects in AIF.[11]

2.1 Diffusion of Quality

The boom in quality (as yet hardly effected by the promotion schemes which have only just begun) can most clearly be observed by the growing number of ISO 9000 certificates given to companies. At the time of writing, there were around 560 certified companies in Germany. In addition, the largest certification body had 500 companies on its waiting list.[12] However, the number of ISO 9000-certified companies is still comparatively low when one considers that there are almost 40,000 companies with 20 or more employees in Western Germany alone.

The certification of quality assurance systems by the DQS is based on DIN/ISO 9001-9003. Table 8 (page 146) gives an indication how the number and distribution of DQS certifications has developed. If individual firms are considered, the main enterprises involved are large companies, which obtained certificates for quality assurance systems in different works, and numerous medium sized firms.

Even though specific certification (particularly in the automotive sector) plays an important additional role, it is apparent that the certification of quality systems is not yet a major factor in the quality competition of German firms. Increasingly, however, customers (particularly foreign companies) require certification to ISO 9000. This is shown in a survey of 900 member companies of the BDI.[13] In this respect, there is a great demand for consultancy support. Some sector and regional industrial associations have already developed services, e.g. quality assurance manuals. Parallel to the certification boom, an enormous increase can be seen in the demand for, and supply of, quality related training (seminars, courses etc.), consultancy, or information (e.g. meetings). The whole situation is doubtless a major challenge for the quality infrastructure in Germany.

Table 8: Development of certification by DQS

	February 91	August 91	December 91	March 92
Total	99	154	224	242
DIN ISO 9001	58	102	150	163
DIN ISO 9002	38	50	71	76
DIN ISO 9003	3	2	3	3
Sectors				
Electrical industry	20	37	60	66
Mechanical industry	14	25	29	30
Chemical industry	44	60	83	90
Precision engineering and optics	2	3	7	7
Paper industry	13	18	22	22
Iron and steel industry	1	1	3	4
Textile industry	1	1	3	3
Food	3	3	3	4
Fireproofed materials	1	3	6	6
Medical devices	-	1	2	2
Services	-	2	6	7
Glass industry	-	-	1	-

Source: Qualität und Zuverlässigkeit, various issues.

3. The Quality Infrastructure

When looking at the institutions which constitute the 'innovation support infrastructure' in Germany, a growing importance of quality-related activities in recent years is obvious. There is an increase in the training offered and a growing emphasis on total quality management. Consultants have begun to specialize in quality questions. New institutions have been founded such as the DQS (Deutsche Gesellschaft zur Zertifizierung von Qualitätssicherungssysteme mbH, German Society for the Certification of Quality Assurance Systems),[14] the TÜVCERT (Technische Überwachungsvereine Zertifierungsgemeinschaft für Qualitätssicherungssysteme, Technical Association for the Certification of Quality Assurance Systems),[15] the FQS (Forschungsgemeinschaft Qualitätssicherung e.V., Quality Assurance Research Association).[16] At the regional level one should mention the several Steinbeis Transferzentrum Qualitätssicherung (Quality Transfer Centres) in Baden-Württemberg,[17] and the QZDO (Qualitätszentrum Dortmund Nordrhein Westfalen, Dortmund North Rhine Westphalia Quality Centre).

For a better understanding of the following report it should be mentioned at this point that institutions for the promotion of quality assurance in Germany are extremely varied in their aims and structures. Organisations include:

- general associations of the most dissimilar branches which have been formed for the representation of common interests (e.g. BDI);
- associations of people from different branches/professional associations (e.g. VDI, Verein Deutscher Ingenieure e.V., Association of German Engineers);
- cross-sectoral associations with tasks and activities in specific areas (e.g. DGQ);
- associations of firms and research institutes for the promotion of joint industrial research (e.g. AIF);
- (often semi-public) organizations for the promotion and support of small and medium-sized firms (e.g. RKW); and,
- several private, commercial bodies, (e.g. GMFT, Gesellschaft für Management und Technologie - Society for Management and Technology).

One thing common to these organizations, which are mainly non-profit-making, is that quality-related activities form only part of their work. These limitations do not apply, however, to the DGQ, which in accordance with its statutes deals exclusively with questions of quality assurance.

Exchange of information and experience takes place centrally through the networking of individual organizations in various committees and higher authorities at a national and sometimes European level, sometimes extending to international cooperation. Two examples illustrate this. In the research field the FQS is a member of the AIF, which in turn is represented in the DFG. The DGQ is the point of contact with similar organizations in other countries when specific issues relating to quality assurance have to be dealt with (e.g. regulations, measures, agreements, etc). It is a member of the European Organization for Quality (EOQ) and has formed personnel links with the International Academy for Quality (IAQ) In this way national aspects can be coordinated with international requirements.

With respect to eastern Germany, the quality issue is definitely more difficult since their standard of product quality has to be considered as relatively low.[18] This is combined with an insufficient performance of many existing products and many other problems of the industrial infrastructure in eastern Germany. Priorities have to be set taking account of this situation and therefore total quality management and similar concepts are not at the top of the list. Nevertheless, it should be mentioned that almost all the organizations of the 'innovation support infrastructure' (RKW, etc.) have established themselves in the new 'Länder'. In the case of the DGQ representatives of the 'Qualitätsfachleute' (quality experts) the groups responsible for quality assurance in GDR firms already contacted DGQ in 1989. In March 1990, a GDR-DGQ was founded and in September integrated into DGQ. There are 14 regional district groups of DGQ in the new Länder. All the west German institutions offer more or less their usual services in eastern Germany. The DQCG (Deutsche Quality Circle Gemeinschaft, German Society for Quality Circles) in 1990 organized its ninth quality circle congress as an east-west German dialogue.[19]

3.1 Education, Training, Research, Consultancy and Promotion

As mentioned above, a number of heterogenous institutions exist, which conduct training, offer services, promote research, etc. in the field of quality in different ways and with different aims. The individual structures and scope of the relevant activities of each actor will not be described at this point. Only a few examples should show the reader the heterogeneity of institutions and activities. Other important organizations will be described in the following sections, where their main activities lie and a selection of the most important institutions active in the field of quality is listed in Section 7.

In the area of further training the DGQ is the most important actor. It conducts courses and seminars on quality all over Germany. Private, commercial bodies offer courses and seminars at central and regional levels, sometimes in cooperation with the relevant chamber of industry and commerce. Their offerings are extremely varied and will not be dealt with in detail.

The AIF is an association of sector-specific research organisations. As an organization of private industry, the AIF supports joint industrial research for SMEs; it is a project administration body of special programmes of the Federal Government, an information centre for the EC COMETT (Community Programme in Education and Training for Technology) programme and acts as assistant to the 'Stiftung Industrieforschung' (Industrial Research Foundation). With regard to its financing, there is a difference between the use made of funds contributed by industry, and public funds contributed by the BMWi (see Section 4.1.1).

The content of consultations on quality performed by private business consultants, by external consultants for the RKW or by consultants of the different chambers of industry and commerce ranges from special questions, such as the introduction of particular quality assurance methods or techniques, to consultancy on total quality management (TQM). Their shares of total consultations are difficult to quantify, as generally no statistics are kept on this aspect.

The target groups of the RKW and the chambers of industry and commerce are SMEs in trade and industry. Some private business consultants offer services nationwide in the area of quality assurance, others only in some regions, some have specialized in advising specific sectors or firm sizes.

Another major player with respect to quality training and promotion is the VDI (Verband Deutscher Ingenieure, Association of German Engineers). VDI societies, which form the basic structure of the VDI at central level are usually run by honourary VDI members. Some are cross-sectoral specialist organizations dealing with practically-oriented methodology, or with scientific knowledge applicable in all areas of technology (e.g. VDI Gesellschaft Produktionstechnik); some are sector-oriented specialist organizations (e.g. VDI Gesellschaft Kunststofftechnik).[20] Accordingly, the main topics they deal with are either trans-sectoral or branch-specific. In addition there are joint committees which act as interdisciplinary steering committees for specialist issues cutting across the main centres of interest of several specialist organizations, and are thus primarily concerned with cross-sectoral and more general problems of quality assurance and optimization. This work is complemented by on-the-spot exchanges of experience by specialized working groups in the VDI 'Bezirksvereine' and 'Bezirksgruppen' (district societies and groups) which form the regional structure of the VDI.

More general aspects and measures, as well as standardization work and recommendations to the federal ministries on promotion measures, are often dealt with at a central level by joint committees of various associations and organizations. For instance, in the joint committees of the DGQ with other organizations, mentioned in Section 4.2, the main activities are discussions and the elaboration of appropriate recommendations, resulting in reports and guidelines.[21]

3.2 Certification, Accreditation, and Standards System

Standards in Germany are established centrally by the DIN.[22] Some other organizations, particularly the VDI, issue 'softer' forms of standards.[23] In principle, standardization in Germany is privately organized, although the DIN has, to some extent, taken on a 'sovereign' character, and numerous public regulations refer to DIN norms. There are several agreements with the public sector, and representatives of public bodies collaborate in the committees and working groups. The work of the DIN is 67% financed by commercial activities (sale of publications etc.), 18% by financial contributions and donations from private enterprises (including membership fees) and 15% public subsidies. However, the main burden is borne by private enterprises via the personnel costs of seconded honourary experts.

Standardization projects are generally conducted by the relevant standardization committee at the DIN, following an application. An application can be made by private persons, institutions or societies. Sometimes they are handed on to DIN via European standards organisations. Nationally valid standards for quality assurance are dealt with in the NQSZ (Normenausschuss Qualitätsmanagement, Statistik und Zertifizierung, Standards Committee for Quality Management, Statistics and Certification within DIN).

The most important aspects of standardization work in the quality field have, up until now, been:

- standardization in the area of measurement technology;
- standardization of concepts and terminology; and,

- standardization of statistical procedures.

- standardization in the area of CAQ, CAQ-modules, interfaces and data formats.[24]

Currently, much stress is put on the completion and adoption of the ISO 9000 series. There is, however, much discussion as to the direction in which further development of these standards should go, i.e. whether they should be made more sector (or product) specific or whether they should keep their general character. The last is obviously the intention of the work of the International Standards Organization Technical Committee 176 (ISO/TC 176). An example of the other approach is that of the DIN 'Normenausschuss Schweisstechnik' (the DIN Standards Committee for Welding Technology) has already delivered a draft standard for quality systems in welding.[25]

An example of an important sector-specific, or more precisely product-specific, standardization activity is the elaboration of DIN 66285 on software quality testing. This is one of many standardization projects in which the costs and organization are shared by institutions of the manufacturers concerned; in this case the Gütegemeinschaft Software e.V, which is dominated by software suppliers.

Both the quality of products and quality assurance systems can be certified. The organizations for the certification of products are very numerous, and will not be considered further within this analysis.

In Germany, there are no public institutions for the certification of quality assurance systems. The private certification organizations such as the DQS and the TÜVCERT perform this task nationwide and at an international level through collaboration with, or participation in, similar organizations. Special financial support from public bodies for the preparation and conduct of certification in firms does not as yet exist though many schemes can be used in this respect. However, the BMFT quality assurance programme now propose a kind of broadly effective promotion of the implementation of quality systems according to ISO 9000.

Under these circumstances the organization of the accreditation of certification bodies is significant. With a view to the European Single Market, an accreditation and certification system is currently being built up which should structure and coordinate the several existing bodies. It has four levels:

- DAR (Deutscher Akkreditierungs-Rat, the German Accreditation Council), will coordinate certification in Germany, represent German interests in European and international committees and implement European harmonization of certification. It is organized as a working group of the federal and the Länder (regional) government, and industry.
- National accreditation bodies are responsible for the accreditation of certification bodies and test laboratories. One of the nine existing ones deals especially with quality: the TGA (Trägergemeinschaft für Akkreditierung GmbH, representative group for accreditation) is a frame organization for the area not regulated by law. It is funded by twelve organizations representing industry, trade and the insurance business

(among which are the BDI, and the DIHK (Deutscher Industrie- und Handelskammem, German Association of the Chambers of Trade and Industry). It accredits certification bodies for quality systems and personnel.

- Accredited certification bodies confirm on request the correspondence of a product, a process or a service with a valid standard or a normative document, e.. that a quality system is in line with ISO 9001.
- Accredited test laboratories correspond to certain fixed quality requirements and can assist certification bodies. There exist public (e.g. as part of public research centres), semi-public and private ones.

The TGA has so far accredited four organizations for the certification of quality systems: the DQS, TÜVCERT, Dekra (a body competing with TÜV in the area of technical observance) and the German Lloyds. In addition, a number of foreign companies (e.g. Het Norske Veritas) operate in Germany. Currently, most certification has been undertaken by the DQS and the TÜVCERT. Both institutions were founded for the certification of quality assurance systems in accordance with DIN/ISO 9000 standard. They are competitors, and both are transnationally active.

At a national level, cooperation agreements have been made between the DQS and some of the TÜV Landesverbände (regional associations), as well as with the VDE Prüf- und Zertifizierungsinstitut (VDE Institute for Testing and Certification).[26] This is typical of the strong interconnection of the various players in the field and underlines an extended independence of regional 'branches' of national organizations.

The certification of quality assurance systems by the DQS is based on DIN/ISO 9001/9003. It should be noted that on request the DQS will test and assess the effectiveness of quality assurance systems according to other relevant norms, and prepare an audit report of the result for the enterprise.[27] There are agreements for the mutual recognition of certificates between the DQS and similar certifying organizations in other European countries. The DQS is a member of the European Network for Quality System Assessment and Certification (EQNET), within which the 14 most important national certifying organizations from 14 west European countries cooperate. The DQS collaborates worldwide with certifying organisations in the USA, Canada, South Africa, Japan, Israel and Turkey, with the aim of cooperation and future mutual recognition of certificates.

Recent statistics from TÜVCERT count 39 certified companies of which 16 are foreign. There is a concentration in metal industries.

The TÜV Nederland B.V. is wholly-owned subsidiary of the RWTÜV (Rheinisch-Westfälischer TÜV, North Rhine-Westphalia regional TÜV), and is recognized in Europe as a certifying company. Its certificates are valid in all the member countries of the European Community, and its services are also available to German firms.[28]

A purely regional certification service for quality assurance systems based on DIN 9000ff does not exist. All institutions are private. The state is only involved in certifications in areas where there is legislation (e.g. some areas of safety).

4. National Quality Schemes and Initiatives

4.1 Global Schemes

At present the only general public promotion measures in the area of quality assurance are at a national level. Important actors are individual ministries such as the BMFT and the BMWi whose promotion programmes are run nation-wide via centrally-acting project administration bodies.

Other important activities at a national level are the promotion measures of the AIF, the DFG, the FQS and the 'Volkswagen-Stiftung' (Volkswagen Foundation), which make (public) funds available for research projects in the area of quality assurance.

4.1.1 Research

The most comprehensive promotion measure in the area of quality assurance with a main focus on research is the 'Programm Qualitätssicherung' of the BMFT. This measure is intended to promote basic research, practically oriented research and cross-field cooperative projects, and technology transfer for the broad diffusion in practice of scientific knowledge on quality; it also supports the work of standardization and the establishing of norms. Cross-sectoral projects are supported, dealing with questions which range from special problems in the area of manufacture, including technology development, to the development of measures for the implementation of TQM in a firm; these projects tend to contribute especially to solving the problems of small and medium sized enterprises. A total of ECU 175 million is planned for the financing of measures by the BMFT for the period 1992-1996. Quality assurance is understood as a cross-sectoral issue. In the promotion of research groups, which is addressed especially to universities, this cross-sectoral approach is complemented by an orientation towards academic disciplines. The 'Programm Qualitätssicherung' is publicly financed by the BMFT, and run by the project administration body, Projektträger Fertigungstechnik und Qualitätssicherung (Manufacturing Technology and Quality Assurance) at the KfK-PFT (Kernforschungszentrum Karlsruhe, Karlsruhe Research Centre) and the DFG. However, not all the elements involve full public financing of each project; thus, for instance, for cooperative projects associated with the 'Programm Qualitätssicherung', a minimum 50% contribution is required from the supported participants. The main content of the programme includes:

- Strengthening of basic research:
    1. Schwerpunktprogramm 'Innovative QS in der Produktion' (focused area programme on innovative quality assurance in manufacturing) which falls a bit outside as it is managed by the DFG.
    2. 'Förderung von Forschergruppen zum Thema QS' (promotion of groups of researchers) from different institutes and universities on the following topics:

        – interaction of quality tasks with organization and shaping of work

- quality assurance in the field of logistics of manufacturing
- knowledge based systems (expert systems) in quality assurance
- quality assurance in the service sector
- quality information systems
- preventative quality assurance in process chains
- interaction of quality tasks and business administration and financial controlling

- Initiation of 'Verbundprojekte' (cooperative projects) on a national and European level. The following aspects should be addressed in cooperation between firms and research bodies in order to develop practically relevant and demand-oriented solutions for SMEs in particular:
  - quality oriented management and motivation structures
  - quality assurance solutions specific to production processes, company structures (SMEs), sectors or products
  - quality assurance with respect to changing production concepts (e.g. automation, CIM)
  - methods of quality assurance in planning, development/design and area before the production stage
  - quality systems taking particular account of the quality factors of employees and organization.

- Broadly effective application of quality expertise through technology transfer via existing scientific bodies. This activity will be prepared by a specific working group which will analyse the current state of knowledge and develop a concept for the transfer and practical application.
- Amplification of research and development related to interfaces/computer aided quality in cooperation of DIN and research bodies.

The intended target groups for the programme are: universities, research institutes, research associations, industrial firms, transfer bodies and industrial firms from any sector. Depending on the particular area and form of promotion activity, public subsidies range from 30% for private enterprises to 100% for universities and non-commercial institutes. The planned budget is given in Table 9 (page 154): figures in brackets relate to the previous 'frame concept'.

A different promotion system is used in research promotion run by private or semi-public organizations, particularly the 'Industrial Cooperative Research' programme of BMWi administered by the AIF. [29]

Table 9: Funding for the 'Programm Qualitätssicherung'

Year	Planned	Previous
1991:		(8)
1992:	13	(5)
1993:	40	(33)
1994:	50	(25)
1995:	30	(25)
Total (ECU million):	175	(104)

Source: BMFT

A precondition for support from the budget of the BMWi is proof that in an earlier period (not connected with the project in hand) the member organization of the AIF has itself made an equivalent contribution in the field of joint industrial research (in terms of money, materials, services, or the financing of research institutions in its own branch). Following a procedure of application, expertise and approval by the AIF, the BMWi will then finance the full costs of a project on recommendation of the AIF; the AIF will run the project.[30] The AIF promotion programme 'Querschnittsforschung Qualitätssicherung', which started in 1989 in agreement with the BMWi in connection with the cross-sectoral 'Initiative Qualitätssicherung', is an example of this type of support system.[31] With the promotion programme 'Querschnittsforschung Qualitätssicherung' (cross-field quality assurance research) the AIF introduced a measure which, unlike its generally 'vertical', sector-related support of joint research, is 'horizontal', i.e. cross-sectoral. This promotion of cross-sectoral research projects, financed by the BMWi, includes both organization-related and technical topics in the area of quality assurance. Work supported under the programme includes:

- Projects and studies that develop strategies for quality assurance which are oriented towards application, as an aim, including their exemplary implementation. Part of these projects can be work on necessary and recommendable organizational structures (structural and procedural organization).
- Projects that deal with the application-oriented systematology of quality assurance in the preliminary stages of production (quality planning).
- Development and further development of measurement, control and evaluation systems, as far as they are discernably components of an existing or projected quality assurance system and will be integrated there.
- Process analyses oriented towards research of the relations between process parameters and the defined product quality. The emergency of defects in order for a quality oriented process control.
- Projects on application-oriented, computer-based information systems for quality assurance.

154

- Development of new hard- and software as far as their industrial application in quality assurance systems is clearly discernable.
- Projects and studies on economic viability of quality assurance systems or modules of quality assurance systems.

The programme is targeted at all members of AIF, ie industrial research and association bodies. The size of project varies, but all receive 100% public funding. Altogether 50 applications were approved between 1989 and 1991; these received support totalling DM 21.8 million. However, a closer look at the projects shows a rather strong sector determination compared with the actual aim. Table 10, below, details the growth in number of projects and funding.

The activities of the FQS are devoted entirely to the formulation and support of practically-oriented research projects in quality assurance and improvement, and the application of their results in practice together with the DGQ. Thus it is involved in the above AIF scheme and plays an intermediate role in the BMFT scheme.

Apart from the 'Programm Qualitätssicherung', measures for the support of research tend to concentrate mainly on technology, and broadly based concepts like TQM play a subordinate role. The support of research projects for specific areas or target groups (e.g. SMEs) is sometimes inherent in the particular nature and interests of the institution providing support.

Table 10: Projects funded under the 'Programm Qualitätssicherung'

Year	Number of Projects	Funding
1989	6	1.8
1990	12	3.0
1991	32	6.6
	(million ECU)	

Source: BMFT

4.1.2 Training and Education

As the level of education is the responsibility of the individual federal Länder, measures and regulations are a matter for the Länder ministries of science or culture. However, professional associations such as the DGQ, in connection with the EOQ have taken the initiative in the formulation of education and training concepts and measures, partly due to the stimulus of recommendations from international organizations (e.g. the IAQ, the International Academy of Quality).

The topic of quality assurance does form a part (albeit a small one) of the vocational training for some jobs (e.g. jobs in industrial metal). Nationally valid teaching frameworks for vocational training, e.g. those for the metal and electrical industries are centrally laid down by the 'Ständige Konferenz der Kulturminister und-senatoren der Länder' (standing conference of the minister and senators of culture of the federal Länder).

There are two instances of measures to improve the further training situation in the area of quality in which central regulation and financing is combined with decentralized implementation by semi-public institutions. These are promotion measures of the BMWi, which are being run by the 'Ländesgruppen' (Länder groups) of the RKW in the various Länder. One is the promotion programme 'Euroworkshop' and the other is the measure MQNBL (Marketing und Qualitäts-verbesserung in den neuen Bundesländern, marketing and quality improvement in the new Federal Länder). In both programmes further training in the area of quality assurance plays a not inconsiderable role. The second measure is a regional one in the sense that, as the name indicates, it only applies to the new Federal Länder.

The aim of the support programme 'Euroworkshop' is to prepare small and medium-sized firms for the European single market. It takes the form of internal workshop-type training measures within the firm, and quality assurance is one of the important subjects covered. In the 'MQNBL' promotion programme, the RKW commissions external consultants to give consultations and carry out professional and in-service training, including the area of quality improvement

The 'Volkswagen-Stiftung has also contributed ECU 2.5 million for the promotion of quality assurance research. These promotion funds have been used as 'initial aid' and 'special provisions' for the installation and consolidation of engineering science chairs of quality assurance at two universities.

The promotion of concepts for the improvement of education is a little neglected, although the above-mentioned support by the 'Volkswagen-Stiftung' represents a first step in this direction.

As already mentioned above, there are deficits in the area of education.[32] In technical colleges and universities, the topic of quality assurance is usually incorporated into the mechanical engineering courses. A database search in Vademecum Wissenschaft listed 88 institutions which had included 'quality assurance' or 'quality management' in their own descriptions of their fields of activity. The great majority of these were engineering science institutions, and only 16 were in the area of business management. However, this information must be interpreted carefully since some of the most relevant BA chairs with respect to quality have not been listed. New chairs of quality assurance also tended to be in engineering faculties. Although it is possible in an engineering course to place emphasis on quality, up till now only one course, a correspondence course of the 'Fachhochschule Berlin' intended for in-service training, has a final exam. leading to the qualification of 'Qualitätstechniker' (quality technician) or 'Qualitätsingenieur' (quality engineer). The titles indicate different education levels. Only a few chairs of business management definitely treat questions connected with quality as a main topic. To our knowledge there is no possibility to specialize in quality in the framework of BA study courses.

A proposal by the International Academy of Quality (IAQ) for the content and organizational inclusion of the topic of quality in education given by colleges and universities is supported by the DGQ, while pointing out the necessity for adaptation to frame conditions and requirements in Germany.[33]

In Germany first steps are being taken at present in the vocational training provided by industry and commerce towards dealing with some aspects of quality assurance, mainly in the areas of manufacturing technology and testing technology. The specific content is already laid down by the teaching frameworks for the various professional orientations, mentioned earlier.

At present only two professional qualifications in this area are recognized by the state: one is 'Güteprüfer' (quality inspector), and the other is 'Qualitätstechniker' (quality technician). Training is carried out by the 'Berufsförderungswerke' (educational and re-training bodies) in cooperation with the DGQ.

The DGQ, which is the most important body with respect to training, provides a self-contained series of courses for use as in-service training. These courses are cross-sectoral, and are constructed to address target groups (e.g. skilled workers, master craftsmen, technicians, engineers and (since 1991) business managers (Betriebswirte). Participation in the courses leads to a DGQ certificate, recognized in industry as a proof of qualification. The main topic blocks dealt with are quality management, quality assurance, quality control/testing and quality technology. There are also special courses dealing with topics of contemporary interest, or devoted to the in-depth treatment of special subjects. In 1991, 419 DGQ courses took place, with a total of 10,540 participants; altogether, more than 28,000 DGQ certificates have been awarded since 1981. As well as these DGQ courses, there is also the possibility of carrying out DGQ licence courses, which is becoming increasingly popular (631 were conducted in 1991, with 13,928 participants). These licence courses are intended for closed communities in technical colleges, other training establishments and DGQ member firms. The number of participants has almost doubled between 1990 and 1991.

The DGQ continues to give sector-specific courses in cooperation with various specialist associations and institutions, e.g. Süddeutsches Kunststoff-Zentrum Würzburg (in the field of plastics), Faltschachtel-Industrie e.V. (in the field of packaging). The seminars offered by the DGQ on topics of contemporary interest in the area of quality assurance and improvement are addressed mainly to entrepreneurs and to managers responsible for quality.[34]

At a Länder level, seminars and courses are held in all the RKW 'Landesgruppen', varying in intensity, content and teaching methods; however, they do not lead to a qualification comparable to the DGQ certificate.

The 'VDI-Bildungswerk GmbH', the 'Landesgewerbeanstalt Bayern' and many similarly organized institutions also offer seminars on quality assurance; however a detailed account of every actor does not fall within the scope of this study.

In summary, it can be stated that training continues to include new areas. Thus, seminars for managers on topics such as the management and organization of quality assurance in firms in the sense of TQM are increasingly being given. However, technical subjects (e.g. CAQ) and the individual instruments and methods of quality assurance and improvement occupy the foreground.

4.1.3 Consultancy

There are no specific national schemes to promote consultancy for quality assurance though consultants play a role in the projects promoted by the 'Programm Qualitätssicherung'.

4.1.4 Promotion and Awareness

In this area it is the various organizations and associations in the semi-public and the non-profit private sectors that have taken the initiative and are most active. No broadly based actions to increase public awareness (such as the 'National Quality Campaign' in the UK for instance) have as yet been carried out by the government in Germany.

Nor, as in other countries, does the public sector in Germany award promotion prizes (such as, for example, the Malcolm Baldridge Award in the USA, which is established in law). Here also the initiative lies in private hands. Every two years the DGQ awards the 'Walter-Masing-Preis' for outstanding and important new ideas and knowledge in the area of quality and quality assurance.[35] Enterprises, especially in the automobile industry (e.g. Ford, VW), also make firm-specific awards to their suppliers.

An event of great significance in Germany was the 1990 Congress 'Initiative Qualität' arranged jointly by the AIF, the BDI, the DGQ and the RKW, which can be considered as the first effective large-scale public event of its kind, with around 1400 participants. It indicated the growing concern about the quality issue in the research, industrial and policy circles and raised general public awareness on quality as a competitive factor.

In the area of exchange of information and experience, too, it is only the associations and organizations that are active, sometimes in cooperation, at an international, national and regional level. Sometimes cooperation results in the organization of joint events, the publication of joint guidelines and recommendations, or in joint standardization work.

The DGQ plays a decisive role in public relations in Germany. It organizes, often together with other institutions, numerous conferences and congresses on the topic of quality, and issues various publications in the form of information brochures, specialist journals and specialist literature. Some associations and common interest groups such as the AIF, the RKW, the VDI, etc. and some private, commercial entities are also engaged in similar public relations activities at a national level. These nationwide activities are complemented to a varying extent by the work of individual regional branches.

In the area of public relations, both general subjects and specialized topics relating to the quality complex are covered. This applies to all the actors already mentioned above, and their conferences, congresses and publications. A few examples will serve as illustrations.

General aspects of quality assurance, rather than individual instruments of quality technology, were the subject of the 1990 biennial quality conference of the DGQ. The following main topics relating to the conference theme 'Quality as an economic factor for Europe' were considered: demands made on industry by the single European market; computer-aided quality management; the quality assurance (QA) element of profitability; the QA element of communication.

For the 1992 specialist congress 'Quality 92', which has been held annually since 1990, the following congress topics were covered: quality management, methods and processes of QA, computer aided QA, software QA, QA of services, measurement and testing technology, national and international aspects of QA, as well as research and promotion.

There are numerous other conferences and congresses devoted to more specialized aspects of individual methods and instruments of quality assurance, or to single specific areas such as measurement and testing technology.

4.2 Sectoral Schemes

There is little point in differentiating the few sectoral activities. Two field-specific promotion programmes are the support of quality assurance projects in space as a part of the 'Weltraumprogramm' (space programme) of the BMFT, and the 'Modellprogramm zur medizinischen Qualitätssicherung' (model programme for quality improvement in medicine), which is part of the 'Fachprogramm Gesundheit' (specialized health programme) of the BMG. These publicly financed promotion measures are administered by public institutions.

At the beginning of 1992 the DFG introduced a priority programme 'Innovative Qualitätssicherung in der Produktion' (innovative quality assurance in production). The BMFT is providing DM 7 million for this programme,[36] which is part of the 'Qualitätssicherung' programme and supports research projects for the manufacturing sector. These include methods of preventive quality assurance, the development of interlinked information processes, and methods for arriving at qualitatively and functionally adequate component descriptions and tolerances.[37] The content of the projects submitted by research institutions for support should generally include a system related aspect of quality assurance. However, the promotion is primarily aimed at chairs of engineering science.

The 'Modellprogramm zur medizinischen Qualitätssicherung' is a public programme, which subsidizes quality assurance projects in a certain service sector: the medical service sector. The programme has been running since 1991, with the BMG providing ECU 2 million per year. The programme is run by the DLR. Projects supported must have the development and use of quality measures as a major objective. The measures have to be developed in such a way that hospital administrations and health insurance companies can agree on them. Projects share the following characteristics:

- within the framework of top medical care (e.g. cardiac and transplant surgery);
- in particular medical disciplines;
- in different fields of care; and,
- in inter-disciplinary fields of care (e.g. hygiene, medical technology).

Sector related questions are also dealt with by the relevant 'joint interest' associations. One example among many is the series of informative publications on 'Qualitätskontrolle in der Automobilindustrie' (Quality control in the automobile industry) issued by the VDA (Verband der Automobilindustrie e.V, association of the automobile industry). Sector-specific QA topics are also handled in particular by the DGQ working groups 'Qualitätssicherung bei Lebensmitteln' (QA in food-stuffs) and 'Qualitätssicherung in der Bekleidungsindustrie' (QA in the clothing industry), and in two joint committees of the DGQ, one with the VDA on 'Quali-tätskontrolle in der Automobilindustrie' (Quality control in the automobile industry) and one on 'Elektrotechnische Konsumgüter' (electrotechnical consumer goods) jointly with the consumer goods associations of the ZVEI.

5. Regional Quality Schemes and Initiatives

5.1 Global Schemes

At 'Länder' and community level there are at present only a few public measures in the area of quality assurance and improvement. Some federal Länder and communities provide investment aid for the founding of 'quality centres'. Examples of this type of institutional promotion of these transfer centres, which are mainly active within their own regions, are the 'Steinbeis-Zentrum für Qualitätswesen' (quality centre of the Steinbeis foundation) in Gosheim and a similar one in Ulm, and the 'Qualitätszentrum Dortmund'.

Under certain conditions projects in the area of quality assurance and optimiza-tion can be supported by the responsible Länder economic ministries, within the framework of promotion programmes whose aims are broader. This can be illus-trated by one example. In the Nordrhein-Westfalen there is the 'Technologie-Pro-gramm Wirtschaft' for the support of small and medium-sized firms in particular in the development, introduction and diffusion of new technologies. There must be technological innovation, and the firm itself must have a share in development. Provided these conditions are fulfilled, products and/or processes for quality assurance and improvement can also be supported.

It is worth mentioning at this point the 'Beratung und Weiterbildung zur Verbes-serung des Produktmarketings und des Qualitätsmanagements in den neuen Bund-enländern' (consultancy and training to improve product marketing and quality management in the new federal Länder). The scheme initially running during 1991 and 1992 is intended to promote consumer goods as well as capital goods of the supply industry in the new federal Länder. The RKW (Rationalisierungs-Kurato-rium der Deutschen Wirtshaft, Rationalization Board of German Industry) argues that producers in the new federal Länder face a competitive disadvantage compared with those in the west because of deficiencies in product marketing and product-related quality management.

The budget has been provided by the BMWi (Bundesministerium für Wirtschaft, Federal Ministry of Economic Affairs). The programme is administered by the RKW and its respective Landesgruppen/Geschäftsstellen (offices) in the new federal Länder. Subsidies are provided for marketing consultancy and in-company training, as well as the creation of experience exchange groups. External consultants are commissioned by the RKW. A maximum of 15 consultation days can be promoted, an additional promotion of internal training is possible. The accepted rates are in case of consultations ECU 900, plus up to ECU 375 cost, and in-house training ECU 600, plus up to ECU 500 costs. About ECU 2.5 million has been spent on the scheme. The intended target group for the programme are SMEs producing manufactured goods exclusively in the new federal Länder.

5.1.1 Research

Several university chairs are mainly concerned with quality research. These include chairs at; Dortmund, Achen, Berlin, Hannover, Stuttgart, Erlangen, Braunschweig, Kaiserslautern, and Chemnitz.

Moreover, there are a number of research groups in several institutes of the Fraunhofer Society (e.g. at Aachen and Stuttgart). Specific regional schemes on quality research have not been identified.

5.1.2 Training and Education

There are no national or regional regulations on education in schools or universities. The universities and 'Fachhochschulen' (technical colleges) are independent in determining the content of their study courses, so that these are regulated autonomously by the relevant university or college in each case, under the supervision of Länder ministries.

The organizational structure of various actors such as the RKW, the DGQ, the VDI, etc., comprising a headquarters and relatively independent regional branches, means that further training in the topic of quality is also approached at a regional level in the form of seminars. However it must be said that the individual regional branches are not all equally active in this field.

5.1.3 Consultancy

Three main situations can be distinguished in the area of consultancy. In the first, public money flows from the relevant Länder economic ministries, within the framework of consultancy programmes, through the semi-public organisations entrusted with the running of the programmes (e.g. the RKW-Landesgruppen, the Steinbeis Foundation, the Landesgewerbeamt Bayern, and chambers of industry and commerce), almost exclusively to SMEs. These consultations are carried out in accordance with the relevant guidelines by lecturers from universities or 'Fachhochschulen' or by freelance consultants, freely chosen by the enterprises or selected from a list cultivated by the relevant institution. In a second type of situation, private enterprises can use the services of these organisations without receiving a subsidy. The third type of situation is where the consultancy originates from a commercial private organization or a private business consultant. Such consultancies may be subsidized where the type of enterprise and content of the consultation fulfils the requirements of public innovation consultancy programmes.

The TÜVs, especially the 'TÜV Rheinland', 'TÜV Stuttgart' and 'TÜV Bayern' (Bavaria), conduct consultancies on quality assurance at a regional level. The IHKs (the chambers of industry and commerce) also sometimes provide consultancy for their own members within their catchment area.

As part of the consultancy programmes of the individual federal Länder for SMEs, consultancies in the area of quality assurance can also receive support, provided they comply with the promotion guidelines. In Nordrhein-Westfalen, for instance, the share of supported innovation consultancies on quality assurance is 10% of all supported innovation consultancies.

5.1.4 Promotion and Awareness

Contact at a regional level is maintained by some regional branches of the various organizations (e.g. the DGQ 'Regionalkreise' (regional circles), the VDI 'Bezirks- vereine' and 'Bezirksgruppen' (district societies and groups), which are relatively independent in their aims, programme planning and cooperation with other organizations.

Practically oriented on-the-spot discussion with firms takes place in regional subdivisions. For instance, the work of the DGQ 'Regionalkreise' is to organize and instigate trans-firm and trans-sectoral discussion rounds.

Almost all specialist and regional subdivisions of the VDI deal with questions of quality assurance and improvement, either trans-sectoral or for specific branches of industry, depending on their main specialist orientation. However, not all subdivisions are equally active in this respect.

5.2 Sectoral schemes

Proper schemes on the regional level aimed at specific sectors do not exist. An example of promotion of quality in a particular sector is the 'Pilotprojekt Qualitäts- management in der Möbelindustrie' (pilot quality management project in the furniture industry). Details of the project are summarised in Figure 17 (page 163). Evaluation of the programme took place in the form of an accompanying research project conducted by the FOCUS-Team. The evaluation was completed in mid- 1992.

6. Overview and Outlook

The activities on quality in Germany are diverse (e.g. by actors, by type of measures and with respect to target groups). Direct, specific activities of the state do not yet play a leading role. In principle, standardisation in Germany is privately organized, although DIN has to some extent taken on a 'sovereign' character. Where federal activities are being implemented, as in the 'Qualitätssicherung' programme of the BMFT, they largely focus on research and mainly address the engineering sciences, particularly with respect to computer aided quality assurance but a view on the complete quality cycle in the research area. Recent amendments in the programme concept have strengthened the TQM and transfer element. Other important quality promoting activities are undertaken by the AIF, DFG, the FQS and the 'Volkswagen-Stiftung'. Education is the responsibility of individual Län- der. However, professional associations such as the DGQ have taken the initiative in formulating training schemes and have proposed changes in education.

Owing to the federal structure of Germany it is difficult to provide a complete overview of regional measures and their respective relevance. It does appear however, that some existing programmes have been flexible enough to allow for the support of quality oriented activities, too. This is particularly true for the public promotion of SME-oriented consultancy services. A particular problem is posed by eastern Germany for which very little up-to-date information is available.

Figure 17: Quality management in the furniture industry,1989-1991

Finance:
Ministerium für Wirtschaft, Mittelstand und Technologie in Nordrhein-Westfalen (Ministry of Economic Affairs, Medium-sized Industry and Technology of North Rhine-Westphalia)
    - ECU 225,000

Implementation:
Projectträger (programme management body): RKW-Landesgruppe NRW (RKW-state grouping/office North Rhine-Westphalia)
'Arbeitsträger' (coordination and cross-firm work performed by): FOCUS-TEAM, Wuppertal

Objectives and rationale:
Aim is to establish total quality management in selected sectors (furniture and plastics) which play a particular role in some parts of North Rhine-Westphalia

Main content and areas of support:
Support is mainly given in the form of training conducted by external consultants:
- information activities on the spot
- training of the 'Qualitätsbeauftragten' (internal quality managers) of the firms
- Six moderators per firm have been educated
- training of the management
- workshops

These activities were partly firm-specific and partly cross-firm oriented

Type of clientele/target group:
Eight medium-sized companies in the furniture and plastics sectors

Average size/share of subsidy:
DM 55,000 per firm, 50% financial subsidy for the costs of consultants

Source: MWMT, Nordshein-Westfalen

Even though most of the specific promotion programmes being implemented have yet to reach the state of broad diffusion, the general awareness of and commitment to quality related activities seems widespread. There is a growing concern for quality management and an orientation towards total quality management concepts (in addition to, and in connection with, the rapidly increasing certification to ISO 9000 standards). This can particularly be observed in the changes and growth of the DGQ and its activities as well as in the growing supply of private commercial organizations in the quality management field.

As in most European countries, apparently the automobile industry and to some extent the electrical industry play the forerunners in quality related activities. Their requirements not least urge even small suppliers to think about advanced quality systems. Another driving force is international and European competition where ISO 9000 is beginning to become a minimum requirement. The 'innovation support infrastructure' which in Germany consists of a very broad mixture of differently organized, financed, and specialized organizations has obviously already largely adapted to the growing demand for offers in the quality field. Public (but rarely state), semi-public, and private bodies both compete with and complement each other. The number of seminars, workshops, conferences etc. being offered in the area is increasing and diversifying rapidly. New institutions are being founded. This process is very much decentralized.

Compared to other industrial countries the German 'awakening' seems to have occurred rather late. But although later than other countries, Germany was probably starting from a more advanced position. Important advantages lie in a highly qualified workforce, decentralized work organization and responsibility, and the commitment to high quality ('Made in Germany') throughout the organization.

7. List of Schemes and Organizations
7.1 List of Significant Schemes

Programm Qualitätssicherung (Programme for the promotion of quality assurance)

Life of scheme: 1992-1996 (1991-1995)

objectives and rationale: Generally to strengthen the competitiveness of German industry. Specifcally, the measure aims to increase and accelerate innovation processes in the field of quality as well as strengthening the related know-how and technology transfer infrastructure.

Main content of scheme:
- Strengthening of basic research.
- Initiation of "Verbundprojekte" (cooperative projects) on a national and european level.
- Application of quality knowhow through technology transfer via existing scientific bodies.
- Identification, in cooperation with DIN and other research bodies of research needs.

Modellprogramm zur medizinischen Qualitätssicherung (model programme for quality assurance in medicine)

Life of scheme: 1991 to date.

Objectives and rationale: Promotion of model projects intended to in the long term put medical quality assurance into practice.

Main content of scheme: As a matter of priority external quality assurance projects with a model character in the fields of directly patient-related medical services in the field of out-patient and in-patient care arc to be promoted.

Querschnittsforschung Qualitätssicherung (cross-field quality assurance research)

Life of scheme: 1989, still running but with no additional funding since 1992 (other than that provided by AIF as part of its normal activities).

objectives and rationale: To promote industrial cooperative multidisiplinary research field of quality assurance.

Main content of scheme: Promotion of research projects that work on questions of quality assurance of products and processes. Besides the technical-scientific importance, the economic importance of the project for SMEs and the measures which are to be taken in order to ensure the transfer into (above all) SMEs have to be pointed out.

Beratung und Weiterbildung zur Verbesserung des Produktmarketings und des Qualitätsmanagements in den neuen Bundesländern (consultancy and training to improve product marketing and quality management in the new federal Länder)

Life of scheme: September 1991 - September 1992

Objectives and rationale: Supporting the marketing of goods from the new federal Länder.

Main content of scheme: Subsidized marketing consultancy by external consultants.

Euroworkshops

Life of scheme: 1990 to end of 1993

Objectives and rationale: To encourage firms to improve their performance in order to exploit the opportunities from the European Single Market.

Main content of scheme: Provision of information.

Qualitätsmanagement in der Mobelindustrie (quality management in the furniture industry)

Life of scheme: 1989 - 1991

Objectives and rationale: The aim is to establish total quality management in selected sectors (furniture and plastics) which play an important role in North Rhine-Westphalia.

Main content of scheme: Support is mainly given in the form of training conducted by external consultants:

7.2 List of Organizations

Name	Address	Telephone/Fax
Arbeitsgemeinschaft Industrieller Forschungsvereinigungen e.v (AIF)	Bayenthalgurtel 23 5000 Koln 51	(0221) 37 680-0
Bundesministerium für Wirtschaft (BMWI)	Heilsbachstraße 16 Postfach 14 02 60 5300 Bonn 1	(0228) 615-1
Bundesverband der Deutschen Industrie e.v (BDI)	Gustav Heinemann Ufer 84-88 5000 Koln 51	(0221) 37 08-00
Deutsche Forschungsgemeinschaft e.v (DFG)	Postfach 20 50 04 5300 Bonn 2	(0228) 885 - 1/(0228) 855 2221
Deutsche Gesellschaft für Qualität e.v. (DGQ)	August Sohanz Str. 21 A 6000 Frankfurt am Main 50	(069) 54 80 01-0
Deutsche Gesellschaft zur Zertifizierung von Qualitätssicherungssystemen mbH (DQS)	Burggrafenstraße 6 1000 Berlin 30	(030) 26 01-0
Deutscher Akkreditierungerat c/o BAM (DAR)	Unter den Eichen 87 1000 Berlin 45	(030) 8104 7421 -7400 -0910/(030) 811 99 12
Deutsches Institut für Normung e.v (DIN)	Burggrafenstraße 6 1000 Berlin 30	(030) 26 01-0
Forderkreis für Angewandle Qualitat e.v (FAQ)	Trelleborger Straße 5 0-1100 Berlin	(0037) 2-47 201 70/(0037) 2-47 210 14
Forschungsgemeinschaft Qualitätssicherung e.v (FQS)	August-Schanz Str. 21A Postfach 50 07 63 6000 Frankfurt am Main 50	(069) 54 08 01 25/(069) 54 89 91 33
Gesellschaft für Qualität und Normung in der Kammer der Technik (CQN)	Trelleborger Straße 5 0 1100 Berlin	(00372) 4 72 01 70/(00372) 4 72 10 14
Ingenieurtechnischer Verband Kammer der Technik e.v (KDT)	Clara Zetkin Straße 115-117 0 - 186 Berlin	(00372) 22 65 0/(00372) 22 65 256
Projektträgerschaft Fertigungstechnik und Qualitätssicherung (KFK - PFT)	Kernforschungazentrum Karlsruhe Postfach 36 40 7500 Karlsruhe 1	(07247) 82-5293
Rationalisierungs Kuratorium der Deutschen Wirtscaft e.v (RKW)	Düsseldorfer Str. 40 Zentrals 6236 Eschbom/Ts	(06196) 495 - 006196-303
Rheinisch Westalischer TUV (RWTUV)	Steubenstraße 53 4300 Easen 1	(0201) 825-0
Steinbeis Stiftung für Wirtachafteforderung	Haus der Wirtschaft Willi Bleicher, Str. 19 7000 Stuttgart 10	(0711) 2 29 09 0/(0711) 2 26 10 76
Steinbeis Transferzentrum Qualitätssicherung	Riewiesenweg 6 7900 Ulm	(0731 9 37 62 0/(0731) 9 37 62 62
Trägergemeinschaft für Akkreditierung GmbH (TGA)	Gustav Heinemann Ufer 84-88 5000 Koln 51 (Bayenthal)	(0221) 37 08 637/(0221) 37 08 730

Verband Deutscher Maschinen-und Anlagenbau e.v (VDMA)	Lyonar StraBe 18 Postfach 71 08 64 6000 Frankfurt 71	(069) 66 03 0/(069) 66 03 511
Verein Deutscher Ingenieure e.v (VDI)	Graf-Rocke-Str. 84 Postfach 10 11 39 4000 Dusseldorf 1	(0211) 62 14-0/(0211) - 575
Volkswagen-Stiftung	Kastanienallee 35 3000 Hannover 81	(0511) 83 81-0/(0511) -344
Zertifizierungsgemeinschaft für Qualitätssicherungssysteme des TÜVV (TÜVCERT)	Reutaratr 161 5300 Bonn 1	(0228) 2 60 98 40/(0228) 2 60 98 44
Rundesministerium für Forschung und Technology (BMFT)	Postfach 20 02 40 5300 Bonn 2	(0228) 59 - 0/(0228) 3601

References

1. The last example here is a comprehensive study on safety and quality in the space industry: Wanduch, V., Schneider, W. (1989), *Sicherheit und Qualität in der Raumfahrt*,VDI/BMFT-Studie, Dusseldorf.

2. Pfeifer, T. et al., (1990), *Untersuchung zur Qualitätssicherung. Kernforschungszentrum Karlsruhe*, KfK-PFT 155, Karlsruhe, KfK.

3. Council Resolution of 7 May 1985 (Official Journal C 136/1 of 4 June 1985) on a new approach to technical harmonization and standards.

4. Council Resolution of 21 December 1990 (Official Journal C10/1 of 16 January 1990) on a global approach to conformity assessment (which followed the communication from the Commission to the Council, COM(89) 209 final - SYN 208, Brussels, 24 July 1989, on 'a global approach to certification and testing, quality measures for industrial products').

5. Pfeifer et al., 1990.

6. E.g. AIF, (1988), 'Initiative Qualitättssicherung, Handlungsbedarf in Forschung und Entwicklung, Kö' ln; DGQ, *Memorandum zur Ausbildung im Bereich Qualitättssicherung*, Frankfurt am Main, DGQ-Schrift Nr. 10-15.

7. RKW(ed.), (1990), *Kongress Initiative Qualitat*, Eschborn, Themen & Thesen.

8. For more detailed information see following sections.

9. This indirect-specific CIM programme included CAQ though CAQ only played a minor role in promoted firm projects (see Lay, G., (1992), 'CIM-Projekte in der Bundesrepublik Deutschland: Ziele, Schwerpunkt, Vorgehensweisen'. *VDI-Z*, no. 3 1992.

10. Ibid.

11. see AIF(ed.), (1989), *Qualitätssicherung in der industriellen Praxis, Herausforderungen und Chancen*, Köln, Dokumentation der 61, Sitzung des Wissenschaftlichen Rates.

12. *Handelsblatt*, 7 August 1992

13. BDI 1992: *Qualitätssicherung in deutschen Unternehmen. Ergebnisse und Bewertunng einer Umfrage des BDI zur Nachfrage nach zertifizierten Qualitätssicherungssytemen von auslandischen Kunden*, Koln, BDI.

14. German society for the certification of quality assurance systems, founded in 1985 by the DGQ and the DIN. Other associates are the VDMA (Verband Deutscher Maschinenund Anlagenbau e.V, Association of German Mechanical Engineering); the ZVEI (Zentralverband Elektrotechnik und Elektronikindustrie, Central Association of Electrotechnical and Electronics Industry); the F+O (Verband der Deutschen Feinmechanischen und Optischen Industrie e.V., Association of German Precision Engineering and Optics Industry); the VCI (Verband der Chemischen Industrie e.V., Association of the chemical industry); and the Hauptverband der Deutschen Bauindustrie (Association of the German Construction Industry).

15. Founded in 1990 by the 'Technische Überwachungsvereine', TÜVs (Technical Supervision Associations).

16. Founded in 1989 at the instigation of the DGQ.

17. The Steinbeis foundation forms an organizational and financial framework for technology transfer bodies.

18. Budde, R. et al., (1990), *Die Regionen der funf neuen Bundesländer im Vergleich zu den anderen Regionen der Bundesrepublik*, Essen, RWI.

19. Bungard, W. et al (Hrsg), 1991: 'Menschen machen Qualtät: Deutsch-Deutscher Dialog.', Dokumentation 9. Deutscher Quality-Circle Kongreß 1990, Ludwigshafen.

20. For a more detailed overview of the specialist subdivisions of the VDI, their main fields of specilization and activity see the VDI's infomative publication *'VDI Fachgliederrungen 1991/1992.'*

21. Cf. DGQ Jahresbericht 1990, p 15.

22. For more details on DIN and the German standards system, see for instance, DIN Jahresberichte (DIN Annual Reports).

23. See for instance, VDI (ed), (1992), *VDI-Richtlinien/Handbücher. Verzeichnis aller gultigen Richtlinien und Handbücher*, Stand Februar 1992 (register of guidelines and handbooks), Düsseldorf, VDI.

24. Pfeifer, T., (1990), *Untersuchung zur Qualitätssicherung.* Karlsruhe, Kernforschungszentrum, KFK-PFT 155, p. 121.

25. Marquardt, D. et al., (1992), 'Vision 2000 - A Strategy for International Standards Implementation in the Quality Arena during the 1990s', *TQM Magazine*, London.

26. Verband Deutscher Elektro-Ingenieure (Association of German Eelectrical engineers) which is part of VDI.

27. Cf. DQS information brochure Die DQS stelt sich vor.

28. Cf. Blick durch die Wirtschaft, 26.11.1990.

28. Cf. Blick durch die Wirtschaft, 26.11.1990.

29. Cf. *BMFT Journal*, (1992), Nr. 1, p. 10.

30. The following remarks on the financing of the AIF are taken from the *AIF-Handbuch 1991*.

31. The results of the projects are published by the AIF in a research report called *Ffentlich Finanzierte Vorhaben*, or in the case of projects financed entirely from own funds of the member organisations, in a research report called *Eigenmittelfinanzierte Vorhaben*.

32. For a more detailed analysis of the education situation in quality assurance in Germany, see DGQ (1989), *Memorandum zur Ausbildung im Bereich Qualit tssicherung*, DGQ-Schrift Nr. 10-15.

33. The IAQ is an association of high-ranking experts from all over the world. The DGQ is also represented in this international organization.

34. Cf. DGQ: *Tätigkeitsbericht 1990*, DGQ-Schrift N 10-90, p 25.

35. DGQ: Ibid.

36. Cf. *BMFT Journal,* 1992, n 1, p 10.

37. Cf. DFG Ausschreibung zum Schwerpunktprogramme '*Innovative Qualitätsscicherung in der Produktion*'.

38. Cf. Pfeifer, T. (1990).

39. Cf. DGQ (1989), *Memorandum zur Ausbildung im Bereich Qualit tssicherung*. DGQ-Schrift Nr. 10-15, p.27 ff.

Greece

Nikolaos Kastrinos

1. Introduction

This section presents trends and developments in quality promotion schemes and measures in Greece. It starts by describing the factors that led to current discussions about the importance of quality in government and industry. The emergence of quality as an issue is followed by a presentation of the quality infrastructure. As the development of this infrastructure is the main aim of public policy in the field, the discussion of quality promotion measures and schemes which follows consists largely of an elaboration of the functions of the quality infrastructure.

The areas of activity covered include standardization, research, training and education, consultancy and other quality improvement promotion activities. These activities are discussed without reference to regional considerations. This is largely due to the fact that initiatives of organizations of a clearly regional character have not been found during the project. While a number of the organizations that are discussed are active at a regional level, their policies are largely centralized.

2. The Emergence of Quality as an Issue

The Greek economy is characterized by a comparatively large service sector and a predominance of small firms and traditional sectors in industry. After an industrialization period that lasted for nearly 20 years, from 1974 industry started losing ground, increasingly concentrating on low value-added, labour intensive activities. Two recent surveys of quality management practices in Greece show that only a very small number of the Greek firms perceive quality as a major issue in their competitive strategies. A 1992 survey by Mouzopoulos found a lack of appreciation of the competitive importance of quality by Greek SMEs.[1] While in general, firms employ some means to ensure the quality of their products that reach the customers, their quality management activities are very limited. EOMMEX, the Organization of SMEs and Handcrafts confirmed this picture, indicating that it has found very limited demand for consultation in quality management practices.

Also in 1992, Vitantzakis and his colleagues questioned the 400 industrial, trading and services firms in Greece, that had the largest turn over in 1989.[2] Some 131 firms responded, 11 of which were subsidiaries of multinationals. While all the respondent firms considered the quality of their products and services essential for their performance some 65% of them did not have a quality manager. A striking result was that only the 11 subsidiaries of multinationals had moved beyond statistical quality controls and were involved in TQM related programmes. Only five firms are certified to the ISO 9000 series, three by ELOT, the Greek Standards Organization and two by the BVQI (Bureau Veritas Quality International). Of these, three are subsidiaries and two are Greek transnational enterprises. This slow start however, has been followed by a number of discussions about the role of TQM in successful competitive strategies and the value of the ISO 9000 series of standards. Another 25 companies have recently applied to ELOT for ISO 9000 certification.

In the public sector, the issue of quality is currently emerging within a largely different framework. Here, the discussions are dominated by the effects of the development of the European standardization system. In this framework, however, standardization acquires a new meaning as the accredited bodies are called to certify compliance of national products to international standards and not the other way around. Thus, standardization is transformed from a means of protecting national markets to a way of accessing international markets. The efforts of the Greek public sector has focused on setting up a 'quality infrastructure' which will enable Greece to satisfy the demands of the emerging European standardization system.

3. The Quality Infrastructure

The quality infrastructure emerges largely through the re-organization of existing institutions, which were set up on an ad hoc basis when the government was faced with specific sectoral demands, in a coherent structure that would be able to satisfy the needs of the European standardization system while responding to the needs of Greek industry. The establishment of new institutions is sought wherever it is necessary.

ELOT, set up in 1976, is the organization responsible for standard specification and certification in Greece. However, its functions have been restricted by the fact that Greek firms have not been at the leading edge of technological developments. Thus, standards have not been a viable industrial policy option for Greek governments. ELOT found itself a new role with the harmonization of national standards in the European Community. The harmonization of Greek standards is specified by working groups consisting of experts from a number of organizations and functioning within the framework of ELOT. Now the quality labels of ELOT certify compliance to European standards.

The National Development Plan 1988/92 calls for an upgraded role for ELOT in the technological development effort of the country.[3] This effort consists of the establishment of a technological development infrastructure which overlaps largely with the quality infrastructure. The re-organization of the research system in 1985 set up a number of research organizations and rearranged existing ones to offer directly or indirectly services to industry. In practice a great proportion of these services was related to quality control, an activity much needed by the bulk of Greek firms which lack a suitable infrastructure.

In the mid-1980s ELOT set up four laboratories to perform its certification tests, in the sectors of low voltage electrical appliances and electronics, electric cable, toys, and plastic pipes. In performing these tests ELOT started using the services of four laboratories of other organizations, which were themselves not accredited to certify compliance with standards. This raised the issue of accreditation which represents a multifaceted policy problem. The pressure comes from a number of laboratories of the public, semi-public and private sectors that perform quality tests and wish to be accredited, as they perceive the cooperation of ELOT with external laboratories as unfair competition. A different type of pressure comes from the changing role of the Greek standardization system. A number of transnational organizations like the BVQI, being accredited by foreign national accreditation systems, operate in Greece and compete with ELOT without being accredited by the Greek government. While this issue can be resolved only in a European framework it created additional pressures for the establishment of a Greek accreditation system.

In 1989 an Accreditation Council was established comprising representatives from ELOT, MIET (The Ministry of Industry, Energy and Technology), SEB (The Federation of Greek Industries), the National Chemical Laboratory of the State, the Association of Greek Engineers, the National Technical University of Athens and one specialist appointed ad hoc from the Board of Directors of ELOT. ELOT holds the Council's Secretariat. Since its foundation the Council has been surveying the laboratories that perform quality tests. While it is estimated that some 25 laboratories comply with the requirements still no accreditation has taken place. This is attributed to functional problems such as lack of staff and flexibility necessary to establish a suitable monitoring system. The lack of a national metrology system is also considered as an impediment. The latter together with the establishment of a number of testing laboratories are being put forward to the European Union for funding under PRISMA, a programme aimed at assisting the industrial structures of the member states in preparing for the Common Market.

4. National Quality Schemes and Initiatives

While the Greek government has not engaged in any explicitly quality promoting schemes, quality improvement has *de facto* been part of various policies to promote the development and modernization of the Greek production system. Furthermore, a number of semi-public and private organizations are involved in activities with an important quality promotion content. In the presentation that follows, global and sectoral activities are distinguished in the areas of research, training and education, consultancy, quality promotion and awareness.

4.1. Global Schemes

Within the framework of Greek public policy-making, sectoral priorities are reflected on the promoted infrastructure rather than on initiatives for the development of specific industrial sectors. The distinction between global and sectoral schemes in the case of Greece can only refer to the activities of organizations performed as part of their belonging to the quality infrastructure.

4.1.1 Research

Engineering research into quality is limited to specific projects in university engineering departments. These are rare and have not been in any sense institutionalized. While the situation is similar in the management community, recently there has been some movement there, driven largely by the initiation of TQM projects by a number of Greek subsidiaries of multinational companies under instruction from their parent companies, together with the publicity TQM has acquired through the press. From this movement a quality management research community seems to have emerged in which the formulation of a Quality Association by the EEDE (Hellenic Management Association) is expected to play an important role.

4.1.2 Training and education

Although in all university engineering departments management courses form part of the curriculum, little importance is attached to quality, quality control being usually part of the statistics course. In management departments the situation is similar. Recently, however, in the University of Pieraeus a quality management course has been introduced. Such a course has also been part of the curriculum at the DEREE College, a private school of management, not recognized by the Greek government as a Higher Education Institution, but the degree of which is recognized in Britain and the US as a Bachelor in Arts.

Quality control and management is increasingly becoming the focus of extra-curricular training activities. During the early 1980s ELKEPA (Hellenic Productivity Centre) started implementing a programme of professional training seminars in a number of topics including quality management. While a number of organizations have launched professional training programmes since then, little attention has been paid to quality management. The number of these organizations has recently multiplied as management and quality management seminars become an attractive business for private consultants because of the increase of European Community funding for training seminars through the European Social Fund.

A major initiative in the field comes from EEDE, which is a member of the EFQM (European Foundation for Quality Management). EEDE is organizing high-level workshops on quality management as part of its training programmes for top management executives. Seminars on quality management have also been introduced in the programmes of the Hellenic Export Promotion Organization (HEPO). Seminar courses, which are addressed to employees of exporting firms, have taken place in a number of Greek cities across the country.

Finally, the Organization of OAED (Employment of Working Potential) administers a part of the national development programme that subsidizes training seminars in enterprises. Those are co-funded by the European Social Fund, OAED and the enterprises. Although executives of ELOT have given seminars in a number of enterprises, it is impossible to estimate the extent in which quality management was touched by this programme as there was not any separate priority attached to it and reviews of the content of the seminars do not exist.

4.1.3 Consultancy

In the public sector both EOMMEX and ELKEPA provide technical and managerial consultancy to firms. During the survey these organizations revealed that they have not faced any significant demand for quality related consultancy. One can only speculate about the reasons for this, given that quality management consultancy is increasingly becoming the field of specialty of a number of private consultancy firms.

4.1.4 Promotion and Awareness

In the field of promotion, the Law 1892/1990 'For Modernization and Development' provides for subsidies in activities, such as upgrading the information technology infrastructure of businesses, and personnel training seminars that, in principle, could support the development of quality management programmes. While the seminars managed by OAED (see above) are funded through the procedures of this law, its subsidies are outside the considerations of the quality community. Characteristically, all the interviewees, who span across the quality infrastructure and relate to virtually all the organizations that have undertaken activities with some sort of quality promotion content, including two large firms that are known for their quality improvement programmes, were not aware of any source of external funding for quality promotion activities.

In the field of awareness, the public sector has left the promotion of the importance of quality and quality management for enterprises to the training programmes referred to above. The information directorate of ELOT is promoting awareness of standards in Greek industries, in a reactive however, fashion. It has developed a data-base accessible on-line including:

- a directory of Greek standards (ELSTAND)
- a directory of Greek technical regulations (ELTEREG),
- a directory of equivalent international, European and national standards (ICONE),
- a directory of announcements of technical standards and regulations in EC and EFTA member states (INFOPRO),
- a directory of technical terms (ELROOT), and
- a directory of technical abbreviations.

The scheme operates through subscriptions. Subscribed persons and organizations are sent all documents published by ELOT, including bulletins with the information contained in the data base. Furthermore, subscribed organizations can use other services provided by ELOT in reduced prices. Although the charges are marginal (in the range of ECU 50), only some 70 organizations from both the public and the private sector have subscribed.

In the private sector, one scheme specifically oriented towards quality awareness was initiated by SEB (the Federation of Greek Industries). SEB, which is also a member of EFQM, launched a campaign called '1991, A Year of Quality for the Greek Industry'. The campaign included the organization of workshops, seminars and conferences on TQM. EEDE was also actively involved in the campaign. It also organized a conference on TQM sponsored by the Japanese firm Toyota. TQM received a lot of publicity during the campaign. As part of the campaign SEB institutionalized two awards for academic and technical press publications related to quality management.

4.2 Sectoral Schemes

4.2.1 Education and Training

ELKEDE, the Hellenic Leather Centre, was set up in the mid 1980s by EOMMEX to provide technological services to firms in the leather sector. It developed quickly into an organization which provides all kinds of technical and organizational assistance, including foreign market forecasts, organization of international demonstration projects and the establishment of a footwear school. This footwear school that provides courses, amongst other things, in quality control, was established in 1989 and has been welcomed by the industry.

4.2.2 Promotion and Awareness

The Greek Aluminium Association has been very active in promoting quality awareness and quality control in its members. During the 1980s it established its own quality labels 'Qualanod' and 'Qualicoat' in cooperation with Euras and Eurocoat, two European associations for quality standards in the sector.

5. Regional Schemes and Initiatives

No regional schemes and initiatives were found.

6. Conclusions and Outlook

Quality improvement is currently an emerging issue in Greece. The discussions are focusing on the development and adaptation of the Greek infrastructure to the demands of the European Community standardization system and on the promotion of TQM amongst Greek firms. The former discussion involves the promotion of an infrastructure that would be able to satisfy the needs of industry in quality control testing and standard certification and refers to developments in the public sector. The latter is enclosed within a relatively small community of subsidiaries of multinationals and large Greek firms.

While a number of developments have taken place at both levels, the quality community in Greece is still small, and the bulk of Greek firms are characterized by a lack of awareness about the importance of quality in competitive performance. It is hoped that an increasing number of institutions and organizations will take part in the 'quality' discussions, widening thus the quality community and diffusing further the quality management practices that will increase the competitiveness of Greek firms.

7 List of Schemes and Organizations,
7.1 List of Schemes

The only action in the form of a scheme that was identified during the project was the campaign: '1991: A Year of Quality for the Greek Industry'

Responsible organization: Federation of Greek Industries (SEB)

Objective and Rationale: To intensify the information flows and the awareness of enterprises and to make the contribution, to their knowledge, which is necessary to implement the new strategies of 'Total Quality' in order to satisfy their customers.

Content:

- Inauguration Ceremony for the 'Year of Quality'
    - This concentrated on the directors of a number of Greek companies in order to promote awareness of Total Quality Management to the top management of Greek enterprises.

- Special Seminar of the Principles and Methods of TQM
    - This seminar was addressed to production or quality managers.

- Ceremony 'Total Quality: A Lever for the Development of Greek Enterprise'
    - The ceremony was intended to promote the importance of TQM.

- Conference 'Principles and importance of Total Quality for every enterprise'
    - The conference was addressed to small firms.

- European Conference 'Quality without Limits'
    - Funded by the Commission of the EC and a number of Greek firms the conference was attended by specialists from Europe and Greece.

- Establishment of two awards, one for academic work, another for technical press publications related to Total Quality.
    - The aim is to stimulate the introduction of quality research in the Greek academic community and its coverage in the technical press.

Target Population: Enterprises

Budget: ECU 130,000 in 1991

Follow on: Activities are continuing. They are complemented by:

- Initiation of research activities into quality management practices in Greece and the other European Union countries.
- High Level Training Seminars in TQM
- Short scholarships to people from industry and academia
- Set up of a network on total quality related subjects.

7.2 List of Organizations

Name	Address	Telephone/Fax
Ministry of Industry	Messogeion 14-78 11510 Athens Greece,	
Hellenic Organisation for Standardisation (ELOT)	Aharnon 313 GR 11145 Athens Greece	30-1-2015025/30-1-5241371
Federation of Hellenic Industries (SEB)	Xenofondos 5a GR-10557 Athens Greece	30-1-3237325-9
Hellenic Management Association (EEDE)	Syggrou Av. 196 & Harokopou 2, GR-17671 Kalithea, Athens Greece	30-1-9373870-5
Hellenic Productivity Centre (ELKEPA)	Kapodistriou 28, GR-10682 Athens Greece	30-1-3600411-7
Hellenic Export Promotion Organisation (HEPO)	Marinou Antipa 86-88 & Agiou Nikolaou, GR-16346 Ilioupolis, Athens, Greece	30-1-9950591
Organization of SMEs and Handicrafts (EOMMEX)	Xenias 16 11528 Athens Greece,	
Organization of Employment of Working Potential (OAED)	Thrakis 8 Kalamaki Athens Greece,	
Greek Aluminium Association	Kipillou Lonkareos 25-27 11475 Athens Greece,	
Helenic Leather Centre (ELKEDE)	Thiseos 7a 17676 Kallithea Greece,	

References

1. Mouzopoulos N. (1992), 'Quality Award and Small-Medium Enterprises', Paper presented in the 3rd European Conference for Education, Training and Research. Rome 9-10 April.

2. Vitantzakis N. et al (1992), *Definition, Measurement and Improvement of Quality in Greek Enterprises*, mimeo, Technical College of Athens.

3. Ministry of National Economy (1987), *National Development Plan 1988-1992*, Athens.

Ireland

Brendan Barker

1. Introduction

The Irish economy is highly dependent on exports. Irish manufacturing industry employs 300,000 people, while the service sector (the largest sector of the workforce) employs more than 625,000 people. Quality has long been recognized as important within the country's manufacturing sector. Increasingly, it is also being seen as important by the service sector as well.

2. The Emergence of Quality as an Issue

In a recent survey of Irish businesses, 81 % of respondents regarded improved quality of service as the key to competitive success. Yet the survey also revealed that only 50 % of Irish companies have service performance standards.

The Irish Quality Control Association was founded in May 1969 (it later became the Irish Quality Association (IQA)). In September 1980, a 'National Strategy for Quality' was prepared by the then Chief Executive of the IQA.[1] In January 1990, the IQA published the document 'Quality Strategy for the 1990s'.[2] The purpose of the document was to identify the means by which quality was to be improved in Irish manufacturing and service industries in the 1990s.

For many Irish companies with large export markets (particularly into the UK) it is essential to their commercial survival that they achieve certification to ISO 9000. With moves to the Single Market based on the harmonization of the various registration processes in Europe, it is likely that this trend will gather pace.

2.1 Diffusion of Quality

The importance of quality is being increasingly understood throughout Irish industry. According to Brian Hoy, head of certification and inspection with the NSAI (National Standards Authority of Ireland), Ireland has the second highest number of companies registered to ISO 9000 in Europe. To date, more than 600 companies are listed in the NSAI National Register of Certified Products and Companies and many others are at an advanced stage in the assessment process. The last two years have seen a four-fold increase in the number of firms registered to ISO 9000 (see Figure 18, page 184). Such growth has been driven by a 'ripple effect':

> *first the bigger or more progressive companies have achieved registration, and then their main subcontractors and suppliers have*

183

followed suit. ISO 9000 is now the norm for companies bidding overseas and in the Irish market.[3]

Figure 18: Growth in ISO 9000 rgistrations by NSAI

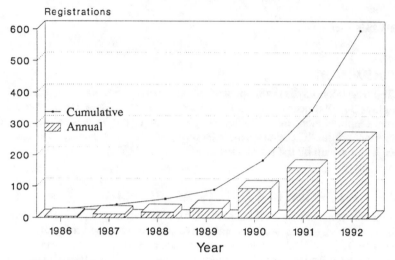

Source: EOLAS

The growth in ISO 9000 registrations in 1990 by sector of industry is shown in Table 11.

Table 11: Growth in ISO 9000 Registrations by Sector of Industry

Sector	Percentage Increase in Registrations in 1990
Mechanical Engineering	29%
Print and Packaging	26%
Electrical/Electroincs	22%
Food	12%
Others	10%

Source: EOLAS

3. The Quality Infrastructure

The National Standards Authority of Ireland (NSAI) is the country's regulatory agency. It is a Division of EOLAS, the Irish Science and Technology Agency. The NSAI is a member of the International Standards Organization (ISO).

ISO 9000 certification is performed by the NSAI. A company registered to ISO 9000 standard is included on the National Register of Certified Products and Companies, maintained by NSAI. It can take a company from three months to four years to organise an ISO 9000 application, depending on company size and quality awareness. Once certification has been applied for, assessment follows within eight to ten weeks. The time needed for pre-licensing assessment depends on company size, but the average is about four days. The application fee for ISO 9000 is I£350 and pre-registration inspection costs I£320 per day plus expenses. Once a quality system has been certified, it costs about I£1,500 annually in registration and surveillance fees to maintain it. The NSAI carries out regular, unannounced assessments three or four times a year.

The NSAI has expanded in recent years to cope with growing demand for its services. As well as processing applications, a staff of 30 organises workshops for companies applying for ISO 9000. 22 workshops were organised in 1991. In addition to specific workshops for the engineering and food processing industries, the NSAI intends to offer workshops specifically for the service and software industries.

The Irish Science and Technology Agency, EOLAS, is the key national body providing developmental and technical support services to the Irish manufacturing and service sectors.

The Irish Quality Association (IQA) is a voluntary, non-profit-making organization first established in 1969 to promote the general concept of quality. The IQA is a national organization with 2000 corporate members and is entirely dependent on members' subscriptions. It publishes *Quality News*, which includes a current awareness service of quality activity in Ireland, Britain and throughout the world by scanning major national and international quality publications. There is also a reference library, a video rental service and a large number of training courses in all aspects of quality. The Irish Quality Association keeps a directory of quality management consultants.

Other organisations involved in the area include:

- IDA (Industrial Development Authority)
- CII (Confederation of Irish Industries)
- ICTU (Irish Congress of Trade Unions)
- FAS (Training and Employment Authority)

For instance, the IDA increasingly takes into account a company's approach to quality when assessing it for assistance. According to Kieran McGowan, managing director of the IDA:

> *Quality is a central strategic issue for Irish industry with a direct bearing on competitiveness, growth and ultimately on job creation.*[4]

The increasing demand for ISO 9000 certification has spawned a sizeable quality consultancy and training sector in Ireland.

4. National Quality Schemes and Initiatives
4.1 Global Schemes and Initiatives

The 1980 IQA document, 'National Strategy for Quality' contained the seeds of many of the present activities of the Association. For instance, considerable emphasis was put on:

- education and training in quality;
- the development of the 'Quality Mark' scheme;
- quality award schemes;
- in-company campaigns for quality;
- quality circles;
- product liability; and
- quality in the services industry.

EOLAS, the Irish Science and Technology Agency, provides several key national support measures to manufacturing and service industries in the field of quality. The measures undertaken by EOLAS (in contrast to NSAI which deals with the quality systems registration and product certification schemes in Ireland) are broad-based strategic developmental initiatives. In order to fully appreciate the significance of the EOLAS quality measures it is necessary to realise that at the time ISO 9000 was issued in 1987, the expertise and awareness in quality management within SMEs and private consultancy practice was considerably lower than it is today.[5]

EOLAS, through its Manufacturing Consultancy Service, set about redressing this deficiency. That the initiatives taken have been successful, is evidenced by the fact that in 1992 approximately 570 Irish companies were registered to ISO 9000 and a considerable number of private quality consultants currently operate in Ireland, indicating the increased level of market demand. The majority of these consultants are 'home grown' through the practical knowledge gained while working in companies currently holding or acquiring ISO 9000 registration.

The national quality measures provided by EOLAS includes:

- quality awareness and training
- graduate placement
- consultancy support

4.1.1 Quality Awareness

EOLAS, through its Manufacturing Consultancy Service, provides in-company and external quality awareness and training programmes which are primarily directed towards the improvement of quality management in industry. The programme includes:

- ISO 9000 quality management systems
- TQM
- quality documentation
- vendor selection and assessment
- internal quality auditing
- quality improvement tools and techniques
- quality module for master of industrial engineering (MIE) degree at University College, Dublin.

The IQA has been responsible for the establishment of a 'Quality Mark'. This is awarded on the basis of a rigorous audit of a company's quality assurance programme. By the end of 1991, 252 firms had the IQA's Quality Mark.[6]

The IQA National Quality Awards were introduced to promote and encourage quality improvement in commercial, industrial and corporate organizations. The awards are presented annually to companies who have demonstrated continuous improvements in quality in a given year. There are eight regional awards and a special Service Quality Award, from which one Supreme award winner is chosen. The selection of award winners is supervized by the Irish Quality Association Approvals Board which consists of the Chief Executive of the IQA as Chairman, and representatives of the CII (Confederation of Irish Industries), FAS (Training and Employment Authority), Irish Congress of Trade Unions, NSAI (National Standards Authority of Ireland), and Shannon Development.

4.1.2 Education and Training

A range of courses are taught in educational establishments. Courses lead to the following certificates:

- Certificate in Elementary Quality Control
- Certificate in Quality Control
- Certificate in Quality Management
- Diploma in Quality Management
- Quality Assurance Degree course
- Post Graduate Diploma in Quality Assurance.

Figure 19 on page 188, lists the institutions offering courses in quality leading to the above qualifications.

Education and training has been a major focus of the IQA's activities. The association has recognized the importance of inculcating quality culture into children when young. In cooperation with school book authorities 'Quality and Hygiene' board games are available for children in the 8 to 12 age range. 120,000 games were distributed in 1990. The IQA also sponsors a national quality poster campaign in the country's secondary schools. The aim of this competition is to promote awareness of quality issues amongst school children.

Figure 19: Courses in Quality

	Certificate in Elementary QC	Certificate in QC Management	Certificate in Quality	National Diploma in QC(PG)	Diploma in Quality Assurance
Athlone Regional Technical College	-	Yes	Yes	-	-
Carlow Regional Technical College	-	Yes	Yes	-	-
Cork Regional Technical College	-	Yes	Yes	-	-
Dundalk Regional Technical College	-	Yes	Yes	-	-
Dublin School of Management Studies, Raime	Yes	Yes	Yes	-	-
Trinity College, Dublin	-	-	-	-	Yes
Galway Regional Technical College	-	Yes	Yes	-	-
University College, Galway	-	-	-	-	Yes
Letterkenny Regional Technical College	-	Yes	-	-	-
Limerick National Institute for Higher Education	-	Yes	Yes	-	-
Sligo Regional Technical College	-	Yes	Yes	Yes	-
Tralee Regional Technical College	-	Yes	Yes	-	-
Waterford Regional Technical College	-	Yes	Yes	-	-

Source: IQA

The IQA has developed links with third-level colleges and universities and an Education and Training Approvals Board has been established. The prime function of this board is to validate courses from education institutions, training establishments and industry. This involves evaluating course syllabuses, approving exam structures and contents and issuing certificates for successful candidates.

The IQA supports a range of national and regional training programmes. Up to 60 evening meetings and lectures are held yearly under its auspices. A Certificate in Management of Quality Control has been established at five third-level colleges, a two-year full-time National Diploma in technology-quality control, and a one-year post-graduate Diploma in Quality Assurance is also available at other third-level establishments. The Quality Assurance Auditor Training is the only indigenous auditor training course which has been specifically developed to meet the needs of Irish industry and services. The course is recognized by the Management Board of the Lead Assessor Registration Scheme, administered by the Institute of Quality Assurance in the UK.[8]

In 1992, approximately 30 Quality Awareness and Training Workshops were carried out by the EOLAS Manufacturing Consultancy Service.

A Total Quality Control open learning programme has been developed by the Training and Employment Authority, FAS. This is aimed at owner/managers of small firms who cannot afford the time to attend courses on quality control, but have identified a need for Quality improvement in their firm.

4.1.3 Consultancy Support

The EOLAS Manufacturing Service provides both 'hands-on' quality consultancy and financial support to assist SMEs to upgrade their quality systems. Financial assistance with quality consultancy costs is provided through the medium of the Technology Audit Programme.

Consultancy is provided by an experienced team of EOLAS quality consultants. The model, developed by EOLAS for the installation of quality management systems in SMEs to the requirements of ISO 9000, is now widely used by most private quality consultants in Ireland.

EOLAS typically provides quality consultancy assistance to approximately 40 SMEs annually. Such consultancy is not exclusively confined to manufacturing SMEs but also includes service companies, which to date include laundry, shipping agents, courier service, hotels, consulting engineers, public utilities and financial services. Indeed the services sector is seen as the major growth area for quality improvement initiatives.

It is also worth mentioning that EOLAS, through its Graduate Placement Programme, subsidizes the placement of graduates in SMEs for a period of one year to undertake quality improvement programmes. Typically, these programmes could involve the installation of a quality management system to the requirements of ISO 9000. Training and consultancy assistance is provided to the graduate throughout the programme by the Manufacturing Consultancy Service Consultants. Fifty graduates were placed on quality programmes in SMEs in 1992.

4.2 Sectoral Schemes and Initiatives

To meet the needs of service companies for quality management certification, the Irish Quality Association has devised a Quality Mark scheme for service companies. The scheme is based on various national and international precedents such as the draft International Standard ISO 10004 Quality Systems, Guide to Quality Management for Services, and the Irish Standard IS 305; the system used in the US for the Malcolm Baldridge National Quality Award, and the IQA's long experience of quality auditing of manufacturing companies.

Whereas it has proved difficult to promote quality assurance approach within the construction industry in the UK, the opposite has been true for Ireland. Irish construction companies with a weak home market are necessarily very international in outlook. They became aware of the certification trend in the UK and demanded a similar approach in Ireland. The Construction Industry Federation took on the role. It is currently the 'only accredited organisation in Ireland'.

Whereas in the UK the CQA persuaded consultants and contractors to demand certification to force construction companies to adopt quality standards, this was not the case in Ireland where the large construction companies took the lead.

5. Regional Quality Schemes and Initiatives

In addition to the meetings arranged by the IQA, it is also responsible for 15 to 20 short courses run in various locations throughout the country.

6. Conclusions and Outlook

The importance of quality is being increasingly understood throughout Irish industry. According to Brian Hoy, head of certification and inspection with the NSAI, Ireland has the second highest number of companies registered to ISO 9000 in Europe. In future, more service companies are likely to apply for ISO 9000. There will also be further harmonization of the various registration processes in Europe. From 1994, ISO 9000 registration will be a prerequisite for product certification.

6.1 Future

The IQA 'Quality Strategy for the 1990s' identified the means by which quality was to be improved in Irish manufacturing and service industries in the 1990s. It focused on a number of new initiatives in education and training and support for quality awards and other promotional activities.

7. List of Organizations

Name	Address	Telephone/Fax
EOLAS	Glasnevin Dublin 9	+ 35 31 370 101/+35 31 379 620
Irish Quality Association	Strand Road Dublin	+ 35 31 269 5255/+ 35 31 269 5820
Construction Industry Federation	Federation House Canal Street Dublin 6	+ 35 31 977 487

References

1. IQA (September 1980), *A National Strategy for Quality*, Dublin, IQA.

2. IQA (August 1990), *A Quality Strategy for the 1990s*, Dublin, IQA.

3. EOLAS (November 1991), 'ISO 9000 Quality Management', Supplement to *Technology Ireland*, Dublin, EOLAS.

4. Ibid.

5. Ibid.

6. Communication from John Murphy, EOLAS.

7. John A. Murphy (1991), *Quality Achievements in Ireland*, mimeo, Dublin, IQA.

8. Ibid.

Italy

Nicola De Liso

1. Introduction

The relevance of issues related to quality in the Italian economy is now recognized by many firms, civil servants, and politicians. Of course, such recognition does not guarantee that the issue itself is being successfully addressed. In terms of quality promotion activities, the Italian government and Parliament have, until recently, been relatively passive, leaving to the private sector the task of adapting to standards of production, as well as the task of fixing standards and quality levels to be met. The situation has recently been partly reversed because of pressures coming from international regulations on the one hand, and competition in markets on the other.

2. The Emergence of Quality as an Issue

A few points concerning quality in the private sector should be emphasized at this point. First, it is necessary to draw a distinction between small and medium-sized firms and big companies. The Italian productive system is characterized by the presence of a number of large companies, like FIAT and Olivetti, which began to tackle the issue of quality relatively early on. FIAT, in particular, started to make use of Quality Teams in production in the mid-1980s, at about the same time it also launched a total quality' campaign. Furthermore, in addition to performing research and development related to quality in its own laboratories, FIAT also cooperates with other research institutions. These activities have had at least two positive effects:

- indirectly, in diffusing awareness of quality-issues at a national level; and,
- directly, in obliging FIAT's suppliers to meet the quality needs of FIAT itself.

Small and medium-sized firms, on the other hand, tend to lag behind in terms of awareness of the importance of quality improvements. Among the reasons for this different attitude are likely to be the much lower level of resources available for research and development, and the different exposure to international competition. In an economic context in which interrelatedness, safety, environmental issues and consumer behaviour are more and more intertwined, small firms producing goods according to required *minimum* standards may be increasingly penalized. Moreover, in many cases the degree of competition found in markets seems to be a good indicator of the quality of goods: the greater the level of competition, the higher the quality of goods.

Second, even taking into account this dichotomy between SMEs and large companies, it is also apparent that the private sector has been more active than the public sector in perceiving the importance of quality. Associations of manufacturers, at both the regional and national level, have sponsored meetings on quality related topics. Typically, the public sector has not been very active, although there are exceptions, particularly when we consider regional schemes sponsored by local authorities.

Third, and here we come to the role of government, the introduction of standards, quality assurance schemes, and certification schemes have been characterized by different routes. These have included safety regulations, mandatory standards, delegation to technical bodies and committees of certification etc. (dicussed in more detail below).

Finally, it is nearly impossible to talk about national schemes without referring to the international context. In the field of quality, in particular, sometimes it is not even sufficient to refer to the European Community area. In a world of growing economic interrelatedness quality standards are becoming increasingly global.

In general terms, there was a delay before the issue of quality *per se* was tackled by the government. While this might not necessarily constitute a problem in a context in which harmonization at the European level is actively pursued via supranational legislation, it does pose difficulties where this legislation takes into account national peculiarities and recognizes national bodies already in existence.

The perception of quality related issues has stimulated a series of initiatives, preceded by case studies. Assolombarda, the manufacturers' association of Lombardy, has recently promoted a study on the application of the principles of quality management within its member firms.[1] Questionnaires were also sent to firms in two other regions, Apulia and Marche.

3. The Quality Infrastructure

As already noted, the Italian situation is still fluid. A national unifying' law does not yet exist, but parliament is working on a bill which will lead to the creation of of an Italian certification system ISIC (Istituzione del Sistema Italiano di Certificazione, Institution of the Italian Certification System). This law will take into account both national and the supranational regulations and those relevant bodies which already exist. Indeed, the Italian scene is already characterized by a series of bodies which create, accredit and certify quality standards, and quality assurance schemes.

Before reviewing the functions of the most important bodies, it will be useful to review some of the routes through which quality enters the productive system:

- The first route is that of safety regulations. In this case ministries, or delegated bodies, fix standards. This constitutes one of the oldest ways of influencing the characteristics of products as well as of processes of production. The influences still exerted by these kinds of regulations should not be disregarded or underestimated.
- A second route is that of national mandatory standards and technical rules, not necessarily referring to safety related aspects, also established by public bodies.

- A third route is that of the official recognition of some body, technically competent and industrially representative, delegated by the government to deal with quality issues in specific sectors. An example is the IGQ (Istituto di Garanzia della Qualita dei Prodotti Siderurgici, Institute for the Quality Assurance of Steel Products), created in 1985, which certifies 60% of Italian steel production.
- A fourth route is the one of supranational legislation affecting quality. Here the relevance of European Community membership is fully apparent.

The system is becoming more and more complex, and some form of coordination is obviously needed.

Among the bodies concerned with quality, carrying on various functions, from quality standard setting to official participation in international bodies, UNI (Ente Nazionale Italiano di Unificazione, Italian Standards Institute) is the most important. UNI was founded in 1921 and was first given official recognition in 1930. It was restructured in 1954 and given new legal status in 1955. UNI is a free association with membership from companies, public institutions, research institutes, and representatives of various ministries (individuals may also join it). It covers all of the productive fields except for the electrotechnical, which is covered by the CEI (Comitato Elettrotecnico Italiano, Italian Electrotechnical Committee). Representatives of ministries, the General Assembly, associated technical bodies, CNR (Consiglio Nazionale delle Ricerche, National Research Council), CEI, and Commissione Centrale Tecnica (Central Technical Commission) are members of the Directing Committee.

UNI's main aims are to create standards, to promote harmonization of Italian industry with European and world legislation and to diffuse the culture of quality at a national level. This last point needs to be emphasized. In fact, UNI stresses a culture of quality that goes beyond its purely statutory responsibilities. In promoting TQM it is attempting to overcome a culture of in which the meeting of minimum standards required to produce and trade commodities is the norm.

Although UNI is undoubtedly important, it is necessary to highlight the fact that though growing fast, members of UNI amounted, in 1990, to only 3080, indicating that quality is still perceived as an important issue by a limited number of companies. Furthermore, the fact that 69% of members are concentrated in Northern Italy must be considered disappointing.

UNI's budget for the year 1990 was over ECU 7 million; 40% of this funding came from the publishing and norms diffusion activities, and another 20% came from membership fees. The CNR is responsible for the payment of expenses related to the participation in supernational bodies.

Other bodies which contribute to quality infrastructure are the metrological institute G. Colonnetti' and the electrotechnical institute G. Ferraris' both of the CNR and both based in Turin, and ENEA (Ente per le Nuove Tecnologie l'Energia, Organisation for New Energy Technologies), a research organisation concerned with new technologies, nuclear and alternative power sources and the environment and which is based in Rome. These bodies are by and large financed by government agencies.

Since 1979 these three 'primary' institutes have recognized a series of other secondary' laboratories, which now constitute SIT (Servizio di Taratura in Italia,

Italian Testing Service) carrying out, the accrediting function with respect to metrological and calibration laboratories.

SIT already has links with the Western European Calibration Cooperation (WECC) which by the end of 1990 numbered nine signatory European countries, including Italy. Member countries are Denmark, Finland, France, Germany, Netherlands, Sweden, Switzerland, and the United Kingdom. This is a multilateral agreement whose central point is the reciprocal recognition of national certification. By the end of October 1991 SIT had accredited 55 centres.

Other relevant bodies operating at a national scale, concerned with accreditation and certification, are SINAL (Sistema Nazionale per l'Accreditamento di Laboratori, National System for the Accreditation of Laboratories), SINCERT (Sistema Nazionale per l'Accreditamento degli Organismi di Certificazione, National System for the Accreditation of Certification Organizations), and AICQ-SICEV (Associazione Italiana per la Qualita' - Sistema di Certificazione dei Valutatori, Italian Quality Association - Certification System).

SINAL was founded in 1988 following an agreement between UNI and CEI, under the auspices of the Ministry of Industry, the CNRl, the ENEA, and the Chambers of Commerce. Its role consists of the accreditation of testing laboratories, ensuring that they comply with all of the required specifications. It also carries out a number of other tasks, the publication of a directory of accredited laboratories, participation in international activities, and the diffusion of knowledge. It participated in the creation of the Western European Laboratory Accreditation Cooperation (WELAC), the basis for which was proposed at a meeting in Amsterdam in 1989. SINAL accredited 20 laboratories during 1991.[2]

SINCERT is also the result of an agreement between UNI and CEI, with the active participation of the Ministry of Industry, the National Research Council, and the ENEA. Its function is the accreditation of certification bodies by means of appropriate methodologies. SINCERT accredited five certification bodies during 1991.

AICQ-SICEV was created in 1989 following an agreement between AICQ on the one hand, and UNI and CEI on the other. This organisation certifies quality inspectors'.

The role played by AICQ alone in promoting the culture of quality must be mentioned. AICQ is a non-profit organization founded in 1955 whose main aim has always been the promotion of total quality management. Being characterized by a relatively long existence, it has accumulated a valuable patronage in terms of the gathering of information and data, and also of relationships established with firms, research organizations and ministries. Moreover, since 1956 AICQ is a full member of the European Organization for Quality. It has been organized on a federal basis since 1982, and Territorial Associations' nearly cover all the Italian territory. Enrolment dues and financial help obtained through cooperation with public bodies constitute the main sources of income for the organization.

Finally, it must be emphasized that either implicitly or explicitly a consultancy activity is always carried out by all of the organizations mentioned in the preceding sections.

4. National Quality Schemes and Initiatives

It is too soon to talk about systematic schemes and initiatives promoted by the government as the situation is still fluid. However, as we have seen, there are many organizations and institutions actively working in the field of quality, and the public sector is playing a relevant role in all of the bodies considered in the previous section.

The year 1990 was declared the Year of Quality', under the auspices of the Presidency of the Council of Ministers (Presidenza del Consiglio dei Ministri), and this fact in itself testifies to the attention devoted to quality issues. Despite recognition of the importance of quality to the production system and the economy a unifying law still has to be passed by Parliament.

However, specific areas have been covered by *ad hoc* legislative measures. An example is a 1988 Act covering producers' responsibilities for the products and services they produce. These kinds of measures have come to cover, at least in part, the area of quality.

Research and development activity is carried out in a series of both private and public organizations which are in some cases already connected, often by participating in joint projects or because they are member of UNI.

The problem is that not enough time has passed to allow for the creation of established networks, and governmental coordination seems to be more an *ex post* activity, rather than an *ex ante* form of planning. This, however, does not necessarily represent a problem in a context characterized by supranational legislation and a private sector ready to catch the opportunities.

As far as training and education activities are concerned, they have been carried out in engineering faculties and polytechnics. In the academic year 1991-92 the engineering department of the Polytechnic of Milan, for instance, offered three courses concerned with quality, one very specific (Quality in Production of Machinery), and two more general (Industrial Management of Quality and Reliability, Quality Control and Maintenance).

The problem here is that there is often too much emphasis on processes and tangible products, while services are largely ignored (although it is true that some methodologies can be applied to services).

Short fee paying courses (four weeks), covering TQM are periodically organised by AICQ. These courses explicitly take into account services. These courses are organised so that it is possible for participants to be officially recognised as quality inspectors/assessors' at the European level in the near future. Other *ad hoc* courses of one or two days duration are also organized, often by regional associations.

Consultancy, and promotion and awareness initiatives are carried out by UNI and associated members, SIT and AICQ. The media mainly used are seminars, conferences, booklets, specialized journals, and books. National conferences are particularly relevant as, given a situation in which the structure is not yet settled, they constitute the occasion to tackle the most important problems and to give rise to actual initiatives to solve the problems themselves.

Specialized journals are regularly published, examples being the quarterly review *Qualita*, and *L'Impresa*. In addition, themes related to quality have entered other journals concerned with industrial policy and economics.[3] Finally other publications are made available to help entrepreneurs to understand and implement quality principles and regulations.[4]

National and regional bodies, as well as regional associations for quality, usually with the financial help of central or local authorities, are organising a rapidly increasing number of initiatives, covering different aspects and particular sectors. Typical are courses run by the Associazione Piemontese per la Qualita and the Associazione Appulo-Lucana per la Qualita.

Sectoral studies are also carried out. The automotive sector is the most studied and active, given the presence of FIAT. Teams are also carrying out research concerning the aerospace, food, chemical and building sectors. These studies, with the exception of the automotive sector, still represent the beginning of a process, the opening of a first path.

5. Regional quality schemes and initiatives

Regional schemes in the field of quality tend to concentrate on small and medium-sized firms. At least four reasons, three 'technical' and one legal, are behind this choice:

- often, big firms and companies have both the financial and human resources to improve and update their products and processes;
- local authorities have limited resources, they cannot hope to support quality improvement in an industry as a whole, even when concentrated in the relevant region;
- small firms generally need help at many levels, not only in financial terms, but also in terms of knowledge; and,
- regional authorities are not allowed to tackle large-scale planning, even at regional level, such as to include any industry as a whole. Such an activity is the responsibility of national authorities.

Having clarified the role played by regional authorities, we have to note that at the moment only three regions, namely Lombardy, Veneto and Piedmont, have implemented policies explicitly concerning quality. Another region, Emilia-Romagna has its regional law waiting to be implemented. Finally also Apulia, a southern region, has started a series of awareness activities and will soon tackle the issue of quality.

It must be noted that there occurs a north-south divide, with northern industrialized regions leading in the field: in fact the regions in which laws concerning quality exist are all located in northern Italy.

In what follows all the comments related to laws and policies must be interpreted in a regional context. In all cases, policies are directed to small and medium-sized firms.

5.1 Lombardy

Situated in northern Italy, Lombardy is one of the richest regions of the country and is highly developed from an industrial point of view.

The Lombard region started its stimulation policy in 1981 by means of a regional law (Regional Law number 33/1981) which concerned the (re)location of industrial and artisan sites. A second law was passed in 1985 (Regional Law number 34/1985) directed to promote innovation within the system of small firms. Finally, a third law, explicitly concerning *quality* was passed in 1990. This is the Legge Regionale 10 maggio 1990, no. 41 concerning Interventi regionali per lo sviluppo dei sistemi di qualita', i.e. Regional Law of 10 May 1990, number 41, on 'Regional interventions for the development of quality systems'.

In this case, particularly with respect to the first indicated law, the original impetus came from the regional public authorities, and not from the enterprises. Moreover, this law precedes national attempts to tackle the same topic, and makes implicit reference to the European norms EN 29000.

The law provides grants of up to ECU 65,000 for firms that intend to develop reliability and quality of their processes and products. The contribution covers the following phases: the realization of the 'quality manual', which has a firm-product specificity; the actual implementation of the 'rules' written in the manual; and the attainment of quality certification by recognized bodies. The regional authorities also offer their help, via laboratories, statistics department, and other useful sources, throughout these phases.

All of the applications are examined by the CESTEC (Centro Lombardo per lo Sviluppo Tecnologico delle Piccole e Medie Imprese, Lombardy Centre for New Technologies in Small and Medium-sized Enterprises) enlarged to two more competent representatives indicated by the associations of manufacturers and artisans. There of course exists an *ex post* form of control exerted by CESTEC itself. In case the firm has not satisfied all of the requirements CESTEC can recommend the partial or total revocation of the grant.

These kinds of intervention have a double benefit: improvements tend to be concentrated in a relatively short amount of time; and imitation of good practice occurs.

To conclude this subsection let us recall a few figures. The regional authorities appropriated ECU 7.5 million for the years 1990 and 1991 for boosting quality projects in the context of the regional law above indicated. The number of applications has been increasing exponentially during the last year. Up to September 1992 about 400 firms had submitted quality-related projects. Of these, 280 projects had been accepted by the region, bearing in mind that acceptance does not automatically mean financial support. The number of projects fully completed and financed was around 45.

Given the success of the law (the number of accepted projects was limited to 280 because of the lack of funds) the region is likely to appropriate some ECU 5 million more for the year 1992.

5.2 Piedmont

Piedmont, located in north-west Italy, implemented its first systematic regional industrial policies in 1986 by means of the Regional Law no. 56 on regional interventions to promote and diffuse technological innovation among small and medium-sized firms (up to 300 employees). The original law aimed at the promotion of innovation with particular reference to new products, services and new techniques of production devoted to improve productive processes as well as increase productivity. This law was improved and updated in July 1991 in such a way as to explicitly include quality as a key objective of regional policies. In an explanatory note the financing of quality related projects is seen as a strategic component to boost the productive system, so that proposals taking total quality management as the final objective are given priority.

The procedure that firms must follow to obtain subsidized loans is characterized by two phases, one technical and one financial. The proposals are submitted to a Technical Committee which is composed of one representative of the regional authorities, one of the financing institutions and a 'technician', such as a member of Turin Polytechnic. When in doubt whether to grant a loan or not the committee can ask extra advice to members of relevant Institutes of the National Research Council or to members of the University, as well as of the Polytechnic. The proposals submitted cannot have a time span of more than three years.

The structure of loans guarantees a reasonably low rate of interest. The loan, in fact, is composed of two halves, the first coming from a regional fund, the second coming from a consortium of 15 banks operating with the regional authorities. On the half granted by the regional fund the annual percentage rate is a symbolic 1%, while the rate of interest charged by the banks is always the prime rate (12% in 1991). A single firm can apply for loans up to ECU 188,000 where half of it is always supplied by the regional fund because quality related projects are given priority.

Once the technical committee agrees to grant a specific proposal the loan must be allocated according to specific rules, i.e. percentages, to buy and cover specific needs. The distribution of the expenditure is as follows:

- up to 40% to gather information as well as to buy specific software, and devices devoted to test and monitor quality of production;
- up to 45% to pay for external consultants to realize quality programmes, testing, technical advice, and so on;
- up to 10% to (re)train staff on quality issues; and finally,
- up to 5% can be allocated to general expenditures.

Information on specific quality promotion activities since the last modification of the law in July 1991 are not, as yet, available. It is possible, however, to discuss what has happened in general since the law was pased in 1986. These past experiences should provide a good indication of what is likely to happen in the near future. Out of a total of 324 applications between 1987 and 1991, 175 projects have either been financed or are in the process of being financed for a total expenditure of nearly ECU 37 million, 12 million of which has come from the regional fund.

Of the industries which have applied for loans, nearly 44 % belong to the mechanical engineering sector, 12 % to information science, 9 % to electronics, 5 % to the textile sector, 5 % to the chemical industry, with a number of other sectors having smaller percentages. The average number of employees of these firms was 36 people.

Finally, it is worth noting that 70 % of the firms having obtained a loan are from the Turin district.

5.3 Emilia-Romagna

Emilia-Romagna, also situated in northern Italy, passed its regional law on quality in 1992 (Regional Law no. 37). ECU 3.3 were initially budgeted, and the indications are that the funding available may be increased.

The law will be fully operative by 1993. Grants cover the phases of information gathering up to ECU 18,500, payments to consultants up to ECU 6,300, implementation of quality systems (hardware, software, etc.) up to ECU 43,700, and finally up to 31,000 ECU for certification.

However, the issue of quality was first tackled a number of years previously. In particular, three institutions operating with regional authorities, namely CERMET (Centro Regionale di Recerca, Regional Research Centre), ERVET (Ente Regionale per la Valorizzazione del Territorio, Regional Organization for Quality) and ASTER (Agenzia per lo Sviluppo Tecnologico, Agency for New Technologies) since 1989 have initiated awareness and consultancy activities. Within these institutions all the relevant actors, from entrepreneurs to the Chambers of Commerce, are represented.

Three conferences were organized by ERVET in September 1990, September 1991 and June 1992 to illustrate to the participants the principles of TQM as well as the need to harmonize production to European quality standards.

CERMET in particular, a regional laboratory accredited by SINAL and SIN-CERT, since 1989 has promoted quality in Emilia-Romagna by means of:

- awareness;
- consultancy and training;
- implementation of pilot projects;
- technology transfer;
- laboratory qualification.

Many firms have thus begun and implemented actions to obtain certification and the right to make use of the quality logo since 1989. At least 100 firms are on their way to being certified despite the fact that specific funding was not made available, at the time, by either central or local authorities.

In many cases certification seems to have been a condition *sine qua non* to have orders; a clear sign of the fact that demand can represent one of the most effective ways of diffusing quality awareness and related activities (ie. of the need to keep up with the latest technologies and techniques of production to survive in highly selective markets).

5.4 Veneto

A different approach was chosen by the north-eastern region of Veneto. In this case the regional authorities approved a sort of general framework, 'Progetto Qualita' (Quality Project), in which lines of intervention were suggested and sketched. The project was discussed and approved in December 1989. The reasons that lie behind this project are explicitly recalled in the preface of the project itself, and are the need to compete on a European scale, the producers' responsibility and the need for small and medium-sized companies to keep up with large companies.

The framework proposed covers broad lines in such a way as to avoid rigidities, and collaboration with the regional small manufacturers' and artisans' associations is explicitly mentioned as a key requirement.

The regional authorities have offered to coordinate, implement and sponsor one or more phases through which the process related to quality improvement must progress. The first steps are awareness and information. It seems that too many small firms do not perceive clearly the relevance of European laws concerning standards and certification. These actions thus make clear that there is no alternative to quality, and supply and diffuse the methodologies pertaining to quality itself. Training and education constitute the second step, ranging from activities like on-the-job training to theoretical courses, at a different level, concerned with quality methodologies and techniques. The project also covers consultancy and accreditation activities.

Among the instruments to implement the policies related to quality, these regional authorities have suggested to strengthen, i.e. appropriate extra funding for, regional laws already existing, some dating back to 1978, on training, education, innovation, and so on. In this way a simplification, rather than a complication in the system should be achieved. Moreover, given the complexity of institutions and regulations already existing at regional, national and international level, an interface activity is explicitly mentioned.

6. Overview and Outlook

The Italian situation is characterized by the presence of relevant organizations whose main activity is to deal with quality in all of its aspects. As we have seen there are institutes and institutions which have a relatively long tradition. The area is thus, from the organizational point of view, already reasonably covered.

As we have seen in some regions, regional laws have already been passed and are operative, and the issue of quality is felt as an important factor of success and growth.

Impetus towards the development of these structures in recent years has come from the growth of a specific interest in TQM engendered by supranational and national legislation, and from R&D activity performed by multinationals and by consumer demand.

All the relevant institutional actors (by which we mean civil servants, manufacturers associations, public and private research bodies, and, in part, firms) are aware of the existence of this 'new' part of the system that must be taken into account.

Though structured in this way, the diffusion of TQM methodologies in the Italian economy is poor, and the *rate* of diffusion is not as high as it should be.

The situation is disappointing when we observe that, once again, there is a north-south divide, with northern firms being more sensitive and leading the field.

Finally, there seems to be too much emphasis on industrial processes of production and on tangible goods with not enough emphasis on the services sector.

Though characterized by some difficulties the Italian quality system has all the premises needed to catch up with its international competitors. Should the distance between Italy and her competitors increase, entrepreneurs would bear the greatest burden of responsibility.

7. List of schemes and organizations
7.1 Quality Schemes

Regional Laws on Quality are already operative in the following regions:

- Lombardy
- Piedmont
- Veneto.

Another region, Emilia-Romagna, has already passed a law concerning quality. The law will be operative by the end of 1992. These laws concern small and medium-sized firms.

Many initiatives related to diffusion of knowledge and sensibilization are carried out mainly by UNI and AICQ.

7.2 Organizations

Name	Address	Telephone/Fax
AICQ - Associazione Italiana per la Qualita	Piazza Diaz 2 20121 Milano	39 02 72003460/39 02 72023085
AICQ-SICEV	Piazza Diaz, 2 20121 Milano	02 72023476
AIPnD - Associazione Italiana Prove non Distruttive	Via A. Foresti 5 25126 Brescia	030 3122762/030 391716
ASTER - Agenzia per lo Sviluppo Technologico	dell' Emilia Romagna Via S. Felice 26 40122 Bologna	051 236242/051 227803
Bureai Veritas QI Italia	Viale Monza, 265 20126 Milano	02 2552441/02 2552980
CEI Comitato Electtotecnico Italiano	Viale Monza 259 20126 Milano	02 257731/02 25773210
CPnD Centro Italiano Coordinamento per Prove non Distruttive	Piazza Diaz, 2 20121 Milano	02 8646418
CERMET Centro Regionale di Ricerca Consulenza Technologica	Via A. Moro, 20-26 40068 S. Lazzaro di Savena Bologna	051 6257570/051 625 7650
CERTIAGRO	Piazza della Repubblica 2 20121 Milano	
CERTICHIM c/o UNICHIM	Piazza Morandi, 2 20121 Milano	02 76004788/02 784236
CERTITEX c/o Federtessile	Viale Sarca, 223 20126 Milano	02 66104012/02 66104012
CESTEC Centro Lombardo per lo Svilupo Technologico e Produttivo delle Piccole e Medie Imprese	via G. Gozzi 1/A 20129 Milano	

CISQ Certificazione Italiana per i Sistemi di Qualita	Milano	
CIT - Consorzio Innovazione Tecnologica Brescia	Brescia	
CNMR - Centro Nazionale Materiali di Riferimento	CSM via di Castel Romano 100-102 00129 Roma	
CNR Instituto di Metrologia "G. Colonnetti"	Strada delle Cacce, 73 10135 Torino	001 39771/011 346761
DET NORSKE VERITAS Certificazione Italia	Srl Viale Colleoni, 21 20041 Agrate Brianza Milano	039 651 1478/039 650161
ENEA Ente per le Nuove Tecnologi, L'Energia e L'Ambiente	Area Ambiente CRE Casaccia CP. P. 2400 00100 Roma	06 30483555/06 30483558
ERVET Ente Regionale per la Valorizzazione del Territorio	Via Morgagni 6 40122 Bologna	051 230567/051 222353
GISI Gruppo Imprese Strumentazione Italia	Via Comerio, 5 20100 Milano	
ICEV Instituto Certificazione Verniciatura	Via Imbriani, 10 20158 Milano	02 3761227/02 3764796
ICIM Instituto di Certificazione Industriale per la Meccanica	Via Giardino 4 20123 Milano	02 72131/02 861306
ICQM Istituto Certificazione Marchio di Qualita' per manufatti in calcestruzzo	Via Zanella 36 20133 Milano	02 7380426/02 7490140
IGQ Istituto di Garanzia della Qualita' dei Prodotti Siderurgici	Piazza Velasca 8 20122 Milano	02 870651/02 8057815
IIP Istituto Italiano dei Plastici	Via M.A. Colonna, 12 20149 Milano	02 3313624/02 3314930
IIS Istituto Italiano della Saldatura	Lungobisagno Istria, 15 16141 Genova	010 853111/010 867780
IMQ Istituto Italiano del Marchio di Qualita'	Via Quintiliano 43 20138 Milano	02 50731/02 5073271
ORSA	Torino	
QUALIFIT	Via Ramazzini, 2 20129 Milano	02 29401364/02 29401847
QUALITAL Associazione di Certificazione Industriale dell' Alluminio	Via Biroli, 1/b 28100 Novara	0321 477572/0321 476464
RINA Registro Italiano Navale	Via Corsica, 12 16128 Genova	010 53851/010 591877
SINAL Sistema Nazionale Accreditamento Laboratori	Via Campania 31 00187 Roma	06 4871141/06 4814563
SINCERT Sistema Nazionale Accreditamento degli Organismi di Certificazione	Via Battistotti Sassi 11 20133 Milano	
SIT Sistema Italiano di Taratura	c/o CNR Istituto di Metrologia "G. Colonnetti", Strada delle Cacce 73 10135 Torino	

TECNOPOLIS - CSATA	Strada Provinciale Casamassima Km. 3 70010 Valenzano Bari	080 8770111/080 6951868
UNAVIA	Via Turati, 10/bis 10128 Torino	011 599201/011 599201
UNI Ente Nazionale Italiano di Unificazione	Via Battistotti Sassi, 11 20133 Milano	02 700241/02 70105992

NB: this list is neither exhaustive, nor official; for full information contact UNI and/or AICQ.

References

1. ASSOLOMBARDA (1991), *Qualita' nell'Impresa*, proceedings of the conference, Milan: Assolombarda.

2. Unificazione e Certificazione (1992), Vol. XXXVI, no. 1, January.

3. *Economia e Politica Industriale* (1990), 67, pp. 5-151, and 68, 7-66.

4. UNI-Ente Nazionale Italiano di Unificazione (1991), *Sistemi Qualita'. Linee Guida per l'Applicazione nel settore Meccanico della Norma UNI-EN 29002*, Milan: UNI.

Other References

Albanesi R. *et al.* (1990), 'Obiettivo Qualita', *L'Impresa*, 4, 69-90.

ASSOLOMBARDA (1990), *Come Cambia il Rapporto Fornitore- Cliente*, proceedings of the conference, Milan: Assolombarda.

Department of Trade and Industry (1982), *Standards, Quality, and International Competitiveness*, London: HMSO.

Economist, The (1992), 'Where Total Quality Management Fails', Vol. 323, no. 7755, 85-86.

Elias G. (1991), *La Regolamentazione del Mercato Unico Europeo dopo il 31 Dicembre 1992*, Milano: UNI.

Fink M. (1992), *Corso di formazione "Esperto Gestione Qualita'" presso Eurosportello - L'Informazione della CEE per le Imprese*, Naples, February, mimeo.

Macdonald, J. and Piggott, J. (1990), *Global Quality. The New Management Culture*, London: Mercury.

Mattana, G. (1990), *Qualita', Affidabilita', Certificazione*, Milano: F. Angeli.

Nicolas, F. (1988), *Common Standards for Enterprises*, Brussels: Official Publications of the EC.

Qualita' - Rivista Trimestrale dell'AICQ, various issues.

Regione Emilia-Romagna (1992), *Legge Regionale 3 settembre 1992 n. 37*, (Regional Law on quality in workshops, small and medium-sized firms).

Regione Lombardia (1990), *Interventi Regionali nel Settore Industriale*, Milano, Regione Lombardia.

Regione Lombardia (1990), *Legge Regionale 10 maggio 1990 n. 41*, (Regional Law on incentives of quality in small firms).

Regione Piemonte (1986, 1991), *Legge Regionale 1 dicembre 1986 n. 56*, (Regional Law on interventions to promote and diffuse innovation in small- and medium-sized firms), modified 2 July 1991.

Regione Veneto (1989), *Progetto Qualita'*, Venice, 22 December 1989.

Secchi, C. and Alessandrini S. (1990), *Affidabilita', Qualita' e Certificazione dei Prodotti*, Roma: SIPI.

SINAL-SIT (1991), *Repertorio dei Laboratori di Prova Accreditati e dei Centri di Taratura in Italia*, no. 1, November.

Taylor F. W. (1911), *Principles of Scientific Management*, reprinted in Taylor F. W. (1947), *Scientific Management*, New York: Harper.

UNI-Ente Nazionale Italiano di Unificazione (1990), *Relazione Annuale*, Milano: UNI.

UNI-Ente Nazionale Italiano di Unificazione (1992), *Catalogo UNI 1992*, Milano: UNI.

Luxembourg

Jean-Jacques Chanaron

1. Introduction

In surface, economic, and population terms, Luxembourg is the smallest of the EC countries. In 1991, the Luxembourg GDP was ECU 9.8 billion. The country covers 2586 km² and in 1992, its population was 395,000. GDP per capita was third (following Denmark and Germany) in Europe at ECU 18,400. Luxembourg's economy is in reasonably good shape. In 1990, the unemployment rate was less than 1.7% of the working population, the annual inflation rate was 2.6% and the GDP grew by 3% on the previous year. Industry exports around 95% of its total output and the balance of trade is strongly positive: ECU 2.9 billion in 1991 (30% as a percentage of GDP).

2. The Emergence of Quality as an Issue

In Luxembourg, there is no national quality scheme or initiative. A working group including representatives from the Ministry of Economic Affairs, the Ministry of Transport, the Ministry of Energy, the Ministry of Employment and the Ministry of the Environment, is currently carrying out a survey in order to set up an official 'Quality Bill'. The purpose of such an act will be to prepare the national administration so that it is able to apply European Commission recommendations on product quality (CE label) and international quality assurance standards (the ISO 9000 series).

3. The Quality Infrastructure

In Luxembourg, there are no national standardization and certification bodies but there are several bodies dealing with sectoral product and process quality control:

- within the Ministry of Transport, the National Service for Automobile Technical Control is dealing with automobile component certification;
- within the Department of Roads and Bridges (Ponts et Chaussées), there is the National Laboratory for the Control and Testing of Building Materials;
- within the Tax Administration there is a National Bureau for Metrology;
- within the Labour and Mines Inspectorate of the Ministry of Labour there is a division concerned with the safety (in working conditions) of industrial devices and equipment.

4. National Schemes and Initiatives

4.1 Standardization and Certification

In Luxembourg, there is neither a standardization office nor an accredited certification body. No testing laboratory or auditing company has been granted ISO 10011 certification. Some private French or German testing and product quality control companies have a representative office in Luxembourg but they need to improve both their organization, and their staff in order to satisfy the ISO 10011 audit requirements.

For product certification, there are some national testing or control units such as the National Laboratory for Control and Test of Building Materials, the National Bureau for Metrology, the Labour and Mines Inspectorate and the National Service for Automobile Technical Control.

In other cases, companies are advised to contact relevant French or German accredited bodies. Thus the Department of Energy has accredited the German TÜV (Köln branch) for low voltage electric devices (although this structure is not accredited in Germany).

Similarly, since companies in Luxembourg export more than 95% of their output, they are advised, when looking for quality assurance certification, to contact internationally recognized and nationally accredited certification bodies (such as the BSI in the United Kingdom, AFAQ in France and DIN in Germany).

Under a law published in April 1991, the Ministry of Employment has certified eight units responsible for audit, test and control for safety in classified plants:

- three are from Luxembourg: LUXCONTROL, LABORLUX and SECOLUX;
- two are based in France: BUREAU VERITAS (Metz) and APAVE ALSACIENNE (Mulhouse);
- two are from Belgium: AIB-VINCOTTE (Brussels) and TECHNICA CONSULTING ENGINEERS (Brussels);
- one is from Germany: TUV-RHEINLAND (Treves branch).

They are all supposed to reach the ISO 10011 standards for auditing consultants.

5. Regional quality schemes and initiatives

Given the small size of the country, there are no regional schemes and initiatives.

6. Overview and Outlook

In Luxembourg, there are no national standardization and certification bodies but there are several bodies dealing with sectoral product and process quality control. Similarly, there are no public quality schemes or initiatives. As already mentioned a working group including representatives from the Ministry of Economic Affairs, the Ministry of Transport, the Ministry of Energy, the Ministry of Employment and the Ministry of the Environment, is currently carrying out a survey in order to set up an official 'Quality Bill'. The purpose of such an act will be to prepare the national administration to be able the apply EEC recommendations about product quality (CE label) and international quality assurance standards (ISO 9000 series).

7. List of Organizations

Name	Address	Telephone/Fax
Ministère de L'Economie	Service de l'Industrie	352-478-1/352 460 448
Inspection du Travail et des Mines	BP 127 26 rue Sainte Zithe 2010 Luxembourg	352 49921 - 2106/352 491447

Reference

Ministère du Travail (1991), 'Règlement ministeriel concernant l'intervention d'organismes agréés dans les établissements classes', *Journal Officiel du Grand-Duche du Luxembourg*, 2 avril 1991.

The Netherlands

Paul Kunst, Jos Lemmink and Ruth Prins

1. Introduction

This chapter describes public activities and measures in the field of quality assurance and management in the Netherlands. In addition to reviewing activities at the national level, a number of significant schemes at the regional level are discussed.

2. The Emergence of Quality as an Issue

In the 1970s, there was growing awareness in the Netherlands that the increased penetration of Japanese products in the European market was, at least partially, due to the attention Japanese companies devoted to the quality of their products. In 1976, the first concerns regarding 'quality' were expressed. In a memorandum, 'Selective Growth 1976', the Ministry of Economic Affairs argued that improved quality control was a necessary prerequisite for the international competitiveness of Dutch businesses.[1] This marked the starting point of a number of governmental support schemes. The first programme was initiated in 1978 at a sectorial level, followed by programmes with a broader exposure and other target groups.

From 1978, quality improvement has been an essential topic in the industrial policy of the Ministry of Economic Affairs.

Although the emphasis of quality policy shifted during the years, the introduction of quality, quality awareness, quality infrastructure and quality training have always been a focus. There are two distinct phases in the development of the quality promotion initiatives. These will be dealt with in turn.

2.1 1978-1987: The Quality Plan

In 1978, the first national programme in the field of quality, the 'Quality Plan', was initiated and supported by the Ministry of Economic Affairs. Quality control, quality assurance and the development of a structure for certification were emphasized. The following activities were undertaken as part of the Quality Plan:

- the introduction of quality systems in five industries; the graphic, packaging, shoe, furniture and precision engineering industries. The programme concentrated on quality costs studies and testing to norms of quality assurance. Three hundred companies participated in this experiment;

211

- the realization of the Dutch series of standards for quality assurance systems by the NNI (Nederlands Normalisatie Instituut, Dutch Standards Institute);[2]
- the preparation of training materials by KDI (Stichting Kwaliteitsdienst, Quality Foundation);[3] and,
- the establishment of an umbrella certification organization, the Raad voor de Certificatie (Council for Certification).[4]

The results of the programme were evaluated by the Quality Plan Advisory Group ('Adviesgroep Kwaliteitsplan') in 1982. It concluded that the improvement of quality policy should be considered an important condition in reinforcing the economic structure in the Netherlands with respect to international competitiveness. The group proposed to the Minister of Economic Affairs that a 'Quality Policy' steering group ('Kwaliteitsbeleid') be established in order to stimulate quality management in Dutch businesses. At about the same time, an advisory committee to the Ministry of Economic Affairs, 'the Wagner Committee' (which was considering the progress of industrial policy) recommended flexibility, productivity and quality as important elements of government industrial policy.[5] On the basis of the advice given by the different advisory groups, the Minister of Economic Affairs decided in 1984 to stimulate the introduction of quality management in Dutch business. Thus quality promotion activities were extended to include quality management.

The programme 'Quality Management' ('Kwaliteitszorg') was conducted between 1984 and 1987. The emphasis of this programme was clearly put on awareness and the development of the knowledge infrastructure. The programme was supported by a large national advertising campaign costing about ECU 650,000. In addition, 20 regional information meetings were organized which were visited by 4,000 persons. The aim of these meetings was to inform participants about quality and to answer their questions in this respect. However, the meetings seemed to evoke more questions than answers. In summary, the main items of the programme were:

- awareness;
- infrastructural facilities (certification, normalization, education);
- support of quality projects in collaborating industries; and,
- the purchasing policy of the government itself which paid more attention to the quality of suppliers.

The target groups of the programme were all industries, including those in the commercial service sector. Thirty projects were carried out and about 1000 companies were given information about the programme. The programme activities were coordinated by the Ministry of Economic Affairs in conjunction with 'NEHEM' (Nederlandse Herstructererings Maatschappij, Netherlands Restructuring Company).[6] NEHEM was responsible for project management while the Quality Policy steering group provided support and advice with respect to programme content. Programme realization costs were primarily carried by the business community. The government provided financial support to encourage companies to develop activities in the field of quality and to create a support infrastructure. The estimated government support in the period 1978 to 1987 was about ECU 4.8 million (see Table 12, below).[7] About ECU 1.6 million was used for awareness and information activities; a large number of advertisements, brochures, videotapes and periodicals were developed and distributed to inform businesses about quality. About ECU 2.6 million was spent on collaboration projects involving small and medium-sized companies in the field of quality improvement. A further ECU 600,000 was invested in research in order to create and improve the knowledge infrastructure.

Table 12: Governmental expenditures on quality programmes in the period 1984 to 1987

Activity	Amount (ECU million)
Information/awareness activities	1.6
Collaboration projects	2.6
Research	0.6
total*	4.8

* Excluding operation costs of NEHEM

Source: Evaluation report 'The Netherlands: time for quality!'

In 1988, an evaluation report, 'The Netherlands: time for quality!' ('Nederland: hoogste tijd voor kwaliteit!'), was published with the results and recommendations for the period 1988-1990.[8] The main conclusion of the advisory group was:

Reviewing the matter as a whole, one can determine that much has been started in the last three years, but a lot of work still needs to be done. Quality still has too little momentum in the Netherlands to continue by itself or at the necessary pace. As an extra consideration, it may count that large-scale quality schemes have also been set up in nearly all surrounding countries because in these countries quality is also considered an essential weapon in the future.[9]

In summary, the advisory group argued that the promotion of quality should be continued in order to introduce quality on a permanent basis in Dutch businesses. The advisory group advised that the Minister of Economic Affairs continue its quality policy by means of a total programme aimed at awareness, infrastructure, education and demonstration projects.

2.2 1988 to 1994: Quality and Logistics

In 1988, a new national programme for the period 1988 to 1991 was launched by the Ministry of Economic Affairs, called 'Quality and Logistics' ('Kwaliteit en Logistiek'). This programme was a conscious continuation following on from the conclusions of the evaluation report 'The Netherlands: time for quality!' already discussed.[10] A budget of ECU 14.7 million was made available by the Ministry for a range of activities. Quality management and logistic management were combined for reasons of efficiency; some similarity being seen in the effect which both have upon the behaviour of firms. However, in practice, it was difficult to combine the two in individual projects and therefore a clear distinction in quality and logistic activities resulted. Of the 90 projects, about 20 were directed to logistics and 40 to 50 to quality (it being difficult to assign the remaining projects specifically to one or other of the areas).

In 1991, the programme was evaluated and prolonged for two more years until 1993.[11] As part of the evaluation a questionnaire was answered by 500 representative Dutch businesses. They were asked questions on their activities and plans concerning quality management and responses were entered into a computer model which compared actual answers with normative ones. The model classified every company in one of four phases of quality management. Although quality awareness had considerably increased (see Section 4, Table 15, page 224), Total Quality Management was applied or fully developed in only 1% of all businesses (see Table 13, below). This seems to be disappointing. More than 80% of the interviewees acknowledged the importance of TQM and are preparing or executing plans and projects. However, even though companies are willing to apply TQM, considerable barriers apparently exist to their doing so.

Table 13: Quality management in Dutch businesses

Phase	Percentage
0. no quality activities	16
1. a first start to put things in order	78
2. internal control, application of instruments	5
3. external orientation, adapt to market needs	1
sample size 500	

Source: Progress report 'Kwaliteit en Logistiek' 1991

The phases of quality are based on a combination of classification schemes developed by the ROA (Raad van Organisatie-Advuesbureaus, Council of Management Consultancies) and by the consultants McKinsey.

3. The Quality Infrastructure
3.1 Quality Organizations

NNI (Nederlands Normalisatie Instituut, Dutch Standards Institute)
The NNI is the national organization responsible for the establishment of standards. The NNI board has its standardization projects delegated to committees. These committees execute standardization activities in specific sectors - construction, chemistry, agriculture and food, environment etc.

Currently, the NNI is being reorganized. This reorganization will change the nature of the institute from one that assists in the establishment of norms on demand (of the government, companies etc.) to a service institute that actively provides information to the business community and supports the initiation and implementation of European norms.

KDI (Stichting Kwaliteitsdienst, Quality Foundation)
KDI works with Dutch manufacturing and service industries to:

* improve quality awareness;
* distribute knowledge and methodology of total quality management; and,
* promote practical application of quality management.

KDI is by far the largest training institute in the field of quality. In addition to training courses, KDI organizes conferences and gives support and advice with respect to the implementation of quality systems in companies. For the non-industrial sector, KDI has developed the KOAF programme ('Quality on all fronts') and the VSOP programme ('Improve Service and Supporting Processes') Since 1957 KDI has represented the Dutch government and organizations in the Council of the European Organization for Quality (EOQ). KDI fulfils an important function in the international quality network.

In 1992, under the national programme Quality and Logistics (see section 4.1), KDI opened a Documentation and Information Centre (DIC). The aim of this centre is to be a national 'one-stop shop' (knowledge centre) for all documentation and information in the field of total quality management.

NVK (Nederlandse Vereniging voor Kwaliteit, Dutch Association for Quality Management)
NVK was originally an association of companies in the mechanical and electro-mechanical industries formed with the intention of supporting affiliated companies in their attempts to introduce and implement quality management systems. Nowadays the association covers the entire industrial and transport sectors. Specifically, NVK promotes also the interests of certification bodies.

MANS (Vereniging Management en Arbeid Nieuwe Stijl, New Style Management Association)
MANS aims to stimulate the Dutch business community to improve the quality of its products, production processes, services and of its labour organization. (MANS has also become the name of the principles developed by the organization

215

itself). MANS organizes orientation days with respect to its philosophy. MANS consultants support companies with the introduction of quality systems.

EFQM/NL (European Foundation for Quality Management/Netherlands)
The EFQM/NL group is the Dutch department of the European Foundation for Quality Management. The group is becoming increasingly important in the quality infrastructure with respect to the promotion of quality as the fundamental process for continuous improvement within companies.

IMK (Instituut Midden en Kleinbedrijf, Institute for Small and Medium-sized Companies)
IMK was established in 1967 by the Ministry of Economic Affairs and SME organisations with a dual purpose: on the one hand, knowledge transfer to SMEs; and on the other, the improvement of the structure and quality of SMEs. IMK has a national network of 40 offices. These offices offer a range of services to companies (in quality related areas, activities include the organization of training courses, workshops and seminars). As part of the programme 'Quality and Logistics' IMK organizes quality workshops for entrepreneurs in the non-industrial sector. The most important target group of IMK is the non-industrial sector (e.g. the building and service industries).

3.1.1 Sectoral Associations

In addition, there are a large number of sectoral associations. These organizations promote the interests of affiliated companies. Sectoral quality projects are often initiated by the sector association. Originally set up in the industrial sector they are increasingly extending into the non-industrial. There were about 40 quality projects carried out by sector associations in 1991.

3.2.2 Regional Organizations

At the regional level the network of eighteen innovation centres (ICs) supports technological innovation in small and medium-sized companies. The network was established by the Ministry of Economic Affairs in 1989 in order to bridge the gap between small companies (up to 100 employees) and knowledge centres (universities, research institutes etc.). The main activity of the centres is technological innovation, but ICs also provide advice in the field of quality. (Specifically the ICs have developed a computer programme, called 'Q-audit' (quality audit), in order to investigate companies with respect to quality.) In total there are about 140 advisors who provide practical and direct advice to companies. The primary target group of the innovation centres is the industrial sector. Free advice to companies is given for two days. Long-term advice (with a maximum of eight days) is offered at a commercial rate. The innovation centres receive an annual subsidy of approximately ECU 17 million from the government.

Also at the regional level there are a number of Quality Centres whose activities concern information, promotion, coordination, advice and training courses in the field of total quality management. Centres help companies in all sectors. Some centres are autonomous and obtain income through their activities, other centres are partly subsidized. For instance, the establishment of the South Limburg Quality Centre was realized with financial support from the European Commission under the EFRO (European Fund for Regional Development) and from the Dutch Ministry of Economic Affairs.

Quality circles

There are twelve regional quality circles. These circles are associations (fora) of companies, institutes and individuals which have as an objective an increase in the quality level of organizations. The circles operate through mutual exchange of experiences and information in an informal way, and some also provide training in conjunction with the Chamber of Commerce. Circles are private initiatives of local businesses, most often found in the industrial sector.

3.2 Activities of Organizations

3.2.1 Standardization and Certification

As mentioned above, the NNI is the national organisation responsible for the establishment of standards. The NNI Stacek committee (Standard procedures and criteria for the evaluation of quality systems in companies) produced the Dutch version of the ISO 9000 norms in the late 1980s. In 1991, the name of the committee was changed to 'Quality Management', and its activities shifted from evaluation of ISO propositions to the more active initiation and development of propositions at the ISO and CEN. NNI is member of the European standardization organization CEN and the international standardization organization ISO. Similarly, the electrical engineering sectoral body, NEC, is a member of CENELEC at the European level and of the IEC at world level. NNI is subsidized by the government, but has an autonomous status. Most of its revenue is realized through sales of standards licenses.

The development of an accreditation system occurred in parallel. In 1973, a study was carried out by the NNI on behalf of the Ministry of Economic Affairs argued that the different certificates and quality marks varied considerably in the methodology applied and also in terms of reliability. The study resulted in an interim report, 'To Guarantee Quality Certification', in 1974. In this report a method was developed by representatives of all organisations involved to organize the different methods of certification. A committee of NNI helped establish a Council of Certification (Raad voor de Certificatie). The council was installed in 1981 and became operational in 1983. The first certification organization was recognized by the council in 1983. In 1986, the first recognition was given to a foreign organization, Lloyd's Register Quality Assurance Ltd. of the UK. Since 1989, there has been close collaboration with the Belgium National Committee for the Accreditation of Certification Bodies which Certify Quality Assurance Systems (NAC-QS) in the joint accreditation of certification bodies.[12]

The objective of the Council of Certification is to regulate, coordinate and advise in the field of certification in the broadest sense. An important part of the task of the council is to examine the application of certification bodies and their certification schemes for compatibility with the recognition criteria. The recognition criteria are drawn up by a representative group of the parties involved and concern the reliability, expertise and impartiality of the certification bodies. Recognition to certification bodies is given for two years, after which an examination takes place again. In 1987, the Council of Certification, as advisor of the Minister of Economic

Affairs, initiated the establishment of STERLAB (Stichting voor de Erkenning van Laboratoria, Institute for the Recognition of Laboratories) with responsibility for certifying laboratories. Similarly, in 1991 STERIN (the equivalent for Inspection Bodies) was established in 1991. With the establishment of STERLAB and STERIN the accreditation structure was complete.

The Council for Certification is financed by contributions from the recognized certification bodies. Since its establishment, the council has also been subsidized by the Ministry of Economic Affairs. In 1990, the subsidy covered 20% (ECU 62,500) of the costs. In 1991, the subsidy was reduced to 10% (ECU 33,000). In addition, the Ministry of Economic Affairs provided a subsidy specifically in support of 'Europe 1992'. In total, over four years, about ECU 422,000 have been provided (ECU 107,000 in 1989; ECU 111,000 in 1990; ECU 103,000 in 1991 and ECU 101,000 in 1992). The council became financially independent of the government in 1992.

The council collaborates in the international field within the EOTC (European Organization for Testing and Certification) for mutual recognition of certificates. The president of the council is the national representative in the EOTC. With respect to the EC Directive for CE testing and certification, the Dutch government can present organizations recognized by the Council of Certification as a 'notified body' to the EC.

Products, services, processes and quality systems are the subjects of certification. Annually, about 100 companies are certificated. The number of certificated companies is 600 in all. There are a large number of certification organizations of which 28 national and international bodies are recognized by the Council of Certification. Quality assurance systems are nationally certificated by 14 recognized certification organizations. The certification of quality assurance systems is based on NEN/ISO 9000 standards. ISO 9000 standards are presently a central issue in Dutch business. Companies are eager to obtain a certificate based on quality assurance norms particularly in the supplier-subcontractor relationship where quality system certification is important.[13]

3.2.2 Promotion, Awareness and Consultancy

The market for information and advice in the field of quality is extensive and difficult to distinguish clearly.[14] The organizations undertake different activities. Some organizations only give advice in the orientation phase, some give advice with regard to the implementation of quality management systems, and other organizations offer a total package of advice and support in the orientation as well as in the implementation phase. There are commercial and non-profit intermediary organizations. Finally, there is a distinction in the primary target group of the different organizations. Some organizations focus on the industrial sector, some on the non-industrial sector, some have just one specific sector as a target group and others focus on all business sectors.

At a regional level, a network of several organizations exists. These organizations provide information and advice and give support with respect to quality projects to small and medium-sized companies. Important organizations in the 'regional' infrastructure are the quality centres, the quality circles, the institutes for small and medium-sized businesses and the innovation centres. The quality centres are intermediary organizations which have been especially established to promote, coordinate and give advice in the field of total quality management, they also provide training courses. The function of the innovation centres and institutes for small and medium-sized companies is the same, but they operate in a broader context, i.e. activities are directed at all management aspects. Quality circles are fora of managers exchanging experiences in the field of quality. In addition, some Chambers of Commerce are active in the field of quality.

3.2.3 Training and Education

The supply of training in the field of quality has considerably increased in recent years. In the last five years the availability of training, by means of courses, workshops and seminars on quality, has doubled.[15] Besides courses provided by schools and universities, training is offered by private schools, consultancy firms and other service organizations, e.g. KDI, IMK, Quality Centres, Chambers of Commerce etc. The NNI also provides courses with respect to certification of quality systems. As a result of the large number of organizations offering training, the need for certification in this field has risen. Such a need was first recognized in 1982 with a study, 'Quality Policy and Organization', carried out in 25 Dutch companies with the objective of determining the situation of quality training in the Netherlands. The situation appeared to be rather disappointing: the general training level of quality managers was low and the training facilities in quality at different levels varied extremely. The NVK tried to improve this situation, e.g. through the preparation of a framework for quality training and the development of a package of teaching material for the training of quality managers.

In 1989, KVP created the CERKOOP institute in 1989 in order to certify training courses as well as the professional skills of persons trained in quality management.

Information about the situation with respect to education and research is available (though rather dated) thanks to the research project 'Total Quality Management in Europe', carried out in 1988 and 1989 by UMIST (University of Manchester Institute of Science and Technology) of the UK, and SQMI (Erasmus University) of the Netherlands.[16] The purpose of this project was to establish the 'state of the art' in teaching and research in European higher education as a basis for future developments in TQM. The project originated from the European Foundation for Quality Management (EFQM) in September 1988. The EFQM stressed that more attention needed to be given to quality and quality management in Europe and especially to the role of European universities and business schools in the teaching of TQM. Thirteen questionnaires were completed in the Netherlands by seven universities and one institute for business economics.

TQM was taught on seven undergraduate courses, on ten postgraduate courses and on three at post-experience level. TQM aspects distinguished in the study were: statistical process control, approaches to TQM, quality costs and cost effectiveness of TQM, customer satisfaction etc. The data indicated that, at graduate level at least, TQM tended to be taught as a part of other subjects. At postgraduate and post-experience level it tended to feature more prominently. The teaching emphasis was mostly on manufacturing and less on services. The academic background of students was mostly business/economic and in some cases technical.

Since 1991 three chairs of quality management have been established in business economic faculties. The first chair 'Quality and Certification' was created at the Erasmus University in Rotterdam (EUR) in 1991 on the initiative of the Council for Certification. The second chair 'Quality Management' was established in 1992 at the University of Groningen (RUG) and the third, also in 'Quality Management' was also established in 1992 at the technical university of Eindhoven (TUE). These chairs have contributed to the number of courses on which TQM is taught. In several schools of intermediary and higher vocational education, courses in quality management are offered. Largely as a result of the education projects developed within the 'Quality and Logistics Programme', the number of courses in which quality management is taught has increased significantly. The Higher Vocational School 'Midden-Brabant' in Tilburg currently offers the only undergraduate course specifically in quality management.

3.2.4 Research

The previously mentioned research project 'Total Quality Management in Europe' questioned the same institutions with regard to their research activities. Research was done on a large number of TQM aspects (statistical process control, quality and business strategy, organizational structures for TQM etc.). The study listed about 165 postgraduate theses (masters and doctorates) in the Netherlands on total quality management, in addition to regular research activities. KDI-Rotterdam is setting up an overview of ongoing research activities in the field of total quality management in the Netherlands.

4. National Quality Schemes and Initiatives
4.1 Global Schemes

4.1.1 Quality and Logistics

At present the only national quality scheme is Quality and Logistics (Q&L, Kwaliteit en Logistiek) Programme initiated by the Ministry of Economic Affairs. The scheme started in May 1989 with the purpose of stimulating the introduction of quality and logistics in management. The intention of the government was not to directly support the development of quality and logistics activities in companies, but to support those organizations, (particularly public and quasi-public, i.e. business group organizations and trade unions) with initiatives already underway. These organizations could ask for a governmental contribution to finance their activities. The programme was originally intended to end in 1991, but has been prolonged until 1993.

The programme covers both the industrial and service sectors. For the period 1988 to 1991 a budget of ECU 14.7 million was made available by the Ministry of Economic Affairs (ECU 14.3 million), the Ministry of Social Affairs and Employment and the Ministry of Transport and Communications. In relation to the prolongation of the programme until the end of 1993, this budget was increased in 1991 by the Ministry of Economic Affairs to ECU 16.9 million.[17] Table 14 (page 221) shows the main topics of the programme, with their budgets.

Table 14. Quality and Logistics Programme Topics

Topic:	Amount (million ECU)
1988-1991	
Information activities to companies	1.7
Knowledge-infrastructure	5.2
Education improvement	3.0
Demonstration projects	4.8
1991-1993	
Integration of management systems (quality, logistics, environment, safety etc)	1.1
Dissemination of programme-products (methods, handbooks, software, videos etc)	1.1
Total	16.9

Source: Projectgroep Kwaliteitsbeleid

Clearly, these topics are closely linked and overlap each other. However, each has its own goal, target group and nature of activities.

4.1.2 Information Activities for Companies

The objective of information activities is to stimulate management to develop systematic activities in the field of quality and/or logistics. Target groups are management and employees of companies in the market sector, sector associations, trade unions, professional associations etc.

Special attention is paid to the building and service (especially transport) industries as well as to small and medium-sized companies because these sectors are considered to lag behind other sectors. The information activities (by means of publications in trade journals, reports, manuals etc.) are undertaken by intermediaries and umbrella organizations (chambers of commerce, innovation centres, consultancies, sector associations etc.). A total of ECU 1.7 million has been reserved in the programme for information activities. (Information has also been an important aspect of the Demonstration Projects - see below.)

An example of an information project is the development between 1989 and 1990 of a videodisc by KDI concerning decision-making and implementation of quality projects.[18] The videodisc is now available for companies: distribution and wide application will be realized by means of workshops and a promotion campaign. Total costs of the project were ECU 313,000. The contribution from Quality and Logistics was ECU 150,000, the remaining costs being paid by KDI.

4.1.3 Knowledge Infrastructure Development

A number of intermediaries play an important role in the knowledge infrastructure. Company familiarity with, and the use of, these intermediaries varies significantly. For instance, small companies are quite familiar with the Chamber of Commerce and their business group associations, but less so with the Innovation Centre and Institute for Small and Medium-sized Companies. Only 50% of the small companies make use of these advisory organizations. The objective of this programme item of Quality and Logistics is to create a structure of knowledge transfer in order to develop, open and spread practice-based knowledge in the field of quality and logistics. Target groups are intermediary organizations. These activities include support for certification and standardization organizations, consultancies, the development of a knowledge information centre by KDI etc.[19] To date, ECU 5.2 million has been made available for this programme item.

An example of a knowledge infrastructure project is the training of advisors and consultants active in the mechanical and electrotechnical sector, and in addition, the promotion of possibilities of innovation trajectories with respect to production and organization in the sector. The project started in 1989 and will end in 1992. The total costs have been estimated at ECU 740,000. Quality and Logistics provides ECU 304,000, with the remaining costs being financed by the mechanical engineering sector.

4.1.4 Education Improvement

The aim of these projects is to stimulate education and training activities in the field of quality and logistics through the development of professional skilled management, curriculums, exams, establishment of specialized schools. The target groups are schools of higher and intermediate vocational education (economic, technical and agricultural). An aim of this programme has been to better fit the supply of graduates qualitatively as well as quantitatively with the needs of businesses and a more structural cooperation between education and businesses results. Additionally, a start has been made with certification in the field of quality training. The programme provides ECU 3.0 million for activities in this field together with other subsidies of the Ministry of Economic Affairs and the Ministry of Education.

An example of an education project is the 'Total Quality Management Pilot Project' of the college of higher education in Enschede. The goal of this project is to increase the knowledge of teachers with respect to total quality management, and also the development of a teaching programme in this respect. The project started in 1989 and is nearly finished. Total costs are ECU 435,000, with the contribution from Quality and Logistics being ECU 217,000.

Similarly, ten projects have been coordinated by the HBO (Higher Vocational Education) Council. The structure of the projects involved three parties; one school (teachers and students), one company and one advisor (see Figure 20, page 223) A company which wanted to improve quality or logistics could call on a school. Students together with their teacher analysed the company for possibilities to improve quality and/or logistics. The school was supported in this by an advisor of a consulting firm. In this way practical advice was provided to the company.

The information acquired as a result of the different projects was distributed by the HBO Council to other schools so that these schools could establish teaching programmes in the field of quality or logistics. About ECU 2.0 million of the ECU 2.8 million budget for education improvement was spent on these projects.

Figure 20: Structure of the HBO quality projects

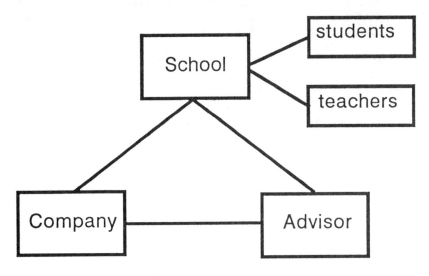

4.1.5 Demonstration Projects

Demonstration Projects are oriented to actual business situations, business groups and sectors, and are set up to provide a good example for other companies and organizations. An important role of the demonstration projects is to improve cooperation between companies in supplier-subcontractor chains (logistics being particularly important in this relationship). In this respect, a direct link exists between the Quality and Logistics programme and the 'Subcontracting' scheme of the Ministry of Economic Affairs.[20] The general objectives of the demonstration projects are:

- to provide practice-based information which is directly applicable;
- to provide information about quality and logistics; and,
- to demonstrate the relation between quality and logistics and other management items. The target groups are industries and service industries.

The demonstration projects are set up by sector associations in association with companies. The projects are of direct interest to participating companies and also other organizations. By means of expert advice the existing business situation is analysed, solutions and methods of decision making are presented, and the actual implementation of quality and logistic management is supported. In this way, practical applied knowledge and new systems are developed. So far, ECU 4.8 million has been made available for the demonstration projects and about 25 projects have been started.

For example, within the scope of the 'MILK' project (Milieuzorg Integratie in systemen van Logistiek en Kwaliteitszorg, Environmental Care Integration in Systems of Logistics and Quality), the efficiency and effectiveness of the integration of environmental protection in quality systems and logistic management is demonstrated in the process industry.[21] The project started in 1990 and will end in 1992. The total costs of the programme are about ECU 326,000 of which the Quality and Logistics programme provides ECU 217,000.

In conclusion, the most important topics are the development of the knowledge infrastructure (ECU 5.2 million) and demonstration projects (ECU 4.8 million, see Table 14, page 221). Actually, ECU 1.4 million and ECU 2.0 million were primarily used for knowledge infrastructure improvement and demonstration projects respectively. In total, ECU 4.6 million was used for integrated quality and logistic activities (see Table 15, below).

Table 15: Realized budget for 'Quality and Logistics' Programme: 1988 to 1991

Item	Budget (ECU million)			
	total	quality	logistics	Q&L
Information activities	1.4	0.8	0.1	0.5
Knowledge infrastructure	4.3	1.4	0.7	2.2
Education	2.8	1.4	1.0	0.4
Demonstration projects	4.1	2.0	0.9	1.2
Total* (ECU million)	12.6	5.6	2.7	4.3

* Excluding operation costs of NEHEM (estimated ECU 1.5 million)

Source: Progress report 'Kwaliteit en Logistiek' 1991

Of the 90 projects, about 40-50 projects were directed to quality improvement and 20 projects to logistic management. Eighty of the 90 projects were completed by the end of 1992. Projects were selected by NEHEM under the auspices of the Ministry of Economic Affairs. The selection criteria were as follows:

- favourable correspondence between costs and spill-over effects to other companies;
- the project has to be carried out by intermediary organizations or a representative business collaboration;
- all information has to be made available;
- proposed projects have to fit in the programme; and,
- quality and logistics have to be the principal items in the project.

4.1.6 Programme Evaluation

Intermediary evaluations of Quality and Logistics were carried out by the Ministry of Economic Affairs. Progress reports were published in 1989, 1990 and in 1991 containing an overview of the activities carried out and the programme results. The overall programme was evaluated as well as individual topics.[22]

The evaluation found that the objectives of the information activities had been attained. However, most of the projects were directed to a single business group or industry. It was noted that the final target group, the business community, was not reached at all levels and in all sectors. The Ministry of Economic Affairs had primary responsibility for the distribution of information. In future, the information and documentation centre of KDI and the recently established 'Nederlandse Kwaliteit' (Dutch Quality) steering group are likely to play an important role.

Some projects in the field of knowledge infrastructure were realized with difficulty and results were obtained with considerable effort. The distribution of knowledge to companies often appeared to be a problem. However, there were also a number of very successful projects, e.g. the realization of 16 workshops in the mechanical and electrotechnical industry, instead of the eight planned workshops.

According to the objectives, a lot of attention has been paid to quality and logistics within the teaching programme of schools of higher and intermediate vocational education (HBO and MBO). In this respect, the ten projects in HBO schools appeared to be very successful. The benefits of the project were many:

- the company was given practical advice in the field of quality or logistics;
- the student were trained in quality/logistics aspects and will enter the labour market as quality or logistic skilled graduates; and,
- the teacher and advisor will become more experienced and specialized in quality and logistics aspects.

In conclusion, the junction between education and businesses with regard to quality has been significantly improved, especially in HBO and MBO. However, most universities do not regard quality as a particular discipline at this moment. As a result, projects in universities appeared difficult to realize. This was also the case for schools of lower vocational education.

Most demonstration projects have not yet been completed and there are no products available at the moment. The financial and time commitments required from companies, financial as well as time, result in a hesitant attitude from potential companies. Most demonstration projects would not have been realized without the financial support of the Quality and Logistics Programme. The distribution to all industries of knowledge obtained in the demonstration projects needs to continue. Most often, adaptations are needed in order to apply the project results more widely or more specifically to other industries. The programme has been prolonged and an additional budget has been made available for these adaptations

The next figures give an idea of the total range of the programme. Because advisors, consultants, teachers etc. are involved in several projects, there can be a double count in some cases. About 700 companies have been actively involved in the execution of the 40 realized projects.

In addition, 900 advisors, consultants and teachers have been trained and about 46,000 companies have become acquainted with the results of one or more projects thanks to brochures, manuals, videodiscs or computer programmes. Governmental support for all realised and ongoing projects was about ECU 13 million by April 1991. The total costs of these projects are expected to be about ECU 30 million.

4.1.7 Effectiveness study of Quality and Logistics

The results of the programme were determined by means of a questionnaire circulated through the Dutch business community. At the start of the Q&L programme, it was found that 78% of Dutch companies paid attention to quality. More recent measurements in April 1991 showed that, in the period of the programme 84% of the companies regarded quality as a central policy issue (see Table 16, below). In addition, the development in the certification of quality systems has been positive. In 1989, approximately 80 new certificates were granted while 370 were granted in 1991 according to the Council for Certification. Although quality awareness among Dutch businesses has been considerably increased, TQM, however, is applied or fully developed in only 1% of all businesses as already indicated in Section 2.

Table 16: Dutch companies for which quality is a central policy issue

		1989	1990	1991
			Percentage	
Total		78	78	84
company size:				
	100	75	76	80
	100-500	82	81	84
	500 +	92	88	96
sector:				
	industry	79	80	83
	construction	78	74	84
	wholesale	70	76	78
	retail		86	86
	transport	75	71	84
	services	86	80	88

Source: Progress report 'Kwaliteit en Logistiek' 1991

4.1.8 'Dutch Quality' Steering Group

Against this background the steering committee 'Nederlandse Kwaliteit' (Dutch Quality) was established by the Ministry of Economic Affairs in December 1991 with the financial support of the Quality and Logistics Programme.[24] The Ministry financed the installation of the steering group and will subsidize its activities for the first three years (1991 to 1994). The secretariat of the steering group is located at the Nederlandsche Maatschappij voor Nijverheid en Handel (Dutch Society for Trade and Industry).

The steering committee consists of top managers in the field of TQM from different sectors, profit and non-profit organizations, and a representative of the Ministry of Economic Affairs. These experienced TQM managers willingly exchange their experiences for the benefit of colleagues. The main goal of 'Dutch Quality' is to stimulate and accelerate the introduction of TQM in Dutch organizations in order to maintain and improve international competitiveness. The objective is to implement total quality management in the private (and semi-public) sectors. The target is top management in relevant organizations with a particular focus on small and medium-sized companies.

The steering group supports top management in actively introducing TQM by means of creating interest, providing information, stimulation and advice. The steering group aims to benefit from the existing interest in quality, the numerous organizations developing projects for quality improvement and/or control and the multitude of quality organizations, courses and consultants. The steering group will cooperate with the existing quality organizations in the field of quality, with consultancy firms and institutes and with quality experts of industrial organizations, innovations centres etc. Activities are primarily directed at the top management of companies and institutions, e.g. seminars, study trips, company visits and information activities. A central activity is the Quality Award corresponding to the Deming Award (Japan) and the Baldridge Award (USA) which is expected to stimulate activities in the field of TQM.

4.1.9 Quality Platform

The relationship between the knowledge infrastructure and the steering group is of great interest, because the support and follow-up of activities of the steering group has to be carried by the knowledge infrastructure in order to operate effectively. A proposition has been developed by the steering group to regulate the coordination between the knowledge infrastructure and the steering group in the form of a 'Quality Platform'. The objectives of this Quality Platform are:

- to advise the steering group with respect to its policy;
- to coordinate activities initiated by the steering group which depend on assistance of the knowledge infrastructure;
- to improve the effectiveness of the knowledge infrastructure by knowledge exchange at national and international level, rejection of market-oriented advice and the realization of collective projects; and,
- to organize yearly a quality manifestation.

All Dutch intermediary organizations active in the field of awareness, consulting, training, knowledge development and normalization/certification concerning total quality management can join the Platform. The establishment meeting of the Quality Platform was held in June 1992.

4.2 Sectoral Schemes

Several sectoral schemes seemed to partly encompass quality activities, but it was extremely difficult to collect information about the exact contribution of these schemes to quality projects.

In most cases quality was only a minor part of projects carried out within the scope of one of the technological subsidy schemes. Only one subsidy scheme 'Subcontracting 1992' included a significant number of quality projects.

The Ministry of Economic Affairs created this scheme with the purpose of stimulating improved cooperation between suppliers and contractors. Quality assurance and logistics are important in this supplier-contractor relationship. Two types of project may be supported:

- *improvement projects,* feasibility studies of cooperation between suppliers, and management improvement projects in the field of quality, logistics, product innovation etc.
- *technological cooperation projects,* aimed at technological research and development work related to product components or production systems characteristic of the product-market combination.

The aim is to involve 300 to 500 companies in demonstration projects. Since the start of the programme in 1988, more than 300 companies have participated. In 1992, seven product-market combinations were targeted under the initiative:

- the automotive industry;
- telecommunication and office machine industry;
- Integrated circuit industry;
- defence industry;
- energy/offshore industry; and,
- equipment for process industry and the audio-visual industry.

Funding for the period 1988 to 1994 is ECU 15.4 million. The subsidy covers the external costs of the improvement project of the company.

A direct link exists between Quality and Logistics and the 'Subcontacting' scheme. As already mentioned, an important part of the demonstration projects in the scope of Quality and Logistics is also aimed at the improvement of the supplier-contractor relationship (see Section 4.1.5).

5. Regional Quality Schemes and Initiatives

A large number of regional schemes and initiatives are set up each year, either publicly or privately. Some of these regional schemes are used for projects aimed at quality improvement. However, information about these regional projects is dispersed and difficult to access. Therefore, it is not possible to give a complete and detailed overview of possible quality projects and initiatives, but it is obvious that in nearly all regions quality stimulating projects have been developed.

An inventory of the available information on regional quality projects shows that most projects are directed to small and medium-sized companies in order to stimulate quality awareness and improvement or to introduce quality assurance systems based on ISO 9000 norms. Practically all projects are sectoral and have industry or the service sector as a target group. The projects are most often carried out by groups of organizations, and not by individual organizations. The innovation centres, quality centres and institutes for small and medium-sized companies appear to play an important role in the initiation and support of the regional projects. They often coordinate projects and take care of funding. The funding of the regional projects is private and/or public. The main stream of privately financed projects is carried by sector associations, although some of these projects may be subsidized as well. There were about 40 business group quality projects in 1991. Publicly financed projects are generally covered by contributions from the individual province, the Ministry of Economic Affairs and the European Union. There are several 'open' regional subsidy schemes of the Ministry of Economic Affairs and the European Union available for quality projects. However, the provinces, the Minister of Economic Affairs and the European Union can also give individual contributions to projects. In most cases, 50% at most of the total costs of the projects are subsidized, the rest being financed by the companies themselves.

The major regional programmes with respect to quality projects are presented in this Section. First some global schemes will be discussed. Then, other regional programmes of interest are described.

5.1 Structure Reinforcing Programmes

The regional programmes are developed within the framework of the regional policy of the government.[25] They are the responsibility of the Ministry of Economic Affairs. The European Union is financially involved in these regional programmes as well. It co-finances the programme with the Ministry of Economic Affairs. The overall objective of these programmes is to reinforce the economic structure of seven provinces: Drenthe, Friesland, Gelderland, Groningen, Limburg, Noord-Brabant and Overijssel. These provinces are considered to be economically underdeveloped in comparison with the western provinces like Noord-Holland, Zuid-Holland and Utrecht. The provinces Zeeland and Flevoland are not taken into consideration in this respect. Study of the regional programmes pointed out that one of the applications of these programmes is quality improvement in companies. These quality programmes are nearly always set up in specific sectors. In order to give an idea of the substance of these programmes an overview of the regional programmes is presented. In addition, a typical quality project carried under the regime of each of the programmes is described.

5.1.1 The OZL programme

The OZL (Oost-Zuid Limburg, East-South Limburg) programme provides a contribution to initiatives aimed at reinforcing the economic structure of East-South Limburg. These initiatives can encompass education/labour market, technology, tourism, export, infrastructure etc. Contributions are given to individuals, companies, institutions and private non-profit organizations in East-South Limburg. Projects are prepared by the province and partly financed by the government. The OZL programme started in 1991 and succeeds the PNL (Perspectieven nota Limburg) programme of 1990, the contents of the two programmes being identical.[26] For the period 1991 to 1994 the budget is about ECU 35 million, including EFRO co-financing.[27]

An example of a project carried out within the scope of the PNL programme is the establishment of the Quality Centre South in January 1990. The objective of the establishment of a quality centre was to realize a more definite result of quality awareness by means of quality management activities. Costs of the project were an estimated ECU 405,000 for the first three years. The project was financed with PNL funds from the Ministry of Economic Affairs and with EFRO funds from the

European Community. Both sets of funds provided ECU 120,000. Companies contributed the remaining ECU 165,000. Financial support was provided on the condition that the centre operated autonomously, and that its activities were only developed regionally. The support of large companies is essential in this context.

5.1.2 The ISP programme

The ISP (Integral Structure Plan) programme is a regional development plan for the provinces in the north of the Netherlands: Friesland, Groningen, Drenthe and Overijssel.[28] The programme began in 1982 and will finish in 1994.

ISP is particularly aimed at the initiation and support of collaborative projects between companies and intermediary organizations. The ISP contributions are not granted to individual companies. Projects are prepared by the provinces and partly financed by the government. At most 50% of a project is subsidized. The fourth phase of the programme (ISP-IV) is running between 1991 and 1993 is currently underway. ECU 130 million has been made available by the Ministry of Economic Affairs including EFRO co-financing. In addition, the Ministry of Agriculture and Ministry of Education are contributing respectively ECU 8.7 million and ECU 326,000 over this period. The ISP-IV programme centres on five fields of related economic activities.[29] One of these fields is small and medium-sized companies. In this field special attention is paid to management improvement, international business, environmental factors and quality. The aim of the quality programme is to increase productivity and to improve service. The following items are distinguished in this respect:

- quality assurance systems;
- practical sectoral training on quality improvement;
- management information and coordination systems;
- supply and sub-contracting; and,
- logistic processes.

Certification based on international standards is the overall objective. The ISP budget for small and medium-sized companies is at least ECU 2.2 million a year (ECU 3.7 million maximum). Project proposals are evaluated by the Ministry of Economic Affairs.

An example of a recently developed project within ISP-IV is the 'Quality and Certification Project for Small and Medium-sized Companies'. The objective of the project is to stimulate about 100 companies annually to obtain certification and to introduce total quality management. The rationale of the project is that only 30 companies are certificated in this region, while more than 60 companies should be certificated based on the national percentage. Target groups are industrial and service organizations with less than 100 employees. The project will be carried out by clusters of companies which work together in one (basic) programme. Each cluster will have one coordinating advisor. The basic programme involves the firms:

- carrying out a quality study, particulary Q-audits based on ISO 9000 norms;
- appointing (quality) advisors for a period of two years;

- making use of junior advisors, trainees of the University of Groningen or schools;
- providing in-company quality training and courses; and,
- organizing meetings in order to exchange experience.

ISP will cover 50% of the company costs of advice, training, testing etc. (and also the costs of certification in some cases) up to an amount of ECU 17,400 per company. The coordination of the project is carried by the regional quality centre in cooperation with business group organizations and intermediaries (innovation centres, institutes for small and medium-sized companies, Chambers of Commerce etc.).

5.1.3 The REP programme

There are three 'regional' (REP) programmes (for the regions Twente, Midden-Gelderland, Noord-Brabant) which are part of the 'structure reinforcing' policy of the government. Initiatives which contribute to reinforcement of the economic structure are considered for REP support. These initiatives have to relate to:

- technology;
- infrastructure;
- small and medium-sized companies;
- tourism; agricultural sector; and,
- education/labour market.

The programme started in 1982 and finished in 1993. The amounts available (including EFRO co-financing) were ECU 4.3 million (Twente); ECU 2,6 million (Midden-Gelderland) and 0.9 ECU million (Noord-Brabant) for 1991 and 1992. All organizations and private institutions are eligible and the size of subsidy depends on the nature and the interest of the project. Project proposals are evaluated by the Ministry of Economic Affairs. Quality projects can be carried out within the context of the different items.

An example of the application of a quality project is 'Quality in the Goods Traffic Transport in the Region Arnhem/Nijmegen'. The project aims to stimulate the introduction of quality management within the goods traffic transport. The final objective is to obtain ISO 9002 certification. The target group was all traffic transport companies. The project proposal contains three phases: an information campaign; company study and advice; and support for the introduction of quality management. The total costs are approximately ECU 128,000. The contributions of the Ministry of Economic Affairs and the Province are: REP (Ministry of EA) ECU 43,500; Province Gelderland ECU 13,000; Chambers of Commerce ECU 6,500; Arnhem/Nijmegen ECU 8,700. Other contributions have come from the companies involved in the project.

5.2 Other Regional Programmes

5.2.1 Stimulation Programme 'Support Market and Innovation Advice South Limburg'

The programme is aimed at supporting small and medium-sized companies in making use of external market and innovation advice.[30] Subsidies (50% of the costs) are provided for advice from market and innovation experts with regard to:

- innovation and product development;
- support of market and strategy studies; and,
- management support.

Quality improvement projects are part of management support. Target groups are small and medium-sized companies with less than 200 employees and with an industrial, building or service character, situated in South-East Limburg and the mine district in West Limburg. The programme is based on the EFRO programme and started in 1989. Total available funding is ECU 870,000 for the period 1989-1993. ECU 435,000 is provided by EFRO and ECU 435,000 by the regional authorities of the Limburg province. At most 50% of the costs of external advice are covered by the subsidy. The project proposals are selected by IMK Limburg.

An example of a project recently developed within this programme is QUATRO ('Quality' Toeleveren Regionaal Ondernemerschap, Quality Supply Regional Entrepreneurship). QUATRO is a regional project aiming to reinforce the competitive position of the local suppliers in the Limburg province. The rationale is that important changes have taken place with respect to quality and specialization in the field of supply and subcontracting. This applies especially to the supply of technical services by the regional suppliers to large industrial subcontractors. The objectives of the programme, which began in 1992, are:

- quality improvement of regional suppliers in the field of technical services;
- introduction of quality systems according to the ISO 9000 series; and,
- certification of these technical service organizations.

The project is supported by EFRO, LIOF (Limburg Development Fund), Province Limburg and the Employers Association of Limburg.

Regional schemes are mainly based on co-financing by EFRO (see Part Four) to improve the regional infrastructure. In a number of cases, these funds are used for quality improvement purposes. Although the total impact compared to the programmes of the Ministry of Economic Affairs is probably of minor importance, a number of interesting examples could be given. A schematic overview of the different regional programmes is presented in Figure 21 (page 233).

Figure 21: Examples of regional programmes and quality projects

Regional Programme	Example of quality improvement	Total Cost (ECU)	Size of subsidy (ECU)
OZL programme	Quality Centre 'South'	405,000	240,000
ISP programme	'Quality and Certification SMO'	?	17,400 (per company)
REP programme	'Quality goods traffic sector	128,000	43,500
Support Market and innovation advice South Limburg	QUATRO	?	?

6. Overview and Outlook

The approach of the government with regard to the different quality programmes changed in the course of time. One can distinguish roughly three phases in the policy of the government: in the first phase, i.e. the period of the programme 'Quality Plan', the government dictated to companies more or less how to improve quality with the emphasis on quality control and assurance . In the second phase of 'Quality Management' the government supported companies which were eager to improve quality. Quality management was emphasized. The third phase can be considered to be the programme 'Quality and Logistics'. The rationale behind the programme was to stimulate companies to come up with ideas themselves rather than be provided with a package of activities composed by the Ministry of Economic Affairs. Active introduction of quality was the responsibility of the companies themselves. The establishment of the 'Dutch Quality' steering group seems to be a more indirect approach of the government to promote total quality management to companies. The government delegates virtually all the actions for quality to the steering group. Figure 22 (page 234) shows the relationship between these different governmental approaches and the evolution over time of the quality concept itself.

Figure 22: Overview of the evolution of government quality programmes 1978 to 1993

Programme	Amount (ECU)	Emphasis	Approach
Quality Plan (1978-82)	?	QC/QA	experimental/ guidance
Quality Management (1984-87)	4.8 million	QM	stimulating
Quality & Logistics (1988-93)	14.7 million	TQM	facilitating
Steering Group 'Dutch Quality' (Quality Platform) (1992-)	1.1 million	TQM widening of concept to labour and environment	delegating

6.1 The Future

The quality concept is increasingly being extended to include environmental and labour aspects. Environmental issues in particular are becoming the subject of an increasing number of quality programmes, partly as a result of the increasing pressure for environmental awareness.

7. List of Schemes and Organizations

Name	Address	Telephone/Fax
National Schemes:		
Quality and Logistics	Ministry of Economic Affairs PO Box 20101 EC s 'Gravenhage	70 37988811
NEHEM	PO Box 90105 5200 MA s 'Hertogenbosch	73132490
Steering Group 'Dutch Quality'	PO Box 205 2000 AE Haarlem	23295703,
Certification:		
Nederlands Normalisatie-instituut NNI	P.O.Box 5059 2600 GB Delft	015-690390
Stichting Raad voor de Certificatie	Stationsweg 13 F Gebouw Vierdaelen 3972 KA Driebergen	03438-12604
STERLAB (Nederlandse Stichting voor de Erkenning van Laboratoria)	P.O.Box 29152 3001 GD Rotterdam	010 4136011
Quality Organizations:		
Centraal Kantoor Innovatie Centra Network	P.O.Box 20104 2500 ECs-Gravenhage	070-3601932
KDI Stichting Kwaliteitsdienst	P.O.Box 84031 3009 CA Rotterdam	010-4554700
IMK Instituut Midden- en Kleinbedrijf	Head Office P.O.Box 112 1100 AC Diemen	020-6901071
NVK Nederlandse Vereniging voor Kwaliteit	P.O.Box 359 5600 AJ Eindhoven	040-432503
MANS Vereniging Management en Arbeid Nieuwe Stijl	P.O.Box 270 2700 AG Zoetermeer	03405-71144
Frits PHILIPS Institute for Quality Management	P.O.Box 513 NL 5600 MB Eindhoven	040-474748
EFQM/NL	Building 'Reaal' Fellenoord 47a 5612 AA Eindhoven	(32) 40-461075
CERKOOP (NvK Institute for Quality Management)	P.O.Box 84031 3009 CA Rotterdam	010-4554700

References

1. Cf. Horning, M.W., en Pruijt, M.W. (1989), 'Het kwaliteitsbeleid van Economische Zaken', *ESB, 1114-1116*.

2. see section 3.

3. see section 7.

4. see Section 3.

5. Advisory Committee Wagner: Committee of 14 experts installed in 1981. Chairman of the committee was G.A.Wagner, former Chief Executive Office of Shell. The task of the committee was to consider the desirability of alterations in the policy of the government with respect to the Dutch industry.

6. NEHEM (Nederlandse Herstructererings Maatschappij, Dutch Society for the Restructuring of Business Groups), founded in 1972 under the Ministry of Economic Affairs. NEHEM became an independent consulting firm in 1991.

7. 1 guilder = 2,30 ECU as of March 1992.

8. Ministerie van Economische Zaken, projectgroep Kwaliteitsbeleid (1987), *Nederland: Hoogste tijd voor Kwaliteit*, Den Haag.

9. Ibid.

10. Recommendations reports with regard to logistics: Coopers & Lybrand Associates (1987), *Logistiek in de logistiek, op weg naar integrale logistiek in Nederland*, Rotterdam; McKinsey & Company (1987), *Resultaatverbetering in het midden en kleinbedrijf door integrale goederenstroombeheersing*, Amsterdam.

11. Ministerie van Economische Zaken/projectgroep Kwaliteit en Logistiek (1992), *Voortgangsrapportage 1991 'Kwaliteit en Logistiek'*, Den Haag.

12. Cf. Gundlach, H.C.W., 'Kwaliteitszorg en Certificatie', *Raad voor Certificatie*, Driebergen.

13. Ministerie van Economische Zaken/projectgroep Kwaliteit en Logistiek (1992), Ibid.

14. IMK (1991), 'Kwaliteitszorg in het MKB, op het goede pad gestuurd', derde druk, *Diemen*, februari 1991.

15. Kluwer Handboek (1991), *Integrale Kwaliteitszorg Beleid-Methodiek-Toepassing,,* Deventer, Kluwer Technische Boeken B.V.

16. University of Manchester, Quality Management Centre, Manchester.

17. 1 ECU = DFL 2.30.

18. KDI (Stichting Kwaliteitsdienst,Quality Organizations), see section 6.

19. The knowledge information centre of KDI will be the national centre of the knowledge infrastruture.

20. Subsidy scheme 'Subcontracting': for more information see section 4.2

21 MILK (Milieuzorg Integratie in systemen van Logistiek en Kwaliteitszorg, Environment care Integration in systems of Logistics and Quality).

22. Cf. Ministerie van Economische Zaken/projectgroep Kwaliteit en logistiek, (1991), *Voortgangsrapportage 1991 'Kwaliteit en Logistiek'*, Den Haag, 1992.

23. Most important are the Steering group 'Dutch Quality" and the Knowledge Information Centre of KDI.

24. Cf. Ministerie van Economische Zaken, Kwaliteit in Bedrijf, Snijders/Van Hilten, Baarn, december 1991.

25. Source: Institute for Small and Medium-sized Companies, 'Kwaliteitszorg in het MKB, op het goede pad gestuurd', Diemen, 1991.

26. PNL: perspectieven nota Limburg. Funds available for the region South-Limburg in 1990: ECU 18,5 million.

27. EFRO; (European Fund for Regional Development)

28. ISP: Integraal Structuur Plan Noorden des Lands.

29. Agricultural business, harbour related activities, tourism and recreation, urban buildings and structure small and medium-sized companies.

30. Subsidieregeling 'Ondersteuning Markt en Innovatie-adviezen in Oostelijk Zuid-Limburg, Westelijke Mijnstreek, Vaals en Wittem'.

Other References

Dijk, van A., 'Innovatie overheidsbeleid: Duwen en Trekken in de industriepolitiek', VU Uitgeverij, Amsterdam, 1986.

Ministerie van Economische Zaken, projectgroep kwaliteitsbeleid, Nederland: Hoogste Tijd voor Kwaliteit, Den Haag, 11 november 1987.

Ministerie van Economische Zaken, Kwaliteit in Bedrijf, Snijders/Van Hilten, Baarn, december 1991.

Ministerie van Economische Zaken/projectgroep Kwaliteit en Logistiek, Kwaliteit en logistiek, Den Haag, 1988.

Ministerie van Economische Zaken/project groep Kwaliteit en Logistiek, Voortgangsrapportage 1991, Den Haag, 1992.

Ministerie van Economische Zaken, Kwaliteitszorg. De hoofdlijnen van het overheidsbeleid, Den Haag, juli 1985.

Ottolander, Drs. M.projectleider, *Overheid en Kwaliteit*, Ministerie van Economische Zaken, Den Haag, 1992.

Portugal

Zulema Lopes Pereira

1. Introduction

This chapter surveys the current situation in Portugal. First, a brief summary is presented which describes the emergence of quality as a national issue in Portugal. Portugal has special funds available from the EC to develop its industry as an aid to integration into the European Union. PEDIP (Programa Europeu Desenvolument Industria Português, European Programme for the Development of Portuguese Industry) is discussed in some detail. The main focus will be the funds that have been spent in quality promotion activities.

Second, the national quality infrastructure is presented mainly with respect to the creation of a National Quality Management System and the activities related to standardization, metrology and certification of both products and company quality systems.

Third, global, sectoral and regional schemes for quality improvement are described. Because the national movement for quality is quite recent in Portugal, only a few examples of entities that have been developing quality activities are referred to, namely with respect to training and education, consultancy and promotion and awareness schemes. In addition some recently created industrial sectoral bodies are also mentioned.

Fourth, the main conclusions of the survey are outlined and expectations for future development are discussed. The final part of the report presents an inventory of the most important quality promotion activities and main Portuguese organizations committed to quality.

2. The Emergence of Quality as an Issue

As in many other countries, quality activities in Portuguese industry were, until recently, directed towards the inspection of the finished product and its corresponding acceptance or rejection. Moreover, many small and medium-sized enterprises (SMEs) did not have any sort of quality control for their products.

The general belief was that Portuguese products would be accepted by national and international markets due to their low cost as a result of cheap labour. As time went by, labour became more and more expensive, and traditional Portuguese products lacked both the quality and low price needed to remain competitive. Table 17 (page 240) summarizes the main exports of industrial products in 1988; in the same year, revenues coming from tourism were approximately ECU 1939 million, which shows that the quality of this part of the service sector is extremely important for the Portuguese economy.[1]

Table 17: Main Portuguese exports in 1988

Activity	Exports (ECU million)
Textiles, clothes, footwear and leather products	3309
Transport equipment and machines	1389
Wood and cork products	1290
Agricultural products and derivatives	707
Chemical products	603
Mineral products, ceramics and glass	238
Others	972
TOTAL	8508

Note: 1 ECU = 180 ESC.

Source: Tome (1991)

For the past few years, the development of the Single European Market has been perceived as a serious challenge by both the Portuguese government and private industry. It was recognized that in order to become more competitive, the entire Portuguese workforce had to participate in a quality improvement revolution. Many managers are aware of the role that a system of total quality management, from the design stage through to the finished product, or service, aimed at satisfying the consumer, can play in the struggle for the survival of their companies. This is particularly important for small and medium-sized enterprises which form the great majority of industrial firms in Portugal. Others, especially in the automobile industry, needed to quickly develop means for quality improvement because their buyers (e.g. Renault, Ford-Volkswagen) were demonstrating it. The government, also aware of the importance of good quality products and services for the Portuguese economy, has adopted, over the last few years, a comprehensive quality promotion strategy. The SNGQ (Sistema Nacional de Gestão da Qualidade, National Quality Management System) was created in 1983 to supervise all activities and methods related to quality. The SNGQ is coordinated by the IPQ (IPQ, Instituto Português da Qualidade, Portuguese Institute for Quality) which replaced, in 1986, the previous General Directorate for Quality.

The General Directorate for Quality (Direcção Geral da Qualidade) was located in the Ministry of Industry and Energy. Its main activities were related to standardization and metrological issues.

The SNGQ was created in order to promote the participation of several public, semi-public and private bodies in the formulation of the national quality policy and other quality related matters. Its top structure is the CNQ (Conselho Nacional da Qualidade, National Quality Council), directed by the Minister of Industry and Energy, with forty members from several organizations. Examples of members are business associations, trade unions, consumer representatives, universities, sectoral standardization and product certification bodies, testing and metrological laboratories.

Recently, the CNQ issued a proposal for a national quality policy in which it argued that traditional practices of inspection and quality control were not sufficient to produce goods that the consumer wanted at a competitive price and that only a total quality management system could guarantee that companies became competitive.[2] The standardization, certification (of both products and quality systems), accreditation and metrology activities are described in the document and the funds spent in their development for the past few years are mentioned. Therefore, the CNQ addresses its important message to several entities, such as trade and industrial associations, health services, tourism, educational bodies, consumer representatives and public administration. It argues that quality improvement at all levels is a national priority and that it depends not only on the commitment of the government, but that it also depends on the common effort made by these entities to increase awareness of the importance of quality. In particular, the policy document notes that producers have to comply with the directives on product liability and other harmonized EC legislation. Education and training are also specifically referred to, and it is recommended that quality matters are taught, as soon as possible, to everyone. Another important aspect emphasized in the document is consumer education, which is, to a great extent, a responsibility of the Association for Consumers Defense. There is also a reference to the need to urgently improve the quality of the public services. The policy document also recognizes that, despite deficiencies which need correction, there also are many signs showing that things have started to change and many people have already recognized that quality is crucial to national economic development.

In fact, particularly in the last five years, there has been an 'explosion' of interest in quality matters. As a result, several firms have started consultancy and training activities. At the same time, and as mentioned earlier, top management of several manufacturing companies afraid of losing competitive strength have initiated accelerated programmes aimed at the certification of their quality systems, either according to ISO 9000-9004 or according to specific standards established by their clients.

It is also important to refer to the PEDIP programme, launched by the EC for the development of Portuguese industry, which has, to a great extent, made possible many of the recent developments in the quality field. PEDIP is centrally managed by the Ministry of Industry and Energy. Although PEDIP is aimed at improving industry in general, it has a special sub-programme for quality (Programme 6). The other sub-programmes have also contributed to the development of quality infrastructures in Portugal the past three years.

In summary, it seems that the desire to improve competitiveness is driving the recent movement towards total quality at all levels in Portugal. The main driving force to promote and diffuse the quality message seems to be the government, and, in particular, the SNGQ in which public, non-public and private entities are represented. Requests by some companies for certified quality systems from their suppliers has also led to a growing interest and activities in the field. Funds that have been available from the EC have made possible the realization of several activities aimed at promotion and implementation of useful quality schemes.

3. The Quality Infrastructure

The SNGQ and CNQ were introduced in the previous section. The main role of CNQ is to develop both the policy and programmes for quality development; it also assists the Government, as a consulting body, in quality matters. The CNQ has an executive commission and four permanent commissions, namely:

- Permanent Commission for Standardization (CPN)
- Permanent Commission for Certification (CPQ)
- Permanent Commission for Metrology (CPM)
- Permanent Commission for Services and Consumer Goods (CPP).

The IPQ (Portuguese Institute for Quality) is the legal framework for quality matters in Portugal, i.e. the IPQ is the national public body that manages and develops the National Quality Management System. As is logical, IPQ is one of the members of the CNQ Executive Commission and of all CNQ permanent commissions. IPQ is responsible for metrological control, calibration and standardization activities. Within the scope of the SNGQ, the IPQ carries out the official certification of products, the certification of company quality systems according to ISO 9000-9004 (or the equivalent EN 29000-29004) and the accreditation of entities.[3] The IPQ also supplies specialized information on quality issues, such as International and European standards, national technical regulations and quality management issues. Figure 23, below, shows the relationship between SNGQ, CNP and IPQ and Figure 24 (page 243) represents the IPQ structure. At international level, the IPQ ensures Portuguese representation in the quality field (e.g. in ISO, CEN, CEI, CENELEC, CECC, etc.).

Figure 23: The National Quality Management System

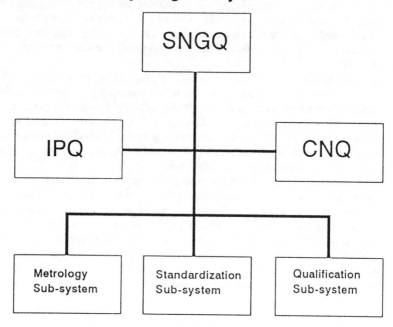

Figure 24: The IPQ Structure

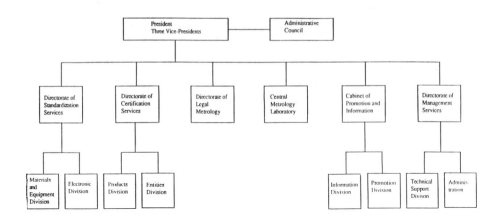

The main IPQ activities are described next, as well as the relationships with other organizations. The IPQ coordinates the activity of primary metrological laboratories, establishes hierarchical chains of measurement standards and oversees the operation of legal metrology. Calibration work is carried out by IPQ itself, by regional offices of the Ministry of Industry and Energy and by associate metrological laboratories. The IPQ applies the NP-EN 45000 standards for the qualification of test and metrological laboratories and inspection bodies. There were, at the beginning of 1992, 48 test laboratories, eight metrological laboratories and seven inspection bodies which had been accredited by IPQ.[4] Recently, the RELACRE, a private association composed of 27 of the 48 accredited test laboratories, was created to represent Portugal within Europe. The RELACRE, however, cannot, for the time being, accredit laboratories.

The preparation of standardization programmes and the approval of NP (Normas Portuguesas, Portuguese Standards) are carried out by IPQ, either directly or in collaboration with ONS (ONS, Orgãos de Normalizaçïo Sectoriais, Sectoral Standardization Bodies). There are two types of ONS: those which have to be approved by IPQ as standardization bodies and those which legally have the right to be standardization bodies (specifically two, the Food Quality Institute and the Portuguese Communications Institute), although the standards prepared by them still need IPQ approval. Standards are usually prepared by the so-called CT (Comissães Técnicas, Technical Committees), being subsequently submitted for IPQ approval. The members of both ONSs and CTs may include representatives of several private entities, namely private companies, universities, certain non-profit organizations and public sector bodies (approximately 1200 people are involved in standardization). There were, by 1992, 35 ONSs.[5]

There are national schemes, based on European procedures, for product certification (either voluntary or compulsory), involving features related to consumer health and safety, and environmental issues. The IPQ establishes and manages marks of conformity to be applied when the product is certified. Besides the IPQ, there are four sectoral certification bodies.

The certification of companies' quality systems complying with NP-EN 29000 (equivalent to ISO 9000) is also carried out by the IPQ, after the audit proves that the system follows the standard requirements. By 1992, there were 16 companies certified, the majority of them according to NP-EN 29002 (two of which were in the service sector).[6] These companies are, however, preparing their systems to be certified according to NP-EN 29001 as soon as possible. The IPQ expects that the number of certified companies will rise to 150 by the beginning of 1994.

Besides the usual European organizations in which all national standardization and metrological bodies are represented (e.g. CEN, CENELEC, EOTC), the IPQ has several other links within Europe. For instance, the IPQ is a member of EQNET (European Network for Quality System Assessment and Certification), within which cooperation agreements with Spain and Denmark have been established and the same with the United Kingdom and Switzerland is expected soon.

At a regional level, the IPQ has established close relationships with the Spanish Ministry of Industry and Energy, with AENOR (Spanish Association for Standardization and Certification) and RELE (Spanish Network of Test Laboratories). As far as training is concerned, the IPQ only develops training programmes for their own auditors and for weights and measurements inspectors of the Ministry of Industry and Energy. The two main concerns of the IPQ, at the moment, is to establish a solid base for future developments in quality and to gain an international reputation and credibility in the areas of standardization, certification, calibration and metrology. Once this has been accomplished, the IPQ may delegate some of its activities to other organizations, such as, for instance, the certification of company quality systems.

4. National Quality Schemes and Initiatives
4.1 Global Schemes

Any company operating in Portugal can be a candidate for a PEDIP programme. As large companies, however, usually have their own resources for quality and productivity improvement, the main beneficiaries of PEDIP funds have been SMEs. PEDIP is not an infrastructure for quality promotion, but it certainly contributed for to it a great extent. The global analysis of PEDIP will help to explain the 'explosion' of quality activities in these recent years. In fact, it would have been virtually impossible, for both the Portuguese government and industry, to develop in such a short timescale the infrastructures and activities necessary for quality and productivity improvement if PEDIP funds had not been available.

The PEDIP Programme is supported by the EC for the development of Portuguese industry. Although PEDIP is aimed at improving industry in general it has a special sub-programme for quality (Programme 6). In addition, the other sub-programmes have contributed to the development of the quality infrastructure in Portugal.

Programme 1 of the PEDIP scheme, Technological Infrastructures, made possible the creation of five regional metrological laboratories (see Section 5, below). The programme also funded new technological sectoral centres for the development of traditional industrial sectors, such as wood and furniture, textiles and clothing, ceramics and glass, footwear, etc. The total investment was approximately ECU 57.2 million, of which ECU 49 million were PEDIP funded.

Programme 2 of PEDIP was directed to training, run either in companies or, in certain cases, in public organizations (e.g. post-graduation courses at universities). Training actions, however, were carried out in several areas, making it difficult to evaluate how much was spent in quality training. Programme 3, Production Investment, had several measures, one of which was directly aimed at quality improvement. In this programme, the total investment, for 278 projects mainly related to the development of laboratories, was ECU 57.5 million, of which ECU 24.3 million was PEDIP funded. Programme 5, Productivity Missions, was aimed at the promotion of the use of new techniques and technologies in industrial companies. As with Programme 2, it includes several actions and it is difficult to estimate how much was spent to specifically improve quality.

Programme 6, Quality Missions and Industrial Design, is specifically addressed to quality issues. Several measures are included in Programme 6. One of them is directed to the implementation and accreditation of new metrological laboratories. Another measure is related to the promotion of campaigns for quality awareness in industrial companies. There also is a specific measure for quality systems certification. The other measures are related to available funds for promotion of measurement instruments calibration; implementation of plans for the development of supplier-client cooperation; development of studies aimed at the diagnosis and characterization of a specific sector or region; support of industrial design promotion activities. The total investment for Programme 6 was ECU 64.3 million (for 477 projects), of which PEDIP provided ECU 46.1 million. Table 18 shows a summary of these projects, according to the promoting body.

Table 18: Promoting bodies for Programme 6 of PEDIP(Quality Missions and Industrial Design)

Body	Projects		PEDIP funding	
	Number	%	Ecus in millions	%
Industrial Associations	89	20	9.094	20
Industrial Companies	241	50	9.144	20
Non-profit organizations	147	30	27.844	60
Total	477	100	46.082	100

Source: APQ

At the moment, the PEDIP head office, where the global management of the programme is carried out, is trying to evaluate the results of the programme. The analysis will be made in three directions: direct audits of promoting entities, inter-sectoral analysis to evaluate the impact of PEDIP in Portuguese industry and the influence of PEDIP on industrial management attitude.

One of the most important organizations in national quality promotion has been the APQ (Associaçïo Portuguesa para a Qualidade, Portuguese Association for Quality). The APQ was set up in 1969 and is a private, non-profit organization. APQ members are individuals, companies and public bodies dealing with quality matters. The central office is located in Lisbon; there are two regional offices, one in Porto (North) and the other one in Faro (South). The main APQ activities have been:

* edition of publications on quality issues;
* organization of seminars, conferences and activities aimed at spreading the quality message throughout the country;
* consultancy;
* education and training activities; and,
* creation and development of sectoral working groups.[7]

The APQ participates in the National Quality Management System and is the ONS (Sectoral Standardization Body) for quality management and assurance standards; these standards are prepared by APQ, before being submitted to the IPQ for approval. APQ is a member of the EOQ (European Organization for Quality), EFQM (European Foundation for Quality Management), EFCQA (European Federation of Quality Circle Associations) and the AECC (Spanish Association for Quality).

Between 1987 and 1991, APQ undertook a project called 'APQ in the regions/Quality in companies'; the main objective of which was to carry out a survey on the manufacturing sector, to spread the quality message in private companies (mainly SMEs) of several Portuguese regions and to motivate their managers towards quality improvement. The work was carried out by the APQ technical department. About 4000 companies were visited by four teams of two people each. Only 1% of the companies were 'large companies'; the other 99% were SMEs (72% small and 27% medium-sized firms). 78% of the firms were industrial; the remaining firms were service (6%), trade (9%), construction (2%) and other non-specified activities (5%).[8]

One of the conclusions from the survey was that, in the period 1987 to 1989, 50% of the firms had some sort of quality activity; nevertheless, less than 5% had set up a proper quality management system. As regards training, 28% had either their own structure or contracts with outside firms for training activities. The survey has proved to be quite useful. APQ had a good picture of the quality related activities already promoted in the country and could therefore establish priorities, in terms of awareness actions, training and consultancy, for the near future. In addition, many SMEs became aware of the importance of quality as a result of the survey and started to demand both training and consultancy from APQ and other bodies. Therefore, in 1990, APQ in cooperation with the IEFP (Instituto do Emprego e Formação Profissional, Institute of Employment and Training) established a training centre (CEQUAL) for quality related matters. Several courses are taught at CEQUAL (Centro de Formação Profissional para a Qualidade, Quality Training Centre) to supervisors, managers and other people interested in learning statistical quality control techniques and other methods for quality planning and improvement. CEQUAL has its main centre in Lisbon and another Porto (in the north). Table 19, below, shows the evolution of CEQUAL activities since 1990.

Table 19: Evolution of CEQUAL activities

Year	Number of actions	Number of people involved	Training hours
1990	56	1 518	6 154
1991*	109	1 685	12, 980
1992*	178	1 861	16,533
*-Estimate			

Source: APQ

CEQUAL training activities can be carried out at the centres or inside the companies. Usually, when this is the case, some sort of consultancy is also performed. CEQUAL has already worked with a few large companies, such as COVINA (glass), MABOR (tyres), MAP (plastics), ALCATEL (telecommunications). As regards the service sector, two actions were carried out in the health and insurance areas.

Another consequence of the survey carried out by APQ was the establishment of the National Quality Campaign, promoted in collaboration with IPQ and funded by PEDIP (Programme 6, approximately ECU 0.9 million). The campaign (1991 to 1992) had as a main objective the creation of a national quality consciousness amongst both consumers and producers. The main activities have been:

- Motivation campaign, at national level, on the need for quality improvement.
- Specific actions in supermarkets aimed at consumers awareness of their rights, product safety, certified product and product quality assurance.
- Information actions in the industrial sector.
- Organization of seminars and conferences on relevant quality matters.
- Institution of a quality award for the best companies, not only for the quality of their products, but also for the quality of their organization and quality management system; there are three types of awards for, respectively, large Portuguese companies, SMEs and subsidiaries of multinational companies.
- Press award for the best reported work on quality.
- Edition of leaflets and posters.
- Edition of the book entitled 'Portugal and Europe in World Quality Market'.

- Production of two videos, one on 'Total Quality' and the other one on 'Quality Assurance'.
- Organization of a Quality Forum for young people and a contest for Portuguese students aimed at stimulating their creativeness about quality issues.

The campaign results have been quite good. In the Quality award for 1992, the APQ received 25 applications, six from SMEs, nine from large Portuguese companies and ten from multinational companies.

Another important project in which APQ has been involved is the Total Quality Project at Oeiras City Council (Oeiras is a small town, approximately 20 km from Lisbon). The work has been carried out in cooperation with FAQ/OUEST (Fédération des Associations Qualité de l'Ouest, Western France Federation of Quality Associations) and the French city of Angers, where a similar project was launched with good results. About 600 people were interviewed during the first phase of the project. The second phase, aimed at implementing new working schemes, is now underway.

APQ has also been involved in a few European projects, directly or indirectly related to quality. One of them is the DELTA (Developing European Learning through Technological Advance) artisan programme, the main objective of which is the development of new learning methods using artificial intelligence. APQ has received about ECU 39,000 for this project. A project within the FLAIR (Food Linked Agro-Industrial Research) is investigating food technology with the aim of improving the quality of food products and increasing the competitiveness of food producers. Within the COMETT (Community Programme in Education and Training for Technology) programme, APQ takes part in MAQUIT, a University-Company Association for training, led by the ISQ (Instituto de Soldadura e Qualidade, Portuguese Welding and Quality Institute). The APQ participates in the coordination of programmes for the several quality courses planned by MAQUIT.

APQ has some short-term development plans, mainly related to consultancy in SMEs. As regards training, APQ and CEQUAL are planning to expand their activities with the creation of four new centres (Castelo Branco, Aveiro, Viseu and Setúbal).

The AIP (Associação Industrial Portuguesa, Portuguese Industrial Association) is another non-profit private organization involved in quality activities. It is interesting to note that the APQ was a section of AIP before it became independent when their activities had grown enough to justify an independent quality association. AIP is one of the members of the SNGQ, specifically within CPQ and CPP.

The AIP has several departments; one of which is the Innovation Technical Department, which deals with technical development and promotes cooperation between Portuguese, European and other international firms. The Department offers advice on appropriate organisations with the necessary expertise to solve any quality or technical problems it members may have. The AIP has created twelve regional associations (see Section 5) throughout Portugal which have also contributed to the promotion of quality activities.

Another important entity is the AI Port (Associação Industrial Portuense, Industrial Association of Porto), which is a private, national, non-profit body. AI Port. is also a member of the SNGQ, participating in the four CNQ commissions (CPN,

CPM, CPQ and CPP). AI Port. maintains close links with IPQ, APQ and CEQUAL. The AI Port. has a specific department which provides technological support to its associates; one of its main activities has been quality promotion within companies. AI Port. started to develop quality activities in 1985, due to its integration in the SNGQ and the growing demand from associate members. Most development occurred between 1987 and 1991; primarily in quality motivation actions and quality education and training.

AI Port. has promoted quality awareness in a number of ways. One was through a 1991 fair, 'Technology, Quality and Design'. Another, was through a quality campaign (1991-92) directed in particular, to AI Port. associate members and, more generally to other industrial firms interested in quality. The main objective was to promote quality within companies with the aim of increasing their competitiveness. The campaign, however, has been mainly directed to specific sectors and will be examined in further detail in Section 4.2.

AI Port. has undertaken a survey to identify the deficiencies and problems faced by firms, especially SMEs. A simple questionnaire was sent to about 1000 companies in several industrial sectors. Questions were asked about the quality departmental infrastructure, the different stages where quality control is conducted, suppliers qualification schemes, quality standards used in the company, plans for the quality system certification, etc.

AI Port. has an educational and training division where several quality courses are taught. Usually AI Port. contracts external people as lecturers. There have also been some training actions carried out in cooperation with CEQUAL. In the future, AI Port. is planning to carry on the quality campaign and to start offering a quality consultancy service.

There are several private organisations which have also been developing quality training and consultancy activities throughout Portugal. Among them one should mention the ISQ. The ISQ is a Sectoral Standardization Body, a member of CPM and CPQ; it also has links with European and other International bodies and has participated in a number of European projects. Since 1984, with the cooperation of the UNL (Universidade Nova de Lisboa, New University of Lisbon) it has been running a one-year post-graduation course on Quality Engineering. The course lasts 350 hours and covers 15 different subjects. The demand has been good with the result that is ISQ running three courses a year, in several regions. Another course is run by ISQ on Quality Costs (this lasts 36 hours), which is sponsored by the European Social Fund.

Because the universities and polytechnics are not nationally regulated, they are free to decide the content of their courses. There appears to be, however, a growing concern about quality, especially in engineering faculties.

Consultancy on quality related activities has been increasing over the past three years. Some commercial organizations offer consultancy services throughout the country. Some freelance consultants have also been carrying out work on quality issues. Apart from the organizations already mentioned, there are other private commercial organizations which have been running short specialized courses on quality. The enterprises either use their own resources or apply for available subsidies.

4.2 Sectoral Schemes

Table 20, below, provides a sectoral breakdown of PEDIP funding (see Section 4.1).

Table 20: Sector of Activity of PEDIP Programme 6

Industrial Sector	Number of Projects	Total Investment (ECUs in millions)	PEDIP funding (ECUs in millions)
Non-metals extraction and industrial rocks	1	0.006	0.006
Food, drinks and tobacco	7	3.511	2.594
Textiles and clothing	37	6.972	3.883
Wood and cork	15	1.661	0.994
Paper industry	7	0.911	0.483
Chemical products, rubber and plastics	33	1.883	1.333
Non-metals industry	88	10.322	7.972
Metallurgy	17	1.711	1.317
Machines and other equipment	151	11.072	8.239
Others	121	26.256	19.256
Total	477	64.305	46.077

Source: APQ

Of significance in their sector is the IQA (Institute de Qualidade Alimentar, Food Quality Institute) of the Ministry of Agriculture, which supervises quality activities in the food sector. IQA also belongs to SNGQ and takes part in CPN, CPM, CPQ and CPP (see Section 3). Food quality standards are prepared by the IQA and submitted to IPQ for approval. The accreditation of food industry laboratories is carried out by IPQ with the collaboration of IQA experts. The IQA is a sectoral product certification body and is also trying to promote within food companies the need for quality systems certification.

It has already been mentioned that several sectoral centres were recently created in traditional areas such as textiles and clothing, footwear, ceramics and glass, cork, wood and furniture. These centres are private and operate nationwide. They develop information material in their specific area and collaborate with firms, mainly SMEs, in relevant technical issues. Quality related activities form part of their work. The majority of them have accredited sectoral laboratories. It is also known that some of them have been organizing short quality courses and promoting seminars on quality topics. One centre is CIVEC (which focuses on clothing). Another centre, CITEVE (textiles and clothing) is starting a survey on quality infrastructures that exist, at present, inside textile firms. CTIMM (wood and furniture) has been promoting seminars on the need for certification of quality systems and has also planned short courses on quality, specifically addressed to the wood and furniture sector. It is believed that these technological centres can become, in a relatively short time, one of the most important promoters of quality within traditional industrial sectors.

The University of Minho also has engineering courses on the textile and clothing industry, contributing to a great extent to the education of experts in this traditional Portuguese sector. AI Port has also been promoting, in cooperation with APQ, sectoral activities aimed at increasing quality awareness and improvement within traditional industrial sectors. In 1991, AI Port started campaigns within the metallurgy, textile, electric and electronic sectors and is planning to do the same during the present year in the cork, special tools, ceramic, glass, furniture, shoes and mechanical components sectors. A one-day seminar and publication of specific information brochures are planned for each sector, followed by visits of AI Port. staff and outside consultants to several firms (mainly SMEs), in order to motivate people towards quality improvement. Results will be evaluated through questionnaires, reports and graphic analysis of data which will allow the identification of the main deficiencies and actions that should be taken for quality and productivity development and the consequent increase in competitiveness.

5. Regional Quality Schemes and Initiatives

5.1 Global Schemes

Programme 1 of the PEDIP scheme, Technological Infrastructures, made possible the creation of five regional metrological laboratories, promoted by the IPQ, as presented in Table 21 (page 252).

Most organizations in the quality field have only recently started to consider future regional schemes and initiatives for quality promotion. However, it is worth mentioning the project led by APQ (Portuguese Association for Quality) and AIP (Portuguese Industrial Association) in the Algarve, with the collaboration of regional entities. The main objective of the now completed project was to motivate managers to increase the quality of both the industrial and service sectors in the region in order to become more competitive. Approximately ECU 105,000 were spent, 80% of which were sponsored by PEDIP. Several actions were realized in a few sectors, such as the food industry, cork, wood, ceramics, plastics and decorative stone. The main actions were the promotion of seminars, identification of standards, equipment and methods that could be applied to each sector and audits to the quality systems implemented in companies. The project had good results and the promoting organizations expect to be able to launch similar projects.

Table 21: Regional metrological laboratories (PEDIP funding)

Region	Total Investment (MECU's)	PEDIP funding (MECU's)
Lisboa	4.436	3.370
Porto	0.987	0.740
Évora	3.515	2.670
Coimbra	4.461	3.389
Faro	4.234	3.216
Total	17.633	13.394

Source: APQ

Table 22, below, gives the regional distribution of Programme 6 (focusing on quality management systems) of the PEDIP scheme.

Table 22 Regional distribution (PEDIP Programme 6).

District	Number	Percentage Projects	PEDIP funding (ECUs in millions)	Percentage
Aveiro	67	14.0	9.711	15.10
Braga	12	2.5	0.970	1.50
Castelo Branco	2	0.4	0.053	0.10
Coimbra	17	3.6	1.160	1.80
Faro	3	0.6	0.267	1.80
Guarda	1	0.2	0.020	0.03
Leiria	29	6.1	1.086	1.69
Lisboa	174	36.5	28.329	44.05
Porto	136	28.5	19.650	30.56
Santarém	8	1.7	0.395	0.61
Setúbal	19	4.0	1.689	2.63
Viana do Castelo	1	0.2	0.004	0.006
Vila Real	1	0.2	0.010	0.02
Viseu	7	1.5	0.960	c1.49
Total	477	100.0	64.305	100.00

Source: APQ

NERA, one of the regional nuclei created by AIP participated in the Algarve project. In fact, AIP has created the so-called 'regional nuclei' (NERs) for several regions of Portugal. These are:

- NERA   Algarve
- NERBE   Beja
- NERCAB   Castelo Branco
- NERVIR   Vila Real
- NERLEI   Leiria
- NERPOR   Portalegre
- NERSET   Setúbal
- NERSANT   Santarém
- NERGA   Guarda
- NERE   Évora
- NERLIS   Lisboa
- NERBA   Bragança

The NERs have been fairly active in promoting several activities aimed at the technical development of regional companies, among which some are related to quality improvement. For instance, NERA, from Algarve, participated in the already mentioned Algarve Project. NERLEI (Leiria) collaborated, in 1989, with the ISQ in the organization of the quality engineering course in Leiria. In the same year, NERLEI organized a 210 hour course for quality control technicians. In 1990, APQ and NERLEI organized two quality awareness seminars for industrial managers. NERSANT (Santarém) and NERSET (Setúbal) have also carried out some actions in the quality area. AIRO (Associação Industrial da Região do Oeste) is a regional, non-profit, industrial association located in the west of Portugal.

AIRO has also promoted a few quality related activities, some with CENCAL cooperation. CENCAL has a training centre and an accredited laboratory for the ceramic industry, which is the most important industry in the region. AIRO and CENCAL have promoted training activities in quality, some with CEQUAL collaboration. AIRO has also promoted seminars and missions inside regional companies, usually with the support of APQ, to motivate managers towards quality improvement. Although the APQ project in the regions was mentioned in Section 4.1 due to its importance for the development of APQ activities at national level, it can also be considered as a central-regional oriented activity, since it took place essentially in five regions (Leiria, Castelo Branco, Santarém, Évora, Portalegre). The same can be said about training activities led by the CEQUAL office at Porto and by AI Port. Although they are open to any company in the country, the main demand comes from the north of Portugal. All these activities are organized by national organizations but the aim is to develop some of their quality actions for companies located in the north. As one might expect, the several courses run by universities located in several regions also have a local impact, although the students can come from any part of the country.

5.2 Sectoral Schemes

The sectoral centres mentioned in Section 4.2 have started to create their own infrastructures in several regions. It is hoped that these entities may become more active in promoting local (regional) initiatives for the development of traditional Portuguese industry, mainly inside SMEs. Cooperation between these regional sectoral centres and the AIP nuclei (NERs) can probably help, to a great extent, the future development, in small and medium-sized enterprises, of both quality and productivity.

6. Overview and Outlook

The increasing market competitiveness felt all over the world has been perceived by the Portuguese government, industry and services as a serious threat in the near future. To become more competitive, Portuguese products and services have to be improved with regard to quality. So, the National Quality Management System, which integrates several public, semi-public and private entities, was created in 1983 to supervise all activities and methods related to quality. This has led to a growing participation of all active forces of the country in a national drive towards the improvement of quality in the industrial and service sectors.

For the past five years, many activities (the national quality campaign, the establishment of quality awards, seminars, conferences and other awareness initiatives) have taken place throughout the country. These activities have contributed to a change in managerial attitude. Several entities, both public and private, made this possible. Among them, one should cite the Ministry of Industry and Energy, the Portuguese Institute for Quality, the Portuguese Association for Quality, the Portuguese Industrial Association and the Industrial Association of Porto. The main achievements have been the creation of several infrastructures for quality improvement, the development of new technological sectoral centres and of regional industrial associations, the increasing awareness of the importance of quality in a competitive Single European Market and the activities already carried out by industrial and services companies for quality improvement. Among them, one can mention training actions both inside and outside the company and the implementation in a few firms of total quality systems. It can then be concluded that the considerable efforts made in the past few years have been successful. There is, however, much more to be achieved, especially with regard to small and medium-sized firms. The technological sectoral centres recently created can contribute, to a great extent, to the technical improvement of traditional manufacturing areas.

As regards regional development, the nuclei created by AIP can also give their contribution to industrial improvement. The cooperation of sectoral centres and regional industrial nuclei will certainly be of great benefit for the achievement of good results both in quality and productivity The national entities directly involved in quality, such as IPQ, APQ/CEQUAL, AIP and AI Port, can certainly cooperate, as already happens at the moment, with these centres and regional nuclei. Cooperation might involve the outline of main guidelines for improvement, technical assistance and collaboration in the promotion of seminars, conferences and training schemes. It has to be noted that APQ and CEQUAL already have plans for the creation of new regional training centres. As regards education at universities, it seems that only a few of these institutions have been committed to quality.

In fact, it is believed that certain faculties, and especially those running engineering and management graduate courses, should introduce into their curricula several quality concepts (e.g. TQM, SPC, reliability, design of experiments and Taguchi methods) which can be very useful in any company. Specialized courses on quality (e.g. post-graduation courses) should also attract more attention; these courses could be run, for instance, with the cooperation of experts from other EC countries. Besides the teaching aspect, research should also be carried out in quality standards, techniques and methods that should be of interest to Portuguese industry and services, especially with regard to their application in SMEs.

To conclude, the continuing activities of the IPQ, APQ and other national organizations, as well as cooperation between sectoral-regional entities, universities and industry, supplier and clients, are having short and medium-term results on quality and productivity improvement. This is essential if Portuguese companies are to play an active role in the European Single Market.

7. Main Initiatives and Organizations for Quality Promotion

7.1 Initiatives

Creation of the Portuguese Association for Quality (APQ): 1969

Creation of the National Quality Management System (SNGQ): 1983

Creation of The Portuguese Institute for Quality (IPQ): 1986

PEDIP project (funding): 1989-present

Project 'APQ in the Regions': 1987-91

National Quality Campaign and institution of quality awards: 1991-92

Promotion of seminars and conferences on quality at national, sectoral and regional levels

7.2 Main Organizations

Name	Address	Telephone/Fax
Main Quality Organizations		
Instituto Português da Qualidade IPQ (Portuguese Institute for Quality	Rue José Estevão 83 1199 Lisboa Codex	(01) 523978,
Associação Portuguesa para a Qualidade APQ (Portuguese Association for Quality)	Plaçã das Indústrias 1300 Lisboa	(01) 363 6443,
Gabinete Gestor do PEDIP (PEDIP Management Office)	Rua Rodrigues Sampaio 13 Lisboa	(01) 315 5548
Associação Industrial Portuguesa AIP (Portuguese Industrial Association)	Praça das Indústrias 1300 Lisboa	
Associação Industrial Portuense AIPort. (Industrial Association of Porto)	Exponor Parque de Exposiçḛes do Norte Leça da Palmeira 4450 Matosinhos, (02) 995 8462/995 6089	
Instituto de Soldadura e Qualidade ISQ (Quality and Welding Institute)	R. Tomás de Figueiredo 16-A 1500 Lisboa	(01) 706361
Instituto de Qualidade Alimentar IQA (Food Quality Institute)	Av. Conde de Valbom 96-98	1000 Lisboa

Examples of CEQUAL Quality Courses

Title	Total Time (Teaching Time)	Locality
Quality Engineering	783 (283)	Lisbon, and Oporto
Quality Management	472 (202)	Lisbon, Oporto
Quality Auditors	119	Lisbon, Oporto
Information Systems for Quality Management	36	Lisbon, Oporto
Quality Audits	21	Lisbon, Oporto
Quality in Services	35	Lisbon, Oporto
Company Certification	35	Lisbon, Oporto
Quality Function Deployment	21	Lisbon, Oporto
Taguchi Methods	35	Lisbon, Oporto
SPC (Statistical Process Control)	28	Lisbon, Oporto
Quality Costs	14	Lisbon, Oporto
Evaluation and Qualification of Suppliers	28	Lisbon, Oporto
Failure Mode Analysis and its Effects	35	Lisbon, Oporto
Managers' Quality Awareness	7	Braga, Porto, Castelo Branco, Lisboa, Setubal, Faro, Aveiro, Viseu, Torres, Novas, Leiria

A.I. Portuguese Quality Courses

Title	Time (Hours)
Preparation for quality system certification according to NP-EN 2900	30
Quality Control and Assurance Systems	30
Quality : Implementation and Strategies	105 (It comprises Quality Management Systems, Value Analysis, SPC, Quality Circles and Motivation)
Quality Audit	30
Quality in Services	21
Quality Manual : Methods and Procedures	100
Note: All courses are run in Matosinhos (North of Portugal)	

University Courses in Quality

University	Course	Subjects
Universidade Nova de Lisboa - Faculdade de Ciencias e Tecnologia	Materials Engineering	Statistical Quality Control, Quality Management, Reliability, Metrology and Standardization
	Industrial Production Engineering, Chemical Engineering	Quality Planning and Control
	MSc Course in Industrial Engineering	Quality Planning and Control
Universidade de Aveiro	Materials Engineering	Quality Control
	Physical Engineering, Industrial Management and Engineering	Industrial Quality
Universidade de Coimbra Faculdade de Ciencias e Technologia	Mechanical Engineering	Reliability and Quality Control
	Electronics Engineering	Reliability and Quality Control
Universidade do Minho	Mechanical Engineering	Physical Quality Control
	Production Engineering Textile Engineering Clothing Engineering	Quality Management
	Textile Engineering	Textile Quality Control I and II
		Reliability and Quality Control
Universidade do Porto	Mechanical Engineering	Quality Management
Universidade de Evora	Biotechnology Engineering	Food Products Control
Universidade Tecnica de Lisboa Instituto Superiod de Agronomia	Chemical Engineering	Quality Control
(Private Universities)		
Electromechanic and Energy Institute	Industrial Management	Quality Control
	(3 year Production Engineering courses)	
	Electromechanic Engineering	
Universidade Autonoma de Lisboa Luis de Camees	Production Engineering	Quality Control
Universidade Catoica (Porto) School of Biotechnology	Food Engineering	Food Quality Control
Universidade Lusiada Vila Nova de Famalicio	Engineering and Industrial Management	Reliability

References

1. Tomé, João Boléo (1991), *Portugal e a Europa no Mercado Mundial da Qualidade*, Lisboa: APQ

2. CNQ (1991); Proposta da Política Nacional da Qualidade.

3. IPQ leaflet (1991), *Portuguese Institute for Quality*, Ministry of Industry and Energy/IPQ.

4. *Qualirama*, IPQ, March/April 1992, 31-35.

5. Anon (1991), 'Apresentação da Associação Portuguesa para a Qualidade', *Forum Calidad*, 22 Mayo 1991, pp 52-53.

6. *Qualirama*, op. cit.

7. APQ. Projecto 'APQ nas regiões-Qualidade nas empresas'.

Spain

Mark Boden (with the assistance of Amaya Sámano)

1. Introduction

From the beginning of the 1980s, the Spanish economy has undergone a number of important and profound changes. Many of these developments are attributable to Spain's membership of the EU, and have given rise to a situation where the competitiveness of Spanish industry has become perceived as a critical issue. Industrial quality has emerged as a key feature in increasing competitiveness, and the formulation and implementation of a large scale orchestrated national policy for industrial quality PNCI (Plan Nacional de Calidad Industrial, National Plan for Industrial Quality) clearly reflects this.

A second important feature of the Spanish situation is the country's political and economic organization into 17 autonomous communities. The variations in the nature of industrial development across these communities is not inconsiderable. The regional dimension of quality in Spain is examined in what are felt to be two contrasting regions, the heavily industrialised Cataluña in the north and the less developed Andalucía in the south.

This Chapter draws on a number of sources. This includes documentation from a number of the organizations involved in the field of quality in Spain at national, regional and sectoral levels and a number of interviews with representatives of these organizations. In particular, much information has been obtained from the Ministry of Industry, Commerce and Tourism MICYT Ministerio de Industría Comercio y Turismo, Ministry of Industry, Commerce and Tourism), the government body responsible for PNCI.

1.1 Evolution of the Spanish Economy

In the context of the country's recent economic developments Spanish industry has experienced a number of structural changes. In particular, there have been measurable improvements in a range of industrial indicators (e.g. employment levels, productivity, labour cost per unit of production, a greater presence in higher value added sectors). There has also been a strong policy orientation towards industrial reconversion. Such positive changes are particularly evident in a number of industry sectors, including energy, food, drink and tobacco. Within the Spanish economy, small and medium-sized enterprises (SMEs) are still of growing importance, particularly in the footwear and clothing industries, and in wood, cork, paper, graphic art and metal products.

With the advent of the European Single Market in 1993, Spanish industry has had to continue its rapid adaptation in order to come to terms with an increasingly competitive market. Enhanced competitiveness is seen as critical, and is the justification for increased investment in organizations, training and education for professionals. Spanish industrial activity has become increasingly centred around a core composed of two principal characteristics: innovation, and the matching of market demand with product quality and price. The salient aspects of the European policy environment, within which the Spanish government administration is attempting to meet the challenges of increased competitiveness and industrial adaptation, can be characterized as follows:

- A free trade policy for goods and services;
- A 'New Approach' in meeting of the requirements of European standards and/or national standards (The 'New Approach' concept is discussed in more detail in Part Four of this book);
- A 'Global Approach' to standardization and certification (again, this is discussed in more detail in Part Four); and
- A competitive policy based on quality improvements.

Spain oriented its industrial activity towards technical assistance in quality control, which subsequently spread to the design and development of new, high value-added products and particularly to technological R&D projects aimed at increasing productivity and thus the competitiveness of Spanish firms.

2. The Emergence of Quality as an Issue

The above developments in the orientation of Spanish industry have led to significant growth in the importance of quality issues in Spain, particularly with respect to their perceived role in enhancing the competitiveness of Spain. This growth in importance is reflected both in the continued development of Spain's quality infrastructure, most notably through the creation or change in responsibility of a number of both public and private quality related bodies during the last decade, and in the scope of government policies for the promotion of industrial quality. This has culminated in the formulation of a broad ranging national plan. Of particular significance is the role played by MINER (Ministerio de Industria y Energia, Spanish Ministry of Industry and Energy) and subsequently MICYT (Ministerio de Industria, Comercio y Turismo, Ministry of Industry, Commerce and Tourism).

In recent years, AECC (Asociacón Española para la Calidad, Spanish Association for Quality), in existence for more than 25 years, has steadily increased its activities across the entire quality field, playing an important role within the national plan. In 1986, Spanish industry supported the launch of AENOR (Asociacón Española de Normalización y Certifición, Spanish Association for Standardization and Certification) to assume the function of elaborating UNE (Una Norma Española, Spanish standards). It was officially recognized by MINER in February 1986. At the same time, RELE (Red Española de Laboratorios de Ensayo (Spanish Network of Test Laboratories), the SCI (Sistema de Calibración Industrial, System of Industrial Calibration) and MINER, and later MICYT, set about improving the industrial structure of Spain through intensive capital investment. A proportion of MINER's investments were focused on the promotion of intangibles, and it is these which provided the basis for the Ministry' initial series of campaigns for industrial quality. Since 1985, there have been a variety of these campaigns aimed at both specific sectors and industry in general. In 1985, a plan was initiated for the promotion of design and style, which essentially aimed to increase the value added in Spanish textile industry. Three years later, in 1988, this was followed by a plan for the promotion of quality, design and style for small and medium-sized manufacturers.

Since 1986, an annual series of 'Campaigns for Industrial Quality' has been implemented. These have aimed mainly at: publicizing quality issues; promoting industrial quality; training and education; information systems - the design of a communication network; and commercialization.

In tracing the historical development of the emergence of quality issues in Spain, recourse can be made to a number of studies, carried out at both national and regional levels, including Andalucía and País Vasco. In 1986, MINER carried out an evaluation of the extent of implementation of satisfactory quality systems using a sample of 500 Spanish SMEs, with between 50-450 employees, distributed throughout different sectors and nine of the seventeen autonomous communities.[1] In this survey, a 'satisfactory quality system' was taken to mean that the minimum compulsory requirements had been satisfied. Some 26.5% of the firms surveyed were found to have satisfactory quality systems. Table 23, below, illustrates levels of satisfactory quality systems in the nine regions covered in 1986.

Table 23: Satisfactory quality systems in 1986
(By Autonomous Communities)

Community	Number of firms evaluated	Percentage satisfaction
País Vasco	86	32.2
Galicia	17	35.5
Madrid	32	34.3
Cataluña	126	27.0
Castilla-Leon	19	21.0
Navarra	24	20.8
Aragon	31	19.3
Andalucía	37	19.0
País Valenciano	43	18.6

Source: MINER 1988

The survey also revealed that the sectoral distribution of satisfactory quality system is similar and reaches approximately 24%. Table 24 (page 264) illustrates this.

Table 24: Satisfactory quality system in 1986 (By sectors)

Sector	Number of firms evaluated	Percentage satisfaction
Automotive	23	52.2
Chemical	33	45.5
Plastics	31	33.3
Electric-electronic	31	29.0
Metal products	64	26.5
Non-metal minerals	43	27.9
Agro-food	57	22.8
Textiles	48	12.5
Paper	27	11.2
Wood and cork	14	7.2
Footwear	25	4.0

Source: MINER 1988

The above table shows that, in 1986, satisfactory quality systems were most common in three interrelated sectors, namely: automobile, chemical and plastics. However, the percentage of satisfactory quality systems decreases when the type of activity changes to the craft industries. Both these tables emphasize the need for substantial work in quality promotion across Spanish industry at the time of the survey. The subsequent policies for quality promotion and related activities enacted by MINER and then MICYT, particularly through the PNCI, have led to significant changes in the levels of awareness and adoption of quality systems and practices. Tables in subsequent sections illustrate aspects of this progress in terms of the aid given to firms and regions under the PNCI.

3. The Quality Infrastructure

Currently in Spain, there are a large number of organizations with some interest or involvement in the quality field. The principal government body, responsible for the PNCI and its implementation, is the Subdirección General de Calidad Industrial (Subdirectorate of Industrial Quality) of the Dirección General de Politica Tecnologica (Directorate General for Technology Policy) of MICYT. There are also a number of public and recognised industrial bodies with responsibilities across the range of quality related activities, a key subset of which is described below. Various public and private laboratories are also integrated into the national and regional infrastructures, (again playing a range of roles in the quality field). Universities and other higher education institutes, particularly engineering and business and management schools, are playing an important role in the education and training dimensions of quality.

There are numerous private consultancy firms active in the provision of managerial and technical advice, training and other services with respect to quality. They operate throughout the country and many of the larger firms have regional offices.

On a regional basis there are centres for the promotion of quality in the autonomous regions, promoting awareness and providing education and training. Like-
wise, Chambers of commerce strengthen the infrastructure at the regional level.

At sectoral level, in addition to the firms themselves, industry associations and
industrial research associations have made contributions to the diffusion of quality
concepts and techniques.

At the heart of the national infrastructure for industrial quality in Spain, particularly with respect to the implementation of the PNCI, are those institutions with
responsibility for standardisation, certification, calibration, testing and inspection.
These institutions have been established or have assumed greater responsibility
during the past decade. The core of the Spanish quality infrastructure integrates
four principal institutions, which are discussed in some detail below: AENOR,
AENICRE (Asociación de Entidades de Inspección y Control Reglamentario,
Association of Bodies for Inspection and Regulatory Control), RELE, and SCI. A
fifth body, AECC also forms an important part of the general infrastructure with its
activities extending across a comprehensive range of quality related concerns.

3.1 Principle Quality Organizations

*AENOR (Asociación Española de Normalización y Certificación, The Spanish
Association for Standardization and Certification)*
AENOR was established in 1985 by and was officially recognized, by MINER,
in 1986. It is an independent private organization. As well as its central position in
the national infrastructure, AENOR also has strong links with a number of international bodies. Thus, in addition to elaborating standards in Spain (UNE), it participates in the elaboration of European standards in the CEN (European Committee
of Standardisation) and CENELEC (European Committee of Electronic Standardisation).

AENOR is recognised by the authorities as the body responsible for carrying out
the controls contained in national regulations and Community Directives. The aims
of AENOR are:

- the promotion of the development of standardization in Spain;
- certification of products and the firms which conform with standards;
- the promotion of Spanish participation in international organizations; and,
- collaboration with the authorities in order to promote standardization and
  certification.

The services provided by AENOR include:

- the exclusive diffusion and sale of both Spanish (UNE) and international
  standards;
- courses and seminars;
- the publication and sale of the Spanish Standards Catalogue;
- the publication of various relevant manuals and other documentation;

- a library and information service at its central offices, providing information on its structure and organization, and certification and standardisation processes.

AENOR produces annual plans for standardization, for certification, and the registration of firms. AENOR's objective is to promote company participation, enabling companies to benefit from public and private purchasers' preferences. The AENOR list of registered firms has been published since 1989.

The AENOR Conformity mark 'N' and the Assurance mark 'S' have been developed in the field of product certification, as well as the Registered Firm mark 'ER'.

At present, 46 Technical Certification Committees have been set up, and these have granted certificates to over 1,500 products in different sectors. Over 200 companies have also been certified under European standard EN 29,000.

AENICRE (Asociación de Entidades de Inspección y Control Reglamentario, Association of Entities for Inspection and Regulatory Control)

AENICRE is an officially recognized private association of 12 companies, (most of which are consultancies). It was created in 1987 to underpin collaboration among its members, to coordinate their activities, and to provide an interface with the Spanish government. Member firms are legally recognised for the application of quality and safety regulations. AENICRE also serves as an instrument for the implementation of the policy of quality promotion. Members have 150 offices in the seventeen autonomous communities, with a number of regional committees. The majority of AENICRE personnel are technically qualified and have professional experience in the industrial quality field. AENICRE aims to:

- assure the greatest degree of homogeneity, level of quality and professionalism in bodies for inspection and regulatory control;
- promote their activities; promote links and collaboration with similar foreign organizations; and,
- establish a system for MICYT to supervise member organizations.

AENICRE has two main areas of activity, namely:

- to audit the manufacturing methods and the integrated quality controls for the production process, and the activities needed for recognition by the MICYT; and
- independent advisory and diagnostic activities for the implementation of quality systems and procedures for diagnosis, improvement of quality plans, training, and promotion of the benefits of adopting quality systems.

RELE (Red Española de Laboratorios de Ensayo, Spanish Network of Test Laboratories)

RELE was constituted in August 1986. It is a private association with the aim of accrediting test laboratories in line with Spanish standards EN45000 and with internationally recognised criteria. Accreditation by RELE is voluntary and can be obtained by all laboratories carrying out testing to the required standard. These include both public and private laboratories and laboratories which are part of large firms or organizations. At least 30 laboratories have so far achieved accreditation. RELE operates across all disciplines and sectors. It is organized along five main industrial sectors: electrical, chemical, mechanical, construction, and electronic.

RELE's activities in Spain are similar to those carried out by the NAMAS (National Measurement Accreditation System) in United Kingdom or by the RNE (Réseau National d'Essais) in France. RELE actively participates in the ILAC (International Laboratory Accreditation Conference).

SCI *(Sistema de Calibración Industrial, System of Industrial Calibration)*

SCI is another officially recognized body and was created in 1981. Its principal objective is to ensure that all measuring instruments used in Spain are adequately calibrated. It integrates more than 30 laboratories which are authorized and classified according to a set of government determined criteria. These laboratories are accredited with the capacity to certify the calibration of instruments used in test laboratories.

AECC *(Asociación Española para la Calidad, The Spanish Association for Quality)*

The Spanish Association for Quality is an independent professional body which has, for more than 25 years, maintained an open forum in Spain for the interchange of information on, understanding of, and techniques for, quality. In recent years, in line with the increasing emphasis placed on quality improvement, its activities have grown and diversified substantially. This recent expansion in activities has included the creation of two new sections in the organization: quality in insurance companies, banks, building societies and financial institutions; and quality in sanitary systems and university education.

The activities of the AECC are quite diverse and include the promotion of awareness of awareness of quality issues, the organization of conferences, courses and seminars, research, liaison with education institutions, and the production of a range of publications. In 1991, the AECC established a quality information centre; one of few comprehensive collections of information on quality in Spain. The association also produces an information bulletin for its members.

The AECC maintains contact with a number of public and private sector organizations, including: various Ministries, the IMPI (Instituto de la Pequeña y Mediana Industria, Institute of Small and Medium sized Firms), and universities and teaching institutions. It cooperates with AENOR on standards for quality management, a collaboration which produces substantial documentation to guide and inform on the implementation of standards, quality assessment, improvement and management across a range of industrial sectors.

AECC seeks to promote awareness of the importance of quality through a number of activities. It is involved in promotional campaigns for the World Quality Day. It organises and participates in various conferences, workshops and seminars, notable among which was the 2nd Iberian and 5th Spanish congresses on quality

The AECC has close links with the education sector. These activities include collaboration with various universities in quality education, the award of Pedro Mendizábal prize for university students studying in the field of quality. Interest from the higher education sector is growing, particularly in terms of students' response to AECC's initiatives. The association has also been stimulating interest in quality issues in schools and secondary colleges.

In collaboration with MICYT, through the PNCI and its funding mechanisms, various activities have been initiated in the AECC, including the execution of studies on the infrastructure, evolution and diffusion of industrial quality, both within Spain and in the wider contexts of the EU, the USA and Japan.

3.2 Other Organizations Relating to Industrial Quality

As the introductory part of this section described, there are a range of types of institutions active in the quality field. Some, such as universities, consultancies, technical and trade associations, and technical institutes, are concerned with a range of issues, of which quality is only one. Others may relate to areas in which quality issues are having an increasing impact. For example, IMPI (Instituto de la Pequeña y Mediana Industria, Institute for Small and Medium Sized FirmsI), is increasingly involved with quality issues as they become relevant to SMEs. Other organizations confine their activities strictly to quality issues, focusing on particular aspects of quality and its consequences, such as ANAVA (Asociación Española de Análisis de Valor, Spanish Association for Value Analysis).

Cutting across our categorization of organizations active in the quality field are groups which focus on specific sectors, such as trade, industry and research associations and institutes, and on the basis of specific geographical regions. Many regional organizations are divisions of national organizations, while others may be set up under the auspices of the governments of the autonomous communities. LABEIN (Laboratorio de Ensayos Industriales, Laboratory for Industrial Testing) which has an active quality department is based in the Basque Country and is supported by the Basque government. However, it also receives funding from MICYT, and has carried out quality related work on a national basis. Finally, the Club Gestión de la Calidad (Quality Management Club) has been created to introduce Total Quality Management (TQM) practices amongst its members.

3.3 Regional Infrastructure

Of the bodies that perform quality related functions on a regional basis, particular attention can be paid to those active in the two selected autonomous regions of Cataluña and Andalucía.

3.3.1 The Quality Infrastructure in Cataluña

As with all regions, quality activities in Cataluña are linked to both the central and regional administrations. Many of the national institutions have offices or representatives in the region. For example, there are 10 AENICRES offices in the region. Cataluña also has its own regional institutes and associations with activities relating to quality. The Centre for Quality Promotion in Cataluña has been based at the ICT (Instituto Catalán de Tecnologia, Catalan Institute of Technology), which carries out a number of quality related activities in education and training and consultancy.

The Industry Department of the Generalitat, the Catalan governing body, has created a network of laboratories spanning an number of industrial sectors, the Basic

System of Test laboratories and Industrial Services in Cataluña, and provides financial aid for equipment and activities to promote quality in-house. The laboratories of this integrated network are:

- IDIADA (Instituto de Investigación Aplicada al Automóvil, Institute for Applied Automobile Research);
- ASCAMM (Asociación Catalana de Empresas Constructoras de Moldes y Matrices, Catalan Association of Mould and Die Manufacturers);
- LEITAT (Laboratorios de Ensayos e Investigaciones Textiles de Condicionamiento Tarrasense, Tarrasa Laboratories for Testing and Research in Textile Conditioning);
- AIATA (Asociación de Investigación Textil Algodonera, Association for Research in Cotton Textiles);
- AIGSTL (Asociación de Investigación, Gestión, y Servicios de la Industria Textil Lanera, Association for Research, Management and Services in the Woollen textile Industry);
- Laboratorio de la Escuela Superior de Tenería de Igualada, (Laboratory of the Igualada College of Tannery); and
- The Centre for Artificial Vision

All of the above laboratories complement the activities of the Catalan General Test and Research Laboratory (LGAI), which embodies 13 laboratories and a new multi-disciplinary section.

ICT (Instituto Catalán de Tecnología, The Catalan Institute of Technology)
Established in 1986, the ICT is just one of number of institutions in Cataluña, carrying out consultancy, education, and training in quality promotion. It has also been host to the regional Centre for Quality Promotion. The ICT is a non-profit organization backed by the Catalan Association of Engineers, the Universidad Politécnica de Cataluña and other universities and professional associations as well as the Catalan and Spanish governments and other bodies. Its principal activities are technical education and the provision of technical advice, and much of this type of work is rooted in MICYT's programmes and those of the equivalent body within the Catalan administration. Retaining an independent stance, it attempts to bridge the gaps existing between the national and local governments and firms. ICT begins with the premise that any serious effort towards quality must be founded on the development of a quality system in line with the ISO 9000 series of standards.

3.3.2 Quality Infrastructure in Andalucía

The regional government (Junta de Andalucía) is responsible for industrial quality through its Directorate-General for Industry, Energy and Mines. Similarly, and in coordination with the PNC), the regional government offers various forms of assistance in the field of quality, financing the analysis, development and implementation of quality systems in Andalusian enterprises.

The infrastructure for quality control relatively underdeveloped. There are only four calibration laboratories in the region, three of which are located within the private sector. These have a very limited technical capacity and most companies in southern Spain when calibrating their test equipment have to send it outside Andalucía (and even abroad in some cases). Quite clearly, this can be a costly affair. The situation with regard to test laboratories is similar.

Like other regions, Andalucía has some satellite offices of national organizations: an example is AENICRE with its 26 offices in the region.

The Centre for Quality Promotion in Andalucía is based at the IAT (Instituto Andaluz de Tecnologia, Andalusian Institute of Technology), which has played an advisory role in the development of quality and other more general innovation infrastructures in the region. Following its recommendations, and with the support of the Andalusian Research Plan, and Information centre for the promotion of standardization and manufacturing has been set up in the Technology Park of Andalucía in Malaga. It aims to provide technological, market and legal information relating to standardisation and certification procedures and projects, and to promote and encourage the participation of industrial sectors in the standardisation and certification processes.

IAT (Instituto Andaluz de Tecnologia, The Andalusian Institute of Technology)
Established in the 1988, the IAT is a non-profit organization backed by the Andalusian Association of Engineers, universities and other professional associations. In addition to being the Centre for Quality Promotion in Andalucía, it holds the vice-presidency of the Spanish Association for Value Analysis (ANAVA) and is AENOR's representative in Andalucía. It also cooperates with the regional and national governments in developing their respective plans for quality. The IAT's Quality Department carries out a large number of information, documentation, training and advisory programmes in the field of quality. These are aimed mainly at SMEs, and the ISO 9000 standard series.

4. National Quality Schemes and Initiatives

4.1. Global Schemes

4.1.1 Plan Nacional

In response to industrial change in Spain over the past decade and the perceived need for Spain to increase its international competitiveness, particularly with the imminent approach of the European Single Market, the role of improving industrial quality to underpin the desired levels of competitiveness has been given particular attention in recent Spanish technology policy. MINER, now reorganised as MICYT, formulated a comprehensive national plan to promote and fund the adoption of all aspects of quality practices by Spanish industry and to develop and strengthen the infrastructure for industrial quality in Spain. The PNCI (Plan Nacional de Calidad Industrial, National Plan for Industrial QualityI) is being implemented over 1990-1993 with a total budget in excess of Pta 12,000 million. Much of the information in this section is drawn from the PNCI, published by MINER in 1990 and the subsequent annual 'Memorias' of its progress published by MICYT in 1991 and 1992.[2]

The plan is essentially a promotion and awareness exercise with the principal objectives being to promote the diffusion of the concept quality management and to create a favourable environment for quality practices, through the following actions:

- creation of demand for quality products and services;
- contribution to the diffusion and international recognition of the quality of Spanish products and services;
- the introduction of systems of quality management; and
- the introduction of demonstrations of quality.

To achieve these objectives there are four main strategies, each of which comprises a set of actions. Each year the actions are prioritised with respect to both the past and the future. These are currently as follows:

Promotion of the use of recognized quality products.
This is enacted through information campaigns directed at users and consumers about product certification, obtainable through AENOR, to improve the public understanding of quality and in particular the aims of the PNCI. So far these campaigns have used a variety of media, including television, and both the general and specialized press. In the first year of the plan's implementation, 70,000 mailshots were sent to Spanish firms and 5,000 copies of the plan were produced. Particular emphasis has been placed on the certification of firms whose quality systems have met with the UNE 66900 series of standard (equivalent to the EN 29000 and ISO 9000 series). In 1990 this strategy accounted for 9.5% of the annual budget for the plan and 5% in 1991. In the first year of the plan, AENOR was one of its principal beneficiaries, enabling the production and dissemination of information on certification and standards, notably their CERTINFORMA document.

Promotion of the recognition of quality of Spanish products and firms in external markets.
This strategy aims to assist mutual recognition between Spanish and foreign bodies active in the quality area and to move towards the integration of systems and procedures, and to support publicity campaigns for Spanish quality abroad. In the past year Spanish organizations such as AENOR, industrial associations and firms themselves have participated in a number of European and International organizations and assemblies. In 1990, these activities accounted for 4.6% of the plan's budget and 8% in 1991.

Promotion of the improvement of quality management systems in firms.
This strategy, which is underpinned by the introduction of quality systems in firms and the industry-wide acceptance of ISO 9000, is being pursued through four main actions and accounts for 34.3 % of the 1990 budget of the plan and 24% of the 1991 budget:

- Awareness activities, directed at top management and across the firm. These have, so far, been assisted by industrial associations and institutes of technology and through various conferences and other fora. The AECC has been active in these awareness activities, particularly in its involvement in the World Quality days.

- Training for all personnel, although much of this has, so far, been directed towards technical staff. The AECC, as described above in the previous section, has run courses on quality techniques and throughout many of the autonomous communities a range of regional technology institutes, industry associations and colleges have received funds for their training activities.

- Information provision, which is seen as essential for success with the aim of constructing a national system of quality information. Recent activities and funding have been directed at providing firms with information through the quality infrastructure and other organizations at national and regional levels producing relevant information. The AECC, for example, has been working on the construction of a database on bibliographic references to quality issues, as has the Cataluña Institute of Technology. LABEIN, AENOR and AENICRE are also amongst the organizations involved in information collection and provision.

- Investment, basically focused on the introduction of quality systems at both firm and sectoral levels. At the level of the firm, all types of firm, are considered and action is carried out in three phases:
    1. Diagnosis of the state of quality in the firm;
    2. Provision of the necessary means to adopt a quality system and to help in the process of introduction;
    3. Evaluation of the system of quality and its conformity with EN 29000.

In 1991, 209 individual firm-level projects received funding, although a further 267 firms also received funding through sectoral channels. The previous year 638 firm projects were supported.

The development and refinement of the quality infrastructure.
This has consumed the largest proportion of the budget so far (60% or Pta 1316 million in 1991 and 45% or Pta 1187 million in 1990) with much of this going to test and calibration laboratories. Strategy Four has led to agreements being made between the principal organizations active in the area. Both AENOR and RELE have entered into agreements with MICYT, but also with each other. AENOR accepts, for certification, the laboratories accredited by RELE. The actions underpinning this strategy revolve around organizations active in the following areas:

- Standardization, which embodies a continuation of current support, annual meeting of collaborators, annual plan of standards with special attention given to providing incentives and reinforcing Spanish participation in Europe.

- Certification, which is being promoted in products and firms and along with standardisation is carried out by AENOR. In 1991, 493 Spanish standards were approved (590 in 1990), 171 firms received certification for their products (230 in 1990) and 47 (16 in 1990) firms themselves became registered as meeting quality standards.

- Quantitative testing, through RELE and other organizations.
- Calibration, which together with testing is being developed to improve the quality and supply of testing and calibration laboratory facilities. Training of laboratory personnel is also ongoing as well as homogenisation of criteria and procedures employed through direct comparison of laboratories. Broader acceptance of RELE's accreditation of both public and private laboratories is also being promoted.
- Inspection, through AENICRE and its member organizations and also the roles played by the individual AENICRE organizations in providing independent quality consultancy in the plan and collaborating in the AENOR certification process.

The above actions are aimed at both consumers and users, with distinctions made between domestic and industrial, national and foreign, with the actions principally aimed at publicity and awareness. Actions towards industrial firms vary according to size, and are based on the following categorisation:

- *Category A* (more than 250 employees), which are seen to require a clearly different type of action. Their collaboration is viewed as especially important given their roles as leaders both through their purchasing activities and as a model for others. Priority actions for firms in this category include: awareness of entrepreneurs and management; presence in international fora; training of technicians in quality; exhaustive and up to date information, principally through the SNIC (Sistema Nacional Información Calidad, National System of Quality Information); and strengthening their relationship with the core of the quality infrastructure (AENOR, RELE, SCI).
- *Category B* (51 to 250 employees). This is where it is hoped that the PNCI will have its most important effects. Important actions here include: information about the use of quality products; awareness of directors and entrepreneurs; training of the workforce in technical quality and quality management; information about the SNIC; and integration into activities relating to quality such as standardisation and certification.
- *Category C* (6 to 50 employees) Actions here are more or less as with Category B firms, with prioritization on the basis of additional criteria.
- *Category D* (less than 6 employees). These firms are treated in the same way as consumers, with actions generally revolving around information and awareness.

As well as firm size, the implementation and targeting of actions also takes into account the following variables: the degree of receptiveness of the firm to each of the actions of the plan; the effects on the firm and/or the sector of developing each of the actions; the prioritisation of activities needed by specific firms and sectors; and the capacity to undertake actions and any budgetary limitations which may exist.

4.1.2 Execution, Control and Continuation of the Plan

The coordination, control and global execution of the plan are carried out by MICYT through its Technology Policy Directorate General (Industrial Quality Sub-DG). Although this requires the support of those public and private organizations which consider themselves suitably qualified to assist effectively in the specified actions. MICYT's aim is to assure that the actions of the plan are carried out in a homogeneous fashion, and that they remain independent from the participating organization, while mediating in the establishment of uniform criteria for application, coordination and control of the actions.

Each action of the plan requires the development of concrete programmes for their execution by the organizations involved. The following aspects of such programmes must be clearly specified:

- planned activities;
- the aims and objectives of these activities;
- details of the organization carrying out the programme;
- personnel and resources; and,
- place, dates and timescale of execution and budget.

The necessity for pilot programmes is also taken into account, with a view to future application in other sectors or geographical areas.

As well the above programmes, the plan makes estimates, on both global and national levels, of the evolution of certain quality related parameters, which assist in the evaluation of the plan's effectiveness. These parameters include:

- levels of investment in quality;
- number of firms which have introduced systems of quality assurance;
- the strengthening of the quality infrastructure; and,
- the cost of lack of quality at both sectoral and national levels.

Table 25, on page 275, provides a breakdown of funding for the four years of the programme.

National Quality Award
Within the National Plan the Ministry of Industry, Trade and Tourism (MICYT) has recently launched the National Quality Award (1992). Following other European initiatives, it aims to develop further the adoption of quality practices and to promote excellence in quality in Spanish firms. The award, which carries no monetary value, is organised by MICYT in conjunction with the Spanish Association for Quality (AECC). Under the scheme, two awards are made: one to firms of more than 250 employees, and another to firms of less than 250 employees.

Table 25: Budget of the PNCI 1990-1993

Areas of Plan's Activity	Budget (Pta million)				
	1990	1991	1992	1993	TOTAL
1. Diffusion of Quality	400	400	419	432	1651
2. Support for the Introduction of Quality Management Systems	900	989	1086	1193	4168
3. Training	150	213	251	302	916
4. Investment in the Quality Infrastructure	1158	1253	1370	1498	5279
5. Studies etc.	25	29	32	35	121
Total	2633	2884	3158	3460	12315

Source: MINER 1990, 1991, 1992

4.1.3 Research

Research in the quality area may be seen to fall into two main categories, research on the technical aspects of quality, and on the diffusion or lack of quality awareness and practices in Spanish industry. In the Spanish quality infrastructure, as described above, there is an obvious interface with relevant technological R&D organizations. Industrial research associations, University Engineering Departments and other higher education institutions, and a wide variety of public and private laboratories can all be seen to be active in the quality field. Various studies on the state of industrial quality in Spain have been carried out over recent years, at the national, regional and sectoral levels.

4.1.4 Training and Education

Under Strategy Three of the PNCI, which aims to promote improved quality systems in firms, training is seen as an important aspect of increasing awareness of quality issues and the effective adoption and implementation of quality systems by firms. Training and education on quality in Spain is available in a variety of forms, relating to both the technical aspects of quality and its management. Courses, seminars and other forms of training have been provided by the full range of national and regional organizations active in the quality field in Spain, including: government bodies (such as in MICYT's own Escuela de Organización Industrial), AECC, AENOR, LABEIN, universities and technical institutes and consultancy firms. The PNCI has provided financial support for the costs of running and attending many of these courses. In 1992, 53 courses were supported by MICYT in the areas of Objective 1, with emphasis on the less developed regions.

In the higher education sector, technical and managerial quality issues are being taught in the form of master's degree courses at various universities and business and engineering schools throughout Spain. The diffusion of quality issues into undergraduate teaching is not so widespread, although awareness of quality amongst university students has been steadily increasing through the activities of the AECC, such as its student competitions and role in world quality days, mentioned above. The AECC has also been promoting awareness of quality in secondary education.

The INEM (Instituto Nacional de Empleo, National Institute of Employment) has, within its Programme for occupational training, a technical course in quality control. The course is aimed at the improvement in the theory and practice of the inspection processes, but also includes quality management issues, quality systems and statistical control.

4.1.5 Consultancy

There are numerous consultancy firms active across the full range of activities in the quality field. For some of the larger firms quality related activities are just one part of their operation, while there are also smaller firms concerned with just one aspect of quality. These activities embrace both the technical and management dimensions of quality, providing technical assistance, training, audits and diagnoses of quality and the introduction and improvements of quality systems. Their domains of activity are similarly broad, both in terms of industrial sectors worked in and regional distribution. Many consultancy firms, although based in Madrid, have offices throughout many of the autonomous communities. There are also a number of firms actually based in the regions. Consultancy activities are also carried out by institutes of technology and other higher education and similar organizations.

Many companies enjoy formal links with the core of the quality infrastructure, assisting these bodies in the pursuit of their activities. AENICRE, discussed above, is principally composed of consultancy firms, which are legally recognised to carry out activities in the field of inspection and regulatory control. There are also links with AENOR in this area. Diagnosis of the state of quality and quality systems in firms is one of the activities of many consultancy firms. It is interesting to note, at this point, the development of an expert system for self diagnosis of quality by firms. This was developed by LABEIN and guides the user through the completion of a questionnaire. The resulting analysis by the computer software should then describe the firm's situation with respect to total quality management, inform them about concepts and techniques, define the degree of variation from the UNE certification system for firm quality and suggest activities to be pursued.

4.2 Sectoral Schemes

4.2.1 Plan Nacional

Of the 650 firms, 75% of which were SMEs receiving assistance under the first year of PNCI support, 38% belonged to only three sectors: metal product manufacturing (15%), chemicals (14%) and mechanical equipment (9%). Other significant sectors showing interest were the electronics sector, machinery construction and metal materials, and automated machinery construction and electrical materials.

This distribution of interest to some extent reflects the large number of firms in these sectors. Some of these sectors are subject to national regulatory controls and directives; some are required by customers to have quality systems; and some with significant export markets are obliged to accept the quality systems of overseas customers.

The PNCI has an explicit sectoral dimension, particularly with regard to the introduction of quality systems on a sectoral basis under Strategy III, which aims at the promotion of improved quality systems in firms and investment in such systems. The management of this aspect of the implementation of Strategy III has been carried out under the auspices of manufacturers' associations, institutes of technology and consultancy firms. The most significant examples include the activities of the Association of Machine Tool Manufacturers, the Paper Industries Association, the Macael Province Marble Association and the Association of Equipment Manufacturers.

However, interest in the funding provision of the PNCI continues to grow in an increasingly broad range of sectors. Behind those sectors listed above, other sectors showing interest include the wood, cork, furniture, food, non-metallic products and plastic processing industries. Table 26 (page 278) illustrates the proportion of financial aid given to each sector, under both sectoral and individual firm initiatives.

In a number of sectors there are general development schemes which cover a range of issues, including quality, in the development of those sectors and which also pay attention to research, training and promotion. A small sample of such sectoral schemes follows.

4.2.2 The Health Strategy Programme 1991-1995

The main objective of the Health Strategy Programme is to improve the quality of public health provision: its planning, training and research activities; and the support for the regional health service.

The first step in attaining these objectives has been the creation of health councils, composed of representatives of the Public Health Department in each zone. Running for a period of four years and across a broad range of health disciplines, the objectives of the Regional Research Health Plan include the pursuit of the following quality related activities:

- the development of new legislation for the accreditation of health centres, similar in its quality requirements to those employed in other European countries;
- the definition of Spanish standards for the extraction and transplant of organs and tissues; and
- inspection services.

Table 26: Sectoral distribution of PNCI funding in 1990-1991

Sector	Percentage of PNCI Budget received	
	1990	1991
Electronics	7.03	4.90
Machinery and electrical eqpt	6.41	13.96
Machinery and mechanical eqpt	9.53	6.84
Metal products	14.31	13.57
Chemicals	16.82	6.66
Non-metal products	5.79	3.88
Automotive		6.12
Rubber & plastics	4.25	2.94
Metal processing	5.19	8.89
Wood, cork and kitchen furniture	5.11	
Textiles	3.20	
Food		8.58
Other sectors	22.36	23.66
(Total	100	100)

Source: *MICYT 1991, 1992*

4.2.3 The Energy Sector

Within the Energy Industries Section of the Spanish Association for Quality (AECC) a guide has been developed for the implementation of UNE 66904 (EN 29004). It contains instructions for the use of the standard by any firm in the sector, and also by other sectors so as to facilitate the introduction of a quality management system based on it.

4.2.4 Manufacturing

The Programa Nacional de Automatización Avanzada y Robótica (National Programme of Advanced Automation and Robotics) was launched in 1980 and is aimed at the provision of new services; the improvement of productivity, quality and reliability; and cost reduction. Its principal objective is to improve productivity and the level of competitiveness of Spanish industry. In order to do so, the adoption of efficient automation processes, the development of flexible manufacturing systems and quality control systems are seen as important factors for companies to take into account. The programme also has a training component for research personnel. This programme has an international collaborative dimension through its relation to the ESPRIT and BRITE programmes of the EC.

4.2.5 The Food Sector

Also worthy of inclusion in this section are some of the main results of a study on the food sector before the total quality management (ISO 9000 series standards) carried out by the Institute of Research and Technology in Oceanography, Fish and Food (AZTI/SIO) and LABEIN. Although both organizations are supported by the Basque government, this study was funded by MICYT under the PNCI. The study adopted a firm-by-firm methodology across the whole of Spain to survey the present quality situation in an industry in a process of continual technological and organizational change. The study aimed to help both firms and public organizations to introduce and improve quality practices and to develop strategies for doing so. It sought to develop a new quality culture within the sector and to provide an impulse to adopt and improve quality management.

4.2.6 Training and Education

Although many of the education and training activities discussed above are either of a general nature or are firm specific, a further reflection of the significance and interest of quality issues is the number and types of organizations offering courses and seminars on aspects of industrial quality. These include research and industrial associations and sector specific engineering and technical schools. Some notable examples in recent years are the Ceramics Industry Research Association; the Wood and Cork Industry Association; the National Asssociation of Electrical Industries; the College of Brewing and Distilling; and the College of Aeronautiocal Engineers.

4.2.7 Research and Consultancy

As mentioned earlier, the organizations performing research and consultancy vary in size, geographical location and scope of activities. Specific sectoral organizations are active with the provision of education, training and awareness, as are specific divisions and subgroups of organizations with broader portfolios of activities.

5. Regional Schemes

As mentioned above, Spain is composed of 17 autonomous communities which exhibit significant variation in their states of industrial development. For the purpose of this survey, the contrasting situations in Cataluña and Andalucía have been selected to illustrate something of the range of this variation. In terms of the diffusion of quality concepts and the development of a regional quality infrastructure, the two areas exhibit significant differences. Some of these are particularly evident in terms of the implementation of the PNCI, although the two regions do share some commonalities which derive from the character of the PNCI as a concerted national and global initiative. Table 27 (page 280) illustrates the effect of the PNCI on all of Spain's regions during 1990 and 1991 and the relative distribution of quality systems in Spain's regions.

Both Cataluña and Andalucía are amongst the autonomous communities that have embarked on formal collaboration agreements with MICYT in implementing the PNCI on a regional level. Both regions had established their own centres for quality promotion, in the Catalan Institute of Technology and the Andalusian Institute of Technology respectively.

In its first year, Cataluña and Madrid were the regions in which the greatest numbers of firms benefited from the PNCI. In that year, 66% of the budget went towards test laboratories and these were concentrated in only four communities of which Cataluña was one. The reviews of the progress of the PNCI also report that, along with Madrid, Barcelona possessed an outstanding level of quality management. At the time of the study there were, in Cataluña, more than 100 companies registered with AENOR to ISO 9000.

While Cataluña has greatly benefitted from the PNCI, in its first year of implementation, it has failed to have quite the same effect on Andalucía. This was seen to be due to a missing 'quality culture' as indicated in the White Paper on Andalucía.[3] Stronger efforts have since been directed towards this region.

Table 27: Distribution of quality systems in the autonomous communities in 1990-1991

Community	% Systems Supported under PNC1		% firms supported	% Petitions
	1990	1991	1990	1991
Cataluña	22.32	16.61	24.19	16.02
País Vasco	13.46	25.11	9.95	16.02
Castilla-Leon	3.99	2.72	5.97	4.33
Madrid	21.53	25.98	19.90	21.21
Galicia		1.98		3.90
Communidad Valenciana	7.75	6.33	7.35	9.09
Navarra		2.37		3.90
Andalucía	6.32		8.11	
Aragon	4.44		5.81	
Others	18.19	18.91	18.72	25.53

Source: MICYT 1991, 1992

5.1 Quality Promotion Activities in Cataluña

Cataluña has a long established industrial tradition from which has emerged its own particular industrial culture. Until recently Catalan industry has been run within a protectionist environment and, as a consequence, in a non-competitive market. The majority of the companies are small and medium-sized firms, a great number of which are run by their owners. As with SMEs elsewhere in Spain, R&D activities are very limited. Tables 28 and 29, below, show the distribution of the SMEs by sector of activity and by numbers of employees.

Table 28: Distribution of Catalan SMEs by Sector

Industrial Sectors	
Mechanical	38%
Textile	19%
Chemical	15%
Electro-mechanical	10%
Plastic transformation	5%
Electronics	8%
Others	5%

Source: ICT

Table 29: Distribution of Catalan SMEs by Size

Number of Employees	
under 100	51%
101-200	23%
201-300	13%
300	13%

Source: ICT

Despite its state of industrial development relative to many other regions, only a fairly limited number of companies had any type of quality assurance system prior to recent developments and promotional activities. These systems were generally a result of pressure from large customers, such as automobile industry as well as the pursuit of firm registration and interest in improving quality and competitiveness.

5.1.1 Global Quality Schemes in Cataluña

Promotion and Awareness

Cataluña has been involved in a series of quality promotion initiatives since the late 1980s. The 1988 Quality Promotion Programme had the aim of spreading information about quality management, and the implementation of quality assurance systems based on the Spanish standard UNE 66900. The ICT was responsible for its implementation.

The 1989 Quality Promotion Programme was created to introduce quality into test laboratories. However, Catalan test laboratories have received significant funding from national government and most have PNCI funds.

The 1990 Quality Programme was based around two main lines of activity: the first was to make companies aware of the importance of quality, through seminars, workshops, conferences, and the publication of the first edition of a magazine, *Industrial Quality*, and the second was directed towards the textiles sector for the implementation of quality assurance systems and diagnosis, with a specific study on the wool sector.

The Industrial Quality Promotion Programme in Cataluña 1991-1993

The Department of Industry and Energy of the Generalitat of Cataluña (Ministry of Industry of the Autonomous Community of Cataluña) has developed an Industrial Quality Promotion Programme in line with the National Plan for Industrial Quality (PNCI). The underlying framework shared by both the present regional and national policies for industrial quality can be seen in the context of the EC's 'Global Approach', which contains guidance for utilization of European standards.

The quality systems currently implemented can be classified into the following four levels, dependent on the degree of involvement of the operating units of the company:

- The first is the non-quality level, which includes those companies that either consider quality as a cost or have no direct contact with clients. Approximately 20% of Catalan enterprises fall into this category.
- The second is the quality control level and is applied by those firms that have established traditional quality control systems and so only implement particular improvements in the manufacturing systems. 50% of Catalan companies have this level of quality.
- Quality assurance is the third level and corresponds to those companies that assure quality in line with international standards. This level of quality is present in approximately 25% of Catalan firms.
- Finally, only 5% of Catalan companies apply the TQM level. These companies have usually established a comprehensive quality system and are often leaders of their respective sectors.

70% of Catalan companies do not reach the quality assurance level, and of those remaining, only 25% have a well defined quality manual.

The promotion of quality management together with the creation and development of the quality infrastructure are the two principal lines of action taken by the Industry Department of the Catalan Generalitat.

Industrial Quality Awards

The annual Quality Awards of the Generalitat were established in 1989 as a means of promoting and encouraging industrial quality, with the objective of distinguishing the most competitive enterprises in Cataluña.

Participating firms are required to have integrated a quality management system based on the UNE 66900 standard. Participation in the evaluation process is free for firms. The award is endowed with Pta 12 million, divided between three prizes:

- First Prize: Pta 6 million
- Second Prize: Pta 4 million
- Third Prize: Pta 2 million

Consultancy

There are various consultancy groups operating in Cataluña, providing education and advice on quality issues, some are the regional offices of national companies, such as AENICRE members and those authorised by AENOR, and some are indigenous. One such example is the Industrial Quality Department of the Instituto Catalán de Tecnología (ICT). In addition to its teaching and education functions, this organization has been working on quality promotion activities, mainly in a consultancy capacity, in accordance with the objectives of the Quality Promotion Programme. Their initial premiss is that any serious effort towards quality requires, as a basis, the development of a quality system based on ISO 9000 series standards. In line with this, they have adopted the following procedure for providing quality consultancy services to firms, which may be seen to illustrate the main concerns and typical methodological approaches of consultancy firms operating in Cataluña:

- The customer company is required to appoint a management representative to collaborate with the consultant.
- An analysis of the organization and of the quality problem is conducted. The requirements of the ISO standards are explained and their implementation studied. A report outlining the major problems outlined is then produced.
- Once the problems have been examined, a draft Quality Assurance Manual is produced in the collaboration with the managerial staff of the firm.
- The consultant follows the programme of this manual during the entire implementation process.
- An audit is performed to evaluate the degree of compliance with the quality system proposed.

In the course of pursuing this type of activity the ICT have identified a number of problems in the implementation of quality systems in both small and large firms.

In the opinion of the ICT, in the case of small and medium-sized firms, particularly those that are family owned, the interests of the owners are at odds with those of the management. Therefore, there may be difficulties in discussing options which could benefit the company. Traditionally, most SMEs in the region target their activities towards local or rather small markets. With a strategy based on product diversification, it is extremely difficult for a small group of technical staff to achieve a deep knowledge of all the products. SMEs are also seen to suffer from organizational problems, particularly that of responsibilities and tasks seldom being well defined.

In the case of large companies the responsibilities of the corporation and those of the local plant are often not clearly distinguished. Quality systems of local companies must be referred to those of the corporation. Very few European multinational companies already have a corporate quality system, which means that the quality systems of local companies may be incomplete, particularly when activities are highly integrated.

The ICT also feel that the achievement of a 'quality environment' cannot progress without cooperation between customers and suppliers. Although, considerable progress has been made since 1987, a quality language common to both sides has not been developed.

They also feel that the adoption of a 'fire-fighter' style to deal with quality improvement in firms is also problematic. Until recently, most of the qualified staff have been occupied in solving everyday problems. Quality assurance and quality improvement oblige technical staff to assume managerial functions and this shift in function is not always easily achieved and requires a combination of both training and a change in attitude.

5.2 Quality Promotion Activities in Andalucía

Much of the following information is derived from the 1991 'White Paper on Andalucía' and related documentation published by the IAT.[4]

The current pattern of industry in Andalucía is very much a two-dimensional one. The strengths of the region can be seen to lie in the creation of new enterprises with high technology and the scope for technology renewal in the region's substantial mature industry. Its weaknesses however are rooted in the slow speed with which processes of renewal, innovation and change take place, and the uneven and heterogeneous nature of the regional development process.

At present, the process of the technological development in Andalucía is constrained by a number of factors. The number of industrial patents, which is currently very limited and largely relates to the agro-food sector, concentrated in Seville. The level of R&D activity is relatively low. Only 30.9% of enterprises with more than 250 employees in Andalucía have an R&D department and these tend to be concentrated in the chemical, machine-tool, electrical, metal products and agro-food sector. However, the investment in R&D has increased since 1988, particularly in large enterprises.

Technology transfer is limited, with the process determined by the size of companies. Andalucía has a large number of SMEs, 95% of them with fewer than 250 employees. Technology transfer in firms with less than 50 employees mainly occurs through the receipt of technical assistance, while in companies with more than 500 employees, which represent the 41% of the technology transfer processes, it occurs through the acquisition of expertise or through specific projects. The region has deficiencies in its information and communications infrastructure. This has been seen as a cause of the region's relatively low initial level of interest in the PNCI and low levels of participation in other national and international R&D programmes and may also explain the uneven geographical distribution of development. The region also has a relatively low level of qualification of human resources.

However, several activities can be identified which aim to strengthen technological development in Andalucía, such as the creation of Technology Centres to support industry sectors, although few of these offer advice on quality issues, the promotion of training programmes by the Administration, the increased use of Information technologies, changes in management attitudes towards new technologies, and participation in technology transfer programmes.

5.2.1 Global Quality Schemes in Andalucía

It is in the above context that the issues of quality promotion and implementation are being considered. The Andalusian administration has outlined three prime objectives regarding the development of industrial quality in the region, namely:

- To provide an incentive to the demand for quality products and services;
- To introduce quality management systems; and
- Increased introduction and use of testing and the development of the regional quality infrastructure.

The IAT surveyed the state of quality in 1400 firms across 300 industries and found that Andalusian industry is still some way from attaining even the minimum requirements for a satisfactory quality situation.[5]

In most companies claiming to have a quality department, approximately two thirds merely consisted of some form of product control and the department was unsuitably situated, with only 2.7% of total personnel dedicated to quality management.

Companies following some type of standards accounted for two-thirds of the total, although the standards applied are rarely nationally or internationally recognized. Access to information on national and international standards was seen as a significant problem.

41.1% of firms have a Quality Manual. 37.7% make use of the calibration and test laboratories, while the remainder do not make any calibrations at all. Approximately 50% of companies do not have procedures to regulate material or services received.

However, certain aspects of industry in Andalucía were seen to offer the potential to improve the region's quality situation. The large and strong companies with quality management systems are highly concentrated and thus can provide good examples for the rest to follow. It was also felt that awareness could be increased amongst younger managers, who are more receptive to promote quality issues, particularly awareness of the promotion and support available from the regional administration through regional, national, and international programmes.

However, there are no quality programmes covering all levels and there is a lack of a solid regional quality infrastructure. SMEs, in particular, exhibit a low level of participation in the quality improvement programmes of the Economy DG and PNCI.

This picture of the industrial quality situation in Andalucía led to a development and modernization policy by the Economy Directorate General of the regional government and the formulation and implementation of a number of regional programmes addressing particular aspects of the situation together with increased participation in national and international schemes. These regional include the following:

- A financial aid programme for technology renewal;
- Subsidies for projects or studies directed towards the identification and implementation of improvements to industry; and
- An aid programme to create quality organizations.

Certification and Standardization

Activities in the areas of certification and standardization are exclusively directed toward companies and include:

- Access to the Certificated Products Systems, AENOR's certification system of the 'N' mark for conformity with UNE standards.
- Introduction of the Firm Registration process, in conformity with the UNE standards 66-901, 66-902, 66-903 (equivalents to EN 29001, 29002, 29003) which define different systems for quality assurance.

An enterprise that obtains its registration after satisfying an AENOR audit, can guarantee its products in the domestic and international markets. A number of Andalusian companies have embarked on the process of registration recently.

Promotion and Awareness Schemes

Awareness of quality issues is being increased through workshops, courses, seminars and other diffusion activities across the quality field. Specific programmes are aimed at improving information, encouraging the adoption of new methods, encouraging certification and the adoption of standards, and encouraging participation in broader based quality-related initiatives.

Community based programmes in collaboration with the Autonomic and Central Administration are facilitating access to and use of information technologies. At present, programmes such as STRIDE (Science and Technology Research into Innovative Developments in Europe), are helping to create integrated telecommunication service centres offering access to information through videotext, on-line databases, telefax etc. Another initiative is the promotion of regional information networks.

Training and Education

As with the national situation, education is available from a variety of organizations. In the higher education field, institutes active in the provision of education on quality issues include the Escuela Técnica Superior de Ingenerios Industriales, the faculty of science of the University of Granada, and the Fundación Universidad Empresa de Córdoba.

Consultancy

As with Cataluña, there are numerous national and regional consultancy firms operating in the Andalucía region, including 26 AENICRE offices. The provision of technological advice has also been enhanced through the creation of technology advisory centres as part of the quality infrastructure.

5.2.2 Sectoral Quality Schemes in Andalucía

There are relatively few sectoral schemes developed in the region, although the regional government is aware of the importance of reaching specific areas of industrial activity. With the collaboration of industry associations, the government wants to organize sectoral programmes to provide: information, technology advice, training and the introduction of quality management systems.

Since 1991, the Asociación Provincial de Marmol de Macael, (the Macael Province Marble Association) has been working on an ambitious project in the field of quality and technological improvement.

6. Overview and Outlook

Spain is undergoing substantial development in many areas of its industry and industrial structure. Membership of the EU has provided Spain with a substantial impetus towards such developments. Of prime concern is the drive towards improved competitiveness, especially on a national level, with industrial quality perceived as a key aspect of improved competitiveness. Recognition of this situation has led to important national and regional policy actions, particularly the formulation and implementation of a large-scale global policy programme primarily aimed at increasing awareness of quality issues and substantially developing and strengthening the national quality infrastructure.

A current strength of the Spanish national position is the way in which quality awareness is being promoted across the full spectrum of industry sectors and the increasing actions and responsibilities of the main organizations which make up the core of the national quality infrastructure.

Surveys of Spanish industry have revealed the enormity of the task facing promoters of quality, with many of the so-called quality systems operating simply basic production controls and practices based in production departments rather than more pervasive awareness of, and commitment to, improved quality at all stages in the firm.

The large proportion of SMEs that make up Spanish industry is also seen as something of a challenge to more widespread awareness of quality issues and adoption of quality practices. They have neither the structure nor the resources to effectively develop quality practices without assistance.

That there are some gaps in systematic quality education has also been noted, although there are numerous post-graduate courses appearing in the area. Additionally, this issue is beginning to be addressed through other specific courses, often at sectoral level.

On the sectoral level there exists some variation with respect to current awareness and levels of implementation. Although the national plan is global, awareness of quality seems greater in more technologically advanced sectors. However, more traditional sectors do account for a substantial part of Spanish industrial activity.

The variation in the quality situation across Spain's regions has been considered, with greater awareness and adoption evident in the northern, more industrialized regions. The political and economic structure of Spain allows regional policies to be formulated and this is indeed occurring with many regional quality initiatives forming part of, or being aligned with, the national programme.

The south is characterized by traditional industries, centred around small firms with slow technology renewal. In addition, the quality infrastructure in the south is much less developed, although moves on both national and regional levels are being made to rectify this.

6.1 The Future

The outlook is good if the objectives of the PNCI are fulfilled and if follow-up actions build on this start with the expiry of the present plan in 1993. The strong emphasis on developing the quality infrastructure would certainly allow for continued development of awareness of quality issues across regions and sectors, and also to facilitate the implementation of quality systems in the future as their nature and importance becomes more widely diffused through development and continuation of the strenuous promotion activities currently in progress.

7. List of Organizations

Name	Address	Telephone/Fax
Asociación Española de Análisis de Valor ANAVA	c/chaurliano 12.14 Bloque B Urb. El Plantio E 28023 Madrid	(9) 1 3878111/(9) 1 3729625
Asociación de Entitdades de Inspección y Control Reglamentario AENICRE	c/María de Molina 60 3 B izqda 28006 Madrid	(9) 5643764/ (9) 1 5630389
Asociación Española de Normalización y Certificación AENOR	c/Fernández de la Hoz 52 28010 Madrid	
Asociación Española para la Calidad AECC	c/Velaquez 24 5° 28001 Madrid	
The Industrial Quality Promotion Programme in Cataluña.	Generalitat de Cataluña	
Generalitat de Cataluña Departmento de Industria y Energia	Paseo de Gracia 105 08002 Barcelona	
Instituto Andaluz de Tecnología (IAT)	Moratin 1 E 41001 Sevilla	(9) 5 4565000/(9) 5 4562355
Instituto Catalán de Tecnología	Plaza Ramón Berenguer Barcelona	
Instituto de Investigación y Tecnología para la Oceanograpia Pesca y Alimentación AZTI/SIO		
Instituto de la Pequeña y Mediana Industria IMPI	Madrid	
Laboratorio de Ensayos e Investigaciones Industriales LABEIN	Cuesta de Olabeaga 16 48013 Bilbao	
Ministerio de Industría Comercio y Turismo MICYT Dirección General de Politica Tecnologica Subdirreción General de Calidad Industrial	Paseo de la Castellana 160 28046 Madrid	3494000/4578066
Plan Nacional de Calidad Industrial PNCI	MICYT	
Red Española de Laboratorios de Ensayo RELE	c/Claudio Coello 73 3 28001 Madrid	
Sistema de Calibración Industrial SCI MICYT	Paseo de la Castellana 160 28046 Madrid	
Club Gestión de la Calidad	c/ Meuendez Pidal, 32 E 27036 Madrid	(9) 1 3459334/(9) 1 3459376

References:

1. Ministerio de Industria y Energía (1988), *Directorio de Entidades que Imparten Cursos y Seminarios sobre Calidad Industrial*, Madrid, MINER

2. Ministerio de Industria y Energía (1990), *Plan Nacional de Calidad Industrial Ejercicio 1990-1993*, Madrid, MINER.

   Ministerio de Industria, Comercio y Turismo (1991), *Memoria del Plan Nacional de Calidad Industrial Ejercicio 1990*, Madrid, MICYT.

   Ministerio de Industria, Comercio y Turismo (1992), *Memoria del Plan Nacional de Calidad Industrial Ejercicio 1991*, Madrid, MICYT.

3. Instituto Andaluz de Tecnología (1991), *White Paper on Andalucía*, Seville, IAT

4. Ibid.

5. Ibid.

Other References:

Instituto de Investigación y Tecnología para Oceanografía, Pesca y Alimentación y Laboratorio de Ensayos Industriales (1992) *El Sector Alimentarion Español Ante la Gestion de Calidad Total (Normas ISO Serie 9000)*, IITOPALEI.

The United Kingdom

Brendan Barker

1. Introduction

This chapter describes the results of a survey of the activities and measures in the field of quality assurance and management in the UK. Although the primary focus of the survey has been the public sector I recognize the significant role played by private organizations (particularly large firms) in shaping the quality 'environment'. Furthermore, industrial and professional associations are actively involved in quality promotion schemes complementing public sector activities in the UK. Where relevant, therefore, I have included such activities in the chapter.

2. The Emergence of Quality as an Issue

The need for improved industrial inspection procedures became apparent during the First World War. The Technical Inspection Association was formed in 1919 and became incorporated as the Institution of Engineering Inspection in 1922. It was only in 1972 that the Institution decided to extend its interests and to adopt its present title of Institute of Quality Assurance (IQA).

Concern over the poor quality of British goods grew after the Second World War. In 1953 a report on a study visit to the USA of the Anglo-American Council on productivity stated that 'there was not the same enthusiasm for quality control in Britain as was evident in America'.[1]

In 1957 Britain became a founding member of the European Organization for Quality Control (EOQC). In 1961 the British Productivity Council formed the National Council for Quality and Reliability (NCQR). It became the sponsoring body for British membership of the EOQC and the driving force behind a number of quality awareness raising initiatives such as the 1966 National Quality and Reliability Year in 1966. In 1981 the NCQR merged with the IQA to form the British Quality Association (BQA).

The UK government has long been active in quality issues related to defence procurement, but only recently has its attention been drawn to the importance of quality in industry generally. In the late 1960s, the government appointed two committees. One, under Colonel Raby, examined quality in the military domain, the other, under Sir Eric Mensforth, recommended measures for wider civilian applications. The Raby report of 1969, although unpublished, had a significant effect on the development of quality assurance in the public sector. The Mensforth report, published in 1970, expressed concern about national arrangements for the attainment of quality in the engineering industries, but had relatively little impact.

In the next two sections we look at the development of quality promoting activities in the defence and civil sectors.

2.1 Ministry of Defence Quality Initiatives

The Raby Committee report of 1969 endorsed quality procedures already used by the Royal Navy, in which responsibility for quality was transferred from the customer to the supplier. Although the report was not published, it had a major effect on the direction and pace of development of quality assurance throughout the public sector.

The years after the appearance of the Raby report saw the reorganization of the purchasing and quality systems in the MOD. Various quality inspectorates were first restyled 'Quality Assurance Directorates' and then placed under the control of a new purchasing administration, the Procurement Executive. Defence quality interests then unified into the Defence Quality Assurance Board (DQAB) and a new industry liaison committee was formed to advise it, the Defence Industries Quality Assurance Panel (DIQAP).

Allied Quality Assurance Publications (AQAPs) first appeared in 1968. The remainder followed over the next two years. The Ministry of Defence adopted the AQAPs and republished them, with a few additions in 1973 as 'Defence Standards 05'.

By 1979, 3000 companies had been approved and placed on a list of assessed contractors, (LAC). Only about a fifth of UK manufacturing industry is involved wholly or partially with the defence market, yet in 1979, the number of firms outside the LAC with a quality system was only about 20, of whom most based their procedures on BS 5179, itself a product of military practice.

Following the appearance of BS 5750 (1979), the pace of second party quality assurance and approval was increasingly set by civilian public sector purchasers. In 1981, the MOD reached agreement with the BSI that third party assessment against BS 5750 was to be considered equal to MOD assessment for defence subcontracting. From 1987, the MOD no longer assessed firms solely engaged on subcontract work. From 1991 it no longer assessed prime contractors (although retaining the right to conduct supplementary inspections).

2.2 Quality in the Civil Sector

The relationship between quality and competitiveness in the civil sector of the economy has long been an issue in the UK. Underlying this interest has been the belief that:

> *a major contributing factor to the success of our principal indus-*
> *trial competitors abroad has been their commitment to standards*
> *and quality.* [2]

In 1970, the committee chaired by Sir Eric Mensworth expressed concern about national arrangements for the attainment of quality in the engineering industries. The Mensworth Report had much less impact than the Raby Report had had within the public sector (and some parts of the private sector).

In the mid-1970s, the Labour government launched an Industrial Strategy with the aim of transforming the United Kingdom into a high output/high wage economy by improving the industrial performance and productive potential of manufacturing industry. In 1977, Sir Frederick Warner, under the aegis of the National Economic Development Organization (NEDO), produced a paper 'The Role of Standards in the Industrial Strategy'.[3] Warner argued that the development and use of standards was potentially a major contributory factor to the competitiveness of British products particularly in relation to their quality and reliability. He went on to argue for a widely accepted third party certified standard for quality. The idea for a quality standard dated from the 1950s when procurement bodies devised standards of manufacture and products. During the 1960s, quality schemes evolved for particular sectors, operated by such organizations as the Central Electricity Generating Board, the National Coal Board and the Post Office. The emphasis, however, was still on inspection, and the direct cost of the schemes was borne by the purchaser. In the late 1970s, after studies of Japanese methods of quality control and following the success of retailers such as Marks and Spencers and of the MOD in requiring suppliers to introduce quality systems, the British Standards Institution (BSI) produced its standard for quality systems BS 5750 (first published in 1979).

In 1978 a meeting of industrialists and government representatives first saw the suggestion of a National Quality Campaign. Subsequently, a consultative document was circulated by the Department of Prices and Consumer Protection. The document 'A National Strategy for Quality' estimated that the cost to British industry of not adopting a quality approach, in terms of unnecessary extra work and replacement due to faults was some £10 billion, or 10% of GDP.[4] The report went on to argue:

> *There is mounting evidence that purchasers in the UK of both industrial and consumer goods are becoming more aware of the importance of quality and total life costs ... [rising] requirements and expectations, coupled with strong competition on quality from overseas manufacturers, underline the importance for British manufacturers of satisfying customers' needs, thus helping to reduce import penetration in the home market.*[5]

The report called for a national quality strategy having three priorities:

- to promote a greater awareness of quality in meeting market needs;
- to facilitate the implementation and assessment of modern quality management systems; and
- to ensure that national arrangements for specification, testing and certification of goods met overseas market needs.

The report suggested that quality promotion activities might include:

- promotional campaigns to develop greater quality awareness, to be organized in collaboration with national organizations;
- review of training and education activities to ensure that they meet appropriate objectives; and the

- provision of advice, through consultancy etc. for SMEs.

Finally, the report made the following suggestions as regards the development of quality management systems:

- some form of national coordination is required to reduce the level of unnecessary multiple assessments;
- in selected areas, assessment of firms' quality systems may need to be undertaken by bodies of acknowledged competence in order to meet overseas market requirements; and,
- some firms may need advice and help in improving their systems.

At the same time the British Overseas Trade Board promoted a series of national and regional trade conferences at which quality featured prominently. This initial push for a national quality strategy lost some of its impetus with the change of government following the 1979 General Election.

In 1982, the Conservative government published the White Paper, 'Standards, Quality and International Competitiveness'.[6] The Paper promoted the assessment to BS 5750 of quality management systems by third party certification bodies and encouraged competition in the third party certification field. A National Accreditation Council for Certification Bodies (NACCB) was subsequently established. The Paper also provided for a closer and more formal relationship between the government and the BSI in particular, the government agreed to make more reference to BSI standards, rather than drawing up its own. Finally, the Paper announced support for a National Quality Campaign.

The following year the then Department of Industry (DoI) announced the launch of the campaign. The campaign led to the creation of a wide variety of promotional literature and videos and the establishment of the National Quality Information Centre NQIC). Financial assistance was made available to firms. An essential part of the campaign were efforts by the DoI to encourage the establishment of a structure to support quality achievement, and make companies better able to demonstrate this to their customers. Registers of quality assessed UK companies and of lead assessors were prepared and a Directory of Quality Education and Training was published. In addition, a British Quality Awards Scheme was created. In 1988, the National Quality Campaign was incorporated within the new Department of Trade and Industry's (DTI) 'Enterprise Initiative'.[7]

It can be seen that throughout this period quality promoting initiatives have been focused on the development and promotion of quality management standards. For this reason, it will be useful to briefly look at the development of quality standards in the UK.

2.3 Quality Standards

Historically, in the UK, as in other countries, major purchasers in the public and private sectors have required their suppliers to meet and document their compliance to certain criteria with regard to process quality, inspection and administration, and to permit regular checks and process audits. During the 1960s, quality schemes evolved for particular sectors, operated by such organizations as the Central Electricity Generating Board, the National Coal Board and the Post Office (and in the private sector by such organisations as Marks & Spencer).

The emphasis in these schemes, however, was still on inspection, with the direct costs of the scheme being borne by the purchaser (second party certification).

Early systems for the management of product quality were introduced into manufacturing industry in Britain by the Ministry of Defence in its capacity as a procurement agent. The Quality Assurance Defence Standards 05-21, 05-24 and 05-29 were based upon US-derived NATO standards. The defence standards were eventually issued for general use of industry as a series of guides (BS 5179). These were not widely accepted outside of the defence sector, however, and various alternatives were developed and used by other organizations. These systems showed a trend away from reliance on simple inspection of incoming goods towards a thorough assessment of the ability of the supplier to satisfy the customer's needs. While arrangements of this type could operate effectively in a simple, single customer/supplier relationship they became increasingly complicated the more complex such relationships became. It became common for larger manufacturers to have to submit each year to multiple assessments of their manufacturing and management capabilities by several major customers.

The problem was examined in Sir Frederick Warner's report on standards and specifications in the engineering industries (see above). The report argued for a widely accepted standard for quality management that could not only be applied by a customer to assess the capabilities of its supplier, but could be operated by independent third party certification bodies. As already seen, BS 5750 provided such a framework.

Although it was recognized that there was more to the achievement of good or better quality than standards, it was felt that the development and application of standards represented one of the most effective ways to approach the problem of improving quality:

> *There is no doubt that the reputation for quality enjoyed by countries such as Western Germany and Japan is directly related to the fact that they enjoy an effective and strong standards system linked with schemes of quality assurance, which commands a respect for, and engineers confidence in, their products throughout the world.* [8]

It is interesting to note that the role of standards as non-tariff barriers to trade was also recognized:

> *... the development of standards-based certification schemes has both an offensive and defensive effect in international marketing terms - offensive, in the sense that the resultant improvement in quality increases competitiveness defensive in the sense that it is conducive to achieving reciprocity of access to markets.* [9]

BS 5750, the UK national standard for quality systems, outlines to both suppliers and manufacturers the requirements of a quality orientated system. It stipulates policies to be adopted in areas such as the review of contracts, traceability of material and the maintenance of inspection and test equipment.

During the period of use of BS 5750: 1979, as a result of trade interfaces and technical links with overseas countries, other national quality standards were introduced in various parts of the world. Many of these standards were substantive copies of the British Standard, some contained amended or additional requirements. This much wider interest in quality standards led to the International Organization for Standardization (ISO) initiating, in 1983, work on an international standard. The work was completed in 1987 with the publication of the ISO 9000 series of five standards.[10]

The ISO standards are largely based on BS 5750:1979 but reflect international requirements and eight years of UK user experience. In the interests of international trade harmonization the ISO 9000 series, published as British Standard 5750:1987 with effect from May 1987, have been adopted for publication without deviation by BSI. Similarly, ISO 9000/BS 5750 is equivalent to European standard EN 29000:1987.[11]

There are five parts to the standard, three of these being the standard and two additional parts serving as guides (see Figure 25, below).

Figure 25: The structure of BS 5750

Standards:

Part 1: Specification for design/development, production, installation and servicing.

Part 2: Specification for production and installation.

Part 3: Specification for final inspection and test.

Guides

Part 4: Guide to the use of BS 5750 Parts 1, 2 and 3.

Part 0: 0.1 Guide to selection and use.

0.2 Guide to quality management and quality system elements.

Source: BSI

A consistent theme in the reports discussing quality during the 1970s was the need for a greater degree of national coordination in the field of standards, and in particular criticism of the extent of multiple assessment. Thus a recommendation in the report 'Standards and Specifications in the Engineering Industries' stated:

I also recommend that the Secretaries of State for Industry and Prices and Consumer Protection should consult all concerned on

*the steps necessary to build a rational structure of quality assurance
bodies with mutual acceptance of approvals to avoid multiple
assessment.* [12]

The National Accreditation Council for Certification Bodies (NACCB) was
established following a recommendation of the 1982 White Paper. Currently, 25
certification bodies are recognized by the NACCB. The emphasis on BS 5750 has
been critised in some circles. For instance, some small firm representatives have
criticized the standard for being unduly complex and for imposing a heavy burden
of management time and cost on small firms. According to a representative of the
Federation of Small Businesses:

*The Standard is written in mumbo jumbo ... Companies have to
take on consultants who regurgitate large chunks from the manuals
and then charge an arm and a leg.* [13]

This belief was also reported by a recent Open University survey which showed
that many small firms feared BS 5750 would push up their costs without improving
the quality of the goods and services provided. [14] At the same time many small
companies feel that they are faced with no choice in having to register for BS 5750
if they want to retain their customers. Large firms and government organizations
increasingly expect their suppliers to meet the standard. However, a recent survey
conducted by PERA International and Salford University Business Services of
companies of all sizes who had obtained certification to BS 5750 seemed to indicate
that cost benefits of improved efficiency generally more than compensate for the
initial consultancy and assessment costs. [15]

The British Standards Institute and other UK certification organizations are also
considering ways of making BS 5750 simpler to implement. The Federation of
Small Businesses initially pushed for a less demanding standard for small firms,
but realizing this would lead to small businesses being labelled as 'second class',
is now pushing for simplified manuals and easier implementation procedures.

*We have been looking at a more appropriate method of applying
the system ... We would like to devise a manual which would allow
a small business to take a step-by-step approach to implementing
BS 5750. It should be possible to [produce these manuals] for under
£50.* [16]

2.4 The Diffusion of Quality Concepts Throughout UK Industry

Companies are coming under increased pressure from their customers to show
proof that they have implemented management systems complying with one of the
current quality assurance standards or certification schemes. In this regard, changes
in public sector purchasing policies have been very important. The Ministry of
Defence is one of many state organizations which now requires most suppliers to
have a certified quality management system.

The major focus of the DTI campaign has been the promotion of BS 5750/ISO
9000 standards. The 1993 DTI Quality Assurance (QA) Register lists around
15,500 companies in the UK and abroad whose quality systems have been assessed

to BS 5750 or an equivalent standard (for instance, the NATO Defence AQAP series standards) by a UK certification body.[17] There is some additional evidence on the diffusion of TQM techniques throughout UK industry. In 1991, 3000 companies were asked about their quality programmes, if any. Of the 15% responded, who nearly all had embarked, or were embarking, on TQM. After seven years or more, only 30% had fully met their objectives in improving competitiveness: only half had improved suppliers' quality to the desired standards: there were also shortfalls in customer service and reducing the cost of failure. A 1991 study by Jay Communications found two-thirds of UK companies viewed quality as a strategic necessity, others responded to pressures from trade associations or purchasers, and a third category were driven by changed market conditions. Only 12% had been spurred into action by export requirements.[18]

Because of the focus in the UK on standards they make a good indicator of the diffusion of quality assurance management techniques throughout industry. There are now more than 15,500 UK organizations assessed and registered by second and third parties against BS 5750 or directly equivalent standards, e.g. Defence AQAP series standards (see Figure 26, page 299). Figure 26, also on page 299, provides a regional breakdown of the 7,500 British companies assessed to BS 5750 in 1992.

There is other evidence on the diffusion of quality assurance and management techniques throughout UK industry. In 1990, TQM experts Develin and Partners mailed a questionnaire to 3000 companies about their quality programmes, if any. 15% of the contacted manufacturers replied, of whom nearly all had embarked, or were embarking, on TQM presumably the main reason they responded to the survey. However, even in this self-selected group after seven years or more, only 30% had fully met their objectives in improving competitiveness: only half had improved suppliers' quality to the desired standards: there were also shortfalls in customer service and reducing the cost of failure.[19]

In the last 12 months there has been what is described as an 'explosion of interest' in quality in the service sector led by local government, health and other public authorities. Management consultants, in particular, have joined the growing number of service providers in applying quality management systems.

3. The Quality Infrastructure

The quality infrastructure in the UK is characterized by a of organizations with specific areas of activity and responsibility but with overlapping membership. In this way, it has been possible to develop a wide consensus as to appropriate activities in the area. The DTI is represented in many of these organizations and fora. The organizations are described in the following section. The quality promotion routes are described later.

Figure 26: Companies certified to ISO 9000 (or equivalent)

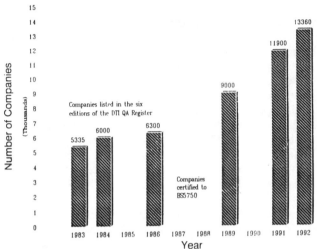

Source: DTI QA Register

Figure 27: Regional distribution of BS 5750 certified companies

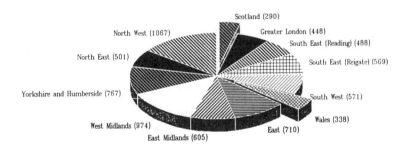

Source: DTI QA Register

3.1 Organizations

DTI (Department of Trade and Industry)

The DTI has actively promoted quality improvement and assisted companies in achieving it through a series of programmes since 1983. These have included the National Quality Campaign (now included within the Enterprise Initiative). There have been two elements to these activities: the promotion of quality awareness (through the 'Management into the 1990s' programme this is discussed in more detail below), and support for consultancy help in implementing quality initiatives (through the Quality Consultancy Scheme). The 1993 DTI QA Register (formerly the Register of Quality Assessed UK Companies) produced by the DTI through the HMSO (Her Majesty's Stationaery Office) lists around 15,500 companies in the UK and abroad whose quality systems have been assessed to BS 5750 (or an equivalent standard) by a UK certification body.

NAMAS (National Measurement Accreditation Service)

The National Measurement Accreditation Service (NAMAS) is a service of the National Physical Laboratory (NPL), the UK national standards laboratory. NAMAS was formed in September 1985 by the amalgamation of the British Calibration Service (BCS) and the National Testing Laboratory Accreditation Scheme (NATLAS). It is responsible for the assessment and accreditation of laboratories carrying out calibrations, measurements or tests in support of product certification, procurements, regulatory bodies and quality assurance generally. Accredited laboratories are included in the NAMAS Concise Directory and in the DTI QA Register.

BSI (British Standards Institution)

The British Standards Institution (BSI) is responsible for preparing British Standards which are used in all industries and technologies. It also represents British interests at international standards discussions to ensure that European and worldwide standards will be acceptable to British industry. Some 70% of BSI standards work is now geared to international alignment. BSI also takes a prominent part in developing internationally agreed criteria for quality assessment and certification.

British Standards are compiled by committees representing those organizations with a close interest in the subject; manufacturers, users, government, professional bodies, safety, research and consumer organisations. There are now over 10,000 publications listed in the BSI Catalogue, including the key standard for quality systems, BS 5750.

The BSI, through its certification and assessment services, provides industry with product certification and company quality assessment schemes.

This provides independent assurance that the firm's quality system complies with BS 5750/ISO 9000/EN 29000 and also with any appropriate quality assessment schedule (QAS). The objective of registration is to establish by means of independent assessment and subsequent periodic surveillance that the firm is capable of consistently manufacturing to specification. Registration entitles the firm to use the BSI registered firm symbol in promotional material.

BSI registration is of general application. In addition, to meet the particular quality needs of an industry or the requirements of a technological discipline, BSI designs and operates special systems having their own rules and scope of application. The BS 9000 system was established before BSI registration to BS 5750 became available. It is designed to meet the needs of the electronic components industry and has its own image and certification and capability assessment, and covers manufacturers, distributors and test houses.

Before applying for certification that a company complies with BS 5750 it has to carry out a survey to establish where it stands as regards quality and what improvements may be required. There are a large number of consultants who are qualified to do this assessment and assist companies in preparing for certification. Some of these consultants have themselves been registered as capable of carrying out assessments on behalf of certification bodies.

Certification follows an in-depth assessment of the company's procedures and the overall management structure for compliance with BS 5750/ISO 9000/EN 29000 using applicable assessment guidance material. Assessment is carried out by a third party certification body. After the company has been awarded its certificate of compliance, the certification body makes regular surveillance visits to ensure that the company is still following the agreed practices.

NACCB (National Accreditation Council for Certification Bodies)

While encouraging the development of private sector certification schemes, discussions with various sectors of industry during 1982-85 led the Government to recognize the advantages of a national accreditation scheme for those certification bodies. The essential features of the scheme were that:

- it should be voluntary;
- accreditation should be open to both public and private sectors;
- it should be a federation, so preserving the identity of accredited bodies;
- accreditation should be against published criteria and subject to periodic monitoring; and,
- it should run on commercial lines and become self-financing.

In July 1985, the National Accreditation Council for Certification Bodies (NACCB) was launched by the Department of Trade and Industry. It is established under BSI's Royal Charter, but is an independent council reporting through the Board of BSI to the DTI Secretary of State. Its activities are quite separate from those of the BSI. Its principal function is the impartial assessment, on behalf of DTI, of certification bodies applying for government accreditation. The organizations represented on the NACCB are listed in Figure 28, page 302.

The government expects that all those certification bodies upon whose services it relies will seek accreditation. In addition it encourages other authorities and purchasing organizations to support the council. Currently, 25 certification bodies satisfying those criteria set out in ISO Guide 40 have already been accredited and thus may use the registered national mark of NACCB.

Accredited Certification Bodies

There are currently 25 organisations accredited by the National Accreditation Council for Certification Bodies (NACCB) - these are listed in section 7. More are being processed.

(ACB) Association of Certification Bodies

The ACB was formed in 1984 with the purpose of working towards the improvement of product quality in British industry by representing the interests of its members and cooperating with British industry and the government in achieving this objective. The Association provides a forum where certification bodies can develop a collective input to issues associated with national accreditation of certification bodies.

Figure 28: Membership of the National Accreditation Council for Certification Bodies

Member Bodies	Number of Representatives
Government Departments	4
Confederation of British Industry	4
National Economic Development Office	1
Trades Union Congress	1
Professional Institutions	1
Insurance/Inspection Interests	1
National Measurement Accreditation Service	1
Certification Bodies, (collectively represented)	3
BSI Consumer Policy Committee (ex-officio)	1
BSI Local Authorities Policy Committee representing the four Local Authority Associations (ex-officio)	1
Nationalized Industry Quality Assurance Liaison Group	2
The Institute of Purchasing and Supply	1
The Retail Consortium	1
Lloyd's Register of Shipping	1

Source: DTI

3.2 Other Quality Bodies

(IQA) The Institute of Quality Assurance
The Institute of Quality Assurance is a professional body established to serve the needs of all those involved with quality assurance. The Institute organizes short courses, seminars and conferences on all aspects of quality, which cover a variety of industries and disciplines. It also administers a structured training course and has details of the colleges which offer part-time and full-time courses based on the Institute's examination syllabus. Details of the post-graduate course on quality assurance and management are also available.

(BQA) The British Quality Association
The British Quality Association (BQA) exists to promote a better understanding of quality throughout industry and commerce. Membership is open to all industrial, commercial and other corporate organizations and is by no means confined to quality professionals. The aim is to make all businessmen and managers aware that the quality of their products or services is a vital factor in ensuring the competitiveness and profitability of their company and to assist in improving quality practices.

(NQIC) National Quality Information Centre
The National Quality Information Centre (NQIC) is operated by the Institute of Quality Assurance. It aims to help industry and commerce obtain the information they need to improve quality in their corporate activities and in the products and services they provide.

(AQMC) Association of Quality Management Consultants Ltd
The Association of Quality Management Consultants Ltd (AQMC) Ltd is a self-regulating body whose members by their training, qualifications and experience, meet requirements designed to establish that they are professionally competent to act as consultants to industry and commerce, on a whole range of quality management activities.

(NSQC) National Society of Quality Circles
The National Society of Quality Circles was formed in 1982 by some 20 organizations in the UK which were operating quality circle programmes. Its aim is 'to encourage the healthy development of quality circles in the UK by combining the experience and energy of people from its member organizations. Membership now extends to approximately 200 companies which together have circles active on thousands of sites in the UK. It provides a network of regional meetings, seminars and conferences for the exchange of informative experience. It also runs regular training courses and an advisory service. Through the European Federation of Quality Circle Associations (EFQCA) the NSQC has links to similar organizations throughout Europe.

3.3 Regional Organizations

3.3.1 Scotland

Scotland operates with two main channels of assistance to industry the Scottish Office Industry Department and Scottish Enterprise.

Industry Department for Scotland
Channel for most parts of the Enterprise Initiative (see DTI). In comparison with the DTI, however, this department has a relatively modest role. Scottish Enterprise is much more important.

Scottish Enterprise
On 1 April 1991, the Scottish Development Agency and the Training Agency in Scotland merged to form Scottish Enterprise. Scottish Enterprise and the local enterprise companies have become a major force in stimulating interest and activity in the field of quality.

3.3.2 Wales

In general the quality promotion schemes and initiatives found in Wales are identical to those in England although implemented by the Welsh Office Industry Department and the Welsh Development Agency. The new Wales Quality Centre in Cardiff has been created to provide a nucleus of quality expertise.

3.3.3 Northern Ireland

Northern Ireland is a Development Area in its own right. Most schemes of support which operate on the mainland have their counterparts in the province, but they usually go under different names. In addition, there are a number of schemes in operation which do not apply in the rest of the UK. Overall, the scale of assistance available to industry matches or exceeds that available elsewhere in the UK.

IAS (Industry Advisory Service)
The Industry Advisory Service provides consultancy support for companies with more than five employees moving towards BS 5750.

LEDU (Local Enterprise Development Unit)
The LEDU provides grants for quality surveys and for implementing their recommendations in small firms (up to 50 employees).

4. National Quality Schemes and Initiatives

4.1 Global Schemes

The Enterprise Initiative is primarily concerned with spreading best-practice management methods in small and medium-sized enterprises (SMEs) in England

and Wales (similar schemes have been introduced in Scotland and Northern Ireland). It has two main elements: awareness and consultancy help. The 'Managing into the 1990s' programme provides practical information and advice on the management of design, quality, purchasing and production. Having a budget of about £3 million per year, it offers a range of events backed up by written and audio/visual material. These include: a 'Strategy Roadshow' a free half-day presentation which identifies factors including quality that will help improve companies' competitive performance; 'Inside UK Enterprise' visits to companies employing best practice in a wide range of areas; workshops and seminars on TQM; and, a booklet 'Total Quality Management and Effective Leadership'. A third main strand of DTI activity in the field of quality has been promotion of BS 5750 and support for the quality infrastructure.

The main focus of the Enterprise Initiative, however, is the provision of subsidized consultancy services. The aim of this is to help companies identify and resolve barriers to their competitive performance. Consultancies cover the following topics: marketing, design, quality, advanced manufacturing, business planning and management of financial and information systems. Under each initiative a maximum of 15 days of assisted consultancy is allowed for each assignment. A 50% subsidy (rising to 66% in regionally assisted areas) is provided toward the cost of the consultancy package. To date, the DTI has received about 100,000 applications for consultancy help. Of the six areas within the Initiative, most applications have been received for help with marketing (38%), and quality (21%). The Quality Consultancy is described in more detail, below in section 4.1.3

From April 1991, firms were limited to a single assisted consultancy project so as to concentrate on those which have not previously been assisted under the Consultancy Initiatives. Provision for the Consultancy Initiatives (including paid publicity) was £54 million in 1991/92, compared with £61 million in 1990/91. The number of completed consultancy projects in 1990/91 is expected to be close to the target of 12,500. A target of 10,000 has been set from 1991/92 onwards, similar to the number of firms assisted in 1990/91.

Table 29: Estimated funding for consultancy initiatives

	1990-91	1991-92	1992-93	1993-94
Expenditure (£ in million)	59.6	61.1	53.9	33.3
Target number of consultancies	12,167	14,000	10,000	7,500

Source: DTI

Independent evaluation of the scheme has indicated that the large majority of assisted firms were well satisfied with their consultancy projects.[20] Within a year of their consultancy project 70% had begun to reap clear commercial benefits and expected to recover their costs within three years (a survey by PERA International the scheme administrators found 90%). The number of completed consultancy projects in 1991/92 exceeded the planned target of 10,000 because of unprecedented demand in the first half of 1991. This was due to several factors, including a rush of applications for second projects before they became ineligible for assistance. The cost of the scheme in 1991/92 was therefore £7million higher than expected. As in 1991/92, the target for 1992/93 is to assist 10,000 small and medium-sized firms.

4.1.1 Research

The DTI Teaching Company Scheme operates through the Teaching Company Programmes which bring together academics, company personnel and graduates. The graduates, known as Teaching Company Associates, work on tasks 'to bring about a substantial change to a company's operations'. Thus, from the company's perspective a Teaching Company Associate often performs a consultancy role. This activity is however, closely related to the research interests of the associate and usually those of his or her academic department. In this way the associate and department gain an insight into real-life problems and the firm gains access to state-of-the art solutions to its problems.

4.1.2 Training and Education

In general, the education of managers in the UK is poor. Most education and training taking place within HE/FE (Higher Education/Furuther Education) colleges and very little in business schools and university departments of management education. Many of these courses are technician-rather than management-oriented. Until recently, there were only three professorships of quality.

Department of Employment

The Department of Employment through its Training Enterprise and Education Directorate (TEED), and the Training and Enterprise Councils (TECs) provide companies with help and advice on training. This includes information on courses and seminars (both full- and part-time) available locally and nationally on quality management.

The Department of Employment Investors in People (IIP) initiative is designed to encourage firms to develop and train their employees to produce a highly skilled and motivated workforce. The initiative has been developed by the National Training Task Force working with the Training and Enterprise Councils (TECs), the CBI (Confederation of British Industry), and other business and training organizations.

The focus of the initiative is the 'Investors in People Standard'. The Standard sets out the policies a company must follow in order to achieve Investor in People status. It stipulates that an Investor in People:

- makes a public commitment from the top to develop all employees to achieve business objectives;
- regularly reviews the training and development needs of all employees;
- takes action to train and develop individuals on recruitment and throughout their employment; and
- evaluates the investment in training and development to assess achievement and improve future effectiveness.

To meet the Standard the employer should have a written, yet flexible, plan setting out business goals and targets, considering how employees will contribute to achieving the plan, and specifying how development needs will be assessed and met. Management should communicate to all employees a vision of where the organization is going and how they will be expected to contribute to its success.

Within the context of business objectives, managers should also regularly agree training and development needs with each employee, and ensure that all new recruits are properly trained. They should review each employee's progress and use of new skills against business targets. As people develop through training, these targets can be reviewed and re-set accordingly.

Investors in People shares a number of similarities with other initiatives such as BS 5750. They are both designed to assist companies to achieve higher standards of quality and productivity. The differences lie chiefly in their particular focus of attention.

Thus, whereas BS 5750 focuses on developing quality management systems and policies, Investors in People concentrates on developing the skills and abilities of the people who must make those systems and policies work for the benefit of the business and its customers.

The Investors in People Initiative is being delivered and monitored through the TECs and LECs. A self-diagnostic pack has been developed to encourage organisations to assess themselves against the Standard. TECs, LECS, industry training organizations and other business and training organisations are developing support for employers involved in the process through consultancy advice, independent progress audits, and guidance to sources of advice and training. When a company is able to provide evidence that it meets the Standard in full, it can then apply to the TEC for recognition as an Investor in People, The adjudication is done by the TEC Boards for which a fee is charged. Once an employer has been recognized as an Investor in People, TECs will have to ensure that continuing development is a reality. This will involve reviews at least every three years. Recognized companies are entitled to display the Investors in People logo.

4.1.3 Other Training and Education Schemes

IQA (Institute of Quality Assurance)
The Institute of Quality Assurance (IQA) runs an extensive programme of 56 courses a year. It is including new modules within both its own training programme and the syllabuses issued for the Institute's qualifying examinations. The IQA

encourages other professional institutions to introduce a quality module into their examination structure.

The Institute maintains a Directory of Quality Assurance Education and Training Facilities in the UK for the Department of Trade and Industry.

The IQA-recognized assessor training courses are run at Cranfield Institute, and Hallam University Sheffield and Portsmouth University (both formerly Polytechnics). Additional requirements have arisen from the application of quality management systems to the IT sector. Working with the British Computer Society, the Institute has agreed plans to validate certification auditors.

Higher Education Institutes

Institutes of higher education ought to have a role in providing appropriate education, training research and consultancy to support industry in its drive for maintaining and improving quality.

The role of the universities and polytechnics in such activities is widespread, but only a few institutions play any significant part. Most education and training takes place within HE/FE colleges and some in business schools and university departments of management education. Many of these courses are technician rather than management-orientated. Most comprehensive educational work is done at post-graduate or post-experience level. At post-graduate level two approaches are discernible:

- specialist technological universities, which teach quality management in the context of their expertise in particular sectors of industry;
- business schools, which teach elements of quality management as a subset of general management programmes.

In general, the business schools tend to stress the motivational and organizational aspects of the subject, whereas the technology-based schools tend to relate the subject more to manufacturing processes and systems and manufacturing management.

4.1.4 Consultancy

Consultancy help is offered under the DTI Enterprise Initiative for independent manufacturing or service companies with fewer than 500 employees. This help is offered in two stages. First an independent Enterprise counsellor carries out a short (up to two days) Business Review. Strengths, weaknesses, opportunities and threats are identified, together with the degree to which the company would benefit from specialist consultancy help, and other types and sources of assistance which may be available. A copy of the counsellor's report is given to the company and sent to one of a number of Scheme Contractors. The contractor matches the needs of the company to a consultant on a list of eligible and suitable consultants. Requests for specific consultants will be accommodated when appropriate. The Scheme Contractor oversees and approves the terms of reference agreed between the company and consultant. The terms of reference contain a detailed programme of work together with a work schedule against which the project can be monitored.

The initial Business Review is free. DTI will pay half the cost of between 5 and 15 days of consultancy. In Assisted Areas and Urban Programme Areas this rises to two-thirds. The company is expected to pay the rest of the consultancy fee. By mid-1992, the DTI had received over 20,000 applications for quality consultancy help under the Initiative.

The quality consultancy provides assistance with the introduction of better or more appropriate quality management systems and procedures. The quality consultancy can help firms with:

- *Quality systems and procedures* Quality control documentation, preparation of quality manuals and systems for implementation.
- *Adoption of quality standards* Advice on how to meet BS 5750 and related standards. The company is encouraged to proceed to assessment and certification to BS 5750 (and therefore EN 29000 and ISO 9000).
- *Quality of supplies* Adoption of supply strategies which will ensure a top quality service from suppliers.
- *Total quality* Assistance with the introduction and implementation of a strategy for company-wide quality improvement. This can include an analysis of company culture and advice on motivational and management techniques designed to enable the company to 'Get it right first time, every time'.

The objective of the quality consultancy is to improve the company's overall approach to quality management. For this reason, it does not cover:

- Advice on specific product assessment, inspection or test methods;
- Assistance with training courses, or quality assurance techniques involving major training inputs;
- The purchase of distance learning packages for the production of quality manuals;
- Industry sectors assistance is not available for whom i.e. agriculture, horticulture, forestry, fishing, primary extraction of coal, oil and gas, and electricity generation.

Also excluded are nationalized industries, other publicly funded organizations, social welfare, charitable and community services, trade unions, professional and trade associations.

PERA (Production Engineering Research Association) International operates the Quality Assurance scheme for the DTI and maintains the list of qualified consultants throughout most of Britain. In the north west of England, the scheme is administered by Salford University Business Services Ltd (SUBS). The scheme offers expert advice on how to introduce a quality management system which meets the right standards for the kind of business the company is engaged in. Strategic advice on total quality is also available.

Since June 1989, the scheme has included support for the development of TQM, providing assistance with the introduction and implementation of a strategy for company-wide quality improvement. This can include an analysis of company culture and advice on motivational and management techniques designed to enable the company to effectively introduce TQM. Advice on TQM is not widely taken up, however. Certification to BS 5750 or equivalent standards is the primary purpose for consultancy in 85% of cases; TQM is the primary purpose in only about 2%. Most of the rest are requested by companies seeking to satisfy specific customer requirements.[21]

Following an evaluation of the first two years of the Consultancy Initiatives, the Government decided to extend them for a final three years, until March 1994. By that time, the consultancy market among small and medium-sized firms is expected to be self-sustaining.

Table 30: Estimated funding for quality consultancy initiatives

	1990-91	1991-92	1992-93	1993-94
Expenditure (£ in million)	12.5	12.8	11.3	11.1
Target number of consultancies	2,500	3,000	2,100	2,100

Source: DTI

Private Consultancy

Many companies make use of private consultancies to help them improve quality and/or apply for BS 5750. A survey conducted in 1991 found that 78% of companies employ consultants to help implement a quality programme. The main reasons given were that they lacked in-house expertise and wished to speed up the process of gaining certification

4.1.5 Promotion and Awareness

The DTI 'Managing into the 1990s' initiative (part of the DTI Enterprise Initiative) provides information on design, quality, production and purchasing and supply. It does this through briefings, demonstration visits, workshops and seminars. These include:

- *A Strategy Roadshow* a free half day presentation which identifies factors including quality that will help improve their competitive performance.

- *Inside UK Enterprise* provides opportunities to visit over 100 leading companies employing best practice in a wide range of areas.
- *Workshops and seminars* including one-day seminars offering an introduction to total quality management by experts and company practitioners in the subject, with the option of a follow-up briefing.
- A booklet *Total quality management and effective leadership.*

The annual budget for this initiative is currently running at about £3 million per year.

In addition, the DTI has provided a small amount of pump priming money to a number of Regional Quality Centres.

4.1.6 'Non-Government' Awareness Initiatives

A number of non-government bodies play a significant role in quality promotion in the UK. Perhaps the most important is the Institute of Quality Assurance (IQA). The IQA played a leading role in the National Quality Campaign. The British Quality Awards scheme was launched in 1984 to give impetus to the government's initiatives arising from the 1982 White Paper. The intention was to create a national award which would encourage the adoption of TQM. Since its inception, 22 companies have won the award. In addition, the IQA runs an extensive training programme and prepares syllabuses for the Institute's qualifying examinations. The Institute maintains a Directory of Quality Assurance Education and Training Facilities in the UK for the DTI. IQA-recognised assessor training courses are run at Cranfield Institute, Sheffield and Portsmouth Polytechnics. Additional requirements have arisen from the application of quality management systems to the IT sector. Working with the British Computer Society and DTI, the institute has agreed plans to validate certification auditors in this sector.

4.2 Sectoral Schemes

4.2.1 Information Technology

Software, together with high technology equipment was identified as a target area for the National Quality Campaign in a review conducted in 1986, shortly after the formation of the National Accreditation Council for Certification Bodies. In 1987 the DTI commissioned two studies. One from Price Waterhouse, looked at costs and benefits. The other, from Logica, examined standards. The reports were well received by the industry which estimates that losses due to poor quality software cost the UK £1 million every hour. The British Computer Society, after extensive consultation, agreed with the conclusion from both reports that the internationally recognised ISO 9001 (EN 29001, BS 5750) standards could be interpreted to meet its members, needs.

The TickIT Programme
In June 1991 the DTI sponsored an industry sector scheme focusing on software and information technology. Under the name TickIT, the programme aims 'to bring

a common understanding of quality management concepts, accreditation and certification to the software and information technology industry'. The industry response to the scheme has far exceeded expectations. John Slater of Logica argued:

> *TickIT is important because it fills a gap in the national certification schemes. ... 'very developed country, every developing country and all major companies in the world have the problem of how to manage software development. The scheme provides a way of showing that the international standard on quality management is understood and implemented.'*[22]

The scheme is seen to offer a model which other industries can follow. The programme has been described by Dr Ivan Dunstan, director general of the British Standards Institution, as a standards body within a standards body':

> *... it manages its programme, its priorities and its resources in a way which is close to the industry itself and to its market-place. We feel this is a trend which will probably extend to other sectors of industry, so standardisation becomes more decentralised.*[23]

BSI Quality Assurance, the commercial certification arm of the BSI, is one of three assessing bodies which issue certificates. The others are Bureau Veritas Quality International Ltd, and Det Norske Veritas.

One feature of the programme is that it requires all auditors to be knowledgeable about this comparatively young and fast-growing industry, and to pass an interview vetting process. Another is that it is owned and led by the industry itself.

5. Regional Quality Schemes and Initiatives

5.1 Global Schemes

5.1.1 Scotland

Research
A number of Scottish universities and HE Colleges are active in quality research. Amongst the most significant are:

- University of Stirling (Scottish Quality Management Centre)
- University of Glasgow
- Heriot-Watt University
- University of Paisley.

Training and Education
The following educational establishments are in the Scottish Quality Network:

- Paisley College of Technology
- University of Glasgow
- Polyed (Napier College)
- Heriot-Watt University
- Edinburgh University
- Stevenson College of Further Education
- Telford College of Further Education
- West Lothian College of Further Education
- University of Stirling
- Falkirk College of Technology
- Glenrothes College
- St Andrews Management Institute
- Robert Gordon's Institute of Technology
- University of Strathclyde.

Promotion and Awareness

In May 1989, the Scottish Development Agency, which had already been involved in work on BS 5750, ran a conference in Glasgow 'Beyond BS 5750 equals TQM'. In November 1989, the SDA sponsored a fact finding mission to Japan for the manufacturing sector of Scottish industry. A tour of the US to study American services companies followed in June 1990.

Scottish Enterprise's Total Quality Group has acted as a catalyst with local businesses and organizations in the establishment of Quality Forums in Scotland with the objective of promoting total quality throughout Scotland. The first of these Quality Forums was opened in Ayrshire in 1989:

- Ayrshire Quality Association
- Central Scotland Quality Forum
- Fife & Tayside Quality Forum
- Grampian Quality Forum
- West of Scotland Quality Forum
- Dumfries & Galloway Quality Forum
- Glasgow Quality Forum
- Lothian Quality Forum
- Lanarkshire Quality Forum
- Highlands & Islands Quality Forum
- ITSA Scottish Quality Forum
- Borders Quality Forum
- Dunbartonshire Quality Forum

Membership is cross-sectorial, e.g. services, professional, financial, health care, educational, manufacturing, the objective being to increase the awareness of TQM leading to implementation at company level. The members meet regularly and informally at events where they have the opportunity to learn from specialists and exchange experiences in quality related matters. Membership is by an annual subscription decided by each forum.

Forums arrange their own programme of seminars, specialist topic evenings and visits which are frequently hosted by organizations in membership. Executive briefings on quality related subjects are arranged regularly and conducted by suitably qualified consultants.

Each Quality Forum is represented by the chairman on the committee of the Scottish Quality Network and members receive the Network Newsletter which is issued each month.

The Scottish Quality Network is comprised of Quality Forums, associations and Organisations in Scotland committed to quality. It has been established to coordinate and enable communication with member organizations committed to spreading the development of quality practices throughout Scotland. The Network represents a total membership of 1000.

5.1.2 Wales

Schemes and initiatives are similar to those found in England. In addition, the Welsh Development Agency has provided support for the Welsh Quality Centre.

5.1.3 Northern Ireland

Northern Ireland is a Development Area in its own right. Most schemes of support which operate on the mainland have their counterparts in the province, but they usually go under different names. But in addition, there are a number of schemes in operation which do not apply in the rest of the UK. Overall, the scale of assistance available to industry matches or exceeds that available elsewhere in the UK.

Between 230 and 240 firms in Northern Ireland are now certified to BSV5750 or equivalent.

Industry Advisory Service

The Industry Advisory Service provides consultancy support for firms moving to BS 5750 for companies with more than five employees - two-thirds consultancy fee for maximum of 15 days.

LEDU (Local Enterprise Development Unit)

The LEDU provides grants for quality surveys and for implementing their recommendations in small firms (up to 50 employees). The surveys cover:

* product and market research;
* product costing;
* plant capacity and production planning;
* products made 'right first time';
* achieving accurate delivery forecasts;

- efficient after sales service; and
- employee commitment to quality.

Grants of up to 55% of the cost (to a maximum of £4,000) of employing management consultants to carry out a quality survey covering all activities available through Better Business Services.

Grants of up to 60% are available towards the cost of implementing an action plan resulting from such a survey. The maximum for these grants is £15,000.

In addition to support for consultancy, LEDU provides 60% of initial registration cost for small firms wishing to undertake quality certification. Until recently such firms had to go to the mainland, the high cost of which acted as major disincentive. The new NICQA presence undercuts the cost of BSI certification.

There is also a Quality Control scheme providing support for consultancy to smaller companies wishing to gain second party (i.e. customer) approval. Two-thirds of the consultancy fee is provided for a maximum of nine days.

LEDU provides assistance on BSI kitemarking (for which there is a need to demonstrate QC system and testing ability) and EC marking (showing that the product meets Community directives). There is increasing harmonization between the two.

LEDU also provides assistance to the Northern Ireland Quality Centre (which performs a similar role to that of the BQA in London).

6. Overview and Outlook

The UK Government has long been active in quality issues related to defence procurement, but only recently has its attention been drawn to the importance of quality in industry generally. A key aim of UK Government policy has been to support the development of a comprehensive quality supporting infrastructure. This has meant closer involvement in standards-making, encouraging the adoption of quality management systems, and of assessment, certification and accreditation schemes. In general, however, recent government philosophy has been against direct intervention. Support for quality consultancy is justified in terms of market failure

The DTI's Enterprise Initiative is primarily concerned with spreading best practice management methods in small and medium-sized enterprises (SMEs) in England and Wales (similar schemes have been introduced in Scotland and Northern Ireland). The main focus of the Enterprise Initiative is the provision of subsidized consultancy services. The aim of this is to help companies identify and resolve barriers to their competitive performance. Consultancies cover the following topics: marketing, design, quality, advanced manufacturing, business planning and management of financial and information systems.

The Quality Consultancy offers expert advice on the introduction of better or more appropriate quality management systems and procedures. Since June 1989, the scheme has included support for the development of TQM, providing assistance with the introduction and implementation of a strategy for company-wide quality improvement.

The Department of Employment, through its Training Enterprise and Education Directorate (TEED), and the Training and Enterprise Councils (TECs) provide companies with help and advice on training. This includes information on courses and seminars (both full- and part-time) available locally and nationally on quality management. The Department of Employment Investors in People (IIP) initiative is designed to encourage firms to develop and train their employees to produce a highly skilled and motivated workforce.

A number of non-Government bodies play a significant role in quality promotion in the UK. Perhaps the most important is the Institute of Quality Assurance (IQA). The IQA played a leading role in the National Quality Campaign. The British Quality Awards scheme was launched in 1984 to give impetus to the government's initiatives arising from the 1982 White Paper. The intention was to create a national award which would encourage the adoption of TQM. IQA - recognized assessor training courses are run at Cranfield Institute, Sheffield Hallam and Portsmouth Universities. Additional requirements have arisen from the application of quality management systems to the IT sector. Working with the British Computer Society and DTI, the institute has agreed plans to validate certification auditors in this sector.

The role of the universities and polytechnics in quality related activities is widespread, but only a few institutions play any significant part. Most education and training takes place within HE/FE colleges and some in business schools and university departments of management education.

Quality promotion activities in the UK have been focused on the development and promotion of quality management standards, particularly BS 5750. While encouraging the development of private sector schemes, the Government recognized the advantages of a national accreditation scheme of private certification bodies. Currently 25 certification bodies are accredited by the National Accreditation Council for Certification Bodies (NACCB).

6.1 Future

The current DTI Enterprise Consultancy Initiative (containing an option on quality) is due to end in March 1994. The original aim of encouraging a self-sustaining market amongst SMEs for consultants is felt to have been very successful. As yet there is little indication as to what, if anything, will follow it, although any follow-up scheme is likely to place more emphasis on TQM.

At the beginning of 1991, the DTI announced that it had set up a committee to examine the scope for a new national award for quality. The committee has now reported and has recommended the introduction of a quality award based on similar criteria to those of the EFQM award.

7. List of Schemes and Organizations
7.1 Schemes

DTI Enterprise Quality Consultancy Initiative

DTI 'Managing into the 1990s'

DTI TickIT Campaign

DTI Teaching Company Scheme

Departmenty of Employment: 'Investors in People'

7.2 Organizations

Name	Address	Telephone/Fax
DTI Enterprise Initiative		
DTI General Enquiries on TQM	Bay 511 Kingsgate House 66-74 Victoria Street London SW1E 6SW	071 215 8142
DTI Advice on BS 5750	1st Floor, Grey Zone 151 Buckingham Palace Road London SW1W 9SS	071 215 1483
Production Engineering and Research Association (PERA) International	The Quality and Assurance Advisory Service (SUBS) Salford	061 736 2843/061 745 8362
Regional Bodies		
Wales	Welsh Office Industry Department New Crown Buildings Cathays Park Cardiff CF1 3NQ	0222 825111
Consultancy help: (North and South Wales)	Enterprise Initiative Section Welsh Development Agency Business Development Unit Treforest Industrial Estate Mid Glamorgan CF37 5YR	0443 841200
(Mid-Wales)	Development Board for Rural Wales Ladywell House Newtown Mid Wales SY16 1JB	
Scotland	Scottish Office Industry Department for Scotland Alhambra House 45 Waterloo Street Glasgow G2 6AT	041 248 2855

Enterprise Services Scotland Ltd	Roseberry House Haymarket Terrace Edinburgh EH12 5HD	031 313 6200
Northern Ireland	Industry Advisory Service (Contact Rodney Hummell)	0232 664 393
Local Enterprise Development Unit (LEDU)	LEDU House Upper Galwally Belfast BT8 4TB	0232 491031
DTI TickIT Project	DTI TickIT Project Office 4th Floor, Green Zone 151 Buckingham Palace Road, London SW1W 9SS	071 383 4501
Department of Employment (TEED)	Management and Trainer Development Room E603 Moorfoot Sheffield S1 4PQ	
Investors in People	Room W828 Employment Department Moorfoot Sheffield S1 4PQ	0742 593427
Ministry of Defence	Directorate General Defence Quality Assurance Royal Arsenal West Woolwich, London SE18 6ST	081 854 2044/081 317 2036
Department of the Environment	Construction Technology Division 2 Marsham Street London SW1P 3EB	071 276 6645

Standards and Accreditation

National Measurement Accreditation Service (NAMAS)	NAMAS Executive National Physical Laboratory Teddington, Middlesex TW11 0LW	+44 81 977 3222 wztn 6672
British Standards Institution (BSI)	Linford Wood Milton Keynes MK14 6LE	+44 908 221166
National Accreditation Council for Certification Bodies (NACCB)	Audley House 13 Palace Street London SW1E 5HS	071 233 7111

Accredited Certification Bodies

Associated Offices Quality Certification Ltd	Longridge House Longridge Place Manchester M60 4DT	061 833 2295/061 883 9965
ASTA Certification Services	Prudential Chambers 23/24 Market Place Rugby CV21 3DU	0788 578435/0788 573605
BMT Quality Assessors Ltd	Scottish Metropolitan Alpha Centre Stirling University Innovation Park Stirling FK9 4NF	0786 50891/0786 51087

BSI Quality Assurance	PO Box 375 Milton Keynes MK14 6LL	0908 220908/0908 220671
British Approvals Service for Electrical Cables	Silbury Court 360 Silbury Boulevard Milton Keynes MK9 2AF	0908 691121/0908 692722
Bureau Veritas Quality International	3rd Floor 70 Borough High Street London SE1 1XF	071 378 8113/071 378 8014
Central Certification Services	Victoria House Midland Road Wellingborough Northants NN8 1LU	0933 441796/0933 440247
Ceramic Industry Certification Scheme	Queens Road Penkhull Stoke-on-Trent ST4 7LQ	0782 411008/0782 412331
Construction Quality Assurance	Arcade Chambers The Arcade Market Place Newark, Notts NG24 1UD	0636 708700/0636 708766
Det Norske Veritas Quality Assurance	Veritas House 112 Station Road Sidcup Kent DA15 7BU	081 309 7477/082 309 5907
Electrical Equipment Certification Service	Health and Safety Executive Harpur Hill Buxton yshire SK17 9JN	0298 26211/029879514
Electricity Association Quality Assurance Ltd	30 Millbank London SW1P 4RD	071 834 2333/071 931 0356
Engineering Inspection Authority Board	Institution of Mechanical Engineers 1 Birdcage Walk London SW1H 9JJ	071 222 4577/071 4222 4557
Lloyd's Register Quality Assurance	Norfolk House Wellesley Road Croydon CR9 2DT	081 688 6882/081 681 8146
National Approval Council for Security Systems	Queensgate House 14 Cookham Road Maidenhead Berkshire SL6 8AJ	0628 37512/0628 773367
National Inspection Council Quality Assurance Ltd	5 Cotswold Business Park Millfield Lane Caddington Beds LU1 4AR	0582 814144/0582 841288
SIRA Certification Service	Saighton Lane Saighton Chester CH3 6EG	0244 332200/0244 332112
The Loss Prevention Certification Board	Melrose Avenue Borehamwood Herts WD6 2BJ	081 207 2345/081 207 6305

BMT Quality Assurance Ltd	Scottish Mokpolita Alpla Centre Stirling Univ Innovation Park Stirling FK9 4NF	0786 50891/0786 51087
Quality Scheme for Ready Mixed Concrete	3 High Street Hampton Middx TW12 2SQ	081 941 0273/081 979 4558
TRADA QA	Stocking Lane Hughenden Valley High Wycombe Bucks HP14 4NR	0494 565 484/0494 565 487
TWI Qualification Services	Abingdon Hall Abingdon Cambridge CB1 6AL	0223 891162/0223 894219
Steel Construction QA Scheme Ltd	4 Whitehall Court Westminster London SW1A 2ES	071 839 8566/071 976 1634
UK Certification Authority for Reinforcing Steels	Oak House Tubs Hill Sevenoaks Kent TN13 1BL	0732 450000/0732 455917
Water Industry Certification Scheme	c/o WRc Swindon PO Box 85 Frankland Road Blagrove Swindon Wilts SN5 8YR	0793 410005/0793 5111
SGS Yarsley Quality Assured Firms	Trowers Way Redhill RH1 2JN	0737 768445/0737 761229

Other Quality Related Bodies

Association of British Certification Bodies (ACB)	c/o BSI 2 Park Street London W1A 2BS	071 495 4193
The Institute of Quality Assurance (IQA)	8/10 Grosvenor Gardens London SW1A 0DQ	071 823 5608
The British Quality Association (BQA)	8 Grosvenor Gardens London SW1W 0DQ	071 823 5608
The National Quality Information Centre (NQIC)	8-10 Grosvenor Gardens London SW1A 0DQ	071 823 5609
The Association of Quality Management Consultants Ltd (AQMC)	The Honourary Secretary 4 Beyne Road Olivers Battery Winchester Hampshire SO22 4JW	0962 864394
National Society of Quality Circles (NSQC)	NSQC 2 Castle Street Salisbury Wiltshire SP1 1BB	0722 26667

References

1. Morrison, S.J., (1990), 'Managing Quality: A Historical Review', in Dale, B.G., J.J., Plunkett (eds), *Managing Quality*, Hemel Hempstead, Philip Allan,

2. Department of Prices and Consumer Protection (1978), *A National Strategy for Quality*, HMSO London:

3. Warner, F. (1977) 'The Role of Standards in the Industrial Strategy', Paper Prepared for the National Economic Development Organisation (NEDO).

4. Department of Prices and Consumer Protection, op. cit.

5. Ibid.

6. Department of Industry, *Standards, Quality and International Competitiveness*, White Paper, London: HMSO, 1982

7. Department of Trade and Industry, 1986 *Quality Counts*, London, DTI.

8. Warner, F. op. cit.

9. Ibid.

10. International Standardization Organization, ISO 9000 series, (1987).

11. BSV5750 series, British Standards Institute, 1987; EN 29000 series, European Committee for Normalization, 1987.

12. Warner, F., op. cit.

13. Personal Communication.

14. Open University.

15. PERA International and Salford University Business Services 1992, *A Survey of Quality Consultancy Scheme Clients 1988/1990*, DTI, September.

16. Personal Communication.

17. Department of Trade and Industry (1993), *Quality Assurance Register*, London, DTI.

18. Commercial report produced by Jay Communications, 1991.

19. Commercial report produced by Develin and Partners, 1990.

20. Segal Quince and Wickstead (1987 & 1989), *Evaluations of the DTI Consultancy Initiatives*. Cambridge, SQW.

21. PERA International and Salford University Business Services, op. cit.

22. quoted in *Financial Times*, 18 November 1992.

23. Ibid.

Other References

Dale, B.G., and J.J., Plunkett (eds): *Managing Quality,* Hemel Hempstead, Philip Allan, (1990).

Department of Trade and Industry, *Quality Counts*, October 1986.

Publications on Quality Produced by the DTI under its Enterprise Initiative

Total Quality Management:

 Total Quality Management - A Practical Approach

 Leadership and Quality Management - A Guide For Chief Executives

 The Quality Gurus - What Can They Do for Your Company?

 The Case For Costing Quality

 The Case For Quality

Quality Assurance:

 BS 5750/ISO9000/EN 29000: 1987 - A Positive Contribution to Better Business

Quality Techniques:

 Best Practice Benchmarking

 Statistical Process Control

 Quality Circles

 Problem Solving For Operators

DTI TickIT Programme

 Guide to Software Quality Management System Construction and Certification using EN 29001

Part Four:

European Quality Activities

European Quality Activities

Brendan Barker

1. Introduction

The European Union is effectively the major actor in quality promotion at the European level. (In 1993, following ratification of the Maastricht Treaty, the official name of what was formerly the European Community became the European Union. However, as the earlier term remains in common use we use the terms interchangeably). Quality promotion activities occur within the context of a clear commitment to the enhanced operation of the Single Market.[1] In particular, the elimination of barriers to trade (one of the principles of the Single Market) demands that any product lawfully produced and marketed in a member state must, in principle, be admitted to the market of every other member state. Thus current European quality promotion activities are dominated by the major task of harmonization between European Union member countries.

The demand for increased harmonization is, in turn, leading to far-reaching changes in technology related legislation, standardization and quality assurance throughout Europe. Up until the recent past, most technical legislation was at the national level, and was different in every country and often formed a significant non-tariff barrier to trade. Voluntary standards were produced by the national standards bodies and few European standards existed (although in a few areas such as information technology standardization was international). Conformity testing and certification were even more fragmented, with most action taking place at the sector level within countries. Other aspects of quality assurance were mainly internal to enterprises, and concentrated on manufacturing defects.

Over the past five years, European standardization has been transformed from a marginal activity to one which is attracting priority attention. The importance that voluntary standards have assumed in the Community's technical legislation has been the driving force behind this change. European standards are not only required for the purpose of removing technical barriers to trade, but increasingly they are also becoming an important factor in the promotion of industrial competitiveness, another key EC policy objective. For this reason, quality promotion goes beyond quality assurance and the associated standards, certification and assessment infrastructure, to include the promotion of more sophisticated quality management approaches having competitive significance.

2. The European Community

The Commission of the European Community has been involved in quality issues for many years. A Directive in 1983 laying down a procedure for the provision of information in the field of technical standards and regulations marked an important turning point.[2] For the first time Member States and the Commission were to be informed of, and given the opportunity to propose amendments to, the technical regulations and standards contemplated by any one member state. In particular, the Directive established the procedures for cooperation between the members of the European Committee for Standardization - CEN and the Commission. It provided for:

- the collection by the European standardization bodies of information from their members concerning their planned and current activity;
- requests from national standards bodies to be associated with the work of another body, or to have work taken up at European level;
- a Standing Committee on Technical Regulations and Standards, composed of member state representatives and chaired by the Commission, in whose work the European and national standards organizations could participate;
- requests from the Commission, after consultation of the standing committee, to the European standardization bodies to draw up standards on specific subjects; and
- best efforts by member state authorities to ensure that national standardization did not continue on subjects for which the Commission had requested European standards.

To further support the goals of a Single Market, the European Community adopted a 'new approach' to technical harmonization and standards in May 1985.[3] This approach identified the harmonization of regulations, mutual recognition of national regulations and the approximation of structures within a system of voluntary certification as important goals in the removal of barriers to trade. Thus the new approach laid the foundations for a Community Quality Policy which emphasized:

- the need for removal of unnecessary technical barriers to trade;
- the restriction of legislative texts to the 'essential requirements' for protection of the general interest (in particular, health and safety, and consumer and environmental protection);
- the use of European Standards or national standards if need be, as a transitional measure for the purposes of defining the technical characteristics of products to satisfy the essential requirements; and the non-mandatory characteristic of the European Standards; and,
- most harmonization occurring within the framework of 'New Approach' directives.

'New Approach' directives cover only essential requirements (safety, environment, etc.), are horizontal across wide ranges of products, and leave technical detail to European standards (to approved national standards as a transitional measure). Products placed on the market in the Community must comply with legislation, but not necessarily with standards; but non-conforming products must be independently tested and certified.

The directives and standards to which they refer are not descriptive specifications but increasingly set performance requirements. The new approach now forms the basis of most Community technical legislation. Under the new approach, EC legislation confines itself to laying down the essential requirements with which products must comply in order to ensure health and safety. European standards are developed in order to provide manufacturers with a set of technical specifications conforming to these requirements. European standards remain voluntary.

While the existence of standards specifying essential requirements is a necessary part of the New Approach, it is not sufficient. Thus, in its resolution in May 1985, the EC Council of Ministers recognised that it was necessary to establish a transparent framework to carry out the conformity assessment of products conforming with EC Directives. Because of the importance of the so-called 'Global Approach' in understanding the Community's Quality policy, it will be useful to describe it in some detail. This we will do in the next section.

2.1 The Global Approach

In December 1989, the Council approved the Global Approach to conformity assessment, which creates, in the context of the Single Market, a technical environment in which public authorities, other economic operators and consumers can all have confidence.[4] The technical environment is composed of product specifications (expressed in the standards and the technical regulations) and structures for the conformity assessment (certification bodies, inspection and quality audit bodies, testing laboratories and the manufacturers' quality systems).

In order to ensure confidence in this technical environment, the Global Approach is aimed at making these structures as homogeneous, transparent and credible as possible throughout the Community. A consistent approach in Community legislation is ensured by a modular approach to conformity assessment and the laying down of criteria for the designation and notification of conformity assessment bodies and for the use of the EC mark the tangible sign of product conformity. A 1990 Council decision, approved the use of this approach for the various phases of the conformity assessment procedures which are intended to be used in the technical harmonization Directives.

Under the Global Approach, EC Directives define the range of procedures open to the manufacturer for ensuring compliance with essential requirements. The modular approach gives great flexibility over the entire production process, allowing the manufacturer to adapt the chosen procedure of conformity assessment to the needs of each individual operation. The eight modules can be combined to form a complete procedure. In one Directive several alternative modules can be applied to the same function provided that they give equivalent results. Conformity assessment procedures usually operate at two levels in the manufacturing process: the design stage and the production stage. Figure 29 (page 328), shows the relationship between the eight modules.

Figure 29: Conformity assessment procedures in EC legislation

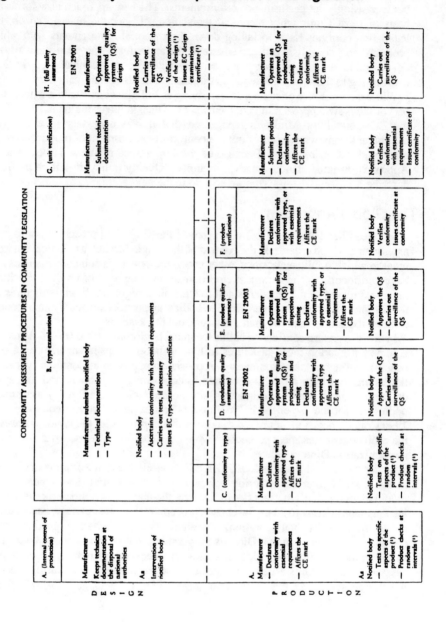

Source: OJ No. L 380, 31.12.1990, p 26

328

The other important element of the Global Approach is the structure for conformity assessment. Member states are required to notify the Commission and other member states of designated bodies undertaking conformity assessment. Verification that these bodies are competent to undertake such assessment may be done by member state national authorities or their national accreditation systems. Notified bodies which can prove their conformity with the EN 45000 series of standards, are presumed to conform to the technical requirements of the Directives.

The Community has given harmonized European standards a prominent role in the opening up of public procurement markets. Community legislation now requires reference to standards in public procurement where relevant. To support these aims, the Certification Unit of DG III was established in July 1992. It is an umbrella organization dealing with quality issues in a 'horizontal' way across the areas of Commission interest. It has responsibility for attempting to harmonize quality criteria throughout the public sector. Although the unit has no formal authority in the private sector, it obviously has a significant impact for most firms operating in the private as well as public sectors.

The unit has formal links with the government officials in the different member states having responsibility for standardisation and certification policy. On an informal basis the unit has strong links with representatives of the private standardization and certification bodies. The unit also has responsibility for negotiating mutual recognition agreements with third countries. Such agreements are based on three conditions:

- assessment bodies in the third countries must demonstrate the same level of technical competence as the Community's notified bodies;
- mutual recognition agreements are confined to reports, certificates and marks drawn up and issued directly by the bodies designated in the agreements; and,
- in cases where the Community wishes to have its own bodies recognized, the agreements establish a balanced situation with regard to the advantages derived by the parties in all matters relating to conformity assessment for the products concerned.

Under 'Cooperation and Technical Assistance Programmes' DG III responds to a number of requests for technical assistance aimed at giving developing countries the knowledge and the necessary means for designing, developing and applying national quality infrastructures.

DG III (in conjunction with DG XIII) is conducting a number of on-going studies. In particular, there is a current study to take stock and review the economic efficiency and competitiveness of the Community Testing, Inspection, Certification and Quality Assurance (TICQA) in services. Other DGs within the European Commission support activities that impinge upon quality related activities. DG XII has launched programmes to support collaboration between testing laboratories of the member states (Community Bureau of Reference (BCR), to examine the interface between developments in science and technology and standards setting and observance (SAST project 2) and a pilot project intended to assist SMEs to identify and assess the impact of new European standardization, certification, and quality requirements they will have to master in order to attain the befits of the internal market. Within DGXIII, the SPRINT programme is relevant in the promotion of quality. Two of the main objectives of the SPRINT programme are to strengthen the European infrastructure for innovation support services and to ensure a rapid diffusion of new technologies to firms throughout Europe. One strand of activities within SPRINT is supporting the formation of transnational networks of Research and Technology Organisations (R&TOs). Another strand within SPRINT is geared towards helping SMEs Manage the Integration of New Technologies (MINT). DG XXIII is running a pilot project under its Euromanagement initiative. These are discussed in detail, below.

3. European Quality Organizations

CEN (European Committee for Standardization)
European standardization organizations have been set up to ensure more effective implementation of international standards by national standardization bodies in Europe, the harmonization of divergent national standards or the preparation of standards where none existed. CEN, an association of European national standards bodies from the member countries of the EEC and EFTA was established in 1961. A stronger regional orientation was given to European standardization after 1983, as a result of initiatives taken by the Community in order to eliminate technical barriers to intra-Community trade.

CEN is a non-profit-making international association of national standardization bodies. The main purpose of CEN is to draw up European standards to promote the competitiveness of European industry throughout the world and to help establish the European internal market. The budget of CEN is voted by the national members, as are its internal rules, work programmes, and decisions on the allocation of resources. In contrast to the situation at national level, the governing bodies of the CEN contain no direct representation of other interests than of professional standardizers. In the period 1985 and 1989, the number of staff has increased from 10 to 70.

The General Assembly has representatives from 18 European national standards institutions:

- Afnor (France)
- BSI (UK)
- DS (Denmark)
- DIN (Germany)
- ELOT (Greece)
- IBN (Belgium)
- IIRS (Ireland)
- Inspection dur Travail et des Mines (Luxembourg)
- NNI (Netherlands)
- UNI (Italy)
- IPQ (Portugal)
- AENOR (Spain)

As already noted, the CEN-approved standards EN 29000 (approved in 1987) and EN 45000 (approved in 1989) forms the basis of the European Community quality assurance strategy. The EN 29000 (equivalent to the ISO 9000) series of standards specify systematic quality assurance at all stages in the product cycle from development through manufacture to delivery and installation. EN 45000 establishes the requirements to be satisfied by the conformity assessment bodies.

EOTC (European Organization for Testing and Certification)
There are many different accreditation schemes throughout Europe and the world, each with its own membership rules (for example, the UK accreditation body the NACBB restricts entry to UK-registered companies. While other schemes are slightly more flexible, the trend is toward restricted, nationalistic policies. There are, however, moves toward a European (or international) accreditation scheme.

A Memorandum of Understanding (MOU) has been signed by the members of the EOTC agreeing a mutually acceptable set of rules the European Accreditation of Certification (EAC) against which companies and their products can be assessed. The agreement is seen as the first step in establishing a method of using certificates that are internationally reliable.

European standard EN 45011/2, underpins the agreement. This specifies the criteria that quality system certification bodies should apply to the management of their own operations. Included are methods of ensuring both impartiality and the competence of assessors.

To provide the environment in which the modules will work, the Community needs a competent and transparent private market in conformity assessment. For this reason, the Community has promoted the EOTC.

EFQM (European Foundation for Quality Management)
Recognising the importance of TQM in underpinning competitive performance 14 of the leading western European firms took the initiative of forming the European Foundation for Quality Management (EFQM) in 1988. As of 1 January 1992 there nearly 200 members from most western European countries and most business sectors. The EFQM is committed to promoting quality as the fundamental process for continuous improvement within a business.

EOQ (European Organization for Quality)
The European Organization for Quality is an autonomous, non-political and non-profit-making international organization. It was established in 1957 and is now domiciled in Bern, Switzerland. At present, membership comprises 25 national European quality organizations, as well as institutions, companies and individuals from all over the world. EOQ aims to improve quality and services. To this end, EOQ initiates and promotes both the theoretical and practical applications of techniques and philosophies in the field of quality. The General Assembly is composed of the nominated representatives of each of the 25 full member organizations and the EOQ officers. This assembly determines the general policies of EOQ and takes the necessary measures to ensure the proper functioning of the organization. Companies and individuals domiciled in European countries become auto-

matically affiliate members of EOQ when joining the national quality organization of their country.

EOQ committees and sections are formed to investigate, on an international scale, the quality needs of specific business sectors and to study general quality-related subjects. EOQ committees and sections active in 1993:

- COM1-Education and Training Committee
- COM3-Dependability Committee
- COM4-Glossary Committee
- COM5-Committee on Statistical Methods
- COM6-Committee on Standardization in QC
- COM7-Software Quality Committee
- COM9-Committee on Metrological Assurance of Product Quality
- COM10-Committee on Quality System Certification and Auditing
- COM11-Committee on Quality Policy
- COM12-Committee on Human Factors in QM
- COM13-Committee on Environmental Quality

- SEC1-Automotive Section
- SEC2-Section for Quality in the Pharmaceutical Industry
- SEC4-Food Section
- SEC5-Section for the Construction Industry
- SEC6-Quality Consultancy Section
- SEC7-Section on Quality in Service

EOQ annual congresses are organized by the national member bodies. The number of delegates are offered a variety of invited lectures on the theme of the conference as well as several parallel sessions within contributions on various specific topics of quality. Overall themes are chosen to provide information of the latest trends in the field of quality management.

EOQ maintains contacts with many international associations and cultivates relations with affiliate societies and with institutional members outside Europe.

EFQC (European Federation of Quality Circles)
The EFQCA is an independent organization representing national bodies whose aim is to promote the adoption of quality circles by industry.

4. European Quality Activities

4.1 Certification and Standardization

An important task in promoting free trade of goods in Europe is the creation of a European infrastructure on testing and certification. It poses a number of challenges to testing laboratories and certification bodies. Uniform regulations and standards are only of a real use if a single assessment of conformity with technical regulations is sufficient for the entire internal market. This requires uniform rules for the assessment of proofs and a European infrastructure for testing, certification and inspection. The Commission of the European Community presented its ideas in the document 'Global Approach for Technical Specifications, Testing and Certification'. Amongst its recommendations were that:

- The quality systems of the companies have to fulfil the requirements of the standard series ENY29000. The testing certification and inspection bodies have to satisfy uniform criteria as they will be defined in the standard ENY45000.
- A new, privately organized European Organization for Testing and Certification(EOTC) will regulate the manual recognition of testing reports and certificates, prevent multiplication of tests and audits, and assure the observance of the uniform criteria within Europe.
- Besides the quality of design, which is evaluated by type testing, the quality control of manufacturing will be demanded and assessed far more stringently than in the past.

Within Europe there are a large number of testing and certification bodies. Within the 12 EU countries alone, more than 10,000 testing and more than 10000 certification bodies operate, each requiring their own tests. Many existing testing and certification bodies operate on a national level and are not well known outside their country. But these difficulties could be overcome by alliances between institutes of different countries, especially if the EOTC would support their cooperation while applying strict quality standards. Much work needs to be done in the area of mutual recognition of test reports, certificates, and the assignment of the EC mark. On the other hand, the EOTC, with its European network of mutual recognition, must be accessible for all testing and certification bodies, as long as they fulfil the relevant requirements and accept the conditions of the EOTC.

Under the new approach to technical harmonization and standardization, legislation is confined to laying down the essential requirements to which products must comply in order to ensure the protection of public health or safety, or the protection of the environment or the consumer. European standards provide manufacturers with a set of technical specifications recognized in each directive as giving a presumption of conformity to the essential requirements. The European standards concerned remain voluntary.

Since the adoption of the new approach, the number of new European standards has increased rapidly from 19 to 1985 to 150 in 1989. This is still low compared to that of unharmonized national standards, and compared to the requirements for the implementation of the internal market programme. Successful standardization implies successful implementation. Credible procedures for certification, inspection and testing play a key role in creating the conditions which allow confidence to grow, and mutual recognition of each member state's procedures to become effective.

4.1.1 The RTOs Strand of the SPRINT Programme

The formation of transnational networks of research and technology organizations (R&TOs) dedicated to technology diffusion activities helps meet these objectives. The aim of R&TOs Networks is to encourage transnational European cooperation between the national R&TO's through common technology dissemination activities. The need for establishing R&TOs networks is justified for several reasons:

- the varying level of development of R&TOs in the different member states;
- the varying level of technological development in the different member states;
- the potential economies of scale to be sought by encouraging transnational cooperation on European scale projects; and,
- the need for common European testing and measurement procedures to facilitate intracommunity trade of goods.

SPRINT is currently providing financial support to 34 transnational projects. Eleven of these networks are specifically concerned with quality and involve more than 60 collective research centres. Projects are concerned with general quality management issues and practices as well as with more specific topics such as certification, quality control, non-destructive testing and interpretation of international quality standards.

4.1.2 Costs of Multiplicity of Certification for Sub-contractors in the European Community

In 1992 a working group supported by DG XXIII (with the participation of DG III) presented its report on 'the cost of the multiplicity of certification procedures for subcontractors in the Community'.[5] The object of the study was to:

- to define the certification procedures imposed on sub-contractors, especially by main contractors, and in particular the type, frequency, organization and conduct of the different audits;
- to measure the cost;
- to evaluate the impact of the conditions for satisfying main contractors' requirements as regards sub-contractors' quality management and production organization; and,
- to find out what sub-contractors expect in this connection.

4.2 Awareness

4.2.1 Euromanagement

Evidence from consultations with SMEs and their representative organizations indicated that the adoption of harmonized standards and associated certification procedures, may pose initial problems of adjustment for enterprises operating within the European Community. Generally speaking, in countries with a limited tradition of standardization, SMEs will have to make greater adjustment efforts, whereas for SMEs in countries with a longer standardization tradition the transition will be easier.

In order to attempt to offset these problems of adjustment and to facilitate the full participation of SMEs in the Single Market, assistance on standardization and certification issues is essential (the notions of quality assurance and health and safety are included in this context).

In June 1992, DG XXIII, again with the participation of DG III announced the launch of a pilot action intended to assist SMEs to identify and assess the impact of new European standardization, certification, and quality requirements they will have to master in order to attain the benefits of the internal market. The pilot action is intended:

- to improve SMEs' awareness of both information sources and requirements regarding standardization and certification of products of particular interest to the SMEs, especially with respect to the pluriannual work programme of the European standardization organizations;
- to assist SMEs to interpret and analyse the new standardization and certification requirements as they apply to their operations;
- to assist those SMEs who potentially could benefit from quality assurance to identify their management problems and to make them aware of the basic concepts of quality assurance; and
- to improve SMEs' awareness and understanding of the requirements of health and safety in the workplace.

The pilot action follows the Euromanagement model established by DG XXIII in the audits of research and development capacities of SMEs. Between 40 and 50 consultants or counsellors in the member states are chosen each to undertake assessments of, approximately, 15 SMEs in the same industrial sector. Assessments are prepared in association with the national sectoral federations and relevant public authorities. An outside coordinator is responsible for setting up and running the programme on behalf of the Commission. Fifty per cent of the costs of the assessments will be covered by the Commission, with the consultants responsible for finding additional financing through local or regional sources or from the SMEs themselves. A total budget of ECU 2 million is estimated for the pilot action, including the costs of coordination.

4.2.2 The European Quality Award

Recognition of achievement is a key activity in supporting the diffusion of quality/improvement activities. For this reason, 1992 saw the inception by the EFQM of a new award consisting of two elements:

- The European Quality Prize which will be awarded to a number of companies that demonstrate excellence in the management of quality as their fundamental process for continuous improvement; and,

335

- The European Quality Award which is awarded to the most successful exponent of total quality management in Western Europe. The trophy will be engraved and held nominally for one year by the recipient.

The European Quality Award is described in more detail in Appendix Two.

4.3 Research

4.3.1 BCR (Community Bureau of Reference) Programme

The BCR (Community Bureau of Reference) programme is a European Community research and technological development programme that helps European laboratories to improve their measurement when there are discrepancies between their results and when these discrepancies are causing disputes and difficulties in the functioning of the Single European Market. The programme is based on the collaboration of laboratories of the member states. Each project concerns a particular measurement problem the study of which is jointly tackled by the competent laboratories. In organizing the projects, the Commission endeavours, with the help of the Advisory Committee, to ensure the participation of laboratories of all member states.

In most cases, the work which is needed is to improve existing methods and improve the way in which the methods are implemented in the various laboratories (quality). Projects are therefore involving laboratories possibly of all member states and some preference is given to laboratories providing calibration. Official control on testing services, as they will have a role in disseminating the expertise resulting from the projects.

The BCR programme does not produce written standards. It complement the process of standardization by providing the technical support needed to ensure the correct method of measurement. The programme has addressed the measurement problems of greatest importance to industry whether they are for classical applications (e.g. thermal conductivity), or advanced technologies (e.g. electronics) or for environmental, food or biomedical purposes.

Generally, the results of collaborative projects are disseminated through publications, such as EUR reports and papers issued in the scientific literature. Additional means of transferring the expertise have been developed for applied metrology. Most member states have a national metrology institute with laboratories which provide calibrations for industry. The results of BCR intercomparisons made between the national metrology laboratories are presented in reports available from the Commission. In general, the results are quickly put into practice, and dissemination to the users in each country is ensured almost automatically through the calibrations provided by the national laboratories.

4.3.2 SAST (Strategic Analysis of Science and Technology)

SAST is one of the activities that comprise the EC MONITOR programme which is organised within DGXII, the Directorate General responsible for science, research and development in the European Commission. MONITOR is an instrument for identifying new directions and priorities for Community Research and Technological Development (RTD) policy. Within that broad mandate SAST's role is to examine specific areas of RTD policy which might be of immediate significance to the Community, the time horizon being about five years.

SAST projects typically combine scientific and technical assessment with the analysis of socio-economic, political and institutional forces influencing scientific and technological developments. Individuals and expert institutions are commissioned to carry out investigations which combine desk research and consultations with other experts, organizations and enterprises who are directly involved in the issue. There are currently nine such investigations. The SAST Project no. 2: 'Standards, Technical Regulations and Quality Assurance Services: What Will Cchange? What Implications for Community Science and Technology?' was intended to analyse the interface between two major areas of community policy:

- science and technology (S&T) including research and technological development, with special attention to pre-normative research; and,
- standards setting and observance (SSO) including legislation, regulations, standardization, testing and certification.

The analysis established a basis for policy decisions relating to the Interface. The target audience was policy-makers at Community, member state and enterprise levels.

Seven major sectors were considered in depth and special studies commissioned for automobiles, construction, medical devices, electronic, electronic components and water resources; a smaller study reviewed the agro-food sector. The leading consultant for the whole project came from the IT and telecommunications sector. These diverse sectors were considered to raise all the main issues, and therefore to provide a basis for general policy decisions. The main objectives were:

- to assess the implications of future developments in SSO on current research directions;
- to identify 'gaps' in research in which the Community has an interest; and,
- to define practical means of achieving closer interaction between standard-setting bodies, certification authorities, testing laboratories, and RTD operators/actors.

The project consisted of three phases. Phase 1 comprised an initial analysis and the identification of those sectors or horizontal aspects of most interest to the Community. Phase II consisted of the more in-depth above-mentioned sectorial studies and consultations through expert workshops and face-to-face interviews in the member states. These were brought together in Phase III when the conclusions and recommendations were finalized. Projects ran from 1989 until 1992. The total budget was ECU 405,740 including 48,780 for travel expenses.

4.3.3 Information Technology Applied to Quality (ITQUA)

The Information Technology Applied to Quality (ITQUA) project is planned and implemented under the auspices of the EOQ software quality committee. It is supported within the DG XIII Esprit III programme.

4.4 Consultancy

4.4.1 Managing the Intergration of New Technology (MINT) initiative

MINT is a consultancy scheme supported by DG XIII within the framework of the SPRINT programme with the aim of providing a diagnosis of the technology and innovation management techniques of participating firms, followed by a planning phase to facilitate the implementation. MINT is intended to provide a complete tool kit for companies wanting to improve their competitive position through innovation and technology transfer. The main objective is to provide companies with an integrated management approach towards acquiring new technologies and using them effectively within the business.

MINT explicitly recognizes the link between innovation and quality. In the diagnostic phase of the MINT scheme, the consultancy process will identify strengths and weaknesses of a company in relation to its quality status and management. This will make it easier, in developing the implementation plan, to target the specific changes required to improve quality.

The initiative will be delivered, administered and operated in each member state in accordance with its own policy and business culture. Approximately twenty organizations have been established as coordinating agencies at regional and national level, in the member states. These organizations will be responsible for selecting, training and monitoring a core group of experts to carry out the individual consultancy assignments. The Commission will ensure harmonization of procedures through exchange of best practice.

Target companies are SMEs in the manufacturing sector with the commitment, operating potential and management resources to take full advantage of the likely benefits resulting from the better use of new technologies. Companies will be selected at a national or regional level by the contractors in each country.

Following a short diagnosis of how the firm is, or could be, using and managing technology within the business, the consultants will assist the firm in developing an implementation plan, taking into account the real needs of the business. As a part of the process, training workshops will be run for groups of firms with common business or technology needs. To ensure that there is follow-through from the consultancy, MINT will relate synergetically with regional and national schemes, so that companies can be guided to other relevant national and Community support programmes.

The Community supports up to 75% of the costs of the innovation diagnosis (to a maximum of ECU 3,500 per assignment). In addition, the Community contributes towards the costs incurred by intermediary organisations in managing promoting and administering the scheme and training consultants (to a maximum of 1300 ECU per assignment). In total, it is envisaged that a maximum of 1000 assignments will be undertaken in the first-year pilot experiment. The aim is to achieve reasonable spread in the emphasis of assignments (e.g. quality, value analysis, design, flexible manufacturing, lean production etc.) as well as geographical spread.

5. Regional Quality Schemes and Initiatives

The European Single Market provides for the achievement of greater economic and social cohesion through the coordinated implementation of Community policies, including the completion of the internal market and the intervention of the structural funds. Within this context, European Community programmes for regional development may include a quality promoting element. Where this is the case, these are described in the relevant country case-study. Nevertheless, given its particular focus on quality, it is worth describing the PRISMA programme in some detail. The PRISMA initiative is designed to help firms in the less favoured regions of the Community to benefit from the completion of the internal market, by improving selected infrastructures and services available to them. PRISMA is complementary to a number of other actions already included in the Community Support Framework:

- INTERREG adaptation of the internal and external frontier areas of the Community to the Single Market;
- STRIDE development of regional capacities in the field of research, technology and innovation;
- TELEMATIQUE services and networks related to data communications; and,
- EUROFORM new qualifications, competencies and opportunities of employment.

PRISMA aims to help SMEs meet quality standards in public and private markets. In particular, it aims to ensure that:

- regions have a satisfactory standard of basic certification and test infrastructures;
- better supporting services are available to help SMEs to meet the new competitive challenges arising from the completion of the internal market.

Particular programmes funded under the initiative are jointly financed by the member states and the Community. The total contribution by the European Regional Fund for the period 1991-1993 is estimated at ECU 100 million. The level of the EC's contribution depends on the quality of the programme, and the needs of the region taking into account the additional facilities and services needed to enable the region's industry to participate fully in the internal market.

6. Overview and Outlook

Large imbalances in the quality culture exist across Europe. Nevertheless, moves towards harmonization in recent years are beginning to see a convergence of national, European and international approaches.

The traditional role of national standards bodies is disappearing especially that of AFNOR, BSI and DIN, which have long been factories for production of national standards. Even the role of defending national interest diminishes as industry becomes less national and as the interests to be reconciled at European level are not between countries but between different interest groups. Over the past five years, European standardization has been transformed from a marginal activity to one which is attracting priority attention. The importance that voluntary standards have assumed in the Community's technical legislation has been the driving force behind this change. The development of a European standards system is, however, an on going process which will take several years to complete.

Efficient procedures for applying standards entail an added gain for competitiveness when they go beyond certification to cover also conformity assessment including testing quality systems and accreditation in addition to certification. It is when control takes place before production (in the course of the development of a prototype or model), or during production (either as surveillance of products or of production processes), that industry gains most advantage. Increasingly, industry is using quality systems as a source of competitive advantage and to diminish costs associated with lack of quality. Third party certification adds credibility to these efforts both internally within the firm and externally for clients.

7. Quality Organizations

Name	Address	Telephone/Fax
European Committee for Normalization	Comite europeen de nomalisation (CEN) rue de Brederode Bruxelles	322 5196811
European Committee for Electrotechnical Normalization (CEN) (CENELEC)	rue de Brederode Bruxelles	322 519681
ISO International Standards Organisation	3 rue de Varembe 1211 Geneva 20 Geneva Switzerland	41 22 7340150
European Organisation for Testing and Certification (EOTC)	EOTC Office rue de Stassart 33 B-1050 Bruxelles	
DG III, DG XII, and DG XXIII Commission of the European Community	Rue de la Loi 200 1049 Brussels	32 2 295 1111
DG XIII Commission of the European Community	Batiment Jean Monnet Plateau du Kirchberg L-2920 Luxembourg	32 4301 34102/32 4301 34544
European Foundation for Quality Management (EFQM)	Building Reaal Fellenoord 47a 5612 AA Eindhoven The Netherlands	31 40 46 1075/31 40 432 003
The European Organization for Quality (EOQ)	EOQ-General Secretariat P O Box 5032 CH-3001, Bern Switzerland	31 21 61 66/31 21 69 51

References

1. Commission of the European Communities (1985), *'Completing the Internal Market'* (COM(85) 310), Luxembourg: CEN.

2. Council Directive of 28 March 1983 laying down a procedure for the provision of information in the field of technical standards and regulations, (83/189/EEC), *O.J. N. C.* 109 of 26.04.83

3. Council Resolution of 7 May 1985 on a new approach to technical harmonization and standards, 85/C136/01, *O.J. N. C*136 of 04.06.85

4. Council Decision of 13 December 1990 concerning the modules for the various phases of the conformity assessment procedures which are intended to be used in the technical harmonization directives, *O.J. N. C* 380 of 31.12.90

5. Commission of the European Communities, Pan-European Forum on Sub-contracting, Working Group 2 (1992), Summary of the study on *The cost of the multiplicity of certification procedures for sub-contractors in the European Community*, CEC, XXIII/743/92-EN, Luxembourg: CEN.

Other References

Commission of the European Communities (1990), *'Industrial Policy in an Open and Competitive Environment (COM(90)556)'*, Luxembourg: CEC.

Mendes, A.S., 'The EC Conformity Assessment Policy', *mimeo*, CEC DGIII, Certification Unit, Brussels, November 1992.

Appendices

Appendix One: Views of the Quality Management Experts

Probably the four most influential quality management experts are Crosby, Deming, Feigenbaum and Juran. Quality management was essentially an American concept, pioneered during the 1950s and 1960s by W.E. Deming and J.M. Juran. It can be argued that it succeeded primarily in Japan, because Japanese companies, unlike their American and European adversaries, were more open to the organizational innovations required to effectively adopt the approaches being proposed.[1] Soon after the war Deming's ideas were rapidly diffused throughout Japanese industry via the Japanese Union of Scientists and Engineers (JUSE). Similarly, in the late 1950s and early 1960s, JUSE played a major role in the diffusion of the Japanese version of Feigenbaum's concept of total quality control, called Company Wide Quality Control (CWQC) or total Quality Management (TQM).

A brief review of the main ideas underpinning the work of the most influential quality management experts is presented below.[2]

1. Deming

Dr W. Edwards Deming is generally considered the father of the Japanese quality revolution. Initially largely ignored in the United States, Deming had a major influence on the Japanese, starting when the Union of Japanese Scientists and Engineers (JUSE) invited him to address them in 1950. This was followed by a meeting with the presidents of 21 major Japanese companies, including Sony, Nissan, Mitsubishi and Toyota.

Deming's approach to quality management is based on the coalescence of two forces: total teamwork and the 'scientific approach'. The scientific approach requires understanding of the nature of variation, particularly its division into controlled and uncontrolled variation due to management-controllable common and worker-controllable special features. It is only by management and workers correctly diagnosing the most important sources of variation, and then reducing or even eliminating them, that quality (reliability, consistency, predictability, dependability) can be improved.

Deming's views on the role of management and a participating workforce are encapsulated in his constantly repeated Fourteen Points. Dr Henry Neave, Director of Research for the British Deming Association, in a pamphlet on the Deming philosophy issued by the UK Department of Trade and Industry, presented Deming's Fourteen Points (listed below).

Deming's Fourteen Points:

1. Constancy of Purpose.
2. The New Philosophy.
3. Cease Dependence on Inspection.
4. End 'Lowest Tender' Contracts.
5. Improve Every Process.
6. Institute Training on the Job.
7. Institute Leadership.

8. Drive Out Fear.
9. Break Down Barriers.
10. Eliminate Exhortation.
11. Eliminate Arbitrary Numerical Targets.
12. Permit Pride of Workmanship.
13. Encourage Education.
14. Top Management's Commitment.

2. Juran

The influence of Dr. Joseph M. Juran on the Japanese has been almost as great as that of Deming, although not so widely recognized in the west.

As long ago as the 1940s Juran was highlighting managerial responsibility for quality and emphasizing that quality was achieved through people rather than techniques. Though a statistician himself, he pointed out that companies could know all about the technical aspects of quality, such as statistical process control, but this did not help them to *manage* quality. He was the first of the quality experts to argue that achieving quality was all about communication, management and people.

Juran outlines the systemic approach to company-wide quality management as follows:

- Establish policies and goals for quality;
- Establish plans for meeting these quality goals;
- Provide the resources to evaluate progress against the goals and take appropriate action; and
- Provide motivation to stimulate people to meet the goal.

The process for establishing goals includes a degree of voluntarism and negotiation. Quality goals are neither uniform nor static. They vary from one organization to another, and from one year to the next. The Juran Institute in Wilton, Connecticut produces video cassettes and develops teaching materials for clients. A number of consultants worldwide are 'licensed' to teach his methods and use the centrally produced materials. They teach a project-by-project approach to quality improvement. Juran says:

> *The project approach is important. When it comes to quality, there is no such thing as improvement in general. Any improvement in quality is going to come about project-by-project and no other way.*[1]

Juran, like other quality experts, has his shorthand for quality improvement, which he encapsulates as follows:

Juran's Ten Steps to Quality Improvement:

1. Build awareness of the need and opportunity for improvement.
2. Set goals for improvement.
3. Organise to reach the goals.
4. Provide training.

5. Carry out projects to solve problems.
6. Report progress.
7. Give recognition.
8. Communicate results.
9. Keep score.
10. Maintain momentum by making annual improvement part of the regular systems and processes of the company.

3. Feigenbaum

Armand V. Feigenbaum marked an important step in the evolution of quality management when he first used the word 'total' in conjunction with quality. He was manager of manufacturing operations and world-wide quality for the General Electric Company of the US when he published the first edition of his book *Total Quality Control* in 1961. In the late 1960s he established the General Systems Company Inc in Pittsfield, Massachusetts, which designs and implements integrated operational systems for improving quality.

Feigenbaum says that the quality of products and services is directly influenced in nine basic areas, or what he calls the 'Nine Ms'. They are:

Feigenbaum's 'Nine Ms'

1. **Markets:** - businesses must be flexible and able to change direction rapidly.
2. **Money:** - reduce quality costs to improve profit margins.
3. **Management:** - responsibility for quality throughout the process and beyond.
4. **Men:** - demand for workers with specialized knowledge.
5. **Motivation:** - quality-consciousness.
6. **Materials:** - require new quality approaches.
7. **Machines and mechanization:** - more complex machines more dependent on quality.
8. **Modern information methods:** - manipulation of information.
9. **Mounting product requirements:** - more demands made of technology.

4. Crosby

The essence of what Crosby teaches is contained in what he calls the 'Four Absolutes of Quality' and in a 14 step process of quality improvement. His various books and other contributions in this area not only develop these concepts but add perceptions on the way management should behave that are not unlike two of Deming's Fourteen Points, 'drive out fear' and 'remove the barriers to communication'. Though not included in the kernel of his concepts, his continual admonition that the job of management is 'to help people' is at the heart of the TQM movement. Crosby argues that to manage quality you must have:

- a definition for quality that can be readily understood by all and the start of a common language that will aid communication;
- a system by which to manage quality;

347

- a performance standard that leaves no room for doubt or fudging by any employee;
- a method of measurement which will focus attentin on the progress of quality improvement.

This provides the premise for Crosby's 'Four Absolutes' for managing quality:

1. **The definition:** Quality is conformance to requirements, not goodness
2. **The system:** Prevention, not appraisal
3. **The performance standard:** Zero defects; not 'that's close enough'.
4. **The measurement:** The price of non-conformance to requirements (Cost of Quality), not quality indices

The Crosby methodology for implementation is contained within the 14 step quality improvement process. This process is clearly based on his experience in implementing quality improvement within ITT in the 1970s. These steps have proved successful in many other companies and therefore demand careful examination. They are, however, at the root of many of the criticisms of Crosby as having little practical application.

Crosby's Fourteen Steps

(as defined in the Philips company publication *'Three of a Kind'*)

1. Management Commitment.
2. The Quality Improvement Team.
3. Quality Management.
4. The Cost of Quality.
5. Quality Awareness.
6. Corrective Action.
7. Zero Defects Planning.
8. Supervisor Training.
9. Zero Defects Day.
10. Goal Setting.
11. Error-Cause Removal.
12. Recognition.
13. Quality Councils.
14. Do It Over Again.

Philip Crosby Associates has built a substantial worldwide organization PCA offices and their concomitant Quality Colleges are spread regionally across America and Europe and are also represented in South-east Asia. Fundamentally his services are based on educational courses, though consultant services are available.

5. Ishikawa

Kaoru Ishikawa, late president of the Musashi Institute of Technology is, perhaps, the best known of the Japanese contributors to the theory of quality management. Ishikawa is known primarily to western management as the originator of the Ishikawa cause and effect diagram, (the 'fishbone diagramme'). This approach to problem solving is the most widely taught and used technique for analysing the likely causes of a known effect.

Ishikawa's influence and contribution goes far beyond the invention of a specific technique. He defined the management philosophy behind quality, the elements of quality systems and what he calls the 'seven basic tools' of quality management, which are:

Ishikawa's 'seven basic tools'

1. Process flow charting: what is done
2. Tally charts: how often it is done
3. Histograms: pictorial view of variation
4. Pareto analysis: rating of problems
5. Cause and effect analysis: what causes problems
6. Scatter diagrams: defining relationships
7. Control charts: measuring and controlling variation.

References

1. Macdonald, J. and Piggot J. : Global Quality: *The New Management Culture,* Mercury: London, (1990).

2. Ibid.

Appendix Two: The European Quality Award

The European Quality Award is sponsored by the European Foundation for Quality Management, the European Organization for Quality and the European Commission. To receive the prize, applicants must demonstrate that their approach to total quality management has contributed significantly to satisfying the expectations of customers, employees and others with an interest in the company for the past few years.

The first step in an application is the collation of a body of quality management data from within the organization. Supporters of the Award argue that there is significant value in this process. Even if the company is not successful in winning the Award, it will enable it to assess its level of commitment to quality. It will also show the extent to which this commitment is being deployed - vertically through every level of the organization and horizontally in all areas of activity.

Application for the Award is open to all companies which meet the competition criteria. Firstly, all applicants must be able to demonstrate a history of significant commitment to western Europe of at least five years. The definition of this commitment is that at least 50% of the applicant business operations have been conducted within western Europe for the past five years. The quality practices on which the application is based must be inspectable in western Europe. Most businesses may apply some, however, may not:

- local, regional, national and government agencies;
- non-profit making organisations;
- trade associations; and,
- professional societies

When the application is received it is marked by a team of up to six assessors all of whom have undergone the same training course thus maximizing consistency. The application is scored on the basis of self-appraisal data supplied by the company with its application. The assessment is used to decide which applicants should be visited for further assessment. Visits involve the verification of the application and the inspection of the quality practices of the leading applicants. After the jury's final review and decision the European Quality Prize is presented to the companies that demonstrate the highest standards of total quality management. The prizes were presented at the EFQM's European Quality Management Forum held in Madrid at the end of 1992. The Forum was also the venue for the presentation of The European Quality Award trophy to the most successful exponent of total quality management in western Europe.

In the year following presentation of the Award winners will share their experience of total quality management at EFQM seminars. These seminars offer an excellent platform for the promotion of their status as leaders in European total quality management.

Appendix Three: Acronyms

General

ISO	International Standards Organization
ISO TC 176	ISO Technical Committee 176 (responsible for development of quality mangement standards)
OECD	Organization for Economic Cooperation and Development
QA	Quality Assurance
QC	Quality Control
R&D	Research and Development
R&TOs	Research and Technology Organizations
SME	Small and Medium Sized Enterprise
SPC	Statistical Process Control
SQC	Statistical Quality Control
TQC	Total Quality Control
TQM	Total Quality Management

Europe

BCR	Community Bureau of Reference
CEC	Commission of the European Community
CEI	International Electrotechnics Commission
CEN	European Committee for Standardization
CENELEC	European Standards Committee In Electrotechnics
EAC	European Accreditation of Certification
EC	European Community
ECU	European Currency Unit
EN	European Standard
EOTC	European Organization for Testing and Certification
EFQCA	European Federation of Quality Circle and Quality Management Associations
EFQM	European Foundation for Quality Management
EFRO/EFRD/EFRU	European Fund for Regional Development
EFTA	European Free Trade Association
EOQ	European Organization for Quality
EOTC	European Organization for Testing and Certification
EQNET	European Network for Quality System Assessment and Certification
ESF	European Social Fund
ETSI	European Telecommunication Standards Institute
EU	European Union
IAQ	International Academcy for Quality
MINT	Manage the Integration of New Technologies (SPRINT programme)
PRISMA	Programme for the Regions Industry for the Single Market
SAST	Strategic Analysis of Science and Technology
SPRINT	Strategic Programme for Innovation and Technology Transfer

Belgium

AWQ	Association Wallone pour la gestion de la Qualité (Walloon Quality Association)
BCK-CBQ	Belgisch Centrum voor Kwalteitsorg-Centre Belgique pour la gestion de la Qualité (Belgian Centre for Quality)
BENOR	Belgian conformance mark
BIN-IBN	Belgisch Instituut voor Normalisatie-Institut Belge de Normalisation (Belgian Standards Institute)
BQS	Belgian Committee for Quality Systems
CEBEC	Belgian Electrotechnics Organization
CKZ	Centrum Voor Kwaliteitszorg (Flemish Quality Centre)
CQ	Centre pour le Gestion de la Qualité (Walloon Quality Centre)
D.O.O.	Dienst Onderwijs Ontwikkeling (Flemish Department of Education)
KCGB-CQRB	Kwaliteitcentrum Gewest Brussel-Centre pour la Gestion de la Qualité de la region Bruxelloise (Brussels-region Quality Centre)
GOM	Provincial Development Society
NAC-QS	National Committee for the Accreditation of Certification Bodies-Quality Systems
NBN	Belgisch Norm Belge (Belgian Standard)
PRACK	Vereniging voor Praktijkgericht en Participatief Management en Integrale Kwalteitszorg (Association for Practice-Oriented and Participative Management and Total Quality Management)
SQMI	Strategic Quality Management Institute, Erasmus University
VCK	Vlaams Centrum voor Kwaliteitszorg (Flemish Centre for Quality)

Denmark

AMU	Centre for Vocational Retraining
BUP	Bedre Udnyttelse af Produktionssystemer (Improved Utilization of Production Systems)
DS	Dansk Standardiseringsråd (Danish Standards Association)
DIEU	Dansk Ingenørers Efternddannelse (Retraining Association of Danish University-Trained Engineers)
KC	Kvalitetsudviklingscenter (Quality Promotion Centre)
DTI	Dansk Tecknologisk Institut (Danish Technology Institute)
KUP	Kvalitets UdviklingsProgrammet (Programme for Quality Development
TUP	Teknologisk UdviklingsProgrammet (Programme for Technological Development)

France

ACFCI	Assemblée de Chambres Française de Commerce et d'Industrie (National Assembly of Chambers of Trade and Industry)
AFAQ	Association Française pour l'Assurance Qualité (French Association for Quality Certification)

AFAV	Association Française pour l'analyse de la valuer (French Association for Value Analysis)
AFCIQ	Association Française pour le Controle Industriel de la Qualité (French Industrial Quality Control Association)
AFNOR	Association Française de NORmalisation (French Standards Association)
AFQ	Association Française des Qualiticiens (French Quality Association)
ANVAR	Agence Nationale de Valorisation de la Recherche (National Agency for Innovation and research and development)
ATPCI	Association Française des Technicians et Professionnels du Controle Industriel, (Association of Industrial Control Technicians and Professionals)
ARACQ	Association Regionale pour l'Amelioration de la Competitive par la Qualité (Regional Association for the Improvement of Competitiveness through Quality)
CEA	Commissariat a l'énergie atomique (French Atomic Energy Agency)
CG	Commission General (AFNOR General Commissions)
CNES	Centre national d'études spatiales (French Space Agency)
CN	Commission Normalisation (AFNOR Standardization Commissions)
CNED	Centre National pour l'Enseignement a Distance (National Centre for Distance Learning)
COS	Comite d'Orientation Strategique (AFNOR Strategic Committee)
CRCI	Chambres Régionaux de Commerce et d'Industrie, (Regional Chamber of Trade and Industry)
EDF	Électricité de France (French Electricity Board)
FAQ	Federation des Association Qualité (Federation of Quality Associations)
FRAC	Fonds Régionaux d'Aide au Conseil (Regional Consultancy Funds)
GRETA	GRoupements d'ETAblissements (Groups of establishments)
IEQT	Instiut de European pour la Qualité Totale (European Institute for Total Quality)
IRDQ	Institut de Recherche et de Dévelopement de la Qualité (Research and Development Institute for Quality)
MFQ	Mouvement Française pour la Qualité (French Quality Centre)
MOD	Ministére de la défence (Ministry of Defence)
MEQUI	Mission pour l'enseignement de la qualité industrielle, (Mission for Teaching of Industrial Quality)
MICE	Ministère de l'industrie et Commerce Estranger (French Ministry for Industry and Trade)
RNE	Reseau National d'Essais (National Network of Testing Laboratories)
RNPQ	Reseau National de Promotion de la Qualité (National Network for the Promotion of Quality)
SQUALPI	Sous-Direction de la Qualité pour l'industrie et de la normalisation (Directorate for Quality of Industrial Products and Standards)
UIMM	Union des Industries Metalliques et Minieres (Union of the Metals and Minerals Industries)

Germany

BDI	Bundesverband der Deutschen Industrie c.V. (national assocation of German Industry)
BMFT	Bundesministerium für Forschung und Technologie (Federal Ministry of Research and Technology)
BMG	Bundesministerium für Gesundheit (Federal Ministry of Health)
BMWi	Bundesministerium für Wirtschaft (Federal Ministry of Economic Affairs)
DAR	Deutscher Akkreditierungerat (German Accreditation Organisation)
DARA	Deutsch Agentur für Raumfahrtangologenheiten GmbII (German Agency for Space)
DAT	Deutscher Akkreditierungsrat (German Accreditation Council)
DFG	Deutsche Forschungsgemeinschaft c.V. (German Research Association)
DGQ	Deutsche Gesellschaft fürr Qualitat c.V. (German Society for Quality)
DIN	Deutsches Institut für Normung c.V. (German Institute for Standardisation)
DLR	Deutsche Forschungsanstalt Luft und Raumfahrt (German Aerospace and Space Research Laboratory)
DOCG	Deutsche Quality Circle Gemeinschaft (German Society for Quality circles)
DQS	Deutsche Gesellschaft zur Zertifizierung von Qualitatssiche rungssysteme mbH (German Society for the Certification of Quality Assurance Systems).
IAF	Arbeitsgemeinschaft industrieller Forschungsvereinigungen c.V. (working group of industrial research associations)
NQSZ	Normenausschuss Qualitätsmananagement, Statistik und Zertifizierung (DIN Standards Committee for Quality Management, Statistics and Certification)
RKW	Rationalisierrungskuratorium der Deutschen Wirtschaft eV, (Rationalization Board for German Industry)
TGA	Trägergemeinschaft für Akkreditierung (Society for Accreditation)
TÜVCERT	Technische Überwachungsvereine Zertifierungsge meinschaft für Qualitätssicherungssysteme, (Technical Association for the Certification of Quality Assurance Systems).

Greece

EEDE	Hellenic Management Association
ELOT	Greek Standards Organization
EOMMEX	Organization of SMEs and Crafts
ELKEDE	Hellenic Leather Centre
ELKEPA	Hellenic Productivity Centre
HEPO	Hellenic Export Promotion Organization
MIET	Ministry of Industry, Energy and Technology
OAED	Organization of Employment of Working Potential
SEB	Federation of Greek Industries

Ireland

CII	Confederation of Irish Industry
EOLAS	Irish Science and Technology Agency
FAS	Training and Employment Authority
ICTU	Irish Congress of Trade Unions
IDA	Industrial Development Authority
IQA	Irish Quality Association
NSAI	National Standards Authority of Ireland

Italy

AICQ-SICEV	Associazione Italiana per la Qualita' - Sistema di Certificazione dei Valutatori (Italian Quality Association - Certification System)
ASTER	Agenzia per lo Sviluppo Tecnologico (Agency for New technologies)
CERMET	Centro Regionale di Recerca (Regional Research Centre)
CESTEC	Centro Lombardo per lo Sviluppo Tecnologico dell Piccole e Medie Imprese Lombardy Centre for New Technologies)
CNR-IMGC	Metrological Institute "G. Colonetti" of the National Research Council (CNR Metrological Laboratory)
ENEA	Ente per le Nuove Tecnologie, l'Energia (Organisation for New Energy Technologies)
IEN	Instituto Elettrotecnico Nazionale (National Electrotechnical Institute)
UNI	Ente Nazionale Italiano di Unificazione (Italian Standards Institute)
CEI	Comitato Elettrotecnico Italiano (Italian Electrotechnical Committee)
SINAL	Sistema Nazionale per l'Accreditamento di Laboratori (National System for the Accreditation of Laboratories)
SINCERT	Sistema Nazionale per l'Accreditamento degli Organismi di Certificazione (National System for the Accreditation of Certification Organisations)
SIT	Sistema Italiano di Taratura (Italian Testing Service)

The Netherlands

CERKOOP	Institute of NVK for Quality Management
EUR	Erasmus University in Rotterdam
HBO	Higher Vocational Schools
IMK	Instituut Midden en Kleinbedrijf (Institute for Small and Medium Sized Companies)
ISP	Integral Structure Plan
KDI	Stichting Kwaliteitsdienst (Quality Foundation)
MANS	Vereniging Management en Arbeid Nieuwe Stijl (New Style Management Association)
MBO	Intermediate Vocational Schools
NEHEM	Nederlandse Herstructererings Maatschappij (Dutch Restructuring Company)

MILK	Milieuzorg Integratie in systemen van Logistiek en Kwaliteitszorg (Environmental Care Integration in systems of Logistics and Quality)
NNI	Nederlands Normalistic Institut (Dutch Standards Institute)
NVK	Nederlandse Vereniging voor Kwaliteit (Dutch Association for Quality Management)
OZL	Oost-Zuid Limburg (East-South Limburg quality programme)
PNL	Perspectieben nota Limburg (Future for Limburg)
Q&L	Kwaliteit en Logistiek (Quality and Logistics)
QUATRO	Quality Supply and Regional Entrepreneurship
ROA	Raad van Organisatie-Advuesbureaus (Council of Management Consultancies)
RUG	University of Groningen
RvC	Stichting Raad voor de Certificatie (National Certification Council)
STERLAB	Nederlandse Stichting voor de Erkenning van Laboratoria (Institute for the Recognition of Laboratories)
TUE	Technical University of Eindhoven

Portugal

AIP	Associação Industrial Portuguesa (Portuguese Industrial Association)
APQ	Associação Portuguesa para a Qualidade (Portuguese Quality Association)
CEQUAL	Centro de Formação Professional para a Qualidade (Quality Training Centre)
CNQ	Conselho Nacional da Qualidade (National Quality Council)
CT	Comissães Tecnicas (Technical Committees)
IEFP	Instituto do Emprego & Formacio Profissional (Institute of Employment and Training)
IPQ	Instituto Português da Qualidade (Portuguese Institute for Quality)
ISQ	Instituto de Soldadura e Qualidade (Portuguese Quality and Welding Institute)
NIR	Regional Nuclei
NP	Normas Portuguesas, (Portuguese Standards)
ONS	Orgãos de Normalizaçïo Sectoriais (Sectoral Standardization bodies)
PEDIP	Programa Europeu Desenvolument Industria Português (EC Programme for the Development of Portuguese Industry)
SNGQ	Sistema Nacional de Gestão da Qualidade (National Quality Management System)

Spain

AENOR	Asociación Española de Normalización y Certifición (Spanish Association for Standardization and Certification)
AECC	Asociación Española para la Calidad (Spanish Association for Quality)
AENICRE	Asociación de Entidades de Inspección y Control Reglamentario (Association of Organizations for Inspection and Regulatory Control)

CPCA	Centro para la Promoción de la Calidad en Andalucia (Centre for Quality Promotion in Andalucía)
ANAVA	Asociación Española de Análisis de Valor (Spanish Association for Value Analysis)
IAT	Instituto Andaluz de Tecnología (Andalucia Institute of Technology)
ICT	Instituto Catalán de Tecnología (Catalan Institute of Technology)
IMPI	Instituto de la Pequeña y Mediana Industria (Institute of Small and Medium-Sized Firms)
MICYT	Ministerio de Industría, Comercio y Turismo (Ministry of Industry, Trade and Tourism)
MINER	Ministerio de Industria y Energia (Ministry of Industry and Energy)
PNCI	Plan Nacional de Calidad Industrial (National Plan for Industrial Quality)
RELE	Red Española de Laboratorios de Ensayo (Spanish Network of Test Laboratories)
SCI	Sistema de Calibración Industrial (System of Industrial Calibration)
UNE	Una Norma Española (Spanish Standard)

United Kingdom

AQAP	Allied Quality Assurance Publications
BQA	British Quality Association
BS	British Standard
BSI	British Standards Institute
DoEmp	Department of Employment
DTI	Department of Trade and Industry
IQA	Institute of Quality Assurance
MOD	Ministry of Defence
NACCB	National Accreditation Council for Certification Bodies
NAMAS	National Measurement Accreditation Service
NEDO	National Economic Development Organization
TEC	Training Enterprise Council
UMIST	University of Manchester Institute of Science and Technology

Appendix Four: List of Interviewees

Belgium

Prof. L. Stals
Post University Centre, Limburg

Mr. C. Horrez
Belgium Centre for Quality (BCK)

Mr. Paolo Caruso
Ministry of Economic Affairs

Ms. I De Clerq
VCK

Mr P Croon
BIN/IBN

Mr. M. Vanqualllie
Walloon Ministry of Economic Affairs.

Mr H Voorhof
Ministry of Economic Affairs

Denmark

Christoffer Svendsen
Industriog Handelsstyrelsen

Kurt Hansen
Industriog Handelsstyrelsen

Torben Juul Jensen
NordTek

Erik Laugesen-Christensen
SEl-Midtjylland

Anette Jensen
Sonderjyllands Amt

Gitte Petterson
Dansk Standardiseringsrad

A.P. Jorgensen
Industri-og Handelsstyrelsen

Mogens Holm
Trade Book International

Preben Moustsen
Teknologisk Informationscenter Aars

Preben Bauer
PLM Haustrup

France

I. Berny
AFAQ,

J. Cavailles
Ministère de la Défense

M. Cieren
ACFCI

H. David
AFNOR

M. Dragomir
SQUALPI

F. Dupre
CDAF, Lyon

G. Callas
DRAFTEX-Industries (Laird Group)

J.L. Jacquinet
FRAC, Rhône-Alpes

R. Laverage
Reseau National D'Essai

J.P. Marleix
Union des Industries Metallurgiques
Electriques et Connexes de l'Isére

A.M. Matherat
Ministère de l'Agriculture et de la Forét

C. Merle
AFNOR

M. Pagny
Association pour la Formation et la Promotion
dans l'Industrie
Grenoble.

M Pepin
Club Qualité, Chambéry.

C. Philippot
Chambre de Commerce et D'Industrie de
Chambéry et de la savoire.

S. Portier
SQUALPI

France cont.

G. Quintaa
AFAV

C. Richet
MFQ, Ile de France

M.N. Thievenaz
CCIG, Grenoble

C. de Tourney
AFNOR

M. Tricoche
AFNOR

Germany

Herr. D. Middeldorf
Arbeitsgemeinschaft Industrieller Forschungsvereinigungen c.V.

Herr Grode
DIN

Herr Freund
Herr Boch
RKW

Herr Dipl.Ing M. Auer
Steinbeis-Stiftung

Herr Dr Dreher
BMFT

Herr Dr Schöttler
Herr Fink
BMWi

Herr Dr Bey
Kernforschungszentrum Karlsruhe GmbH

Herr Fuhr
DGQ

Herr Dr Petrick
DQS

Herr Dipl. Ing. V. Wanduch
VDI

Herr Dorr
RKW

Herr Dipl. Ing. (FH) E Frey
Steibus-Transferzentrum

Frau Dr. occ. A. Giewoleit
DQS

Greece

Mr A. Kofinas
ELOT

Ms M. Pitsika
ELOT

Mr Melargakis
ELOT

Ms Y. Komodromou
EOMMEX

Mr G. Fryssalakis
Ministry of Industry

Ms N. Moustaka
Ministry of Industry

Ms D. Velissariou
Association of Greek Industrialists

Ms P. Nikoloudaki
EEDE

Ms A Garyfallou
HEPO

Dr N. Vitanzakis
OTE

D. Economou
Greek Aluminium Association

Mr Kefalas
OAED

N. Mouzopoulos
Deree College

Mr D Papakonstantinou
EL.KE.DE.

Ms Kotsida
ELAIS

Mr A. Spanos
Interamerican

Dr N Logothetis
TQM Hellas Ltd

Italy

Dr Lucia Barberis
Servizio Sviluppo Sistema Inustriale

Prof. Luigi Crovini
CNR-Instituto di Metrologia 'G. Colonetti'

Dr Enrico Martinotti
UNI

Dr Giovanni Mattana
AICQ

Dr S. Moneghel
Regione Veneto- Dpt Problemi Lavoro

Mr Eraldo Oelati
Regione Lombardia - Assessorato all'Industria

Ms. Patrizia Rolli
Ministero dell'Industria

Ms Federico Zampese
IRER

Dr Zini
ERVET

Drs J.J. de Vries
Ministry of Economic Affairs

Portugal

Eng. Cândido dos Santos
Instituto Português de Qualidade

Eng. Oyilia Vieira
APQ

Eng. Beja Cardeiro
Cabinete Gestor do PEDIP

Eng. José Bruno
AIP

Eng. Silva Pereira
AIP

Eng. Cristina Pescada
AIP

Eng. Moreira da Silva
AIP

Ireland

Mr Sean Murphy
EOLAS

Mr Anthony McInerney
EOLAS

Professor John A. Murphy
Irish Quality Association

Terry O'Callaghan
Irish Quality Association

Mike Jones
Construction Industry Federation

The Netherlands

Drs M Ottolander
Ministry of Economic Affairs

Ing. S.A. Torjuul
NEHEM

Drs J A J Balk
Secretary Steering group 'Dutch Quality'

Spain

Mr Miguel Barcelo
ICT, Barcelona

Mr Alberto Urtiaga de Vivar Ministerio de Industria, Comercio y Turismo

Mr Timoteo de la Fuente Garcia
Ministerio de Industria, Comercio y Turismo

Mr Javier Iglesias
IAT, Sevilla

Mr Miguel Angel Luque
IAT, Sevilla

Mr Rafael Carvajal Raggio
IAT, Sevilla

Mr Joan Rotger
ICT, Barcelona

United Kingdom

David Ellis
Department of Trade and Industry

Mr. Ron Richards
Pera International

Mr. Brendan Vickers
Pera International

Mr Claude Garner
Salford University Business Services

Mr. Rodney Hummell
ASI, Belfast

Mr A Woodall
MacGregor Associates

Mr Albert McKeaveney
LEDU, Belfast

Mr Les Price
Ministry of Defence

Dr Brian Moore
Manchester Business School

John Slater
TickIT

Mr Brian Taylor
Institute of Quality Assurance

David Stack
Construction Quality Assurance

Commission of the European Communities

Mr Silva Mendez
DG III/B/2

Mr Robin Miege
DG XIII/C/4

Mr Gerhard Braunling
DG XIII/C/4

Mr Jose Ramon Tiscar
DG XIII/C/4